UNDERSTANDING TREES

UNDERSTANDING TREES

By

Dr. H. Shivanna

Professor & Head

Deptt. of Forest Biology & Tree Improvement

College of Forestry

SIRSI, Uttar Kannada

Karnataka (India)

DISCOVERY PUBLISHING HOUSE PVT. LTD.

NEW DELHI-110 002

Published by:
Tilak Wasan

DISCOVERY PUBLISHING HOUSE PVT. LTD.
4831/24, Ansari Road, Prahlad Street
Darya Ganj, New Delhi-110002 (India)
Phone: +91-11-23279245, 43764432
Fax: +91-11-23253475
E-mail: parul.wasan@gmail.com
info@discoverypublishinggroup.com
discoverypublishinghouse@gmail.com
web: www.discoverypublishinggroup.com

First Edition: 2011
ISBN: 978-81-8356-866-1

Understanding Trees

Printed at:
Shree Balaji Art Press
Delhi

PREFACE

The present title "*Understanding Trees*" provides a structured approach to learning by covering all the important topics in a uniform, systematic format. The book has been comprehensively designed incorporating recent advances in this fast moving field. It is written to provide accessible information on trees in compact form for undergraduate students in biology and related life sciences. It will be useful for both beginning students and those who are more advanced. In addition, busy lecturers who require a quick reference compendium will find it useful, particularly for tutional planning. Simple, yet hopefully clear figures and tables are provided throughout the book.

The over-riding goal of this book, and indeed of the whole *Understanding series,* is to present the essential information concering microbiology in a compact, readily accessible form which leads itself to student learning and revision. The convergence of various approaches has generated a rich panorama of detail, the significance of which we are still attempting to unraval. The present text has been written as an introduction to this rapidly growing field.

To make the work more comprehensive and informative, the author has consulted many authoritative books, research journals, abstracts, monographs etc., so there can be no claim to originality except in the manner of treatment.

The author expresses his thanks to his friends and colleagues whose continue inspirations have initiated him to bring out this book.

The author expresses his gratitude to Mr. Wasan and staff of M/s Discovery Publishing House Pvt. Ltd. for their whole hearted co-operation in the publication of this book.

In the mean time, the author will remain sincerely responsible for any shortcomings of the book and be grateful to the readers for their suggestions and constructive criticism for the continuous betterment of the book. He takes this opportunity to appeal to the readers to send their suggestions straightaway to his Publisher.

Author

CONTENTS

1 Chapter EARLIEST PLANTS

The Earth was formed approximately 4600 million years ago and within 1800 million years cellular life had evolved. Palaeoenvir-onmental reconstructions suggest that global temperature and the earliest composition of the atmosphere, ocean, and land would have provided a challenging combination of environmental extremes for the onset of biological evolution. However, evolutionary change was such that by 540 million years ago (Cambrian) an array of multicellular organisms, both plant and animal, had evolved. This chapter outlines the patterns of change in these early environments (3500-540 million years ago) and the processes leading to the development of the first forms of multicellular plant life.

THE EARLIEST ENVIRONMENTS

Geological evidence indicates that the continental crust started to form by 4200 Ma and that by 1900 Ma a large, single, lens-shaped body had amassed. This supercontinent has been named 'Rodinia' and is thought to have been located around the equatorial belt, in roughly the same position as present-day Africa.

Initial splitting up of Rodinia occurred from approximately 1000 Ma, resulting in three major parts, Laurasia, East Gondwana and West Gondwana (principally parts of South America and West Africa).

The early continental crust would have been thin and extremely hot due to heat flow from the mantle. An estimate of

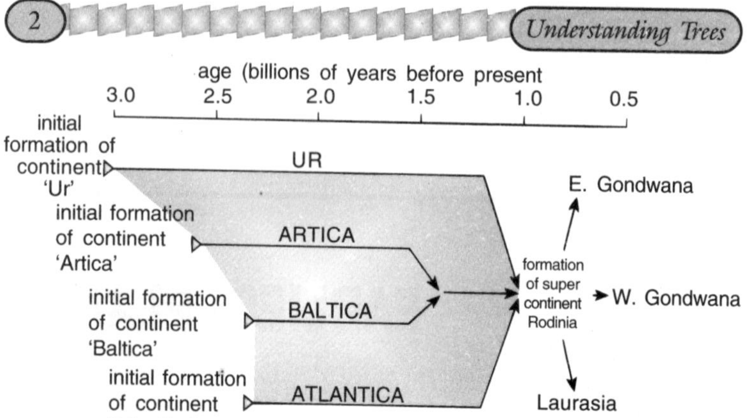

Figure 1.1: Diagrammatic representation of major continental development and movement in the Earth's early history.

Earth's heat production in the early Archaean (4000-3500 Ma), suggests that it was two or three times greater than present. However, there is also metamorphic evidence to indicate that by 3000 Ma, the heat had subsided sufficiently to allow the development of a continental crust, up to 40 km in thickness.

This crust was composed of igneous rock, weathered sediments (including volcanic sands), and meteoritic compounds resulting from intense cometary bombardment.

Although the continental crust was hot, it has been calculated that endogenic heat supplied only an extremely small fraction (< 0.001 %) to the Earth's energy budget, and that this was not an important factor in controlling surface air temperatures.

Rather, surface air temperatures would have been strongly influenced by the high levels of atmospheric methane (CH_4) and carbon dioxide (CO_2) from volcanic degassing.

Therefore, even though the sun was considerably less luminous than today (solar luminosity has increased by approximately 25% since the origin of the solar system, high levels of atmospheric CO_2 and CH_4 would have blocked outgoing long-wave radiation, promoting greenhouse warming.

Climatic model-ling suggests that CO_2 greenhouse warming could have been responsible for global temperat-ures between 30 and 50°C in these early environments (3500-3200 million years ago).

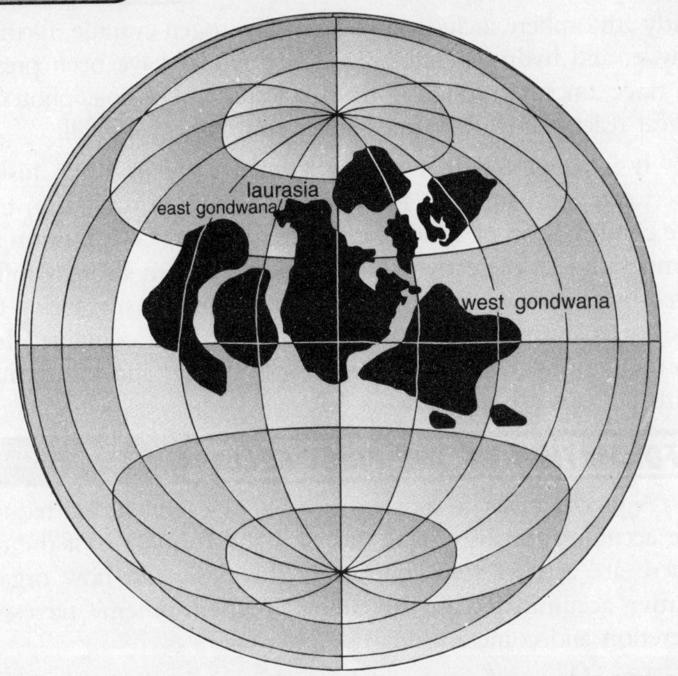

Figure 1.2: Splitting up of supercontinent Rodinia from approximately 1000 million years ago resulting in Laurasia, East Gondwana, and West Gondwana.

In contrast to the high levels of carbon dioxide, early atmospheric oxygen (O_2) was extremely low. Some estimates suggest that before 2200 Ma (early Proterozoic) the O_2 content of the air accounted for 1 % of total atmospheric composition, and was probably a major limiting factor for organic evolution.

One of the most restrictive factors associated with extremely low levels of oxygen would have been the lack of an ozone layer, and therefore no protection for terrestrial organisms from incoming solar radiation. Between 2200 and 1900 Ma (middle Proterozoic), however, various sedimentary deposits that require free oxygen for their formation become apparent in the geological record. These include red-beds (sandstones and shales with red iron oxide) and highly oxidized palaeosols, and are taken to be indicative of increasing amounts of atmospheric O_2.

Other gases contributing to the overall composition of the

early atmosphere included hydrogen, hydrogen cyanide, formaldehyde, and hydrogen sulphide. These would have been present in trace amounts, resulting from volcanic outgassing, photochemical reactions in the atmosphere, and cometary infall.

It is suggested that oceans formed early in Earth history (between approximately 4400 and 3900 million years ago) from the condensation of atmospheric water vapour. Composition and temperature of the early oceans would have been strongly influenced by mantle outgas-sing, with some estimates suggesting that they were warm (between 80 and 100°C) and contained high concentrations of ferrous irons, dissolved CO_2 and bicarbonate, with perhaps a pH as low as 6.0.

FORMATION OF THE FIRST CELL

A precondition to any form of biological evolution requires the accumulation of organic material and formation of the cell. There are at least two contrasting theories as to how organic matter accumulated in the prebiotic environment: terrestrial accretion and cometary infall.

The oldest and most widely cited theory is that of terrestrial accretion. This theory, first proposed by Miller in 1953, is based on the principle that, under laboratory conditions, when gases such as hydrogen, carbon dioxide, methane, and ammonia are heated with water, and energized by electrical discharge for at least 24 hours, approximately half the carbon originally present in the methane gas will be converted into amino acids, sugars, and other organic molecules, including purines and pyrimidines (required to make nucleotides). Amino acids and nucleotides can associate to form polymers, including polypeptides (proteins) and polynucleotides (RNA and DNA) thus forming the first building blocks of the cell.

An alternative theory is that the first organic material on Earth came from other planets and entered the Earth's atmosphere via meteoritic input. This idea was originally viewed as better suited to the realms of science fiction. However, there is increasing evidence to support the theory that meteoritic and cometary infall provided the first organic material on Earth. Analysis of the present-day meteorites on the ice beds of the Antarctic (carbonaceous chrondrites), for example, indicate that they typically contain between 1 and 4% carbon, mainly as graphite but also as much as 1% organic molecules. Organic compounds contained within the carbonaceous chrondrites include hydrocarbons, amino acids, carbon, hydrogen cyanide and amphiphilic molecules.

In the literature, there is considerable debate as to which process is more probable. Critics of the terrestrial accretion mechanism suggest that although such processes may occur under laboratory conditions, there is no conceivable environmental equivalent of a closed glass flask in which such reactions could occur. On the other hand, critics of the meteoritic theory argue that the extremely high atmospheric pressures (as a consequence of the high levels of atmospheric carbon dioxide) would have resulted in organic materials in these rocks burning up before reaching the surface of the globe. Recent calcula-tions, however, indicate that although this might be the case for large meteorites, very small micrometeorites, in the size range 10^{-6} to 10^{-9}g, lose relatively little of their mass during atmospheric entry and could

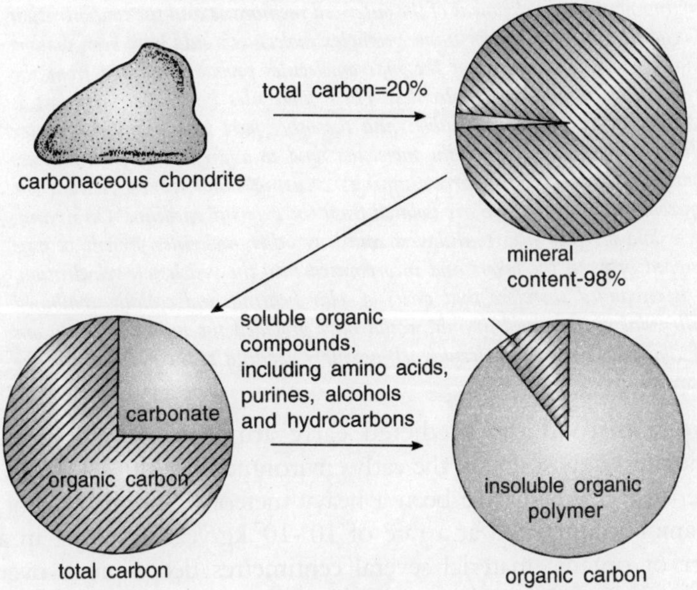

Figure 1.3: Composition of carbonaceous chrondrites.

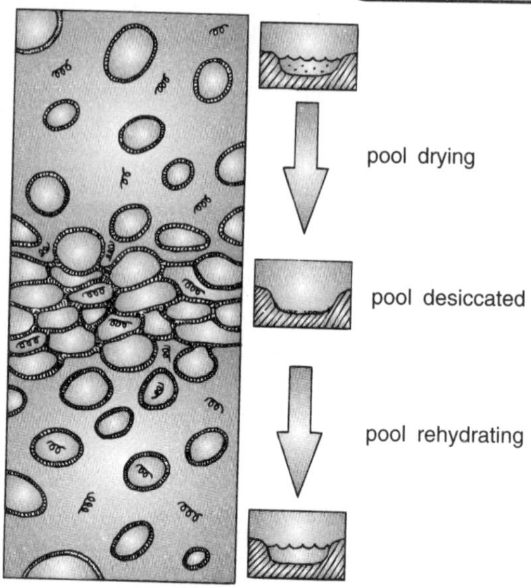

Figure 1.4: Formation of outer cell membrane and containment of the macromolecules within the cell. It is suggested that an extremely important environment for development of the outer cell membrane and the concentration of organic compounds to form more complex molecules would have been shallow tidal pools. Containment of the macromolecules probably resulted from the presence of amphiphilic molecules. These molecules have one part that is hydrophobic (i.e. water insoluble) and the other part hydrophilic (i.e. water soluble). In water, amphiphilic molecules tend to aggregate to form bilayers (with the water-soluble parts aligning) creating small, closed vesicles, the aqueous contents of which are isolated from the external medium. On drying, these bilayers fuse into multilayers and any other molecules present become trapped between the layers and incorporated into the vesicles on rehydration. It is envisaged therefore that cycles of solar heating and cooling, combined with tidal wetting and drying, would have provided the necessary conditions for concentration and molecular self-assembly, leading to the formation of the first cell.

have withstood the predicted early atmospheric pressures. Estimates suggest that in the early environment (4700-3500 Ma), when there would have been a heavy meteoritic bombardment, organics accumulated at a rate of 10^6-10^7 kg/year, resulting in a layer of organic material several centimetres deep spread over the surface of the earth.

Another crucial event in the formation of the first cells would have been development of the outer cell membrane, since without this there would be no means of simple containment of the macromolecules within the cell. There is also the question of how organic compounds became sufficiently concentrated to form more complex molecules. An extremely important environment for both processes to occur would have been shallow tidal pools, where cycles of solar heating and cooling, combined with tidal wetting and drying, would have provided the necessary conditions for concentration and molecular self-assembly.

Containment of the macromolecules probably resulted from the presence of amphiphilic molecules. These molecules have one part that is hydrophobic (i.e. water insoluble) and the other part hydrophilic (i.e. water soluble). In water, amphiphilic molecules tend to aggregate to form bilayers (with the water-soluble parts aligning), creating small, closed vesicles, the aqueous contents of which are isolated from the external medium. On drying, these bilayers fuse into multilayers and any other molecules present become trapped between the layers and incorporated into the vesicles on rehydration. It is envisaged therefore that wetting and drying cycles in the prebiotic tidal pools may well have provided an ideal environment for formation of an early protocell.

A more recent, and just as controversial, third theory is closely associated with the terrestrial accretion theory, in that it suggests that the evolution of the first cell took place on another, planet, possibly Mars. These cells were then carried to Earth via meteoritic bombar-dment. Again it is acknowledged that most organic material would have perished in space, but it is also noted that 'it only takes one cell to infect a planet'.

THE FIRST PROKARYOTES

Of all the organisms presently on the Earth, prokaryotes are the simplest in structure, smallest physically, and most abundant in terms of number of individuals. They range between approximately 1 and 10 gm in size, are single celled (although many types have cells joined together within a mucilaginous sheath), lack an organized nucleus surrounded by a nuclear envelope, and reproduce by binary fission (i.e. each cell increases in size and divides into two). Prokaryotes also tend to have one

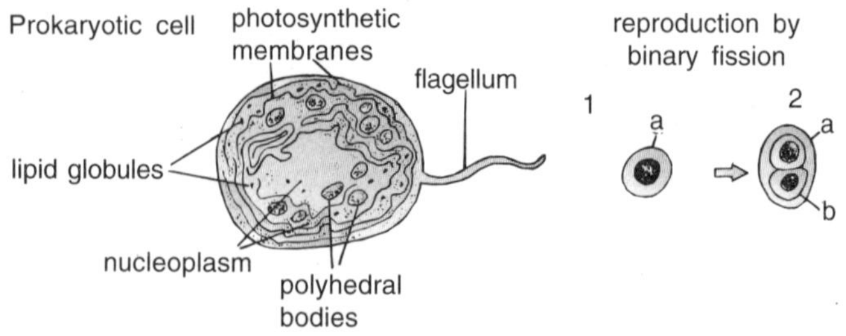

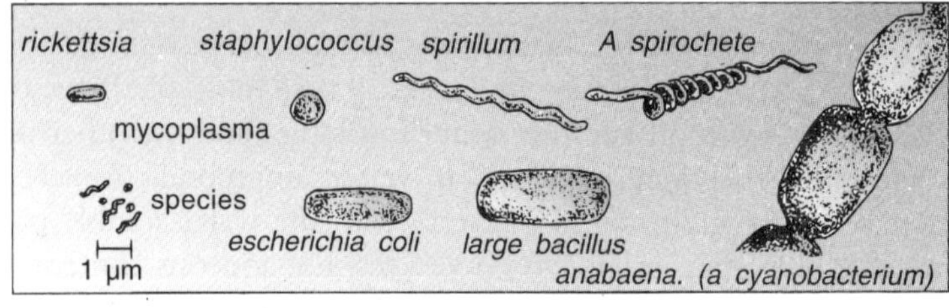

Figure 1.5: The most common cell shapes of prokaryotes.

of three basic cell shapes: a straight rod shape (bacilli); a spherical shape (cocci); or a long, coiled shape (spirilli).

Evidence for some or all of these characteristic features (shape, size, arrangement of organelles, and method of reproduction) is apparent in the earliest fossil records, suggesting that by 3500 million years ago, a complex system of prokaryotes had developed on planet Earth.

Evidence from Stromatolites

Stromatolites, some dating as far back as 3500 Ma, are found in localities ranging from Spitsbergen and central East Greenland to South Africa, Australia, and parts of Antarctica. They are composed of numerous alternating light and dark layers of sediment and are thought to represent the trace fossils of ancient microbial mat communities (algal/bacterial mats).

One of the most widely cited examples to explain stromatolite formation are the stromatolite beds presently accreting in Shark Bay on the west coast of Australia. Here, laminated cushion-like structures can be seen in the intertidal zone, composed of alternating layers of calcium carbonate and filamentous and coccoid micro-organisms (algal mats). These layers are formed when algal mats spread over the ocean substrate and trap and bind a layer of sediment particles. A layer of calcium carbonate forms on top due to microbially mediated precipitation, and the light-requiring micro-organisms respond by growing upwards.

A subsequent layer of sediment is trapped by the newly formed algal mat, and thus through time, a layered structure will develop. This is, however, just one example, and research indicates that stromatolite organisms are extremely diverse and colonize both hard and loose substrates, preparing a broad spectrum of benthic environments for stromatolite construction. Such structures appear to form today only in hypersaline environments which exclude the grazing invertebrates that now inhibit their formation in other marine settings. Their Precambrian equivalents had no such grazers to contend with.

The distribution and composition of stromatolite communities are strongly determined by ecological factors, including temperature, pH, salinity and water potential, light intensity, and the ability for anaerobic growth. Subtle differences in these environmental factors determine the microbial communities present and this, in turn, affects the shape of the stromatolite.

For example, many coneshaped stromatolites (Conophyton) have been found in fossil deposits dating as far back as 3500 Ma. Broadly similar structures have been found forming in the hot springs of the Yellowstone National Park in Wyoming, USA, where the thermal waters have temperatures of between Sand 59°C and pH values of 7-9.

The predominant micro-organisms responsible for the formation of these 'conophytons' in the Yellowstone springs have been identified as filamentous cyanophytes (blue-green algae), but other photosynthetic filamentous bacteria are also present (e.g. *Chloroflexus*).

The presence and shape of the fossil stromatolite beds dating back to the Proterozoic have therefore been used to infer a number of features. These include the early presence of prokaryotes, the probable types of microbial communities represented, evidence of early prokaryotic metabolism (especially photosynthesis), and the type of environment in which they were formed.

Until recently, information from the fossil stromatolite beds was always inferential since they rarely contained direct evidence of the micro-organisms responsible for their accretion.

However, ancient biomolecules have recently been extracted from 2700 million-year-old rocks that are characteristic of cyanobacteria, thus confirming the early presence of organisms capable of oxygenic photosynthesis.

Most geologists would still agree, however, that they are a better indication of the long-term evolution of the Earth's environment rather than the microbial communities associated with them.

Evidence from Cherts and Shales

Fossil micro-organisms have also been extracted from other early sedimentary deposits, including cherts and shales. Some of the earliest examples are found in the Warrwoona Group in Western Australia, where filamentous and colonial fossil structures have been reported from carbonaceous cherts dated between 3500 and 3300 Ma.

These fossils, which are predominantly small spheres and filaments, indicate close morphological comparison with extant prokaryotes, based on both cell size and also structure (i.e. whether single cells or in colonies, whether the colonies are sheath enclosed, etc.).

The micro-organisms contained within the Warrwoona Group sediments have therefore been 'classified' as photoautotrophic cyanobateria (oxygen-producing blue-green algae) and taken to indicate the presence of organisms capable of oxygen-producing photosynthesis as far back as 3500 million years ago (early Archaean).

Cell size and structure have not been the only factors used to identify these early micro-organisms as prokaryotes; evidence of their reproductive mode has also been discovered. There are now many examples in the early fossil record of cells that have been preserved while in a state of cell enlargement and division, suggesting binary fission.

Younger Proterozoic deposits (between 2500 and 540 Ma)

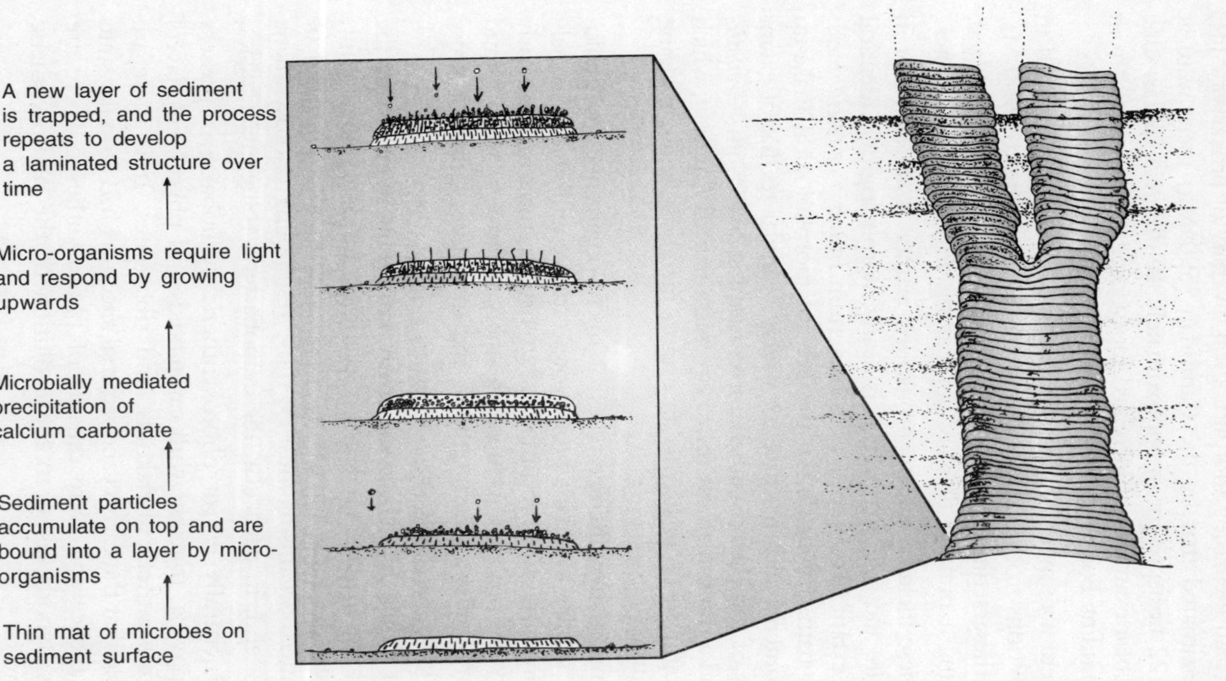

Figure 1.6: Process of stromatolite formation on the west coast of Australia.

indicate an increasing morphological diversity of prokaryotic life. It is estimated that by the Cambrian (590 Ma) there were at least 122 taxa present in approximately 40 different biotas. One of the best examples of increased morphological diversity is from the Gunflint Formation in southern Ontario, Canada.

Here a number of micro-organisms have been identified in thin sections from black carbonaceous chert dating to 1900 Ma. From these sediments at least 12 species have been recognized, including a number that are comparable to extant prokaryotes.

These include: a filamentous form named *Animikiea*, that in structure and cell organization is nearly morphologically identical to the extant filamentous cyanobacterium *Lyngbya or Oscillatoria;* a type named *Gun flintia*, the general morphological make-up (cell contents and structure) of which is similar to that of extant species of the chemosynthetic, iron-forming bacterium, *Crenothrix*; and a multi-filament micro-organism named *Eoastrion*, which is thought to be related to an extant, metal-oxidizing, budding bacterium.

Thus many different types of micro-organisms, morphologically similar to extant prokaryotes, are recognizable extremely early on in the fossil record. Characteristic features of these early prokaryotes probably included an ability to ferment, to withstand hot temperatures (thermophily), and to respire without the use of oxygen (anaerobic respiration).

All would have been extremely important requisites in the earliest environments. From a plant evolutionary viewpoint, however, the most interesting of these numerous examples of early micro-organisms must be those resembling photosynthetic bacteria and, in particular, the cyanobacteria (blue-green algae).

Structurally extant photosynthetic cyanobacteria possess chlorophyll a, together with carotenoids and phycobilins, layers of photosynthetic thylakoids, and ribosomes. It is therefore probable that the early cyanobacterial ancestors had a similar suite of organelles and were capable of photosynthesis. There are various hypotheses as to the evolution of the photosynthetic pathway.

One of the most plausible is that the evolution of photosynth-

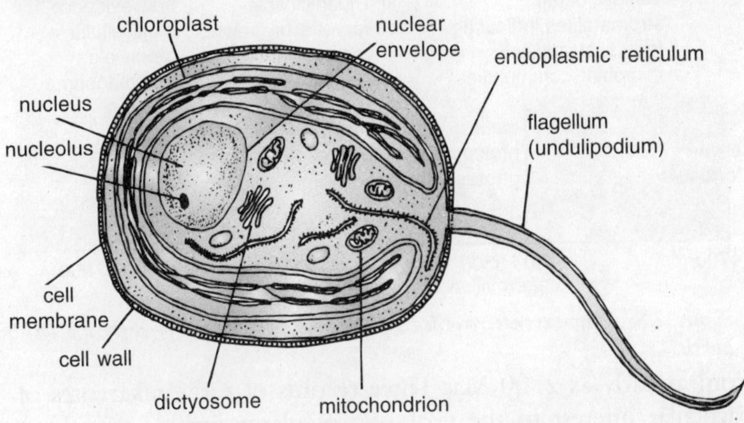

Figure 1.7: Cross-section of a eukaryotic cell.

esis paralleled the evolution of the structural mats (stromatolites). Thus, as organisms grew in the more productive but more dangerous uppermost layers of the microbial mats, new forms evolved that had the biochemical pathways to utilize the energy of the sunlight and the electrons from the water to convert atmospheric CO_2 into organic compounds (i.e. photosynthesis). The splitting of the water molecule in this reaction would have resulted in the release of O_2 into the atmosphere—a process that was essential for the evolution of aerobic life on Earth.

EVOLUTION OF THE EUKARYOTES

Eukaryotes differ from prokaryotes in that they have a membrane-bound nucleus in which the DNA is contained, organelles including mitochondria, integrated multicellularity, and sexual reproduction (sometimes). They constitute the three major groups of multicellular organisms (plants, animals, and fungi), along with many groups of the Protista, including species of red, green, and brown algae. Because of the diversity and importance of eukaryotic organisms to life on Earth, it is often stated that the evolution of eukaryotes was one of the most important events in the history of life.

Geological Evidence

Evidence for eukaryotes (from fossil organisms and ancient biomolecules) suggests that they were probably present on Earth

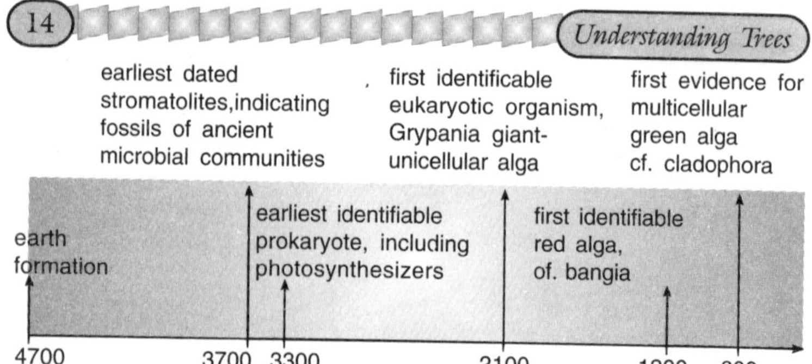

Figure 1.8: Major events recorded in the geological record of early life on Earth.

from as early as 2700 Ma. Three records of early eukaryotes of particular interest to the evolution of plants include the oldest recorded alga *Grypania*, dated to 2100 Ma, fossil bangiacean red algae, dated to approximately 1200 Ma, and cladophoralean green algae, dated to between 800 and 700 Ma.

Grypania

The oldest recorded alga *is Grypania*, which was discovered in the banded iron formations of northern Michigan and dated to approximately 2100 Ma.

This fossil, which is a coiled cylindrical organism, 0.5 m in length and 2 mm in diameter, has a number of morphological characteristics, including its large size, morphological complexity, and structural rigidity, to suggest that it represents a giant unicellular alga.

A suggested modern-day analogue is *Acetabularia*, which is a dasycladalean (green algae) and a photosynthetic autotroph.

Bangiophyte Red Algae

Some of the earliest evidence for eukaryotic organisms bearing a close resemblance to extant species of red algae comes from the silicified carbonate rocks of the Huntington Formation in arctic Canada.

These rocks, dated to approximately 1200 Ma, contain fossils that are extremely close in morphological detail to the extant red algal genus *Bangia*. Because of the exceptional preservation of the fossils in this formation (they are permineralized), it has been possible to cut thin sections both transverse and perpendicular to the bedding plane. Perpendicular cross-sections have revealed unbranched, uniserate filaments, 15-45 mm in diameter and up to 2 cm long.

The filaments appear to consist of stacked disc-shaped cells enclosed in a relatively transparent enveloping sheath and, in some sheaths, constrictions are apparent. Examination of these filaments in transverse section has revealed that they are composed of up

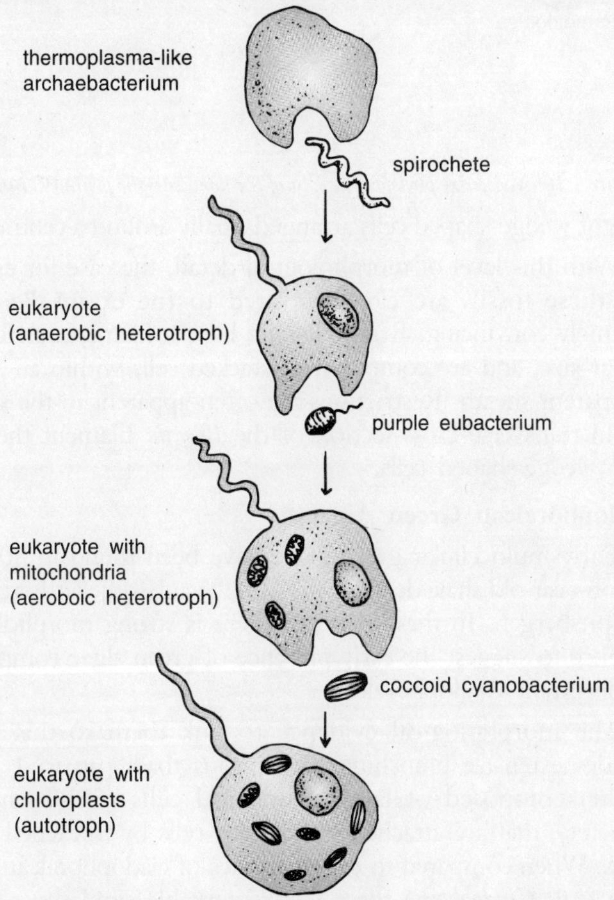

Figure 1.9: Proposed endosymbiosis of cyanobacteria and purple non-sulphur bacteria, leading to the acquisition of chloroplasts and mitochondria in the eukaryotic cell.

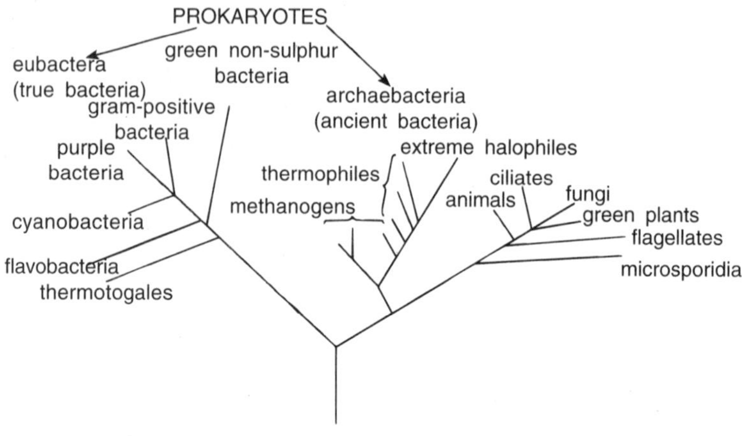

Figure 1.10: Molecular phylogenetic split of the domains: the primary kingdoms.

to eight wedge-shaped cells arranged axially around a central core.

With this level of morphological detail, the case for arguing that these fossils are closely related to the extant *Bangia is* extremely convincing. Extant *Bangia* have a filamentous form, a similar size, and are composed of stacked cells within an almost transparent sheath. Restrictions are often apparent in the sheath, and in transverse cross-section of the *Bangia* filament there are eight wedge-shaped cells.

Cladophoralean Green Algae

Early multicellular green algae have been found in 800-700 million-year-old shale deposits from the Svanbergfjellet Formation on Spitsbergen. In these deposits there is strong morphological evidence to suggest the early presence of green algae comparable to the extant Cladophorales.

The morphological evidence to link them to this group includes extensive branching filamentous thalli (up to 1 cm in height) composed of large cylindrical cells (50800 mm in diameter), that are attached to adjacent cells by thickened septal plates. When compared to extant species of cladophoralean green algae (e.g. *Cladophora*) there is a remarkable similarity.

It is interesting to note that present-day classifications divide the green algae (over 7000 species) into five classes (Charophyceae, Chlorophyceae, Pleurastrophyceae, Prasinophyceae, and

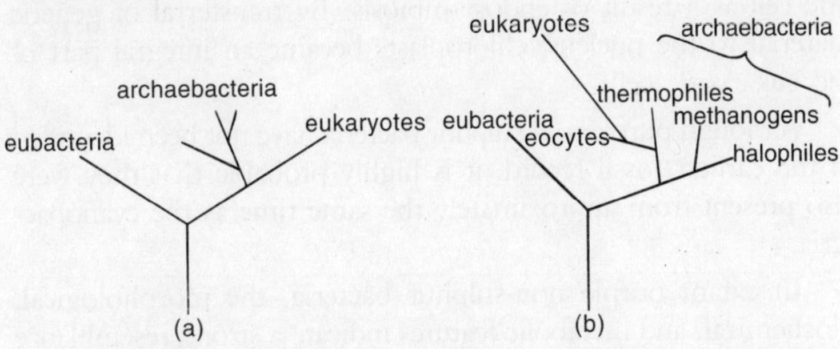

Figure 1.11: Two theories based on molecular phylogenies to explain the origin of eukaryotes: (a) molecular phylogeny proposed by Woese et al., and (b) the new phylogeny indicating that the eukaryotes share a most recent common ancestor with only the eocytes.

Ulvophyceae). Each is thought to represent a separate evolutionary line. The Ulvophyceae, which clude the cladophoralean green algae, are predominantly marine (and include the green seaweeds). They contain a number of species that form 'algal mats' in tropical reef areas.

Geological evidence has therefore provided many pieces of the jigsaw to understanding the earliest evolution of life on Earth. It gives a first estimation as to what was around and when. However, further insights into the evolutionary relationship between the early prokaryotes and the eukaryotes have been gained not by looking at the fossil record, but by examining extant forms at both a structural and a molecular level.

Comparison with extinct forms

Structural comparisons

From a structural viewpoint, extant forms of the fossil prokaryotes, resembling the cyanobacteria (blue-green algae), are some of the most interesting. Certain species of extant photosynthetic cyanobacteria bear a remarkable similarity, both in terms of intracellular structure and molecular make-up, to chloroplasts.

These similarities have led to the generally accepted theory that the early cyanobacteria may have been instrumental in evolution of the first eukaryotic cells. It is suggested that the cyanobacterium became incorporated into a pre-existing eukaryotic cell as a result of endosy-mbiosis. By transferral of genetic material to the nucleus, chloroplasts became an integral part of the eukaryotic cell.

Although purple non-sulphur bacteria have not been identified in the earliest fossil record, it is highly probable that they were also present from approximately the same time as the cyanobacteria.

In extant purple non-sulphur bacteria, the morphological, biochemical, and metabolic features indicate a strong resemblance to mitochondria. Endosymbiosis of a purple non-sulphur bacterium is therefore suggested as another probable process that led to the formation of an integrated and functioning eukaryotic cell.

Molecular comparison

As species diverge from a common ancestor, they accumulate genetic mutations (usually substitutions in the genetic code), resulting in species becoming more genetically different over time. Thus by comparing the genetic difference between two groups, it is possible not only to relate them to a common ancestor but also to calculate the amount of time that has elapsed since they diverged from that ancestor.

Using evidence attained from the geological record as to which groups to examine (i.e. those first present), a number of molecular studies have been carried out in recent years to determine both the probable evolutionary pathway to, and time of divergence of, the earliest eukaryotes.

By comparing base sequences of ribosomal RNA (rRNA) among a large selection of bacteria (more than 1000 species have been analysed), as well as a number of protein sequences, a number of interesting molecular relationships have emerged.

These have upset the traditional two-kingdom classification of eukaryotes and prokaryotes. The main conclusions drawn from these molecular studies to date are as follows.

Prokaryotes have a deep phylogenetic split between archaebacteria and *eubacteria* Molecular evidence has established that there are two distinct groups of bacteria that are as genetically distinct from each other as each is from the eukaryotes. These two groups have been named the archaebacteria (ancient bacteria) and eubacteria (true bacteria). The archaebacteria include the extreme halophiles (salt-tolerant bacteria), the methanogens, and the extreme thermophilic (heat tolerant) sulphur-metabolizing bacteria (eocytes). The eubacteria include cyanobacteria and purple sulphur bacteria. To date there is direct evidence in the geological record for numerous cyanobacteria (eubacteria) but not, as yet, any archaebacteria. However, carbon isotope signatures from ancient sedimentary carbonates indicate that the onset of methane cycling occurred from at least as early as approximately 2800 million years ago, thus providing indirect evidence for the early presence of at least the methanogens.

The molecular result that prokaryotes have a deep phylogenetic split between archaebacteria and eubacteria thus has significant implications in understanding eukaryotic evolution and, in particular, suggests that the traditionally cited evolutionary pathway of the eukaryotes evolving from the prokaryotes may be too simplistic.

Eukaryotes bear a specific phylogenetic relationship to archaebacteria Molecular evidence also indicates that the eukaryotes are phylogenetically closer to the archaebacteria than the eubacteria.

That is, the archaebacteria either separated early from the eubacterial lineage and/or the eukaryotic lineage branched from the archaebacteria after they separated from the eubacteria. Further molecular phylogenetic work on the archaebacteria has also revealed that it is probably the eocytes (that is the extreme thermophilic, mostly sulphur-metaboliz-ing bacteria) that are the closest bacterial relatives to eukaryotes.

Thus, rather than the eukaryotes sharing a common ancestor with all three main groups in the archaebacteria (the halophiles, the methanogens, and the eocytes), the eukaryotes only share a most recent and common ancestor with the eocytes.

Eukaryotes are an ancient group almost as old as the prokaryotes Using a molecular clock based on DNA sequences, dating of the split between the three major lineages (eukaryotes, eubacteria, and archaebacteria) suggests that diversification occurred at around 3500 million years ago (or earlier). The earliest eukaryotes evolved at, or very shortly following, the split of the archaebacteria and eubacteria. However, these 'early' eukaryotes, including those that are in the lowermost branches of the phylogenetic tree and therefore most similar genetically to the archaebacteria, are simple microorganisms that have no mitochondria and are confined to oxygen-free environments.

The middle branches of the tree (i.e. the next most similar), which have a calculated molecular age of between 2800 and 2400 million years ago, include protists that contain mitochondria but no chloroplasts. It is not until a calculated molecular age of 1000

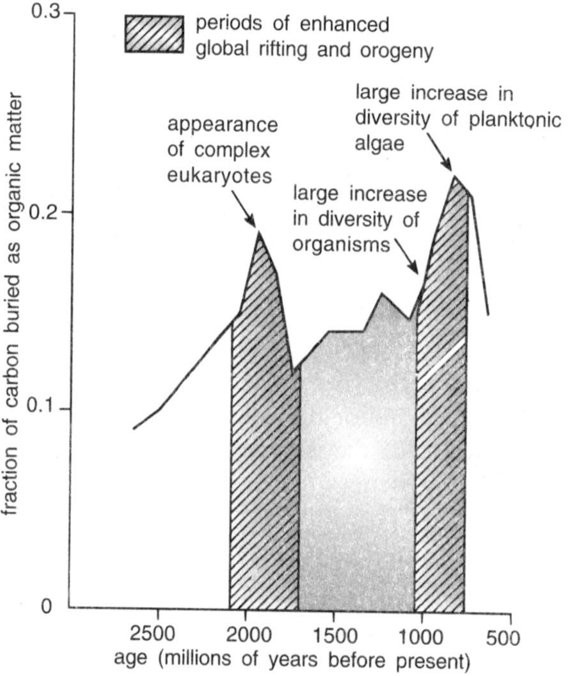

Figure 1.12: Organic carbon burial between 3000 and 500 million years ago measured through the isotopic analysis of carbonate carbon in sedimentary rocks. When organic carbon is buried, it effectively becomes shielded from oxidation, causing the oxygen that was previously bound to it as CO_2 to become 'free' to enrich the atmosphere. This has been used as a proxy record of levels of atmospheric oxygen between 2600 and 600 Ma. Also indicated are periods of enhanced global rifting and orogeny and the timing of major events in eukaryotic evolution.

million years ago that major radiation of multicellular organisms, especially photosynthesizers, is believed to have occurred.

The pattern of this preliminary phylogeny raises some interesting questions as to the rate and process of evolution of life on Earth. In particular, the fact that the major clades (animals, fungi, plants) appear to branch near a common point implies a rapid burst of evolution.

This, along with other lines of evidence, has led to the suggestion that the major epochs in eukaryotic evolution are in some way causally linked to significant geological events in the early period of Earth's history .

POSSIBLE TRIGGERING MECHANISMS OF EUKARYOTIC EVOLUTION

A number of researchers have suggested that the combined geological/molecular record demonstrates a general trend of episodic increases in biological diversity through the Archaean and Proterozoic (3500-540 Ma). Six major biological events, which are specific to the plant fossil record are recognized, including

(i) the origin of life on Earth and diversification of anaerobic archaebacteria and eubacteria at or around 3500 Ma;

(ii) origin of photosynthetic organisms around 3300 Ma;

(iii) the appearance of organisms capable of aerobic metabolism and cellular acquisition of the organelles mitochondria and, later, chloroplasts, between 2800 and 2400 Ma;

(iv) the appearance of complex eukaryotic organisms in the geological record from approximately 2100 Ma;

(v) the large increase in diversity of organisms and radiation of acritarchs—a group of organic-walled microfossils, the majority of which are thought to represent reproductive cysts of green algae or alage cysts, from approximately 1000 Ma;

(vi) the large increase in diversity of planktonic algae from approximately 540 Ma.

The question therefore arises as to whether it is possible to relate these periods of evolutionary change to evidence in the geological record for environmental change. A number of tentative links have been suggested for events (1) and (2), including decreasing meteoritic bombardment between approximately 4000 and 3800 Ma and rapid accretion of continental crust at around 2700 Ma.

However, more detailed consideration of the environmental conditions associated with tectonic activity and also climatic conditions associated with periods of glaciations have been given for the changes apparent from 1000 Ma (in particular rising levels of atmospheric oxygen resulting from increased burial of organic carbon).

Rising Levels of Atmospheric Oxygen

It has long been suggested that a rise in atmospheric oxygen could have been one of the triggering mechanisms responsible for the appearance of complex eukaryotes.

In order to examine a possible causal link, it is necessary to have a means of measuring levels of atmospheric oxygen other than by increases in the number of aerobic organisms, which involves a circularity of argument.

Two geochemical methods that provide independent records are the measurement of the isotopic fractionation of carbon and sulphur in ancient sedimentary rocks.

Isotopic analysis of carbonate carbon in sedimentary rocks can give an indication of times of burial of organic carbon. When organic carbon is buried, it effectively becomes shielded from oxidation, causing the oxygen that was hitherto bound to it as CO_2 to become 'free' to enrich the atmosphere.

Results suggest that episodic increases in the burial of organic carbon occurred between -2200 and 1800 Ma and 1100 and 700 Ma. In contrast, measurement of the isotopic composition of biogenic sedimentary sulphides can be used to detect the process of sulphide production and whether it occurred in conditions with or without the presence of oxygen.

Comparison of deposits dated between 1050 and 640 Ma with younger deposits (i.e. < 540 million years ago) indicate a change in the process of sulphide production, from one driven within anaerobic conditions to one within aerobic conditions.

Both lines of evidence therefore point to increasing availability of atmospheric oxygen between "2200 and 540 Ma, and the former to episodic bursts of increase.

When the proposed times of increase in atmospheric oxygen (measured through carbon burial rates) are compared to geological evidence for periods of global rifting and orogeny, it becomes apparent that there might be some causal link between the two.

Thus increased atmospheric oxygen may be related to periods of tectonic activity. Such a process is therefore proposed for the earliest environments, whereby during periods of major global tectonic activity, atmospheric oxygen increased, and this was in some way causally linked to eukaryotic evolution.

Changing Environmental Conditions Associated with Glaciations

Geological evidence suggests that as many as four major glacial periods occurred in the late Proterozoic (1000-540 Ma), the final one, the Varanger ice age, taking place between approximately 610 and 590 Ma.

During the Varanger ice age, more acritarch extinctions occurred than originations, resulting in a decline in overall species number (75% reduction). Following the ice age, there was a large increase in species number and many new and highly ornamented acritarchs appeared.

A tentative link has therefore been suggested between the acritarchs and environmental/oceanographic changes (e.g. changing patterns of marine sedimentation) that accompanied the end of the Varanger glaciation.

Although just two examples are provided above, there are many other suggestions in the literature of bursts of evolutionary activity occurring at or around the same time as significant geological events in this early period of Earth history.

However, it is also highly probable that in these early environments there would have been spiralling ecological relationships.

Without a doubt, these would also have had a major impact on species diversity and number, resulting in the development of a complex marine ecosystem of plants and animals by the beginning of the Cambrian period, 590 Ma.

FLOWERING PLANT ORIGINS

Flowering plants (angiosperms) are the dominant plants in the world today, accounting for between 300 and 400 families and between 250 000 and 300 000 species (compared to approximately 10 000 species of pteridophytes and 750 species of gymnosperms).

However, in evolutionary terms, flowering plants are relatively recent, with fossil evidence indicating their first appearance at around 140 million years ago in the early Cretaceous, followed by rapid diversification and radiation in the mid-Cretaceous.

By the early Tertiary (~65 Ma), only 60 to 70 million years after their first appearance, angiosperms had attained ecological dominance in a majority of habitats and over a wide geographical area. As a group, therefore, even though they evolved some 300 million years later than the first vascular plants and 220 million years later than the first seed plants, they are of profound evolutionary interest.

This chapter examines the evidence for the first flowering plants, considers various theories as to why their appearance was so late in the geological record and discusses the proposed evolutionary pathways leading to angiosperm evolution.

EVIDENCE FOR THE FIRST ANGIOSPERMS

Features used to separate extant angiosperms from other seed plants include the enclosed nature of the ovary (the carpel or

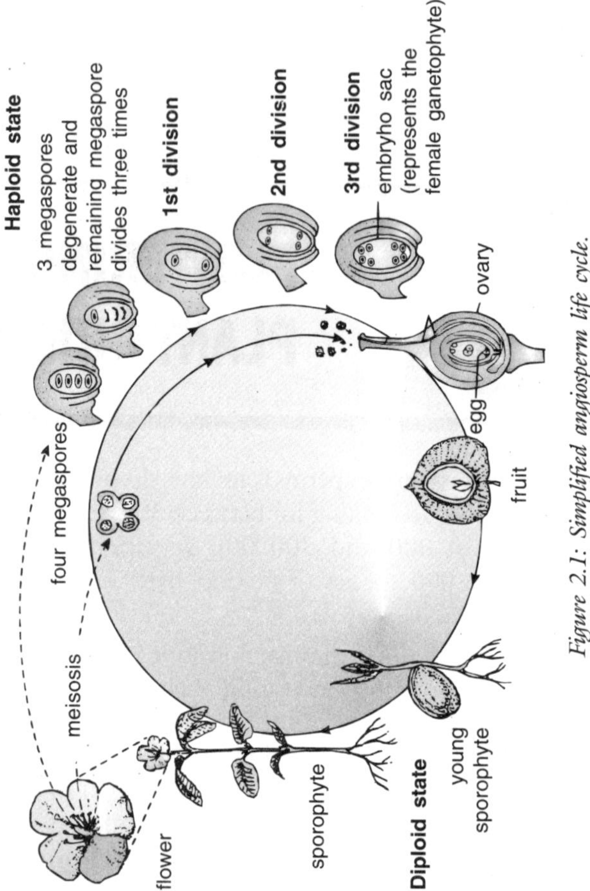

Figure 2.1: Simplified angiosperm life cycle.

carpels), the presence of flowers, specialized conducting cells in the xylem and phloem, ovules that have a doublelayered seed coat (two integuments), and pollen with a distinctive grain wall made up of columellae.

A number of characteristics of the angiosperm life cycle are also distinctive, including a process of double fertilization, whereby two sperms are released from the pollen tube into the ovary (which has one or several ovules inside it).

One sperm fuses with the egg to form the zygote (which divides immediately after fertilization to form the embryo), and the other sperm fuses with the embryo sac to produce the primary

Table 2.1: Distinguishing characteristics between monocotyledons and dicotyledons.

Characteristic	*Dicotyledons*	*Monocotyledons*
Flower parts (usually)	In fours or fives	In threes (usually)
Pollen	Usually with three	Usually having one pore
pores or furrows	or furrow	
Cotyledons	Two	One
Leaf venation	Usually netlike	Usually parallel
Primary vascular bundles in stem	In a ring	Complex arrangement
True secondary growth	Commonly present	Commonly absent with vascular cambium

endosperm (the storage tissue in the seed). The angiosperms were traditionally divided into monocotyledons and dicotyledons; however, this division is no longer supported by recent systematic studies.

Instead, two major monophyletic groups are now recognized, the monocots and the eudicots (which contain most, but not all, of the dicotyledons and are characterized by a pollen type with three apertures). The remaining dicotyledons constitute a third, smaller group, the magnoliids, which have pollen with a single aperture.

Although the similarities between the two major groups are far greater than the dissimilarities, the features that group angiosperms as a division and separate monocots from eudicots appear to have persisted from early stages of angiosperm evolution.

Evidence from the geological record suggests that angiosperms first appeared approximately 140 million years ago in the Valanginian, with their major radiation, leading to a global distribution, during the Albian-Cenomanian (~100-90 Ma). The earliest fossil evidence for angiosperms is represented in the record as flower parts, fruits, leaves, wood, and pollen.

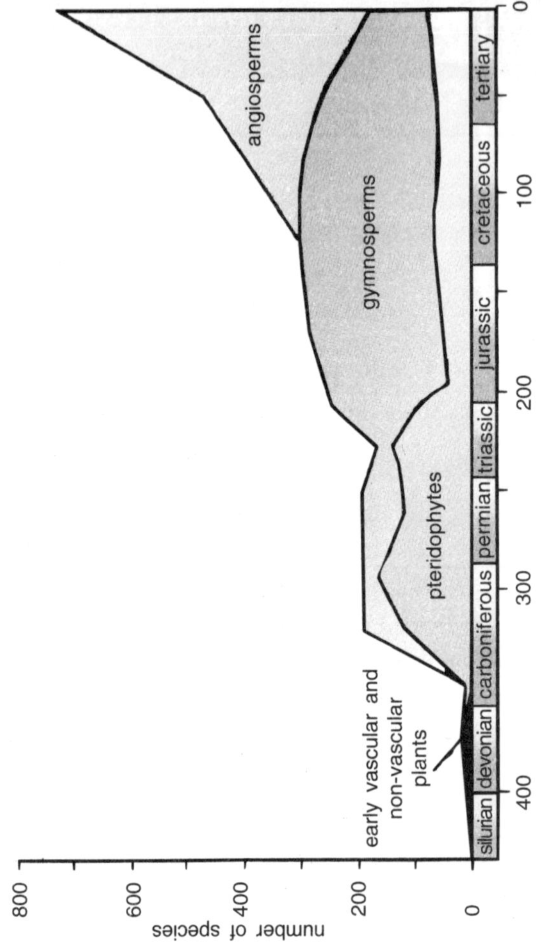

Figure 2.2: Evidence for the appearance and major expansion of the angiosperms from ~140 Ma and a dramatic increase in the number of angiosperms through the mid-Cretaceous.

Flower Parts

Some of the earliest known fossil flowers, dating back to approximately 127120 Ma, have been found in deposits from Portugal (Barremian or Aptian) and near Melbourne in Australia (Aptian). The fossil flowers from Portugal show character combinations that indicate magnoliid or monocotyledonous affinity.

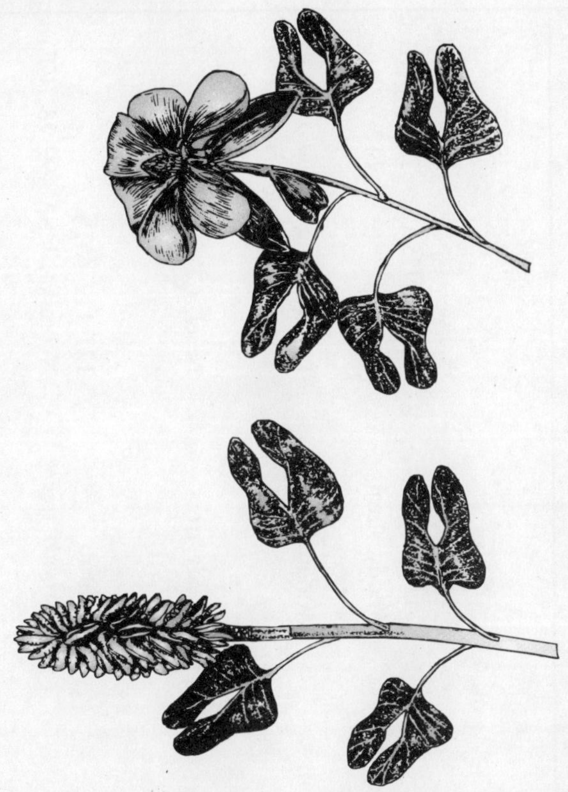

Figure 2.3: Fossil Archaeanthus linnenbergeri (~100 Ma), indicating many similarities with members of extant Magnoliaceae.

Those from Melbourne appear to be similar in floral arrangement to extant perennial herbs in the Piperaceae family, and probably grew in marshy habitats. Although such early finds are rare (the majority of evidence for fossil angiosperm flowers dates back only to approximately 100 million years ago), they show the greatest potential for further insights on early angiosperm biology, ecology, and evolution.

Most early fossil angiosperm flowers can be subdivided into two broad groups. Group (i) includes features such as relatively few flower parts (stamens, carpels, number of ovule/seeds per carpel, number of perianth members) and small (< 1 mm diameter), possibly unisexual flowers.

Table 2.2: Some of the earliest angiosperms in the fossil record.

Order/family/species	*Fossil evidence (leaves, pollen, flowers, wood)*	*Tree, shrub or herb*	*Fossil localities*	*Age (Ma)*
Dicotyledons				
Magnoliales				
Lesqueria	Fruits, flowers	? Herbaceous	Kansas, USA	112(99 (AL)
Archaeanthus	Fruit, leaves	? Herbaceous	Kansas, USA	112-99 (AL)
Protomonimia wood	Reproductive organ,	Woody shrub or tree	Japan	112-99 (AL)
Prisca	Fruit, leaves, stem or shrub	Woody tree	Kansas, USA	*99-93* (CE)
Winteraceae				
Walkeripollis	Pollen, wood or shrub	Woody tree (AP/AL)	Israel, California	121-99
Laurales				
Amborellaceae	Fruit	? Shrub	121-112 (AP)	
Crassidenticulum	Leaves shrub	? Woody tree/	Nebraska, USA	99-93 (CE)

(Table 2.2 Contd.)

(Table 2.2 Contd.)

Mauldinia	Flowers shrub	? Woody.tree/	North America	99-93 (CE)
Chloranthaceae				
Chloranthus	Flowers, pollen, seeds	? Herbaceous	North America	112-99 (AL)
Hedyosmum-like	Flowers, pollen	Herbaceous	Portugal (BA/AP)	127-112
Piperales	Flowers, pollen	Herbaceous	Portugal (BA/AP)	127-112
Platanaceae				
Platanus potomacensis	Flowers, pollen tree/shrub	? Woody	North America, Sweden	112-99 (AL)
Hamamelidales				
Hamamelidae	Leaves	? Herbaceous	Patagonia, Argentina	127-112 (BA/AP)
Monocotyledons				
Pandanaceae	Leaves	?	?	71-65 (MA)
Palmae	Leaves, pollen, and stem	Tree/shrub	New Jersey	89-85 (CO)

Such flowers are compared to those of existing angiosperm families such as Chloranthaceae, Piperaceae (the pepper family), and Platanaceae (the plane-tree family). In comparison, group (ii) has numerous flower parts and large, bisexual flowers (up to 65 mm in diameter).

These flowers are compared with those of extant angiosperm families such as Magnoliaceae, Degeneriaceae, and Winteraceae. An example of a fossil flower classified in this second group is *Archaeanthus*. This has a fossil record dating back to the Albian (~100 Ma), and demonstrates many features in common with extant species of *Magnolia*, such as numerous stamens (between 50 and 60) and free carpels (between 100 and 130).

It was originally suggested that the first flowers to evolve were similar to extant *Magnolia*, with numerous bisexual flowers (therefore those classified above in group (ii)), and that group (i) originated either by extreme reduction in the floral parts from group (ii) or from two different sources in the gymnosperms.

Fossil evidence, however, indicates that both types of flowers were present at around the same time. Also, in extant orders of angiosperms, extreme variations in the number of floral organs are not restricted to comparatively unrelated orders or families, but can occur within a genus, and even a single species, thus indicating that floral organization is very plastic.

It is highly probable therefore that the number and arrangement of floral organs changed many times during evolution, and that extremes in these features in the earliest angiosperms was not necessarily an expression of distant relationship.

Fruits

Earliest evidence for fossil angiosperm fruits dates back to the Aptian and Albian (~121 Ma), with examples from localities in Asia and North America, including fruits of ceratophyllales, juglandales, and ranunculids.

Many of these early seeds were small (1-40mm in length) in relation to later groups in the fossil record-a feature that is thought to be indicative of the 'weedy' stature of these early flowering plants.

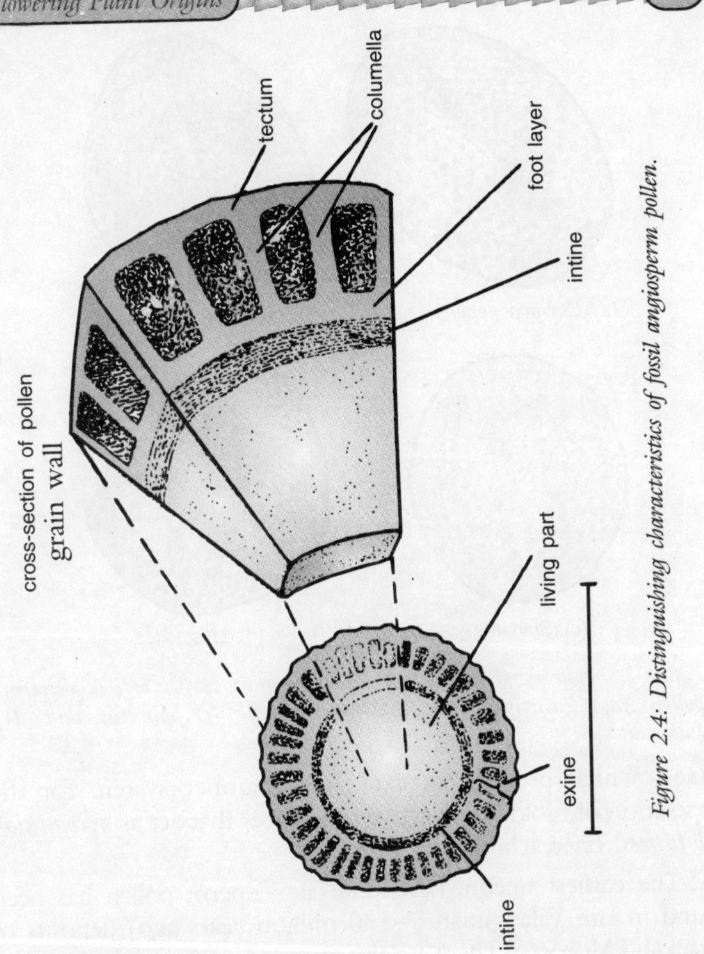

Figure 2.4: Distinguishing characteristics of fossil angiosperm pollen.

Comparison of seed sizes in extant floral groups, for example, broadly demonstrates that small propagules with thin seed walls and little storage material are associated with early successional plants that can be classified as 'r' strategists (weedy generalists.

Pollen

Angiosperm pollen is non-saccate (without bladders), and in the eudicots has numerous symmetrically arranged pores and furrows. In all angiosperms the pollen wall is divided into an outer layer (the tectum) supported on numerous short, radial structures (looking like columns and often referred to as colum-

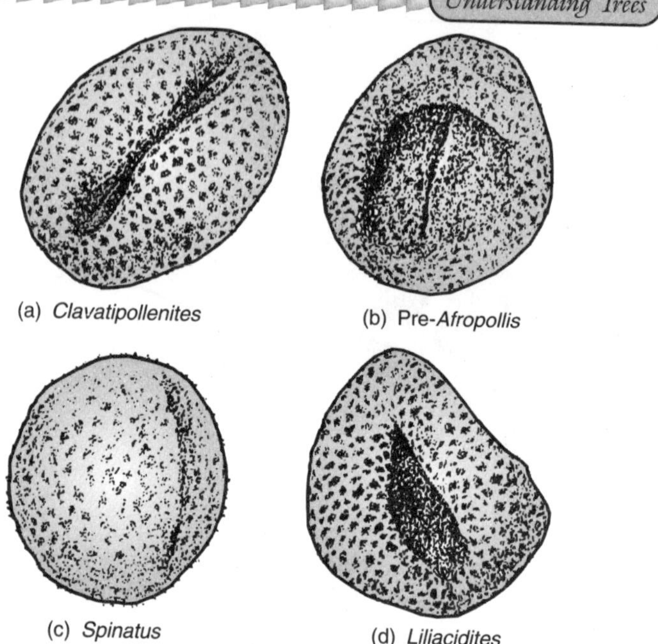

Figure 2.5: Four morphological types identified in the earliest fossil angiosperm pollen: (a) Clavatipollenites; (b) Pre-Afropollis; (c) Spinatus; and (d) Liliacidites.

ellae), which provide an extensive chamber system for the deposition of biologically active substances that act as '*recognition substances*' on reaching the stigma.

The earliest unequivocal fossil angiosperm pollen has been found in late Valanginian (~130 million years ago) deposits of Israel and Morocco. There are also reported occurrences of angiosperm pollen from older sediments in Libya (Berriasian, ~140 Ma) and China (Hauterivian), but the ages of these sediments are not well constrained.

All the earliest angiosperm pollen grains are small, between 10 and 50 μm in diameter, and distinguishable by their wall construction and the number and types of germination-furrows. Four morphological groups have been identified in the earliest angiosperm pollen, namely *Clavatipollenites*, Pre-A *fropollis*, *Spinatus*, and *Liliacidites*.

Those classified in the *Clavatipollenites* group have a characte-

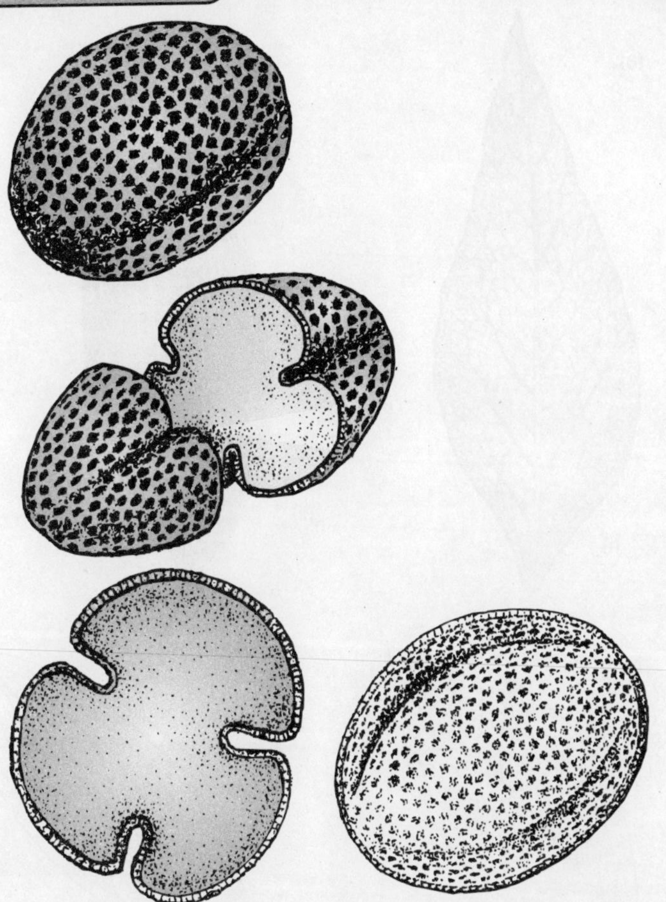

Figure 2.6: Fossil Tricolpites pollen, equatorial and transverse view. These grains were approximately 50µm in diameter.

ristic columellate wall with usually one germinationfurrow. Those in the Spinatus group can be distinguished, along with other features, by short spines on the margin of the grain.

The *pre-Afropollis* group contains grains that are inaperturate (i.e. no furrows) but have a grain wall pattern that is described as wedge-shaped, with fluted walls. Finally, those in the *Liliacidites* groups are distinguished by their larger size (up to 50 μm in diameter), their single germination-furrow, and a cell wall composed of very high columellae. A number of associations have been

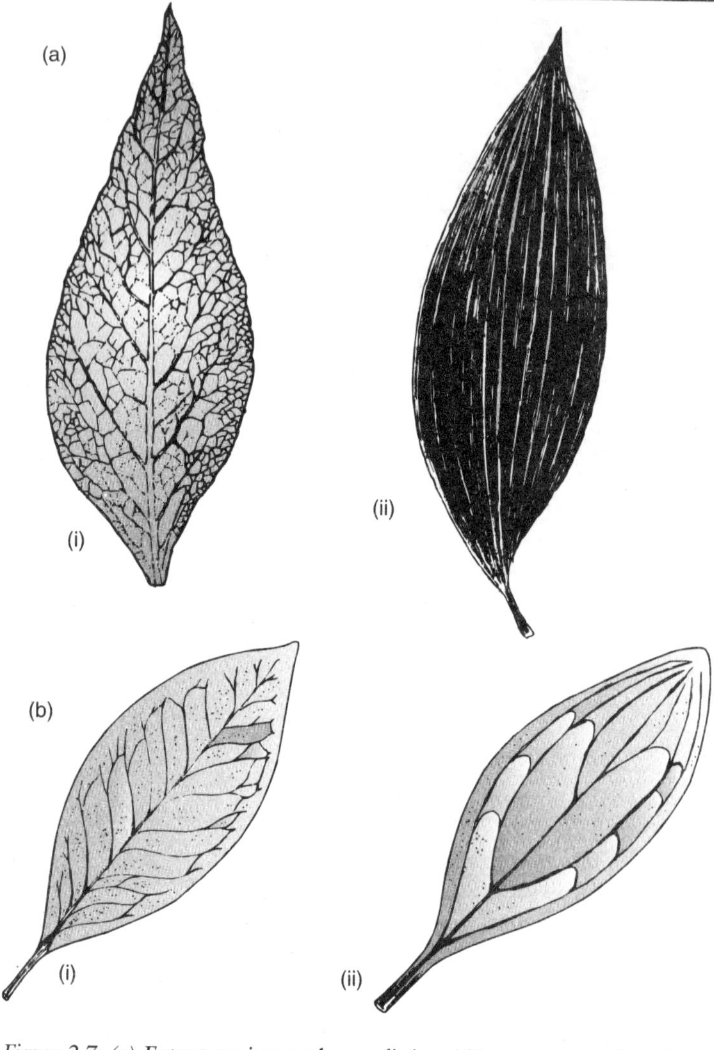

(a)

(i)

(ii)

(b)

(i)

(ii)

Figure 2.7: (a) Extant angiosperm leaves: distinguishing characteristics include (i) reticulate venation forming areoles on dicotyledon leaves, together with veins that end blind within the areoles, and (ii) parallel major veins arranged in sets of various sizes and interconnected by smaller veins on the lamina of monocotyledons. (b) Primitive angiosperm leaf types from the early Cretaceous: (i) dicotyledon, showing pinnate venation and entire leaf margin; (ii) monocotyledon, showing convergence of main veins at top of leaf and interconnecting veins.

made between the early fossil angiosperm pollen and extant types.

The fossil grains of *Clavatipollenites*, for example, apparently bear a close morphological resemblance to pollen of the extant family Chloranthaceae. *Clavatipollenites* has also been found within fossil flowers identified as members of the Chloranthaceae family, supporting the suggestion that it is associated with this family.

Those in the *Liliacidites* group, in comparison, have an outer layer (the sexine) that is similar in structure to that of extant monocotyledons such as Liliaceae. In increasingly younger sediments (Barremian/Aptian boundary), there is the appearance of more complex fossil pollen grains with various arrangements of pores and furrows.

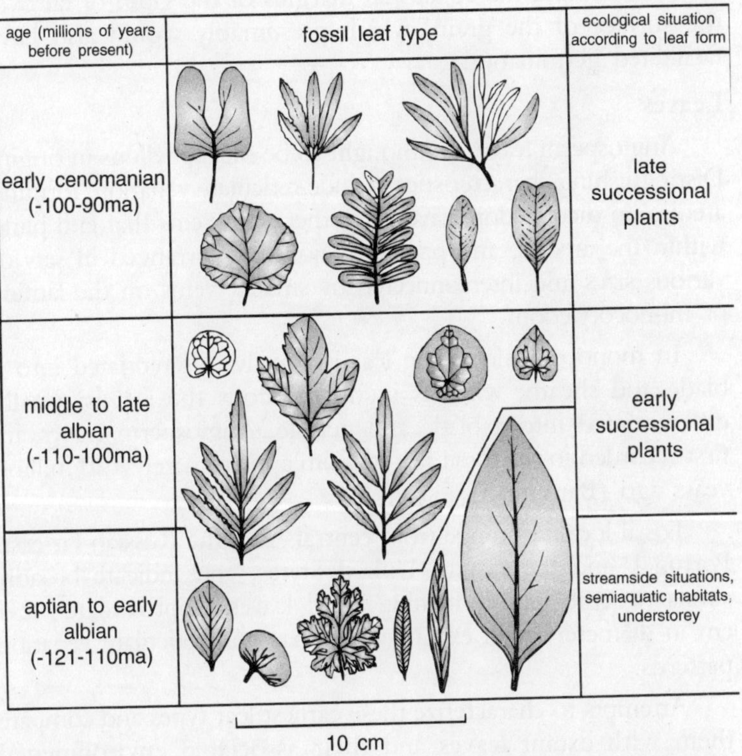

age (millions of years before present)	fossil leaf type	ecological situation according to leaf form
early cenomanian (-100-90ma)		late successional plants
middle to late albian (-110-100ma)		early successional plants
aptian to early albian (-121-110ma)		streamside situations, semiaquatic habitats, understorey

10 cm

Figure 2.8: Trends in the earliest fossil angiosperm leaves through the Cretaceous and classification of their probably ecological situation according to leaf form.

One type, named *Tricolpites*, for example, had three symmetrically arranged furrows (often referred to as tricolpate). Evolution of three furrows is thought to be an adaptation that facilitated germination on a stigmatic surface, as any orientation of a tricolpate grain would result in at least one germination furrow being positioned near or on the surface of the stigma. *Tricolpites* pollen grains have been found inside the anthers of fossil Platanaceae flowers, indicating a probable association with this family.

Another type of pollen grain to appear from the Cenomanian (~95 Ma) was spherical with numerous apertures resembling pores. These grains, known as polyporate, had pores either arranged around the equatorial margins of the grain or all over the surface of the grain, which presumably would also have facilitated germination.

Leaves

Angiosperm leaves are thought to be megaphyllous in origin. Distinguishing characteristics include reticulate venation, forming areoles on dicotyledon leaves, together with veins that end blind within the areoles, and parallel major veins arranged in sets of various sizes and interconnected by smaller veins on the lamina of monocotyledons.

In monocotyledons, the leaf is usually differentiated into a blade and sheath, whereas in dicotyledons the leaf is usually differentiated into a blade and petiole. Angiosperm leaves are first recorded in the fossil record from approximately 120 million years ago (Barremian).

Fossil localities range from central Asia, the Russian far-east, Portugal, and the eastern United States, and indicate broadly similar assemblages containing small leaves (approximately 2-4 cm in diameter) with expanded laminae and reticulate venation patterns.

Attempts to characterize these earliest leaf types and compare them with extant leaves and their associated environmental conditions (based on features such as presence/absence of driptips, entire or dissected margins, size of leaf blade) has led to the suggestion that most were similar to plants that grow in streamside situations, semiaquatic habitats, or as an understorey. In comparison, fossil leaves present in younger assemblages of Albian age (~110-100 Ma) possessed features characteristic of extant early successional plants, namely pinnately compound leaves, palmately lobed leaves, and shallow cordate leaves with serrated margins and palmate venation.

Leaves present in deposits of Cenomanian age (~100-90Ma) included leaf physiognomies (shape and size) that in extant species are typical of late successional plants.

These marked changes in angiosperm leaf physiognomy spanning the latter part of the early Cretaceous has led to the suggestion that although angiosperms were initially early successional plants, within a matter of 20 million years they had formed the canopy of late successional forests.

NATURE AND DISTRIBUTION OF THE EARLIEST ANGIOSPERMS

Trees, Shrubs, or Herbs?

Various lines of evidence from the fossil record, including fossil flowers, fruits, leaves, pollen, and also wood, suggest that by 100 million years ago (Albian/ Cenomanian) there was an increasing diversity of angiosperms in the global flora.

There is some difficulty, however, based on the available fossil evidence, in determining whether the earliest angiosperms were trees, shrubs, or herbs. Many of the earliest fossil families (i.e. *Chloranthaceae*, *Piperaceae*, *Platanaceae*, *Magnoliaceae*, *Degeneriaceae*, and *Winterace-ae*) have both arborescent and non-arborescent forms.

Hence, many competing hypotheses on the likely vegetative morphology of ancestral angiosperms have been proposed. These fall broadly into three schools of thought. According to the first, the earliest angiosperms were arborescent shrubs or small trees.

The second suggests that they were herbaceous and rhizomatous in habit, such as in extant Chloranthaceae or Piperaceae. A third intermediate hypothesis suggests that they were most probably herbaceous, weedy, small shrubs.

Increasingly, evidence from the fossil and molecular record

appears to support the third hypothesis. Angiosperm wood is rare in the early Cretaceous fossil record compared with that of gymnosperm wood, and it is not until the late Cretaceous (~70 Ma) that a diverse angiosperm wood flora is apparent. Most of the specimens of early Cretaceous angiosperm wood are also extremely small (< 10 cm in diameter).

It is generally assumed, therefore, that this lack of angiosperm fossil wood is a reflection of the herbaceous nature of the earliest angiosperms. This assumption is further supported by the fact that, in the fossil record, the earliest angiosperm seeds tend to be small (1-40 mm in length) with thin seed walls, and the leaves, small (2-4 cm in diameter) with expanded laminae and reticulate venation.

All of these characteristics in extant plants are usually indicative of small, weedy plants with a rapid life cycle. This evidence therefore appears to also support a herbaceous hypothesis.

However, recent molecular phylogenetic analysis, based on evidence from mitochondrial, plastid, and nuclear DNA in extant plants, has identified *Amborella*, a small shrub, as the basal branch of angiosperm phylogeny.

This finding therefore supports the intermediate hypothesis, that the earliest angiosperms were herbaceous, weedy, small shrubs. It is interesting to note, however, that the second most basal group identified by the molecular study of Qui *et al.* (1999) are Nymphaeales, which are aquatic rhizomatous herbs. These results therefore also lend support to the herbaceous origin hypothesis.

Dicotyledons or Monocotyledons?

In the fossil record, the earliest flowers and most of the leaves and pollen appear to be from dicotyledons and, although several lineages of monocotyledons are now known from both the palynofloras and megafloras of Barremian-Albian age (127-112 Ma), early monocotyledon fossils are rare.

Various suggestions have been made as to why there is this apparent paucity of early monocotyledons. First, it has been suggested that the majority of the monocotyledons were herbaceous (as is the case for extant monocotyledons) and therefore

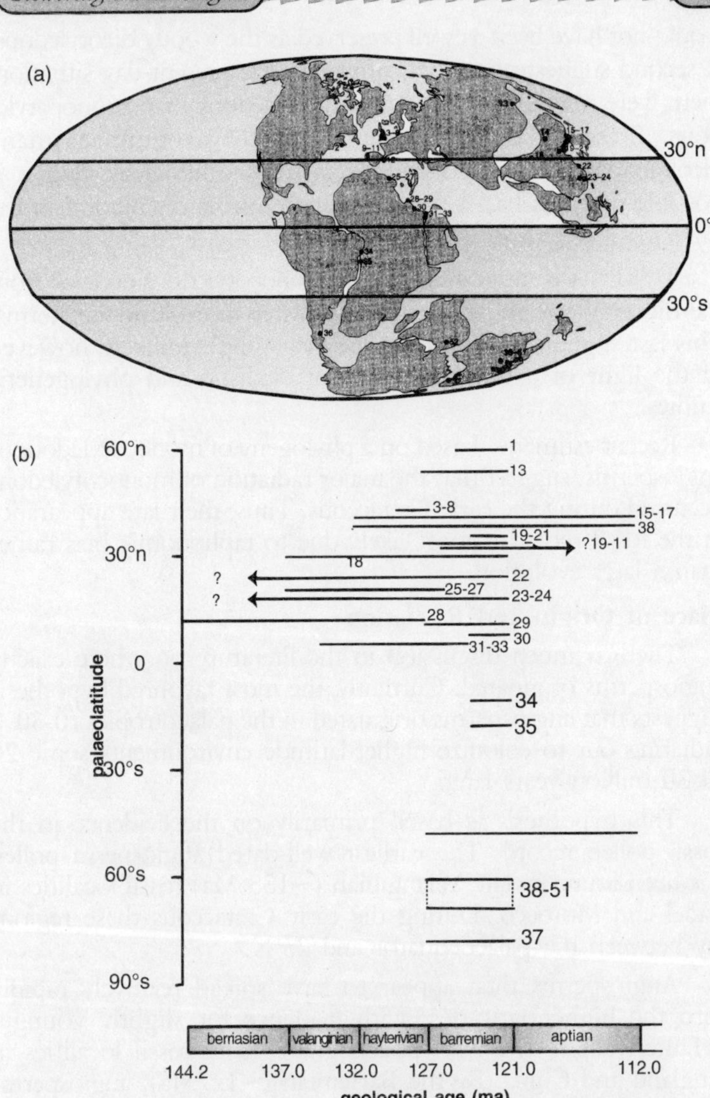

Figure 2.9: (a) Global distribution of earliest angiosperm occurrences (pre-Aptian, < 121 Ma) recorded in the fossil pollen record, plotted onto a palaeogeographical map of age 135 Ma (Valaginian). (b) Graphical representation of the data presented on the map above. Horizontal lines represent the temporal ranges suggested for the specific angiosperm taxa, the numbers correspond to the localities listed on the map.

would not have been as well preserved as the woody dicotyledons. A second suggestion is that, similar to the present-day situation, there were many more genera of dicotyledons than monocotyledons. Presently there are approximately six times as many dicotyledons as monocotyledons in the world's flora, and it is possible that this had a major influence on representation in the early fossil record of angiosperms.

Thirdly, it is suggested that the monocotyledons evolved from the dicotyledons and therefore were later in evolutionary terms. This last suggestion appears to be increasingly unlikely, however, in the light of a number of recent cladistic and phylogenetic studies.

Recent estimates, based on a phylogeny of monocotyledonous angiosperms, suggest that the major radiation of monocotyledons occurred during the early Cretaceous. Thus, their late appearance in the fossil record is most likely due to taphonomic bias rather than a later evolution.

Place of Origin and Radiation

There is much discussion in the literature on where exactly angiosperms originated. Currently, the most favoured hypothesis suggests that angiosperms originated in the palaeotropics (0-30°), radiating out to colonize higher-latitude environments some 20 to 30 million years later.

This hypothesis is based primarily on the evidence in the fossil pollen record. The earliest well-dated angiosperm pollen has been found in late Valanginian (~135 Ma) fossil localities in Israel and Morocco. During the early Cretaceous these regions lay between the palaeoequator and 25°N.

Angiosperms then appear to have spread relatively rapidly into the higher latitudes, with evidence for slightly younger (Hauterivian, ~132 Ma) pollen grains from fossil localities in England and China. By the Barremian (~127Ma), angiosperms appear to have been widespread, with fossil localities in central Africa, Australia, Europe, and China.

Although angiosperms appear to have spread relatively quickly, they did not become floristically prominent in the low palaeolatitudes (between ~30°N and 30°S) until the Aptian (~120 Ma), and in higher palaeolatitudes (between 40 and 65°S) until the Cenomanian (~100 Ma).

However, differences in both diversity and abundance between the low and high latitudes persisted for at least another 30 million years. In the Maastrichtian (~70 Ma), for example, angiosperms dominated low latitude pollen assemblages, accounting for 6080% of pollen, whereas in the high latitudes, they accounted for only between 30 and 50% of the total pollen.

The remaining percentage of pollen in high-latitude floras was made up of gymnosperms and pteridophytes. The apparent paucity of early angiosperms in these high-latitude environments is thought to be due, in part, to limitations of light and temperature for a substantial part of the year.

Such environmental conditions would have offered few opportunities for the replacement of existing well-adapted vegetation, dominated by conifers and ferns, by '*weedy*' angiosperms.

Angiosperm diversity and abundance in the high latitudes increased slowly through the early and mid-Cretaceous, most probably as a function of their biology rather than due to slow migration rates. Even today in the tundra and boreal biomes of the high-latitude regions of North America and Eurasia, for example, angiosperms are of relatively low abundance compared to gymnosperms, in particular the conifers.

Although the early angiosperms were not an invasive element in the highlatitude environments, for later angiosperm groups the high-latitudes appear to have been centres of origin. Southern Gondwana, in particular, appears to have been a centre of origin for *Nothofagus*. *Nothofagus* is presently an important element of the southern hemisphere flora, and according to the fossil record of this genus, evolved in southern high latitudes during the Maastrichtian (~70 Ma).

WHY SO LATE?

Even though angiosperms were present from as early 140 Ma (BerriasianValanginian), in plant evolutionary terms this is late. The first unequivocal evidence for angiosperms in the fossil record is up to 300 million years later than the first vascular land plants, and, as a group, they are therefore the most recent.

The 'enigma of angiosperm origins' and their late arrival in the fossil record have long been areas of palaeobotanical interest

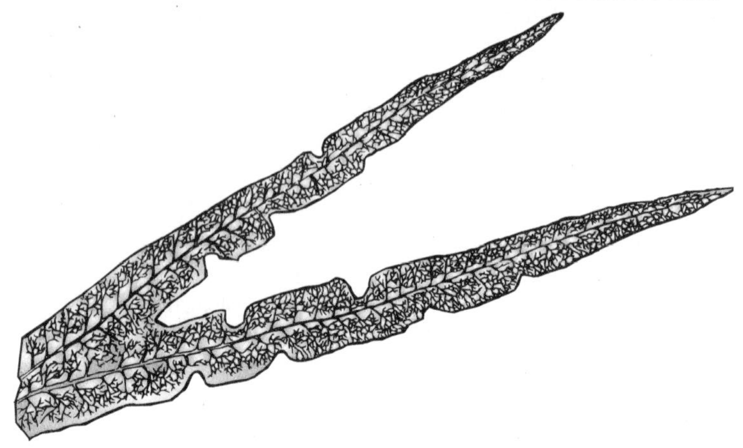

Figure 2.10: Fossil Furcula leaf.

and research. There are a number of hypotheses are to why they appear so late in the fossil record.

These include bias in the fossil record (therefore they evolved much earlier but went undetected), and the suggestion that their evolution was triggered by a particular set of environmental conditions, and/ or biotic interactions (such as co-evolution with faunal groups). A broad overview of these different hypotheses will be considered in the following section.

Nature of the Fossil Evidence

One commonly cited explanation for the late appearance of angiosperms is due to taphonomy. It is suggested that there is a bias in the fossil record against the preservation of the earliest angiosperm vegetative or reproductive parts.

Thus it is argued that angiosperms may have been part of the global vegetation much earlier than the Cretaceous, but were situated in dry upland environments, where preservation potential would have been poor.

Both fossil and molecular evidence exists to support this hypothesis, although neither is particularly convincing. Fossil evidence for a pre-Cretaceous origin of angiosperms is based on early examples of angiosperm-like pollen, fruiting axes, and leaves.

Angiosperm-like pollen, recognized by a tectate pollen wall, has been found in deposits dating as far back as the Triassic (~220 Ma) and includes several species of grains with a single furrow that have been classified loosely in the *Crinopolles* group. However, many discount this evidence since this early 'pollen' has never been found within angiosperm flowers.

In addition, other morphologically similar types of early pollen, originally classified as angiosperm-like, have since been demonstrated to belong to earlier groups (i.e. gymnosperms or pteridophytes), or be contained in deposits that were stratigraphically misplaced and much younger than originally thought.

Fossil evidence for angiosperm fruiting axes has been described recently from a late Jurassic fossil locality in China. The angiosperm megafossil named *Archae fructus liaoningensis*, and placed within the Magnoliophyta division, displays a number of key angiosperm features, including, for example, ovules (seeds) that are completely enclosed in carpels, and leaf-like structures subtending each axis, which are probably flowers.

However, there has been much debate about the age of the formation in which this 'early' angiosperm is preserved. The fossil was extracted from the lower part of the Yixian Formation of the Liaoning Province, China, which has been dated by biostratigraphical correlations to late Jurassic (~145 Ma).

However, other lines of evidence, including radiometric dating (^{40}Ar-^{39}Ar) and palaeontological evidence, suggest that the lower part of the Yixian Formation is of late early Cretaceous age (~125 Ma), casting some doubts on the claim that this is the first unequivocal pre-Cretaceous angiosperm megafossil.

Angiosperm-like leaves have been found in deposits dating back to the late Triassic (~210 Ma), the most commonly cited being a leaf-type named *Furcula*. This leaf appears to have a typical angiosperm-like venation pattern. However, *Furcula* leaves also display forking laminae, which are much more common in certain pteridosperms.

The classification of this leaf type as angiospermous therefore remains ambiguous, and from the fossil evidence alone (pollen, fruiting axes, and leaves) there is a justifiable scepticism concerning the pre-Cretaceous occurrence of angiosperms. However, evidence

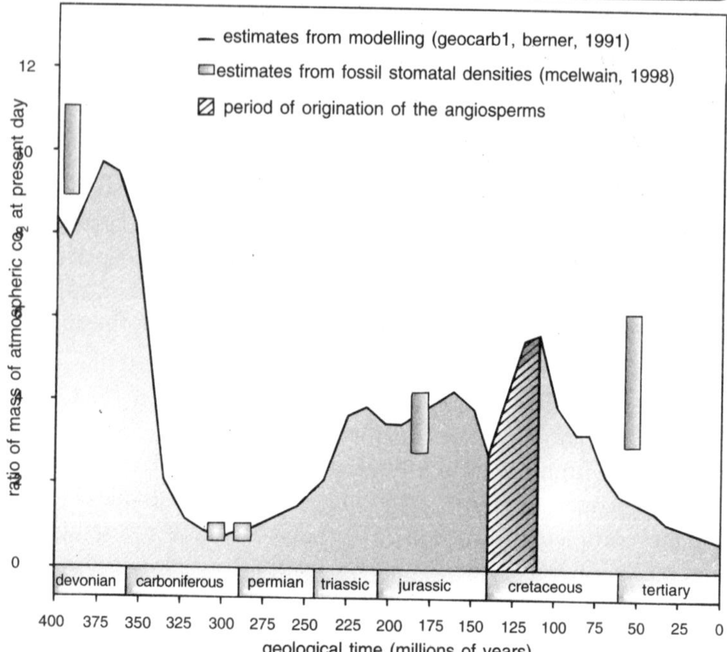

Figure 2.11: Estimated variations in atmospheric CO_2 during the past 400 million years. The general direction of the trends are supported by independently derived results from carbon isotope analysis of palaeosols and stomatal densites on fossil leaves. For comparison, the latter are indicated on the graph. Both are plotted against ratio of mass of atmospheric CO_2 at time t to present day (where present day is taken at the pre-industrial value of 300 p.p.m.v.). The early to mid-Cretaceous rise in atmospheric CO_2 is highlighted, along with the major change apparent in the plant fossil record during this time.

from molecu-lar analyses has rekindled some support for a pre-Cretaceous origin for angiosperms.

Construction of a molecular clock, based on the number of substitutions that have occurred since the divergence of monocotyledons from dicotyledons, suggests that this event may have occurred as early as 300 million years ago in the late Carboniferous. Thus by inference, this study suggests that angiosperm origins must have occurred much earlier in plant evolutionary history.

But a note of caution must be added since the method used in this study compared the number of substitutions that occurred

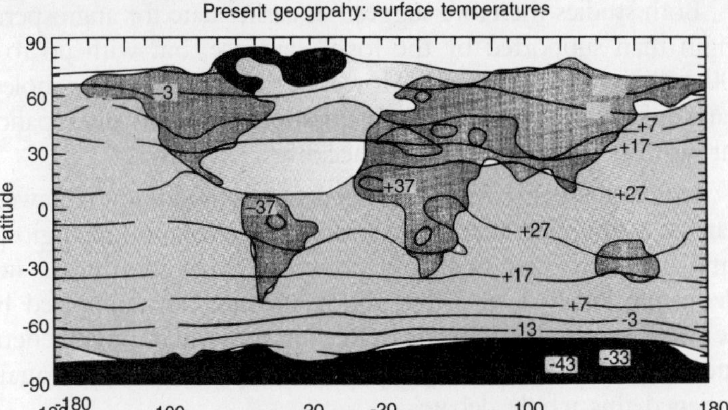

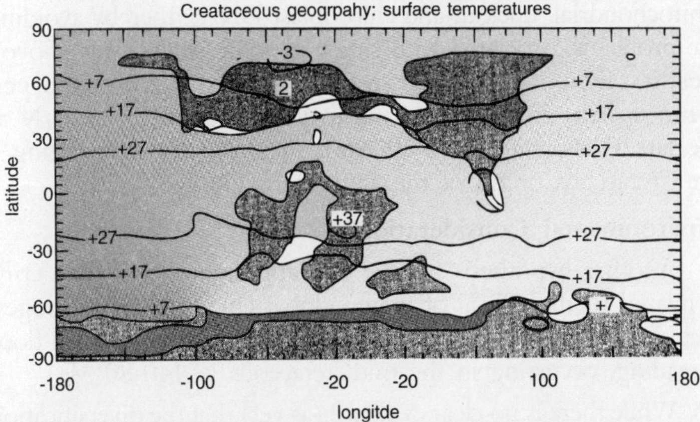

Figure 2.12: Computer-simulated model of mid-Cretaceous surface temperatures (~100 Ma) compared to present. The model used predictions of Cretaceous topography, ice cover (stippled), continental positions, and sea-level in comparison with the present day in order to determine global surface temperatures. From this model it is predicted that the average global temperature during the Cretaceous was approximately 4.8°C warmer than present. Temperatures are contoured in °C.

in DNA of a slowly evolving glycolytic enzyme in nine extant species. When the same question (i.e. divergence of monocotyledons from dicotyledons) was asked using DNA from chloroplast sequences of extant species, the molecular clock suggested a date of between approximately 250 and 200 million years ago (Triassic).

Both studies therefore suggest an earlier date for angiosperm origin than supported by the fossil evidence, but with up to a 100 million year discrepancy. However, the results of these molecular studies have not only been questioned on this discrepancy, but also on a number of other accounts.

It is argued that their phylogenetic methodology is flawed, that the assumption that rates of molecular evolution in angiosperms has remained relatively constant through time is not adequately justified, and that the results are not supported by the angiosperm fossil record. Recent molecular phylogenetic studies of 106 extant angiosperms, however, have yet again reopened this whole debate.

This study analysed gene sequences for all three plant genomes (mitochondrial, nuclear, and chloroplast DNA), thereby avoiding the problems associated with single genome analysis (as above). Results from this study suggest that the split between gymnosperms and angiosperms may have occurred as early as the late Carboniferous (~290Ma), therefore also supporting a pre-Cretaceous origin of the angiosperm lineage.

Environmental Considerations

Another hypothesis for the late appearance of angiosperms is related to the effects of major global environmental changes, including oceanic anoxia, increased tectonic activity, and sea-floor spreading, occurring in the midCretaceous (~140-80 Ma).

While there is no clear evidence (as yet) that the diversification and radiation of angiosperms was triggered by these environmental events, a number of floristic changes in mid-Cretaceous vegetation do correlate broadly with them.

It is suggested that these major environmental changes may have conferred competitive advantages to the angiosperms at the expense of the previously dominant gymnosperms and pteridophytes. In particular, the period between 124 and 83 million years ago (Aptian to Campanian) saw a dramatic change in continental configurations.

Although the supercontinent Pangea had started to break up by the early Jurassic (~200 Ma), a period of rapid plate spreading was initiated in the Aptian (~124 Ma) until the Cenomanian

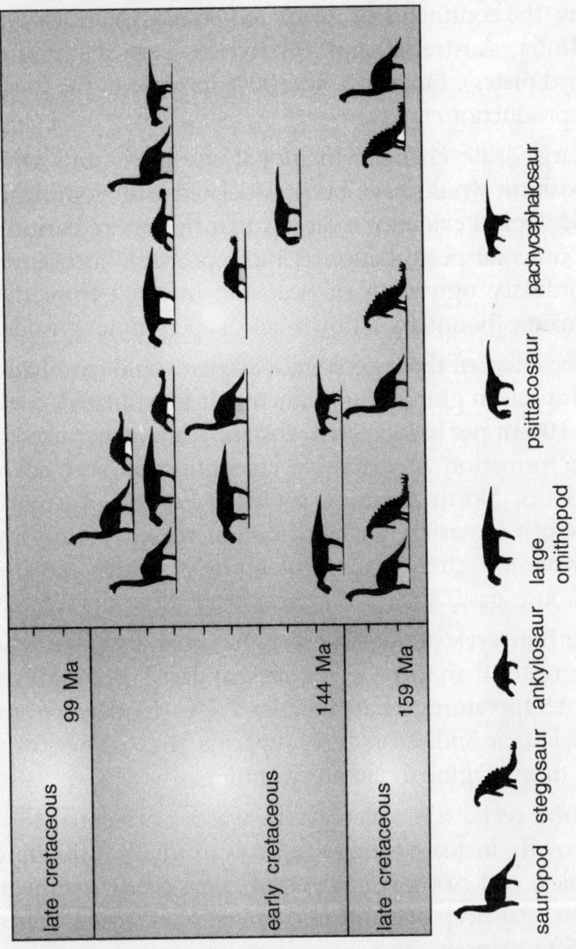

Figure 2.13: Stratigraphic record of herbivorous dinosaurs through the late Jurassic/early Cretaceous. It is proposed that the transition from highbrowsing forms to low browsers in the early Cretaceous resulted in increased mortality among the gymnosperm seedlings and thinned out the forest structure, thus creating gaps in the canopy and highly disturbed environments. Early angiosperm traits, such as small structure, rapid life cycle, and high colonizing ability, would have given them the competitive advantage on these disturbed substrates, thereby promoting their radiation.

(~83 Ma). This resulted not only in changing continental configurations (the continents of Africa and South America were formed, and India, Australia, and Antarctica were distinguishable as attached plates), but also a 50-100% increase in the Earth's ocean crust production.

Large-scale changes in global sea levels and atmospheric composition would have been associated with continental break-up. Geological evidence indicates that this entire period of major environmental perturbation is most probably attributable to an extraordinary upwelling of heat and material from the Earth's core-mantle boundary, known as a superplume episode.

The effect of these geological events would have had a significant impact on global environments. It is estimated, for example, that a 100-m rise in long-term eustatic sea level occurred, resulting in the formation of extensive epicontinental seas covering the interiors of North America, southern Europe, Australia, Africa, and South America. In addition, increased volcanism, which accompanied the plate movements, would have pumped greenhouse gases into the atmosphere, most notably CO_2.

Carbon cycle modelling indicates that CO_2 levels were 4-5 times greater than those of the present day. This could have raised global temperatures by as much as 7.7°C. Evidence from various palaeoclimatic indicators also supports the suggestion that this was a time of global climate warming.

Coral reefs, for which warm water is essential for survival and growth, increased their ranges as much as 1500 km closer to the poles, and isotopic analysis of deep ocean sediments ($5^{18}0$) suggests that deep ocean water, presently hovering near freezing, was 15°C warmer.

There is also no evidence for polar ice during this period of time. But why should increasing warmth promote angiosperm evolution or favour their diversification and radiation? A number of key innovations are recognizable among angiosperms which may have made them more drought resistant and therefore at a competitive advantage.

These include tough, leathery leaves that were commonly reduced in size; a tough, resistant seed coat that protected the young embryos from drying out; vessel members providing much more efficient water-conducting cells than in previous groups; and a deciduous habit.

The latter characteristic would have been critical in periods of drought but is not, however, unique to angiosperms. For instance, a number of gymnosperms (e.g. glossopterids, Ginkgo-ales, and Cycadales) are thought to have been deciduous, particul-arly at higher latitudes.

The predominance of drought-resistant features, as well as a weedy life history and rapid reproduction, in the early angiospe-rms may have given them a competitive advantage in increasingly disturbed environm-ental conditions and warm climate.

An alternative explanation, is that dramatically accelerated speciation rates, which are characteristic of the angiosperms, simply led to an overwhelming diversity of adaptive types.

Biotic Interactions

Dinosaur-Angiosperm Coevolution

One hypothesis proposed for the late appearance of the angiosperms is that their evolution was closely associated with the'large-scale radiation of certain groups of tetrapods, and that dinosaur feeding behaviour promoted the evolution of flowering plants.

This hypothesis is based on apparent evidence in the fossil record to suggest that a change in herbivore communities from high to low browsers occurred at approximately the same time as the initial evolution and radiation of angiosperms.

Dinosaur fossil evidence suggests, for example, that approxi-mately 160 million years ago, in the late Jurassic, 95% of the preserved biomass of dinosaurs was made up of sauropods and stegosaurs. These were high-browsing herbivores with a diversity of cranial and dental adaptations indicating a diet of a wide range of conifer tissue.

It is argued that these high-browsing forms would have put intense pressure on the canopies of the mature trees, but permitted the development of gymnosperm saplings. However, from approximately 144 million years ago (Jurassic/ Cretaceous

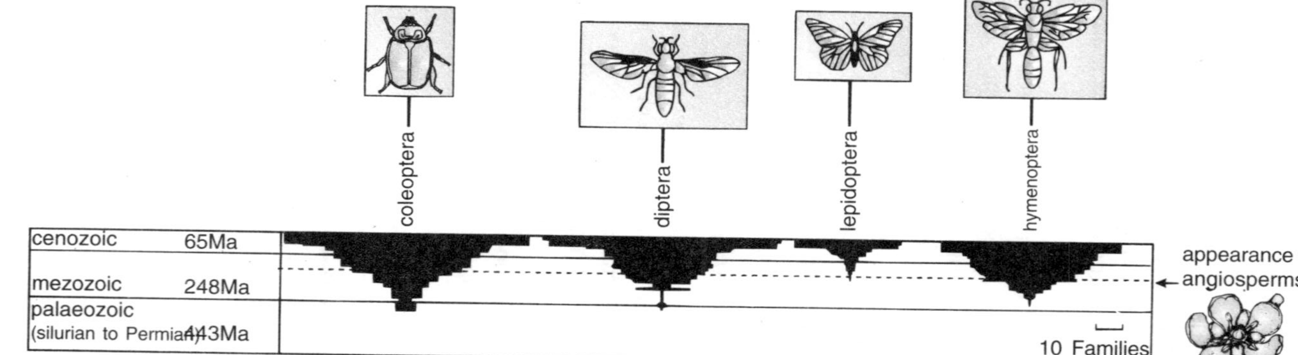

Figure 2.14: Spindle diagrams to display diversity of fossil insect families Diptera, Coleoptera, Lepidoptera, and Hymenoptera from the Silurian (~443 Ma) to present. The temporal position of the first appearance of angiosperms in the fossil record is also indicated.

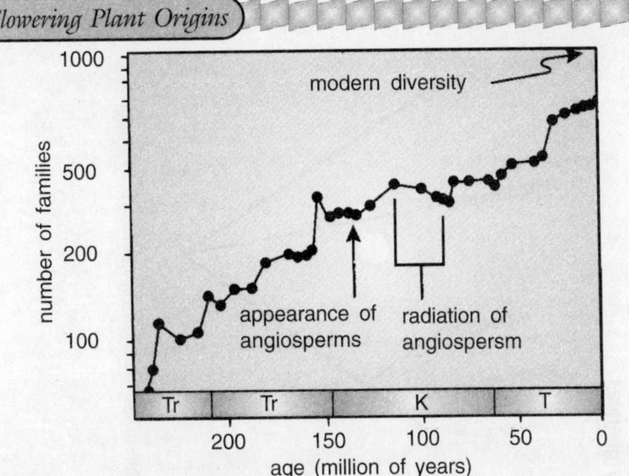

Figure 2.15: Insect familial diversity from the Triassic (~248 Ma) to present, plotted on a semi-logarithmic scale. The temporal position of the first appearance of angiosperms in the fossil record, and their subsequent radiation, are also indicated.

boundary) the herbivore communities changed considerably and new groups of big, low-browsing ornithischian dinosaurs appeared in the fossil record.

It is suggested that these intense low-browsing dinosaurs would have increased mortality among the gymnosperm seedlings and thinned out the forest structure, thus creating gaps in the canopy and highly disturbed environments. Early angiosperm traits, such as small structure, rapid life cycle, and high colonizing ability, would have given them the competitive advantage on these disturbed substrates, thereby promoting their radiation.

Additional work on plant-herbivore interactions adds further detail to the above in suggesting that it was the mechanics of chewing among herbivores that aided angiosperm evolution during the Cretaceous.

In particular, the radiation of ornithischian dinosaurs between 160-120 million years (mid-Jurassic-midCretaceous) may have played an important role, since these were the first group of herbivores to develop a transverse chewing motion (which ground the food before passing it into the gut), thereby enabling these animals to exploit more fully the newly evolving plant resource.

However, recent work comparing the timing and location of

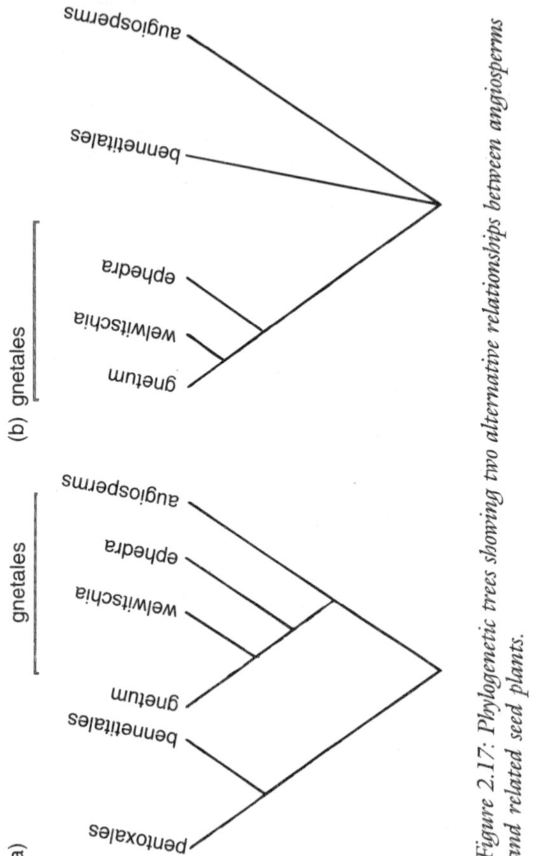

Figure 2.17: Phylogenetic trees showing two alternative relationships between angiosperms and related seed plants.

the evolution of angiosperms with major events in the evolution of dinosaur herbivory has rejected this hypothesis, for a number of reasons. First, the fact that angiosperms did not comprise a significant proportion of the global flora until the late Cretaceous suggests that it is highly unlikely that they formed a major constituent of dinosaur diets during the early Cretaceous.

Secondly, detailed examination of the timing of the dinosaur fossil record suggests that no major event in the evolution of herbivorous dinosaurs can be correlated with angiosperm origins. Innovations in chewing and the onset of factors such as low browsing, for example, either precede or post-date the appearance

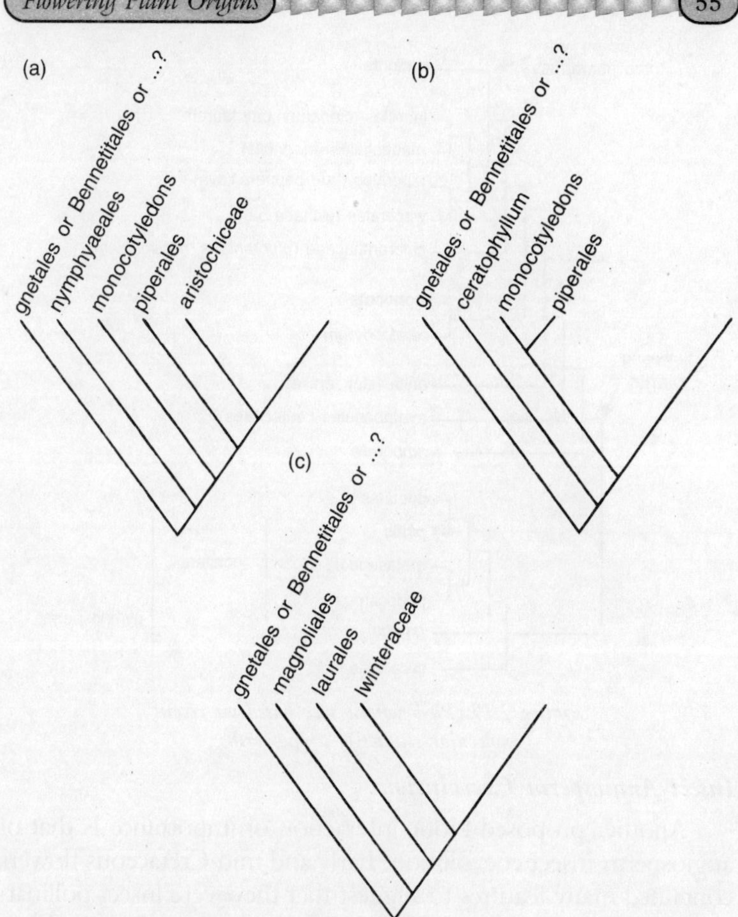

Figure 2.18 (a-c): Phylogenetic trees to indicate alternative relationships for major basal clades within the angiosperms.

of the first angiosperms in the fossil record. In addition, changes in dinosaur browsing behaviour at the Jurassic-Cretaceous boundary may not have been so marked as previously suggested. Thirdly, fossil evidence currently available suggests that there was no spatial overlap between the earliest angiosperms and the major clades of herbivorous dinosaurs.

Most early Cretaceous dinosaur localities, for example, were situated at palaeolatitudes higher than 30°N and 30°S, with only around 10% of the total number within 20° of the palaeoequator, where the earliest angiosperms occurred.

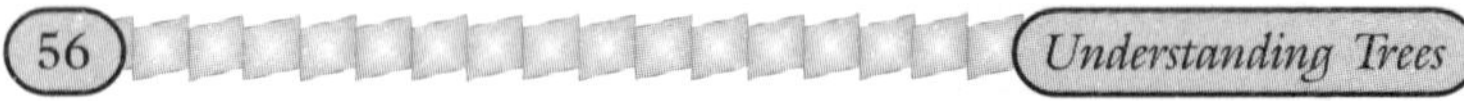

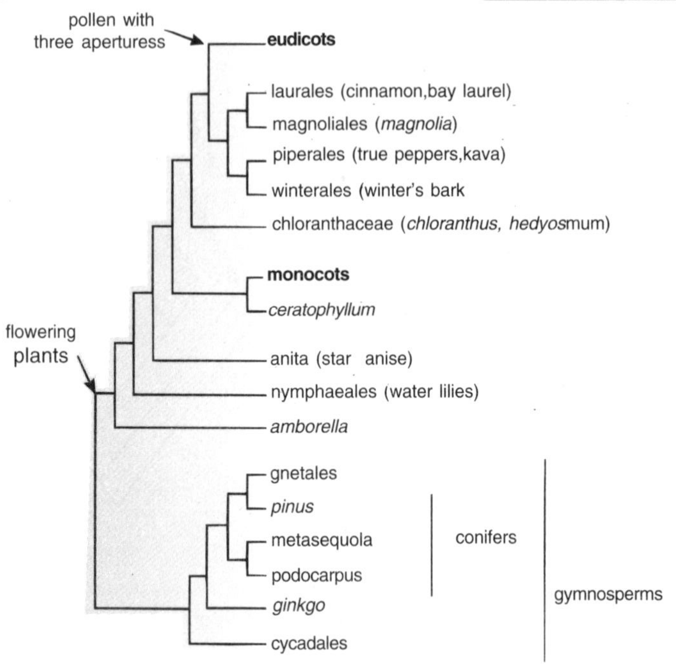

Figure 2.19: Phylogenetic tree based on recent molecular studies of angiosperms.

Insect-Angiosperm Coevolution

Another proposed biotic interaction of importance is that of angiosperm-insect coevolution. Early and mid-Cretaceous flowers contained many features to suggest that they were insect pollinated, including stamens with small anthers and low pollen production, and pollen grains often covered with pollenkitt-like material, and they were larger than the most effective size for wind dispersal.

Insect pollination would have been highly advantageous to the early angiosperms, enabling genetic exchange between widely spaced individuals or small populations. Furthermore, the suggestion that self-incompatibility mechanisms were present in the earliest angiosperms makes processes such as insect pollination even more critical for cross-pollination.

It is therefore suggested that the late evolution of angiosperms is closely related to that of insect evolution. Fossil evidence for

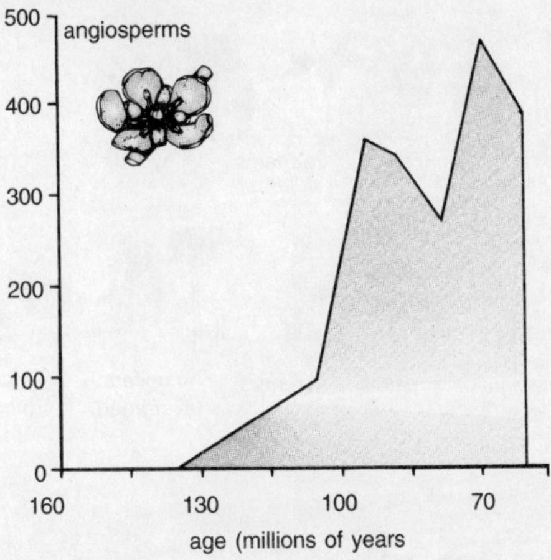

Figure 2.20: Evidence from fossil leaf assemblages (summed genus and species diversity) indicating the major expansion of the angiosperms from ~140 Ma and a dramatic increase in the absolute number (summed diversity) of angiosperms through the mid-Cretaceous (~10Ma).

the coevolution of pollinating insects with angiosperms is ambiguous. There is some fossil evidence for insect herbivory on Cretaceous angiosperms, such as leaf mines and other damage to leaves caused by feeding.

However, comparison of the times of appearance of innovations in insect feeding systems with the timing of angiosperm radiation does not indicate a strong relationship. The advanced pollinator groups, including some *Hymenoptera* (certain wasps that are the sister group of the bees) and *Lepidoptera* (butterflies and moths), indicate a certain amount of synchronicity between their first fossil appearance (from approximately 140 million years ago) and that of angiosperms.

However, other early groups such as *Diptera* (*e.g.* crane flies and fungus-gnats), *Coleoptera* (beetles), and some *Hymenoptera* (*e.g.* saw-flies) have a fossil record indicating that their first appearance pre-dates that of the angiosperms, whereas other species of *Hymenoptera*, including the *Apoidea* (honeybees), have a fossil record that only extends as far back as the Albian (~100 Ma).

Moreover, in analysis of insect familial-level diversity through

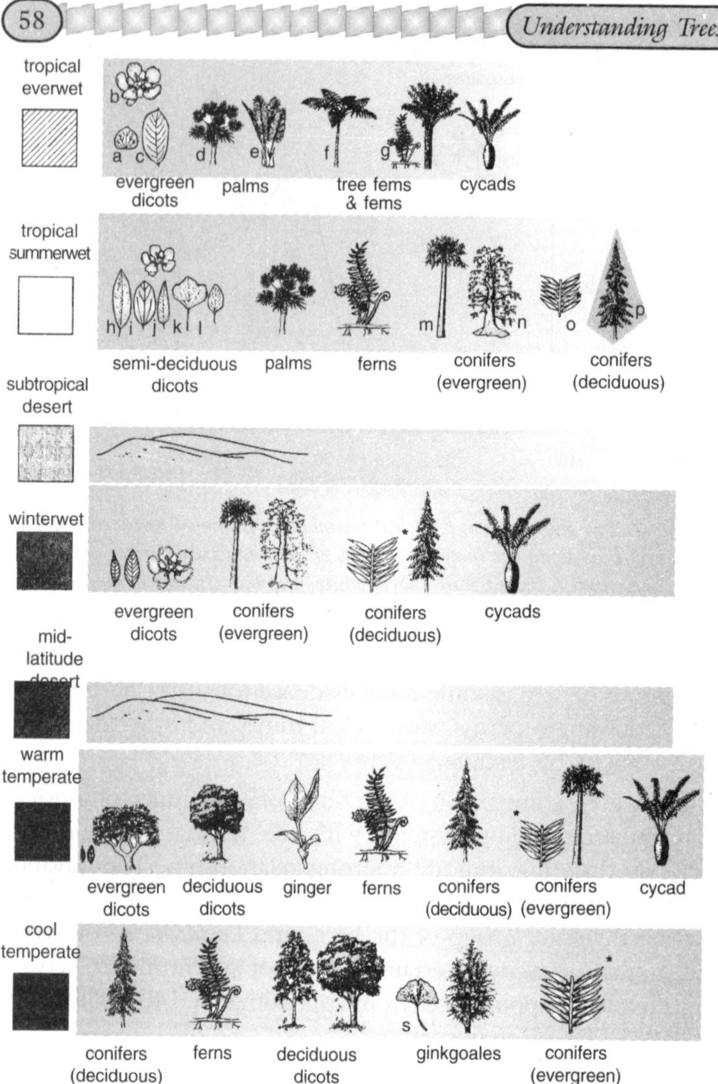

Figure 2.21: Suggested biomes for the late Cretaceous, with representatives of the most abundant and/or dominant fossil plant taxa shown. The biomes are superimposed on a global palaeogeographic reconstruction for the Maastrichtian (~70 Ma) (courtesy of A. M. Ziegler, PaleoAtlas Project). (a) and (c) Stylized megaphyllous leaves; (b) generalized Cretaceous flower; (d) Sabalites palm; (e) Nypa palm; (f) Cyathea; (g) Dicksonia; (h) Myrica leaf; (i) Ficus leaf; (j) Dryophyllum leaf; (k) Viburnum leaf; (1) Grewiopsis leaf; (m) Araucaria; (n) Cheirolepidaceous tree; (o) Podocarpus leaves; (p) Taxodiaceae conifer; (q) stylized microphyllous leaves; (r) generalized deciduous tree; (s) Ginkgo leaf. See Appendix 5 for sources of plant reconstructions and line drawings. Dominant or abundant in the southern hemisphere.

time there is no marked increase in insect diversity with the time of angiosperm origin. There is increasing evidence to suggest, therefore, that advanced pollinators (wasps, bees, and moths) may have played an important role in the coevolution and major radiation of certain groups of flowering plants, but that the timing of angiosperm evolution as a whole cannot he explained by insect coevolution alone.

EVOLUTIONARY TRENDS: GYMNOSPERMS TO ANGIOSPERMS?

Two questions that inevitably arise when discussing angiosperm origins are, from which lineage did they evolve, and when and how did divergence of the monocotyledons from the dicotyledons occur? Originally these questions were tackled by examination of only the fossil record, but more recent techniques, including morphological and molecular phylogenetic analyses of extinct and extant groups, have allowed the construction of detailed evolutionary relationships between the gymnos-perms and angiosperms, and the monocotyledons and dicotyledons.

Despite early suggestions that angiosperms were of a polyphyletic origin (a number of difference ancestors), almost all recent evidence (morphological and molecular) suggests that angiosperms were derived from a single common ancestor (that is they had a monophyletic origin).

Two of the earliest suggestions for possible evolutionary pathways between gymnosperms and angiosperms were via the Bennettitales. Evidence for Bennettitales as the precursor to early angiosperms was based upon the fact that certain species in this fossil group had flower-like bisexual reproductive organs and similar wood anatomy.

One species in particular that is often cited is *Williamsoniella.* This late Jurassic fossil plant had a reproductive organ that consisted of a bisexual reproductive axis bearing naked ovules above a series of pollen-bearing structures, the whole enclosed by large bracts.

These large bracts were thought to be the equivalent to petals in an angiosperm flower. Also, the position of the reproductive organ, erect and at the end of the branch, bore some similarities to extant insect-pollinated flower structures. *Coleoptera* and *Diptera* flies have been suggested as pollinators for this plant. Gnetales are present in the fossil record from the early Cretaceous (~140 Ma).

The group has three extant genera in biogeographically distinct regions of the world: *Ephedra* (35 species), which exists in arid and semiarid regions, including parts of the Mediterranean, Asia, and the Americas; *Welwitschia mirabilis*, which is restricted to the Namibian desert; and *Gnetum* (30 species), which is exclusively tropical, occurring in Asia, Africa, and South America.

Morphological similarities between many species of Gnetales and angiosperms first led to the suggestion that they were probably close in evolutionary terms. These include, for example, reproductive organs that are bisexual (in some species), the presence of vessels, leaves with a venation pattern closely approximating that of dicotyledons, and a pollen wall (e.g. in certain species of *Ephedra*) that is tectate. Some extant Gnetales are also insect pollinated.

Phylogenetic analysis based on these shared characteristics, in both extant and extinct species, also confirmed a close relationship between angiosperms and Gnetales.

More recent cladistic analyses, which also include the molecular characteristics of extant species, are in agreement with the earlier morphological analysis and demonstrate a close relationship between Bennettitales, Gnetales, and the earliest angiosperms. The phylogenetic trees obtained from these analyses indicate that angiosperms from a Glade with Bennettites and/or Gnetales but also sometimes with an extinct group, the Pentoxylales.

However, the majority of studies suggest that the Gnetales are the most likely closest living relative of angiosperms. There are a number of hypothesis as to which of the earliest angiosperms forms an evolutionary link with the Gnetales.

Most suggest that early members of the Nymphaeales and Piperales were the evolutionary link between Gnetales and angiosperms; others have suggested a single genus, *Ceratophyllum*, within the Nymphaeales, and members of the Laurales.

However, there is also strong support for woody Magnoliales. More recent and extensive molecular studies of angiosperm phylogenetics have, however, turned a number of these relationships on their head. In the first instance, the results of both studies do not support the hypothesis that the Gnetales are the closest living relatives of the angiosperms.

Instead, these analyses group the Gnelates with the conifers. Secondly, the results do not agree with any of the existing ideas about which angiosperms are most primitive. Instead, the analyses indicate that *Amborella trichopoda*, the only extant species of Amborellaceae, represents the most primitive (basal group) of all flowering plants.

This is followed by the Nymphaeales, and then a group including Illiciaceae, Trimereniaceae, *Austrobaileyaceae*, and Schisandraceae. Together they have been referred to as ANITA.

Evidence from the various cladistic analyses described above have also indicated the relationship between early monocotyledons and dicotyledons. Again, the analyses support the fossil evidence in suggesting that monocotyledons were an early branch in angiosperm evolution. However, the species or group that forms the evolutionary link between the monocotyledons and dicotyledons is still under debate.

BIOGEOGRAPHICAL DISTRIBUTION OF GLOBAL VEGETATION DURING THE LATE CRETACEOUS (~84-65 MA)

During the late Cretaceous (~100-65 Ma) angiosperms increased in both species number and diversity. Angiosperm trees and shrubs evolving during this time included a number of families that constitute a significant part of the present-day global flora.

Evidence from the fossil record suggests, for example, that a number of extant northern and southern hemisphere families appeared for the first time. These include Ulmaceae (including evidence for *Ulmus*), Betulaceae, Juglandaceae, Fagaceae (especially *Nothofagus*), and Gunneraceae.

The striking number of angiosperm fossils present by the late Cretaceous with close affinities to extant families has led to the suggestion that eventually it will be discovered that all angiosperm families originated during this remarkable period. The majority of trees to appear in the late Cretaceous (~100-65 Ma) have a present-day distribution that is mainly tropical or subtropical.

It is interesting to note that most present-day angiosperm families are basically tropical in their requirements, with over one-half of angiosperm families confined to tropical regions and over three-quarters of all angiosperm families attaining optimum development and diversity in a tropical environment.

Therefore, although many may now be classified as northern/southern temperate species by their distribution, it is probable that they still possess the traits that would enable them to survive in conditions similar to those characteristic of the early environments where they originated.

Detailed 'biome level-analyses' of global plant biogeography and palaeoclimate have been carried out for the late Cretaceous (Maastrichtian, ~71-65 Ma). Six global biomes are recognized, as follows.

Cool Temperate Biome

The cool temperate biome in the Maastrichtian coincides roughly with the present-day Arctic circle, comprising Canada, Greenland, and Siberia in the northern hemisphere and Antarctica in the southern hemisphere.

The vegetation of the cool temperate biome has also been referred to as polar deciduous forest and was clearly one of three remaining biomes in the late Cretaceous not dominated by angiosperms.

Instead, vegetation in this region was dominated by deciduous and evergreen conifers with ferns and ginkgos. Angiosperms are believed to have been present as understorey and included members of the Betulaceae and Juglandaceae.

The prevalence of leaf-shedding among the angiosperm species, relative low-diversity floras, evidence for growth rings, and the presence of some, but not abundant, coals, supports the suggestion of seasonality, typical of a cool temperate climate.

Members of the Pinaceae and Taxodiaceae (*Sequoia* and *Taxo-*

dium) were common conifers, and the fossil record also includes evidence for 'modern' genera such as *Pinus* and *Abies.* Other conifers, widely spread but less significant in terms of their representation, included Cupressaceae, and Araucariaceae.

In the southern hemisphere, the cool temperate biome was characterized by an abundance of podocarpacean and araucarian conifers and the angiosperm dicot genus *Notto fagus* (southern beech). The abundance of *Notto fagus* pollen has led to the suggestion that the climates of Antarctica and southern Australia were cooler and drier than those of the southern hemisphere lower latitudes.

Warm Temperate Biome

The warm temperate biome between 45° and 65° palaeolatitude, encompassed present-day northern North America, southern Greenland, parts of western Europe, Russia, and northern China in the northern hemisphere, and Australia and coastal Antarctica in the southern hemisphere.

The vegetation characteristic of this biome included abundant dicotyledonous and monocotyledonous angiosperms, evergreen and deciduous conifers, ferns, and cycads. Upchurch *et al.* (1999) have ,referred to the vegetation of this region as ›sub-tropical broad-leaved evergreen forest and woodland' as many of the fossil leaf shapes are common among modern subtropical plants.

However, due to the palaeolatitudinal position of this region, well outside the subtropics, Horrell's climatic assessment and interpretation of this region as warm temperate rather than subtropical is used here. Common angiosperms included members of the Fagaceae (e.g. *Castanea*), Betulaceae (e.g. *Betula*), Juglandaceae (e.g. *Juglans*), Ulmaceae (e.g. *Ulmus*, *Zelkova*), Proteaceae (southern hemisphere only), and Winteraceae among the dicotyledons and corphoid palms were abundant monocotyledons. Conifers included Araucariaceae and Taxodiaceae.

The high diversity of angiosperm dicotyledons in fossil floras from this region was thought to indicate their dominance. However, detailed analysis of a fossil flora from Wyoming, preserved *in situ* by an ash fall, has shown that although dicotyledons constituted 61% of the total floral diversity, they accounted for a mere 12% of cover, compared with 49% by ferns. It is apparent, therefore, that although angiosperms had reached a dominant position in stream-side vegetation of the warm temperate biome by the Maastrichtian (~70 Ma), ferns still maintained dominance in certain habitats, even after 30 million years of angiosperm diversifi-cation and radiation.

This study also demonstrates the complexity and mosaic of different habitats that exist within each individual biome, and highlights the importance of taking into account preservational biases when undertaking biogeographical analyses.

Winterwet Biome

The vegetation between palaeolatitudes of approximately 30° and 45° was markedly less diverse than that of the warm temperate biome, and is characterized mainly by the occurrence of evergreen dicotyledons together with both evergreen and deciduous conifers with some cycads.

A notable feature of the vegetation of this region was the relatively lower abundance of monocotyledons. Floras from the winterwet biome indicate the presence of abundant *Araucaria* and cheirolepidaceous conifers, and evidence from fossil wood suggests that angiosperms may have formed part of an understorey of both shrubs and small trees rather than large canopy trees.

In the southern hemisphere, Patagonian floras contained abundant ferns and angiosperm families such as Lauraceae. The presence of huntite, a mineral which today is only formed in warm environments with high rates of evaporation, typical of Mediterranean climates, together with an absence of clear growth rings in fossil woods, provides good support for the designation of a winterwet biome to this region.

However, this is not supported unanimously and Upchurch *et al.* suggest that the absence of fossil leaves with spinose margins, which are typical of the modern winterwet biome vegetation, questions whether this biome really existed during the late Cretaceous.

It is worth noting, however, that despite the absence of one vegetative characteristic, a number of model simulations of the late Cretaceous climate indicate that a Mediterranean (i.e. 'winterwet') climate may indeed have prevailed in certain areas during this time. The northern limit of the winterwet biome in the northern hemisphere is marked by coals, whereas to the south it is marked by the presence of evaporites, indicating humid and arid conditions, respectively.

It is thought therefore that this biome represents a transition between the arid desert biomes of the lower latitudes and the humid biomes of the higher-latitude temperate belts.

Subtropical Desert Biome

Evidence for extensive evaporite deposits during the late Cretaceous (~70 Ma), indicating high rates of evaporation over precipitation, mark the subtropical desert biome. These deposits occur in a northern hemisphere belt which incorporates present-day north Africa, China, and the Yukatan peninsula, and in the southern hemisphere include present-day south-western Africa and southern South America.

No fossil floras have yet been found in these biomes, most probably reflecting both the low diversity and productivity which would have been apparent, but also the low preservation potential of fossil plants in arid environments.

Tropical Summerwet Biome

The tropical summerwet biome incorporates the majority of present-day Africa, South America, and India, from palaeolatitudes 0° to 25° and is characterized by a 'tropical semi-deciduous forest' type vegetation. Common elements in the vegetation of this region include dicotyledons and monocotyledons, ferns, conifers, and cycads.

Evidence from fossil pollen and wood suggest that common conifers included members of the Araucariaceae, Cheirolepidaceae, and Podocarpaceae. India contained floral elements typical of both the southern hemisphere (e.g. *Notofagus*, Proteaceae, and Podocarpaceae) and also elements of the northern hemisphere vegetation, leading to the suggestion that by the late Cretaceous, the Indian plate was already part of the equatorial biogeographical region, even though in terms of palaeogeography it was still 30°S.

The combined evidence from fossil floral composition, leaf physiognomy, and sedimentological indicators suggests that this region was characterized by a hot, subhumid to semiarid climate typical of present-day summerwet or savannah regions.

Tropical Everwet Biomed

The tropical everwet biome of the late Cretaceous was much reduced in comparison with the present-day extent of tropical rain forest, and was restricted to an area including present-day subequatorial west Africa and Malaysia and possibly Somalia, in east Africa and Colombia in South America.

Palynological assemblages recovered from these areas suggest that during the late Cretaceous the equatorial region was dominated by species of Arecaceae (palms), including the extant genus *Nypa*. Other angiosperms present included Proteaceae and many other dicotyledon groups, while ferns and tree ferns were also abundant.

A striking feature of this biome is the almost complete absence of evidence for either evergreen or deciduous conifers, with the exception of Araucariaceae in Malaysia.

Comparison of the biogeographical patterns present in the late Cretaceous (~70 Ma) with those from the early Carboniferous (~360 Ma), middle Permian (~267 Ma), and early Jurassic (~196 Ma) reveals a consistent pattern, whereby the tropical everwet biome is either absent or severely restricted in extent.

This phenomenon has also been observed for the early Cretaceous (~137 Ma). In contrast, however, the extent of the tropical everwet biome during the late Carboniferous (~300 Ma) spans from the equator to approximately 25°, similar to the observed extent of this biome today.

It is noteworthy that the features common to both the upper Carboniferous and present day are the presence of polar ice caps, high latitudinal temperature gradients and comparatively low atmospheric CO_2 concentration. It can therefore be suggested that these characteristics may be important global environmental prerequisites to the development of an extensive '*tropical rainforest*' biome.

THE FIRST FORESTS

Between 395 and 286 million years ago (early Devonian to late Carboniferous) the terrestrial flora evolved from one composed of small vascular and nonvascular plants to a vegetation that included trees towering to over 35 m.

During this time significant changes were also occurring to the global environment. This chapter examines the evidence for these environmental and evolutionary changes and discusses the possible evolutionary pathways from the earliest vascular plants to trees.

It concludes with a consideration of the biogeographical distribution of the first multi-storied forests and the factors influencing their distribution.

MID-DEVONIAN TO LATE CARBONIFEROUS

The period between 395 and 290 Ma was one of active plate movement. It was also a time of dramatic global climatic change. The continental blocks that had formed the Gondwana and Laurussian groups during the Silurian moved northwards, resulting in the formation of the supercontinent Pangea by 300Ma and global climates altered from warm, humid, and ice-free, to cooler, drier climates with extensive glaciation in the high latitudes of the southern hemisphere. Various links between the changing continental configurations and this period of dramatic global climate change have been suggested.

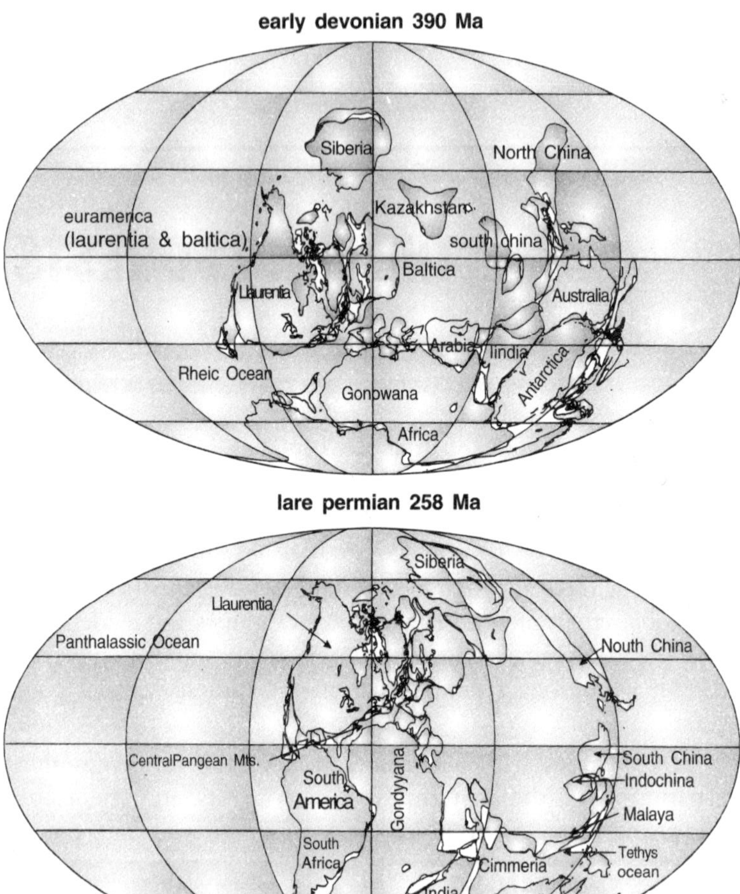

Figure 3.1: Continental plate changes between 390 and 258 million years ago, showing assembly of Pangea.

During the early to middle Devonian (~395-360 Ma) the South Pole was situated either over Central America or South Africa. This would have resulted in extensive warming and retention of heat at the pole. Estimated January temperatures at the South Pole, for example, were between 20 and 24° C and at the equator up to 32° C.

From the late Devonian (~360 Ma), however, the South

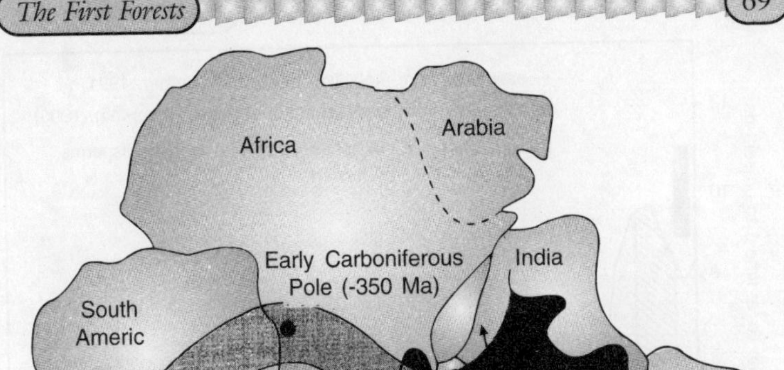

Figure 3.2: Postulated polar wander across Gondwana during the Carboniferous and Permian (~350-248 Ma). The large arrow indicates the direction of wander. Also indicated (stippled) are major glacial centres during this time and ice flow directions (small arrows) reconstructed from glacial pavement studies.

Pole became much closer to the coast and modelling suggests that this would have caused significant global cooling. The larger heat capacity of the water would have suppressed the magnitude of warming on the adjacent land masses, and resulting summer temperatures might therefore not have reached above freezing in the high latitudes of the southern hemisphere.

This would have led to the formation of a large southern hemisphere ice sheet, with increasingly cool and arid conditions in continental interiors. At least four periods of southern hemisphere glaciation have been recognized between approximately 360 and 290 Ma.

Initial areas of glaciation were in South America and Africa, but then it became more widespread, with evidence for continental glaciation also occurring in Antarctica and Australia. During times of glaciation, sea levels were lowered by an estimated 100-200 m and there was aridity in the high latitudes.

Although continental climates became generally drier, fossil

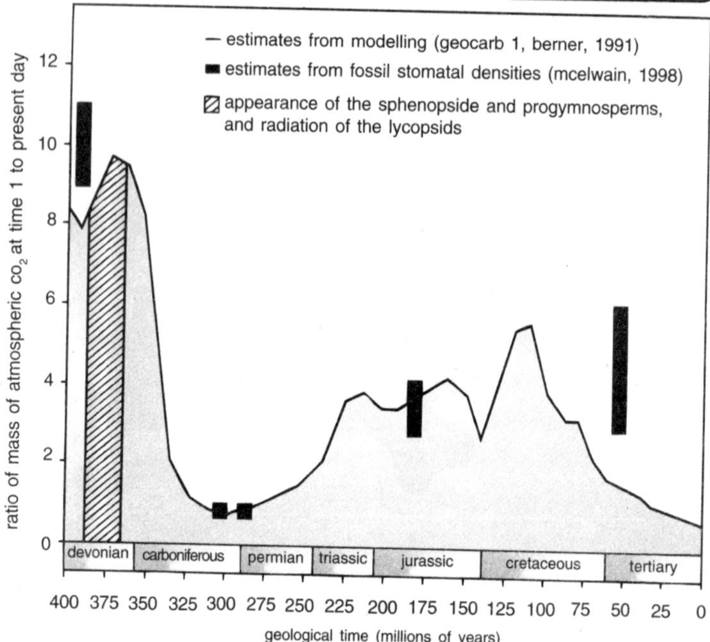

Figure 3.3: Estimated variations in atmospheric CO_2 during the past 400 million years. The general direction of the trends are supported by independently derived results from carbon isotope analysis of palaeosols and stomatal densities on fossil leaves.

evidence also suggests that precipitation became enhanced in a narrow equatorial belt. High year-round wetness in this tropical belt is thought to be partially responsible for the development of extensive lowland swamps, resulting in the formation of coal deposits in eastern North America, western Europe, and parts of Russia during the Carboniferous.

The effect of the continental plate movements is also thought to have been responsible for this. Extensive mountain-building episodes resulted from the continental plate collisions. The formation of the Central Pangean Moutains at tropical latitudes, at approximately 305 Ma (Westphalian), for example, resulted in a mountain range over 3 km in altitude.

Modelling indicates that this uplift would have had a significant impact on global circulation and precipitation. In particular, there would have been enhanced local precipitation in palaeoequatorial latitudes, thus accounting for the formation of extensive coal deposits at this time.

Another factor affecting the global climates during this period (395-290 Ma) was less directly related to the continental plate movements and was a result of the widespread colonization of the land by plants. Estimates of atmospheric CO_2 in the early Devonian indicate that levels were up to 8-9 times higher than those of the present-day, in fact at its highest level in the past 400 million years. This would have had a considerable effect on global warmth through an enhanced greenhouse effect.

However, between 360 and 286 Ma modelling estimates that atmospheric CO_2 levels plummeted from 3600 p.p.m. to 300 p.p.m., such that by the late Carboniferous, levels of atmospheric CO_2 were comparable to those of the present day.

This declining atmospheric CO_2 concentration would also have made a significant contribution to the pattern of global cooling evident from approximately 360 million years onwards.

One of the main processes thought to be responsible for this rapid decline was the global expansion of vascular plants and the effect that they would have had on the acceleration of silicate rock weathering and the production of bacterially resistant organic matter (e.g. lignin).

Both of these processes are thought to have contributed significantly to a decline in atmospheric CO_2. It is envisaged that with the widespread colonization of land surfaces by vascular plants and their associated release of organic acids (e.g. released through root mycorrhizae, humic and fluvic acids) would have greatly increased chemical weathering of silicate rocks.

This process is one that uses atmospheric CO_2 (CO_2 + $CaSiO_3 \leftrightarrow CaCO_2 + SiO_2$), resulting in a transfer of carbon from the atmosphere to carbonate minerals. These would then be washed away and eventually deposited on the ocean floor where they would subsequently become buried and therefore removed from the atmospheric pool.

In addition, it is suggested that the large increases in plant organic matter composed of organic polymers such as lignin, that were highly resistant to decay, would have exceeded the

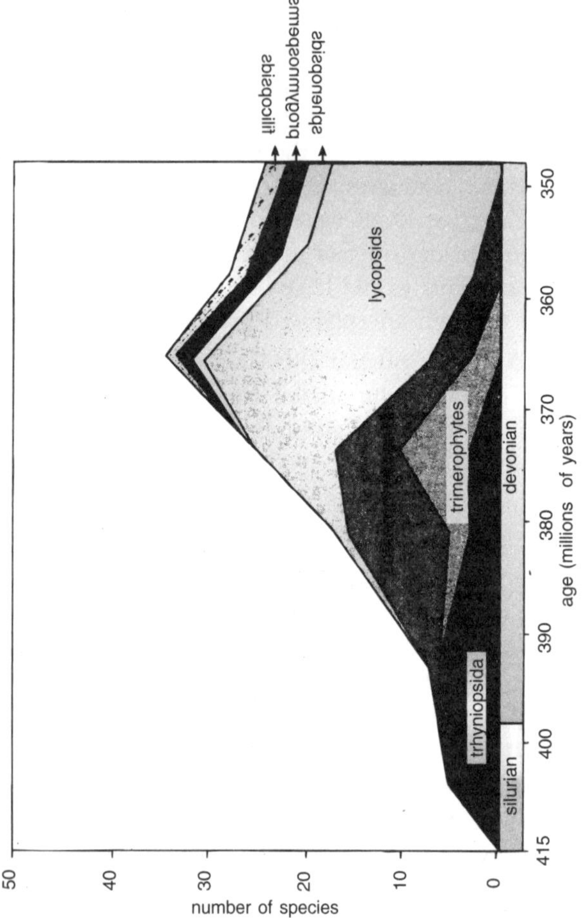

Figure 3.4: Evolution and diversification of vascular land plants during the mid to late Devonian (~390-365 Ma). Data are taken from a compilation of approximately 18 000 fossil plant species citations.

numbers of primary decomposers (e.g. various fungi). This would have led to a scenario where rates of accumulation would have exceeded those of decomposition. Burial of these vast quantities of organic material would again have resulted in the removal of carbon from the atmosphere, but this time by locking it away in long-term carbon sinks, namely coal.

PLANT FOSSIL RECORD

During this period of dramatic global environmental change, major changes and innovations were occurring in the terrestrial vegetation. The period spanning the middle to late Devonian (~390-365 Ma) was a time of emergence of new plant groups, and relatively rapid increase of species numbers. Estimates suggest, for example, that within a matter of 20 million years, the numbers of spore-producing plants had increased threefold

This pattern of increasing diversity was not to last, however, and by the late Devonian (~360 Ma), numbers of new species started to plateau such that there were less originations than extinctions, leading to a slight drop in overall species number.

This reduction in overall species number occurred at a time (late Devonian, Frasnian/Famennian) when there was a mass extinction event in the animal record.

Throughout this period (~390-365 Ma) the plant fossil record also indicates that major innovations were occurring in land plant morphology. In particular, terrestrial plants were getting much bigger and acquiring more refined reproductive structures.

There is also evidence for the evolution of a more advanced vascular system for the transport of water and nutrients, additional supporting mechanisms, advanced rooting systems, and leaves. Evolution of these features would have facilitated the large increases in vascular plant size and structure.

The fossil evidence for these morphological changes will therefore be discussed first, followed by a description of some of the earliest trees on Earth and their biogeographical distribution.

PLANT ADAPTATIONS TO LAND DWELLING

Advanced Vascular System (stelar evolution)

In order to attain greater height, one of the most important adaptations would have been the development of the central conducting cylinder (the stele) for the effective transport of water and nutrients around the plant.

Evidence from the geological record suggests that the stele of plants became progressively more complex with time and that by the late Devonian (~374 Ma) at least three different stele types were apparent.

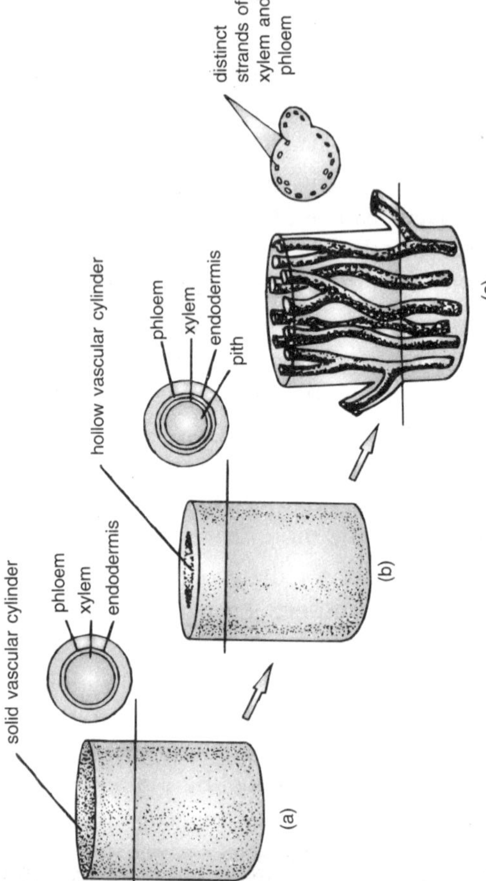

Figure 3.5: Morphological differences between the early stele types apparent in the plant fossil record: (a) protostele, apparent in the earliest vascular plants from ~420 Ma; (b) siphonostele, apparent in the fossil record from ~395 Ma; (c) eustele, apparent in the fossil record from ~380 Ma.

Protostele

The earliest stele found in the fossil record is the protostele; found in most of the earliest vascular plants and also some early lycopsids and sphenopsids. This stele is composed of a solid strand of vascular tissue in which phloem (food-conducting tissues) either surrounds the xylem (water and mineral conducting tissues) or is interspersed within it.

Siphonostele

A more complex stele, termed the siphonostele, became apparent in the geological record in the Emsian (~395 Ma). This stele was made up of xylem and phloem forming a cylinder around a central core filled with pith, and has been found in fossil filicopsids, lycopsids, and some sphenopsids.

Eustele

A third stele type, termed the eustele, first emerged in the fossil record in the Givetian (~380 Ma). This stele appears to be the most complex of the three structures in that it was composed of distinct strands of phloem and xylem, separated by parenchymal tissue.

These strands were arranged either in a circle or throughout the ground tissue. The eustele first occurred in the progymnosperms (the precursor to the seed plants). Evidence from the geological record thus suggests that the stele of plants became progressively more complex with time. It is also notable that with increased stelar complexity there was an increase in stem diameter and height.

As shown in the previous chapter, the earliest vascular land plants were small and narrow-stemmed, and the transport of water and nutrients in the plants occurred through specialized tracheids. The central stem therefore contained the tissue for support, transport of water/nutrients, and also photosynthesis.

Calculations indicate that the best arrangement of tissue for these three functions would have been a photosynthetic 'rind' of tissue just beneath the surface of the stem and a central water-conducting strand running through an inner core of non-photosynthetic tissue.

This type of arrangement is seen in the protostele, where the xylem cells would have provided mechanical support and the phloem cells would have transported sugars and nutrients.

These two layers were then surrounded by an outer layer of photosynthetic tissue. However, calculations indicate that in order to attain greater heights the required thickness of the xylem cells (to provide mechanical support) would eventually present a barrier between the photosynthetic and water-conducting tissues.

Therefore, beyond a certain size it would have been necessary to compartmentalize functions of the plant body into organs devoted to photosynthesis and organs devoted to mechanical support and water conduction.

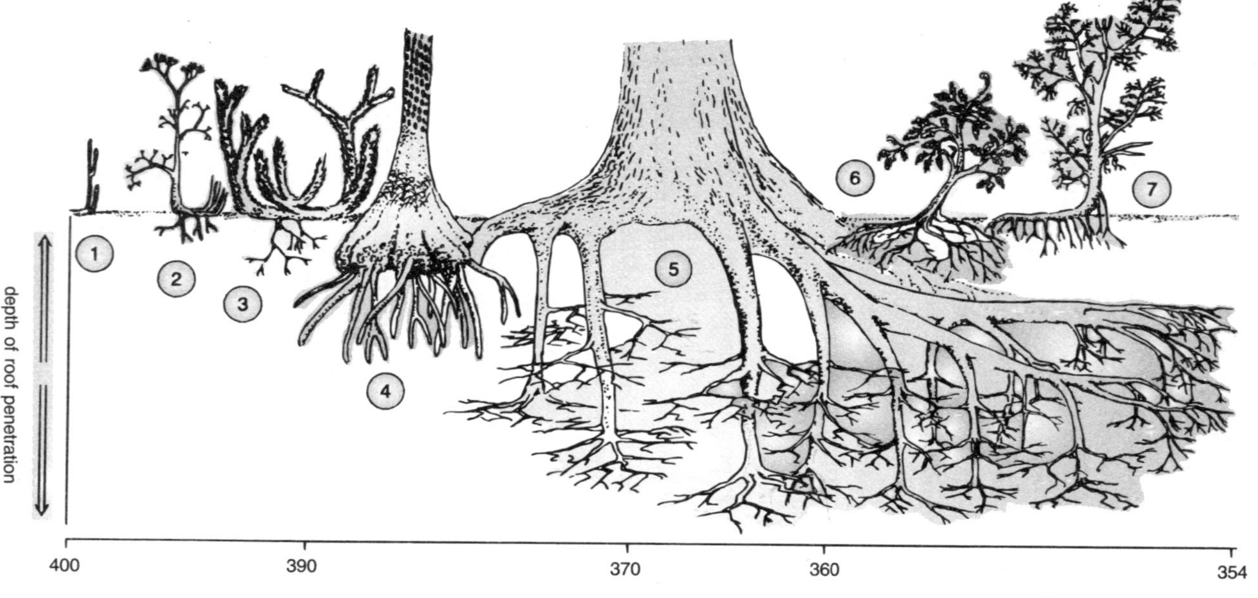

Figure 3.6: Relative sizes, shapes, and penetration depths of root systems druing the early, middle and late Devonian (~400-354 Ma; age axis is not drawn to scale)

Increasing complexity of the stele in combination with innovations in supporting mechanisms and the evolution of true leaves (discussed in the next section) are therefore regarded as fundamental to the evolution of arborescence (a woody habit) in plants. Ultimately this would lead to the appearance of well-stratified forested ecosystems on Earth.

Additional Supporting Mechanisms

Arborescent forms in the extant flora display a variety of different supporting mechanisms, ranging from thickening of the trunk with wood and bark, to above-ground root mantles and extensive underground rooting systems.

Fossil evidence suggests that many of these supporting mechanisms developed from as early as 380 Ma. Probably the most common form of support for extant trees is achieved by thickening of the trunk through the growth of wood.

Wood results from the growth of secondary xylem and phloem from lateral meristematic zones known as the vascular cambium. Evidence from the fossil record suggests that the formation of secondary xylem and pholem first occurred in the middle Devonian (~380 Ma) and enabled some of the earliest known trees (e.g. *Archaeopteris*) to achieve heights of up to 30 m.

However, palaeobotanical evidence indicates that in other early trees, thickening of the trunk for increased stature was achieved in other ways. These included the development of large quantities of inner bark (usually referred to as secondary cortex) and the development of greatly thickened stems as a result of numerous leaf bases (e.g. *Lepidode-ndron*).

Another mechanism for support appears to have been the development of abundant mantles of roots, that were thickest at the base of the trunk. These would have acted as guy-ropes, tethering the tree to the ground and enabling much greater stature to be achieved (e.g. *Psaronius*).

In addition to above-ground root mantles, evidence from palaeosols (fossil soils) indicates the development of at least seven morphologically distinguishable below-ground rooting systems during the Devonian and Carboniferous.

They ranged from highly branched systems extending up to

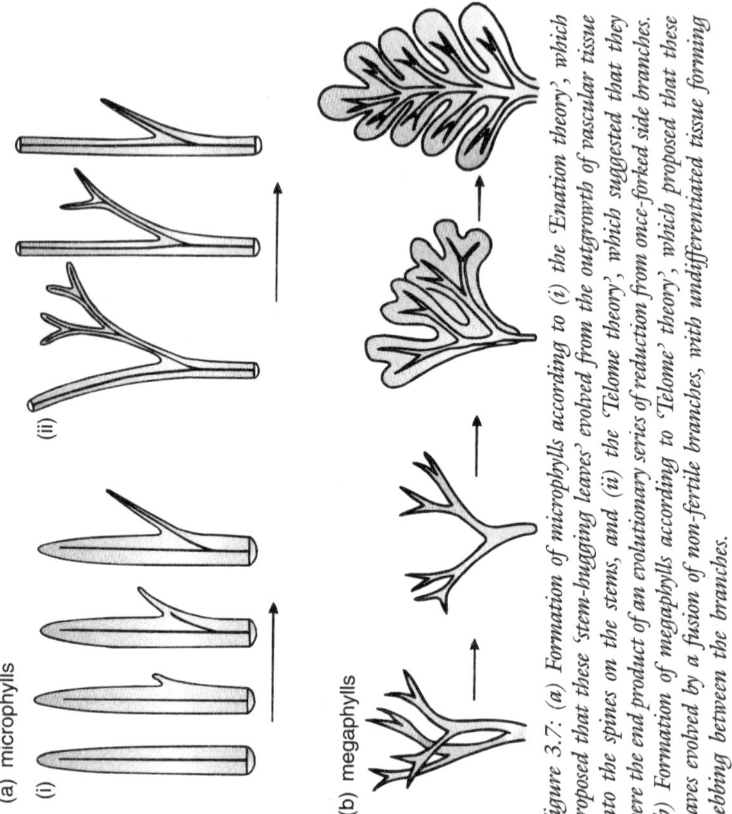

Figure 3.7: (a) Formation of microphylls according to (i) the 'Enation theory', which proposed that these 'stem-hugging leaves' evolved from the outgrowth of vascular tissue into the spines on the stems, and (ii) the 'Telome theory', which suggested that they were the end product of an evolutionary series of reduction from once-forked side branches. (b) Formation of megaphylls according to 'Telome' theory', which proposed that these leaves evolved by a fusion of non-fertile branches, with undifferentiated tissue forming webbing between the branches.

1 m into the substrate to small annulated-segmented roots from which long root hairs grew at the point of segmentation. These rooting systems would have been vital, for both support and the increased uptake of water and nutrients.

They would also have had a significant impact on weathering rates and processes, increasing the depth of mature soil profiles. The variation between different root types is thought to reflect the need for anchorage and support, and also the different environmental conditions in which the plants grew.

Leaves

The earliest land plants possessed stomata and cuticles in their stems and were therefore photosynthesizing from these axes. For at least the first 40 million years of their existence land plants were therefore leafless or had only small, spine-like appendages.

However, leaf-like structures and true leaves, primarily devoted and optimized for the photosynthetic process, started to appear in the fossil record from the mid to late Devonian (~390-354 Ma), respectively. There were two early forms of leaf type-microphylls and megaphylls-and the differences between them can still be seen in plant groups today.

Microphylls

These are generally relatively small leaves (although there are exceptions) that grow out directly from the stem. They contain only a single strand of unbranching vascular tissue and tend to be associated with stems possessing protosteles.

It is proposed that they evolved from one of two hypothetical pathways, termed the Enation theory and the Telome theroy. The 'Enation theory' proposed that microphyll leaves evolved from the spiny stems of the earliest land plants, such as *Sawdonia.*

Lateral outgrowth of vascular tissue into the spines (enations) resulted in the spines 'fleshing out' and the formation of microphyllous leaves. The 'Telome theory', on the other hand, suggested that microphylls represented the end product of an evolutionary series of reduction from once-forked side branches, which became aligned (planation).

Such 'stem-hugging' leaves, with a single vascular strand and no petiole, are typical of extant species of lycopsids such as *Lycopodium* and were the characteristic leaf-type of the earliest, but now extinct, lycopsids, such as *Baragwanthia.*

Megaphylls

These are leaves associated with stems that have either a siphonostele or eustele, and are attached to the stem by a petiole. Their evolution is thought to be closely linked to the three-dimensional vegetative branching pattern (i.e. branches with no sporangia on them) of the earliest vascular plants (e.g. *Psilophyton dawsonii*). According to the Telome theory (Zimmerman), megaphylls are thought to have evolved by a fusion of these non-fertile branches, with undifferentiated tissue forming webbing between the branches.

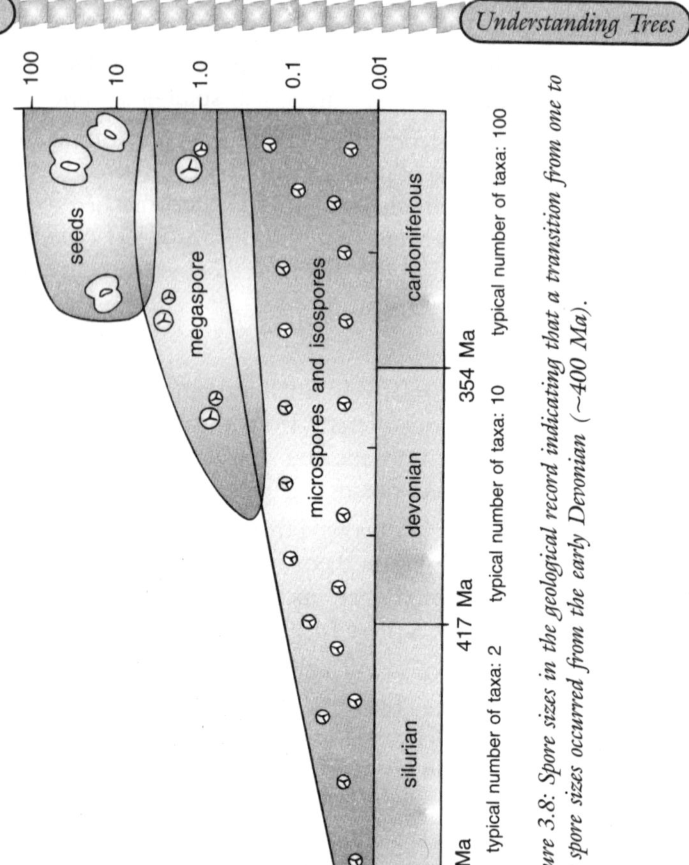

Figure 3.8: Spore sizes in the geological record indicating that a transition from one to two spore sizes occurred from the early Devonian (~400 Ma).

The former branches would thus provide vascular tissue into the megaphyll leaf, resulting in the evolution of a broad leaf containing many vascular strands. Early and extant filicopsids (ferns), a number of extinct sphenopsids (horsetails), and all flowering plants possess megaphylls.

Recent studies based on morphological observations and modelling of the biophysical principles of plant physiology suggest that evolution of the megaphyll leaf may have occurred in response to the massive reduction in atmospheric CO_2 during the late Devonian and early Carboniferous.

It is suggested that in the high CO_2 world of the early and mid Devonian (~417-370 Ma), the evolution of a megaphyll leaf would have been detrimental to plant survival, as leaf temperatures would have exceeded lethal threshold limits. It was not, therefore, until the late Devoninan/ early Carboniferous, when CO_2 levels plummetted, that increased leaf size would have been advantageous to land plants.

FURTHER ADAPTATIONS TO THE PLANT LIFE CYCLE

Alongside the morphological innovations that were taking place in plant vegetative structures, the period between 395 and

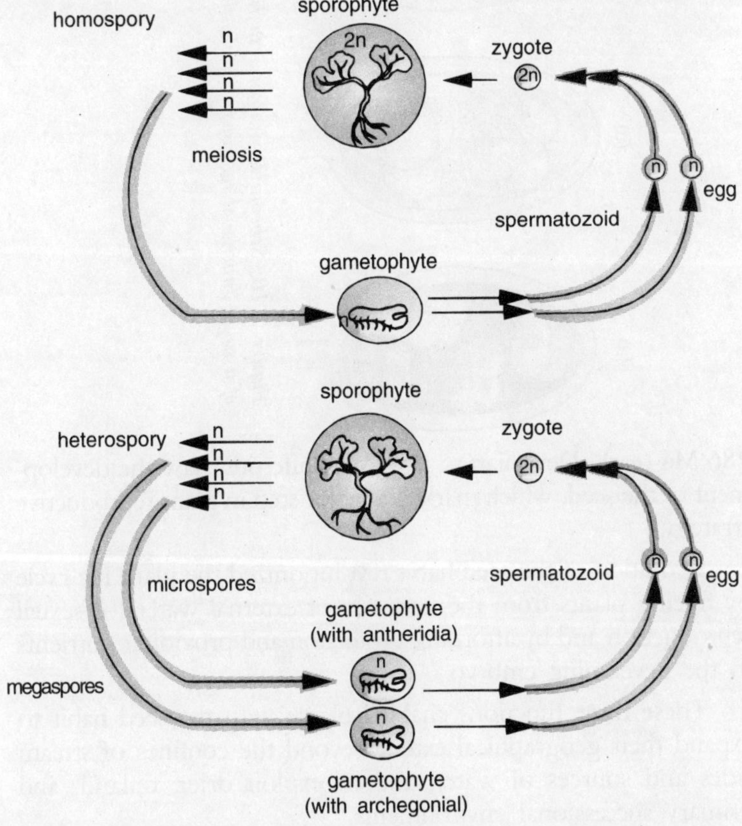

Figure 3.9: Schematic diagram to indicate the proposed transition from homospory to heterospory in the vascular plant life cycle, leading to the development of seed-bearing plants.

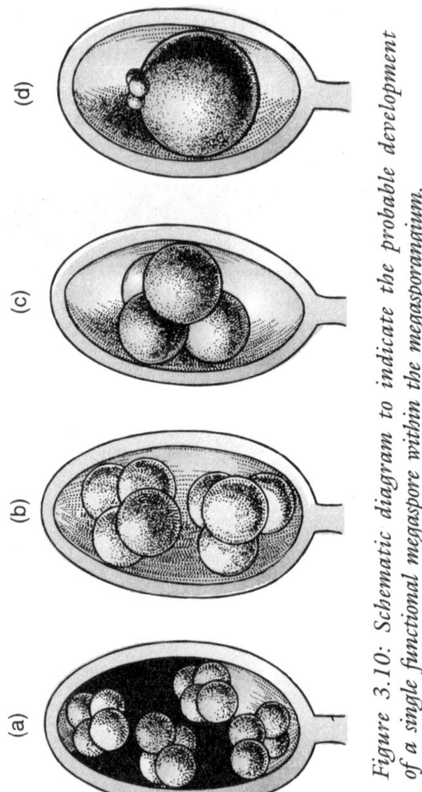

Figure 3.10: Schematic diagram to indicate the probable development of a single functional megaspore within the megasporangium.

286 Ma (early Devonian to late Carboniferous) saw the development of the seed, which marked a major step in plant reproductive strategy.

Evolution of the seed habit revolutionized the plant life cycle by freeing plants from the necessity of external water for sexual reproduction and by affording protection and providing nutrients to the developing embryo.

These three functions enabled plants with the seed habit to expand their geographical extent beyond the confines of stream sides and sources of water, and to exploit drier, upland, and primary successional environments.

Homospory to Heterospory

Evidence from the fossil plant record indicates that plants

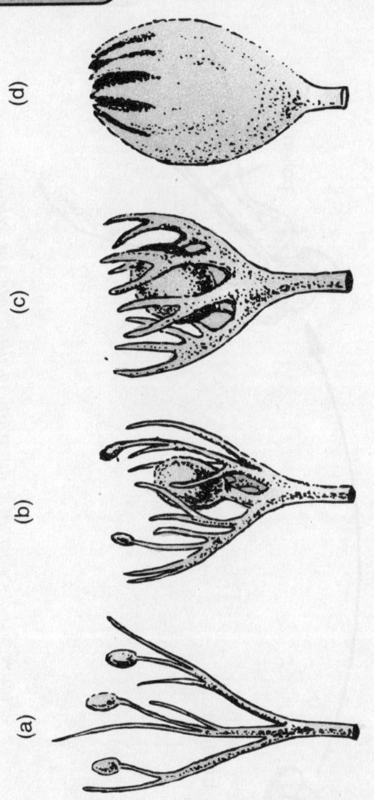

Figure 3.11: Development of the seed coat from sterile telome trusses.

were producing sporangia yielding two kinds of spores from the early Devonian onwards. These include megaspores that were between approximately 150 and 200 μm in diameter and microspores that were usually <50 pm. The transition from plants that were homosporous (one spore size) to heterosporous (two spores sizes) is considered one of the most important evolutionary trends in the development of seed-bearing plants.

It is postulated that the larger spores of heterosporous plants were the precursor of ovules, and the small spores, the precursor to pollen. There is much discussion in the literature as to the formation of megaspores.

The most widely accepted theory is that mutation resulted to two spore sizes developing in a sporangium. Evidence from the geological record would appear to support this theory in that

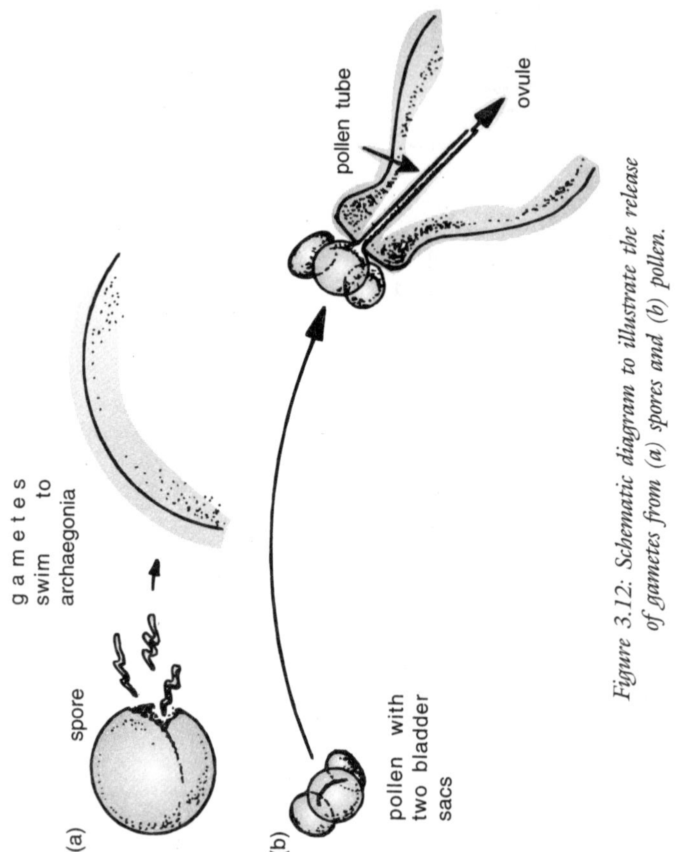

Figure 3.12: Schematic diagram to illustrate the release of gametes from (a) spores and (b) pollen.

records of dispersed spores of two size classes (anispory) indicate a gradual increase in occurrence of heterospory through the Devonian.

An early example in the fossil record of a heterosporus plant is *Chaleuria*. Specimens of this late Devonian plant have been shown to contain two types of sporangia, those that produce spores between 30 and 48 μm and others that produce spores between 60 and 156 μm.

Ovule Evolution after the Onset of Heterospory

Evidence from the plant fossil record indicates that by the end of the Devonian heterospory had progressed to the point that development of megaspores involved the abortion of three out of the four spores in a sporangium, with all the energy going into the remaining spore to form a single functional megaspore.

Retention of the megaspore in the megasporangium was the first step in the direction towards evolution of the ovule. The second step would have been the development of a seed coat.

Development of a Seed Coat

Analysis of late Devonian fossil megaspores has revealed an outer protective coating. This would have protected the megasporangium from desiccation and attack.

According to taxonomic nomeclature, once an outer coat or integument has formed around a megasporangium, it technically becomes an ovule, since in structure it now represents an unfertilized seed.

Seed coats probably resulted from the envelopment of the

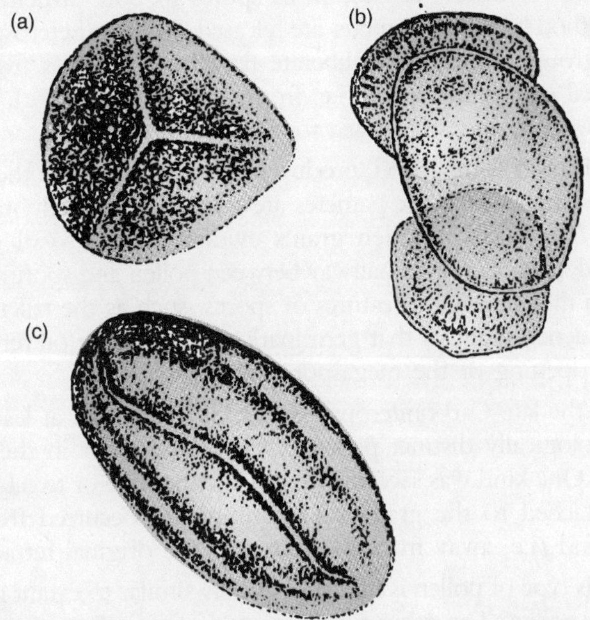

Figure 3.13: (a) Earliest spores with trilete scar; (b) saccate pollen, with two bladder sacs attached to the grain; (c) monolete pollen, with a long suture running down the distal edge. All grains -20-60 μm in diameter.

megasporangium by sterile telome trusses (another use in addition to the formation of megaphyllous leaves), which fused around the megasporangium to encase it, so forming an ovule.

Many of the early ovules were further enveloped by stalked cupules, with up to four ovules within a cupule. Again, the cupule was thought to have developed from fusion of a vegetative branching system.

Evolution of Pollen Grains

In association with the development of the ovule (from the megasporangium), palaeobotanical evidence indicates the evolution of pollen from approximately 364 million years ago (Famennian).

Evolution of pollen represents adaptation of the male part of the plant life cycle, since prior to this time only spores had been found in the fossil record.

Pollen is distinguishable from spores in both structure and the method by which gametes are released. In exant heterosporous plant groups, microspores liberate flagellated gametes from the proximal end of the spore (i.e. from the trilete aperture), which then swim to the archegonia for fertilization.

Pollen, in comparison, produces a pollen tube from the distal end, through which the gametes are transferred directly into the ovule. The earliest pollen grains evident in the fossil record (termed 'prepollen') are halfway between pollen and spores. They contain morphological features of spores, such as the trilete scar, but evidence suggests that germination occurred on or very near to the opening of the megasporan-gium.

By the late Carboniferous (-31 O Ma), however, at least two morphologically distinct pollen types were present in the fossil record. One kind was saccate (i.e. it had either one or two bladder sacs attached to the grain) and germination occurred from its distal end (i.e. away from the centre of the original tetrad).

This type of pollen is morphologically similar to extant gymnosperm pollen. The other type consisted of a single grain with a long suture running down the distal edge, presumably from where germination occurred.

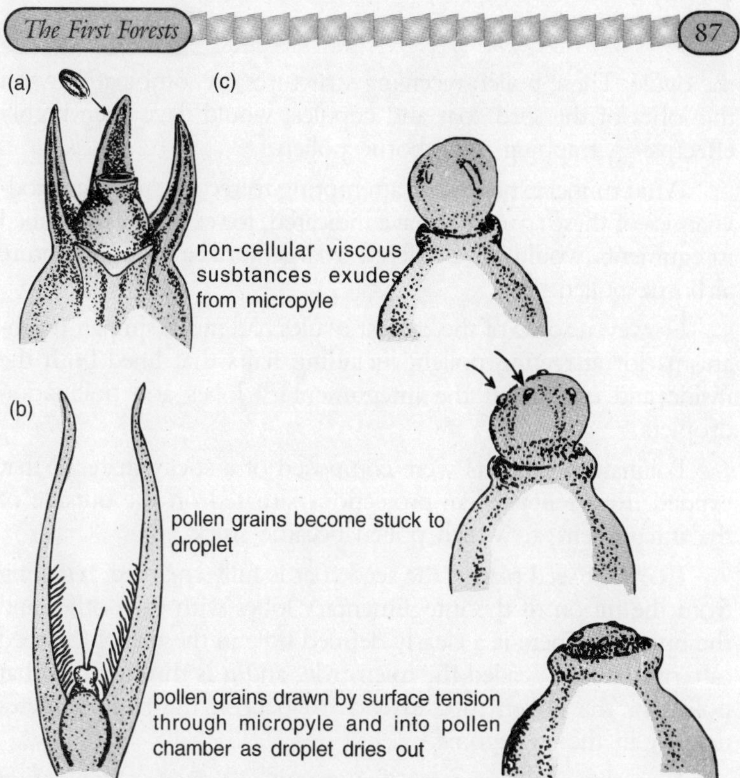

Figure 3.14: Development of pollen reception mechanisms visible in the fossil record: (a) adaptation of funnels to channel pollen towards the ovule; (b) hairs; (c) schematic diagram to indicate the 'pollination drop' mechanism.

This morphological type of pollen grain is known as monolete. Both monosaccate and monolete pollen in the early fossil record are attributed to members of the pteridosperms and cordaites.

Development of Pollen Reception Mechanisms

With the encasement of the ovule in a seed coat, it would have been necessary to develop a mechanism by which the pollen could reach the egg contained within the ovule, for germination.

In the earliest seeds, where the integumentary envelope was only fused at the base, there is evidence for evolution of various elaborate structures at the neck of the megasporanium.

In effect, these acted as a funnel to channel the pollen towards the ovule. These pollen-receiving structures, in combination with the lobes of the seed coat and cupules, would have been highly effective in trapping wind-borne pollen.

Wind tunnel experiments attempting to reconstruct the aerodynamics of these structures have indicated, for example, that lobed integuments would have offered a large surface area to capture airborne pollen.

However, some of the earliest ovules had much simpler mechanisms for attracting pollen, including hairs that lined both the inside and outside of the integumentary lobes and pollination droplets.

Pollination droplets were composed of a sticky material that exuded from tentacle-like projections situated on the outside of the integument, to which pollen became stuck.

In extant seed plants, the seed coat is fully enclosed, resulting from the fusion of the integumentary lobes with each other and the nucellus. There is a clearly defined hole in the top of the seed (a terminal pore) called the micropyle, and it is through this that pollen or the pollen tube extends to deposit the male gametes near or in the archegonia.

In extant gymnosperms, for example, a sugary 'pollination drop' exudes from the micropyle in which wind-blown pollen becomes trapped. As the pollination drop is withdrawn back into the nucleus, the pollen is taken in with it.

Evidence in the fossil record suggests that development of an enclosed integument and associated micropyle occurred in the late Devonian. The advantages of an enclosed integument were threefold.

First, it would have provided much greater protection to the megasporangium against predators and desiccation.

Secondly, it would have increased the efficiency of wind pollination; a more fused morphology and reduced lobes would have conferred aerodynamic efficiency for deflecting windborne pollen into the pollen drop, and thence into the micropyle.

Thirdly, it would have aided the dispersal of mature seeds. The evolution of true seeds would therefore have enabled much greater chance of lateral dispersal away from the parent plant and greater potential for survival, once dispersed, in the newly created, drier, primary successional environments.

In summary, therefore, it is apparent that throughout the early Devonian, major innovations were occurring in vascular plant morphology.

These would not only have enabled greatly increased size and stature but also the ability to reproduce and survive in more arid environments over a wider geographic distribution.

It is interesting to note that these innovations occurred during a dramatic transitionary phase in global climates, moving from a period of high global temperatures and high atmospheric CO_2 to one of cold glacial climates, with a rapid and major decline in atmospheric CO_2.

However, these climate changes did not merely provide a background to vascular plant evolution but, rather, vascular plant evolution played a significant role in altering the global climates as the terrestrialization of the earth resulted in a draw-down of atmospheric CO_2 which in turn contributed to global climatic cooling.

EARLIEST TREES IN THE FOSSIL RECORD

The term 'earliest trees' must be used fairly loosely since the record of when and where the first trees were located is strongly influenced by the fact that certain regions provided better preservation potential, such as in areas of lowland swamps, and therefore the record is somewhat biased.

However, two irrefutable facts emerge about the vegetation of this time. First, that the earliest arborescent forms of plants (trees) appeared in the middle Devonian (~380 Ma).

Secondly, from this time on until the late Carboniferous, forests composed of sporeproducing trees (sporophytes) plus two groups of early seed-producing trees dominated large regions of the continents.

Earliest Spore-producing Trees

The spore-producing trees, shrubs, and herbs that evolved

during this interval (~380-290 Ma) can be classified into four main groups, namely lycopsids, sphenopsids, filicopsids, and progymnosperms.

The progymnosperms are extinct, but the other three groups all have extant members, indicating the remarkable length of the fossil record of some groups. It is beyond the scope of this book to describe in detail all fossil members of each group.

However, the features of one common fossil type from each group are described in the following section to provide a preliminary picture of the composition of vegetation in the earliest forests.

Lycopods

Although there is evidence in the geological record for small, herbaceous, homosporous lycopsids from as early as 410 million years ago (e.g. *Baragwanathia longifolia*), and many subsequent forms, lycopsid trees were first present in the Frasnian.

Table 3.1: Cladistic classification of land plants.

Infrakingdom embryobiotes (land plants)

Superdivision Marchantiomorpha (liverworts)

Division Marchantiophyta

Class Marchantiopsida

Superdivision Anthoceromorpha (hornworts)

Division Anthocerophyta

Class Anthocerotopsida

Superdivision Bryomorpha (mosses)

Division Bryophyta

Class Bryopsida

Superdivision Polysporangiomorpha

Class Horneophytopsidat

Aglaophyton major

Division Tracheophyta (vascular plants)

Class Rhyniopsidat

Subdivision Lycophytina

(*Table 3.1 contd.*)

Species *Zosterophyllum myretonianum incertae sedist*
Class Lycopsida (lycopsids)
Order Drepanophycalest
Order 'Lycopodiales'
Order Protolepidodendralest
Order Selaginellales
Order Isoetales
Class Zosterophyllopsidat
Order Sawdoniales
Family Sawdoniaceaet
Family Barinophytaceaet
Family 'Gosslingiaceae
Family Hauaceaet
Subdivision Euphyllophytina
(fern-equisetum-seed plant Glade)
Eophyllophyton bellum
Psilophyton dawsonii
Infradivision Moniliformopses
Class 'Cladoxylopsida' (early fern-like plants)
Subclass Cladoxylidaet
Subclass Stauropteridaet
Subclass Zygopteridaet
Class Equisetopsida (sphenopsids)
Class 'Filicopsida' (ferns)
Subclass Ophioglossidae,
Infrakingdom embryobiotes (***land plants***)
Subclass Psilotidae
Subclass Marattiidae
Subclass Polypodiidae
Infradivision Radiatopses
Pertica variat
Supercohort Lignophytia
Order 'Aneurophytales' (progymnosperms)

(***Table 3.1 contd.***)

Order 'Archaeopteridales' (progymnosperms)
Order 'Protopityales' (progymnosperms)
Cohort Spermatophytat (seed plants)
Family 'Calamopityaceae't (pteridosperms)
Family 'Hydraspermaceae' (pteridosperms)
Family 'Lyginopteridaceae' (pteridosperms)
Family Medullosaceaet (pteridosperms)
Subcohort Euspermatoclides
Infrascohort Cycadatae (cycads)
Family callistophytaceaet (pteridosperms)
Infracohort Coniferophytatae
Superclass Cordaitidrat (cordaites)
Superclass Coniferidra (conifers)
Family Glossopteridaceaet (glossopterids)
Infracohort Ginkgoatae (ginkgos)
Family 'Peltaspermaceae' (pteridosperms)
Family 'Corystospermaceae' (pteridosperms)
Family Caytoniaceaet (pteridosperms)
Infracohort Anthophytatae*
Order Pentoxylalest
Order Bennettitalest (bennettites)
Superclass Gnetidra
Superclass Magnolidra (angiosperms)
Class 'Magnoliopsida'
Class Lilliopsida
Class Harnamelidopsida
Subclass Ranunculidae
Subclass Hamamelididae
Infraclass Caryophyllidna
Infraclass 'Rosidna'
Infraclass 'Dilleniidna'
Infraclass Lamiidna
Infraclass Asteridna

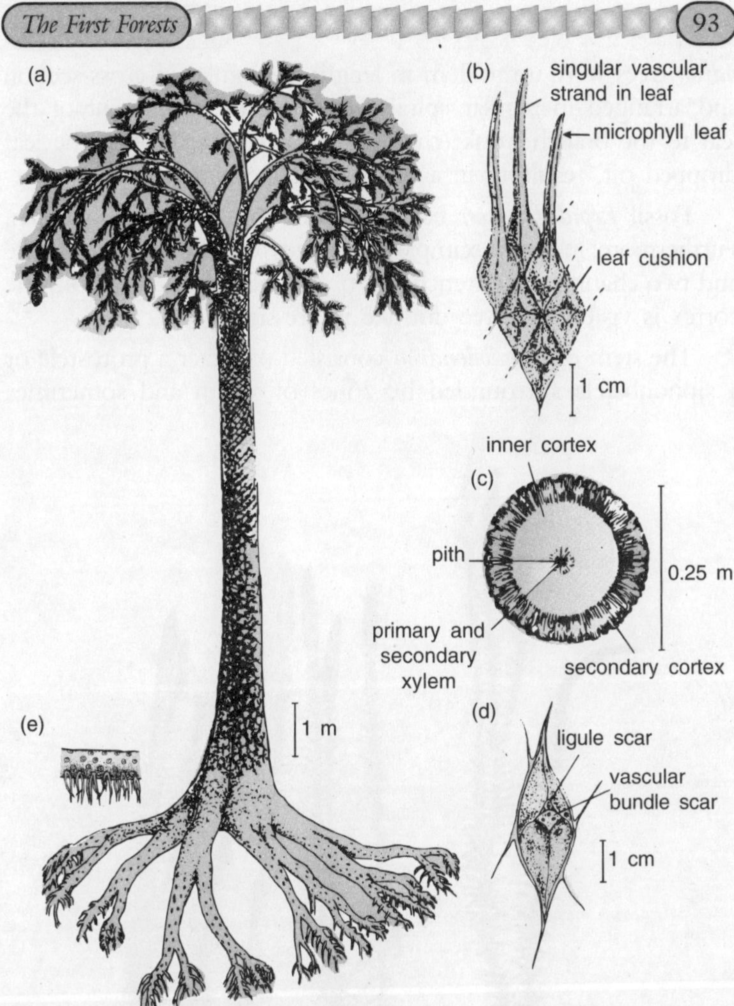

Figure 3.15: Lepidodendron tree: (a) habit; (b) bark pattern with leaves; (c) cross-section of stem with cortical tissue; (d) details of leaf scar; (e) roots.

One of the most common arborescent lycopsids in the fossil record was the giant *Lepidodendron* tree, which achieved heights of between 10 and 35 m and had a trunk up to 1 m in diameter. The upper part of the trunk was branched many times to form a dense crown covered in simple microphyll leaves that grew directly out from the stem (i.e. without a petiole), leaving the swollen leaf base or 'leaf cushion' when shed. Leaves of *Lepidode-*

ndron trees were up to 1 m in length, triangular in cross-section and arranged in regular spirals. The area of attachment of the leaf to the branch/trunk (the leaf base) remained when the leaf dropped off, resulting in a diamond-shape pattern.

Fossil *Lepidodendron* bark indicates this distinctive pattern. Furthermore, in many examples the area where the vascular bundle and two channels of parenchyma tissue entered the leaf from the cortex is visible as three dot-like impressions.

The stem of *Lepidodendron* consisted of either a protostele or a siphonostele surrounded by zones of xylem and sometimes

Figure 3.16: Extant Lycopodium, indicating the characteristic microphyllous leaves on the stem.

secondary xylem. However, the main tissue contributing to trunk diameter and providing support was bark (periderm), in extensive layers.

The rooting system of the *Lepidodendron* tree was in many ways as impressive as the above-ground part of the plant. It consisted of four or more radiating arms (axes) that were extensively branched and, although not deeply penetrating into the substrate, extended up to 12 m in length.

These axes, referred to as stigmaria, were composed of large amounts of secondary xylem and cortical tissues, and bore spirally

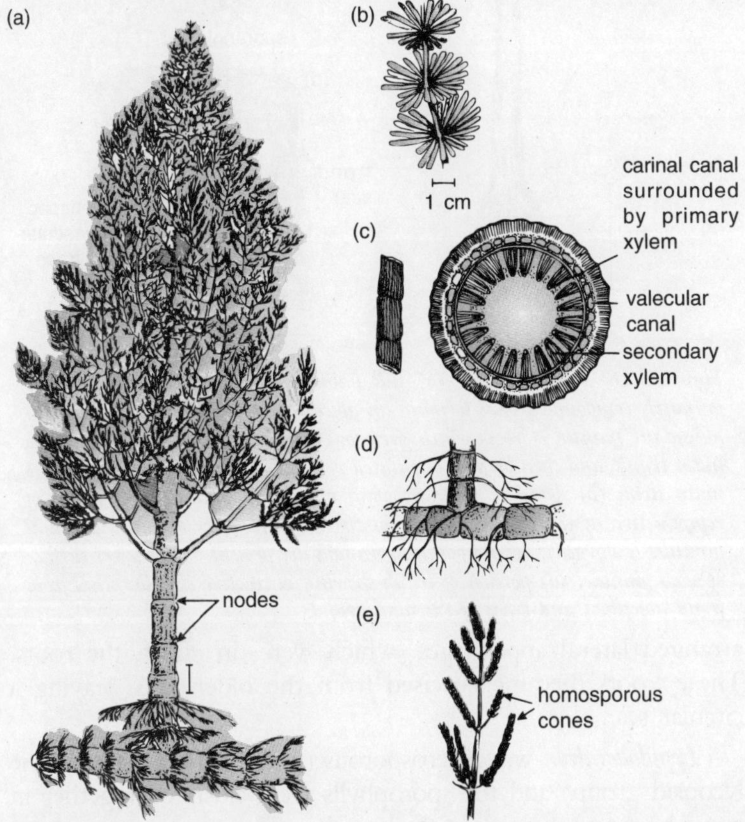

Figure 3.17: Calamites tree: (a) habit; (b) leaves; (c) stem and cross-section of stem; (d) roots; (e) reproductive structures.

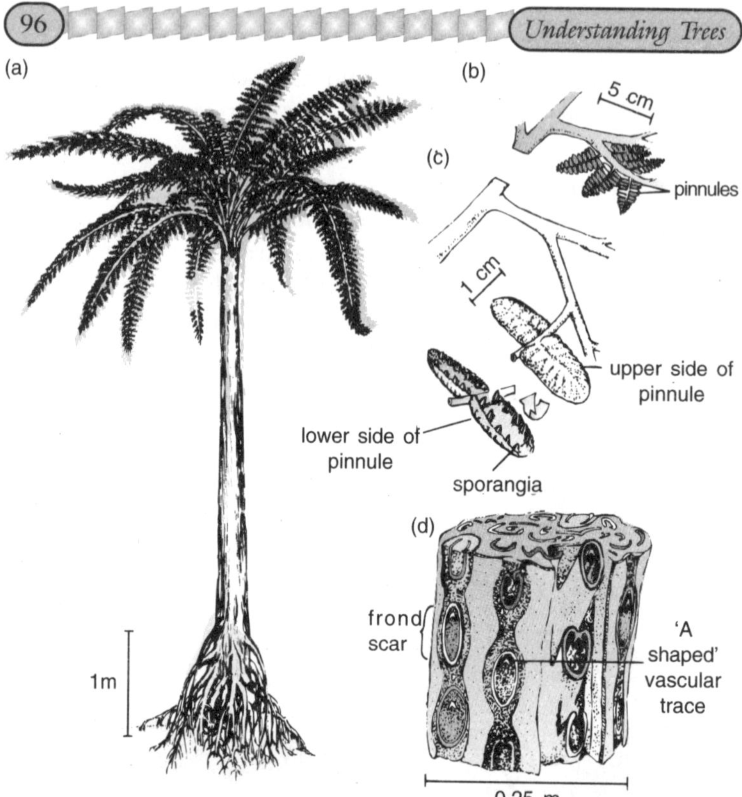

Figure 3.18: Psaronius tree-(a) full habit showing attachment of large pinnately compound fronds forming an apical crown. Also illustrated are an abundant mantle of roots which grew out as lateral appendages from the main trunk, and then became orientated vertically downwards parallel to the main stem; (b) detail of frond showing individual pinnules; (c) detail of reproductive structures (synangia) on the lower surfaces of two individual pinnules (enlarged), 10 individual sporangia are present on the lower surface of each pinnule; (d) portion of trunk showing distinctive circular scars from frond abscission and trace of vascular strand.

arranged lateral appendages, which were, in effect, the roots. These 'roots' became abscised from the older axes, leaving a circular scar.

Lepidodendron was heterosporous (unlike earlier plants in the lycopsid group) and the sporophylls were clustered together in cones borne on the ends of the branches. These cones were composed of a central axis with helically arranged sporophylls and were between 1 and 3.5 cm in width and 5 and 40 cm in length.

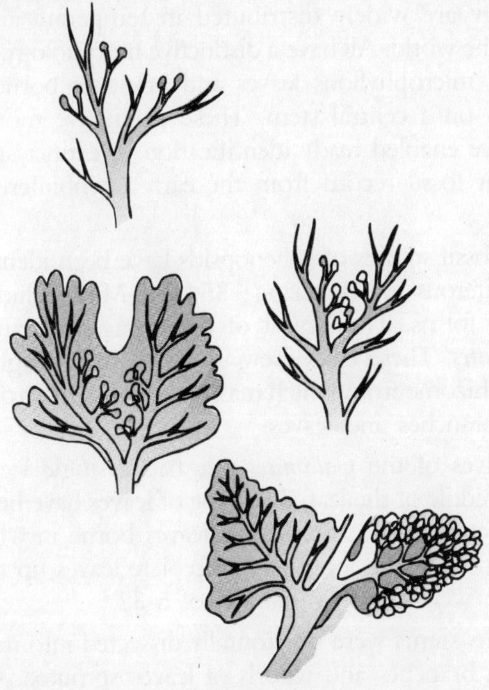

Figure 3.19: Formation of fertile fronds.

From these cones the megaspores and microspores were shed. Following their evolutionary radiation, arborescent lycopsids greatly increased in number to become a dominant component of the world flora. They formed a significant part of the organic material deposited in the coal measures of the late Carboniferous, leading to estimates that they accounted for over two-thirds of the earliest global forests.

There were also numerous herbaceous and shrubby forms of lycopsids. Extant lycopsids include a number of genera, including *Lycopodium* (clubmoss), *Selaginella*, and *Isoetes*. All three are herbaceous plants with microphyllous leaves, ranging from small epiphytes to large climbing plants. However, no extant members of this group are arborescent.

Giant Horsetails

Presently there are approximately 20 extant species of sphenopsids, all of which are herbaceous and belong to a single extant genus. They are widely distributed in temperate and tropical regions of the world. All have a distinctive morphology, comprised of whorled microphyllous leaves and branches borne as lateral appendages on a central stem. These distinctive morphological features have enabled ready identification of extinct sphenopsids in the plant fossil record from the early Carboniferous (~354 Ma).

Many fossil species of sphenopsids have been identified from the Carboniferous and Permian (~354-248 Ma), including several arborescent forms. The largest of these was the giant horsetail tree, *Calamites*. These trees grew up to 18 m in height and had a creeping rhizome from which massive aerial stems arose, bearing whorls of branches and leaves.

The leaves of the *Calamites* tree had a single vien running down the middle of the leaf. Two type of leaves have been identified in the fossil record: needle-like leaves borne in whorls of 4-40 and up to 3.0 mm long, and lanceolate leaves up to 8.0 mm long, which were borne in clusters of 5-32.

Calamites stems were horizontally dissected into many nodes from which branches and whorls of leaves sprouted. The upper branches also bore whorls of leaves.

In structure the stem was a siphonostele with a central pith. This was surrounded by vascular bundles of primary phloem and xylem, which were then surrounded by secondary xylem. Fossil evidence suggests that in many examples this secondary thickening was at least 12 cm thick.

Calamites possessed a complex root system composed of large underground rhizomes, which were segmented, and from which arose the aerial stems, root branches, and root hairs. Some *Calamites* were homosporous but there is strong evidence for heterospory in late Carboniferous *Calamites*.

Similar to *Lepidodendron* trees, the spore-bearing structures were aggregated into cones. Location of the cones varied greatly, with evidence suggesting single cones, clusters at nodes, or several cones on fertile appendages at the end of lateral branches.

The evolution of heterospory in the sphenopsids appears to have paralleled that of *Lepidodendron*, with evidence for megaspo-

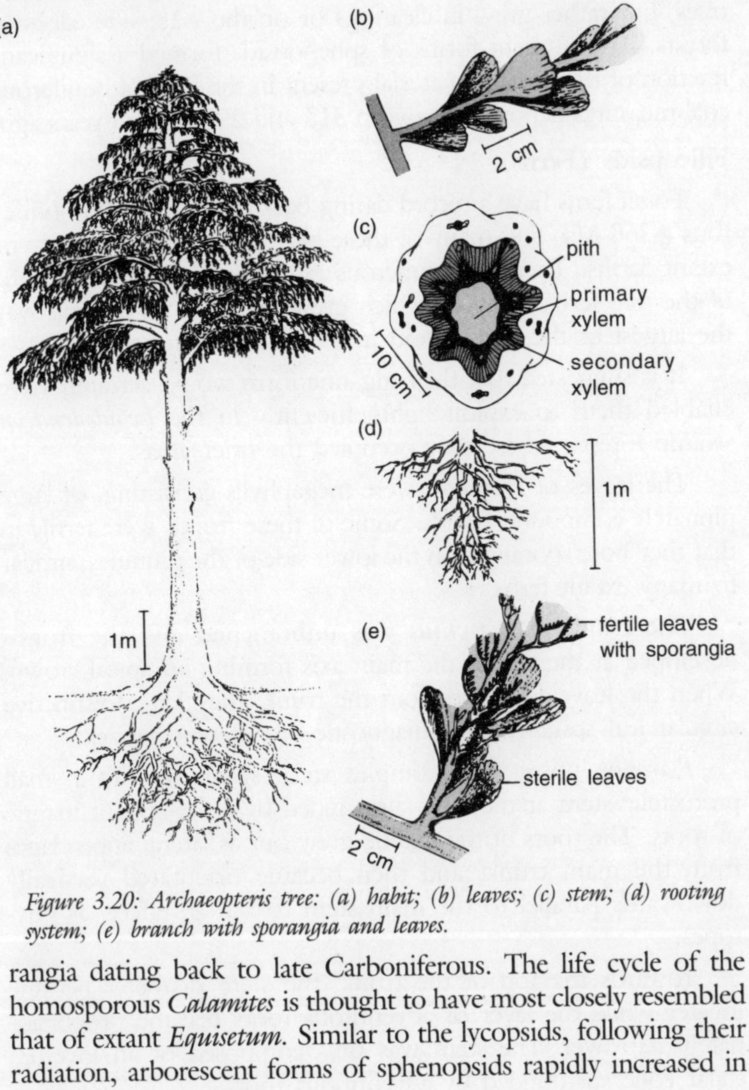

(a) 1m

(b) 2 cm

(c) pith, primary xylem, secondary xylem, 10 cm

(d) 1m

(e) fertile leaves with sporangia, sterile leaves, 2 cm

Figure 3.20: Archaeopteris tree: (a) habit; (b) leaves; (c) stem; (d) rooting system; (e) branch with sporangia and leaves.

rangia dating back to late Carboniferous. The life cycle of the homosporous *Calamites* is thought to have most closely resembled that of extant *Equisetum*. Similar to the lycopsids, following their radiation, arborescent forms of sphenopsids rapidly increased in number and diversity.

These trees flourished in wet, swampy conditions and their large underground rooting rhizomes would have provided an ideal base from which aerial stems could force their way through the swamp.

They probably did not form an understorey to the lycopsid

trees, but rather grew in clearings or on the waterside edges of forests. Arboresecent forms of sphenopsids formed a significant fraction of the organic material present in the late Carboniferous coal measures deposited between 315 and 290 million years ago.

Filicopsids (Ferns)

Fossil ferns have a record dating back to the early Carboniferous (-360 Ma) and many of these bear remarkable similarity to extant forms. There are numerous examples in the fossil record of the tree fern *Psaronius*, which grew up to 10 m tall and was the largest of the ferns found in the coal-measure swamps.

It is suggested that their gigantic form would certainly have enabled them to exploit light efficiently in the *Lepidodendron* swamp forests, where they occupied the drier areas.

The leaves of *Psaronius* were megaphylls consisting. of large pinnately compound fronds. Some of these fronds were fertile in that they bore sporangia on the lower side of the pinnules, similar to many extant ferns.

The trunk of *Psaronius* was unbranched and the fronds developed at the top of the main axis forming an apical crown. When the leaves abscised from the trunk, they left a distinctive circular leaf scar, which is diagnostic of different species.

Psaronius possessed a complex stelar structure with a small protostelic stem at the base surrounded by an abundant mantle of roots. The roots of the mantle grew out as lateral appendages from the main trunk, and then became orientated vertically downwards parallel to the main stem to act, in effect, as guy-ropes.

Towards the top of the trunk, the stem diameter became greater while the layer of adventitous roots became proportionately narrower. The stem was thus composed of an inverted stelar cone surrounded by adventitious roots.

The construction of the stele was also complicated in the fact that each of the leaf bases received an extensive leaf trace consisting of several strands of vascular tissue. This resulted in numerous concentric leaf gaps visible in cross-sections of the stele.

There was no secondary vascular tissue (wood) in the trunk.

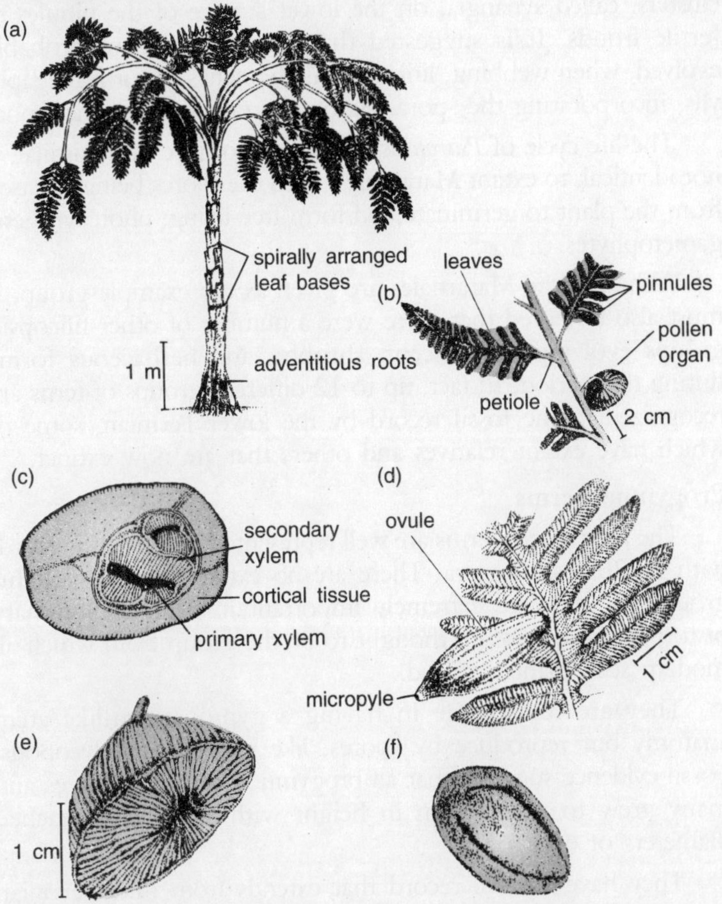

Figure 3.21: Medullosa noei tree: (a) habit; (b) leaves; (c) stem and stelar structure; (d) ovules; (e) pollen organ; (f) monolete pollen (up to 600 sm in diameter).

Rather, their tree-like stature was made possible by the supporting strength of adventitious roots as in all extant tree ferns, which share the same structure.

Palaeobotanical evidence suggests that in some specimens, the root mantle reached 1 m in diameter at the base of the stem. The majority of extinct ferns, including *Psaronius*, were homosporous.

In *Psaronius* the sporangia were large and arranged in fused clusters, called synangia, on the lower surface of the pinules of fertile fronds. It is suggested that this arrangement probably evolved, when webbing, linked fertile branches to form megaphylls, incorporating the sporangia on the underside of the frond.

The life cycle of *Psaronius* is thought to have been similar, if not identical, to extant Marattiales, with the spores being released from the plant to germinate and form free-living, photosynthetic gametophytes.

Although the Marattiales are given as the example group, it must also be noted that there were a number of other filicopsid groups evolving arborescent, shrubby, and herbaceous forms during this period. In fact, up to 12 different groups of ferns are recognized in the fossil record by the lower Permian, some of which have extant relatives and others that are now extinct.

Progymnosperms

The progymnosperms are well represented in the fossil record, with 15-20 fossil genera. There are no extant members of this group, but they are extremely important in plant evolutionary history because they are thought to be the group from which all modern seed plants evolved.

They are remarkable in having a gymnosperm-like stem anatomy but reproduce by spores, like in ferns and lycopods. Fossil evidence suggests that all progymnosperms were trees and many grew to up to 8 m in height with stems that reached diameters of over 1.5 m.

They have a fossil record that extends from mid-Devonian to early Carboniferous (~390-340 Ma). One of the first fossil trees to be documented as a progymnosperm was *Archaeopteris.*

Helically arranged, deciduous branches grew out laterally from the upper part of the main trunk, on which grew laminate leaves. Progymnosperm foliage is not dissimilar to the fossil fern fronds of *Psaronius* described previously, and for many years these leafy branches were regarded as large pinnate fronds (compound leaves).

It was only when fossil examples of these 'fronds' were found attached to trunks, with clear evidence of thick secondary xylem, that it became apparent that they were part of a different evolut-

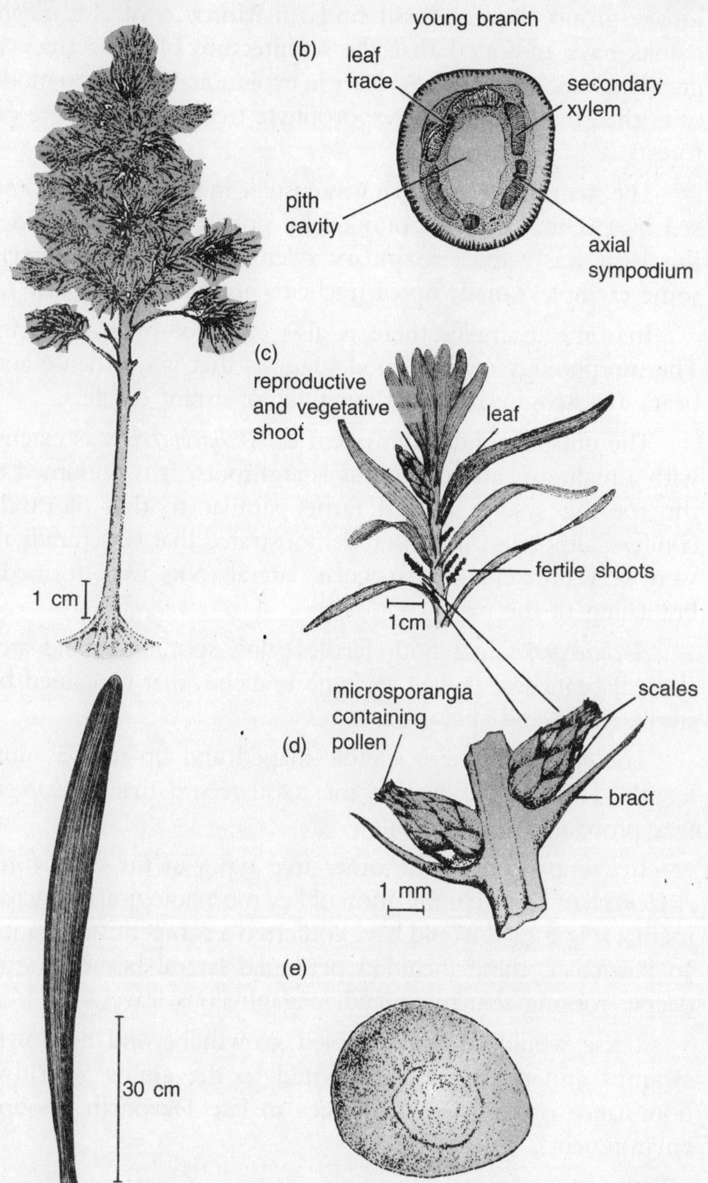

Figure 3.22: Cordaitales tree: (a) habit; (b) stem stelar structure; (c) branch with leaves and reproductive shoots; (d) reproductive structures; (e) pollen (45-65 μm in diameter); (f) leaf.

ionary group. Recent fossil finds in Morocco of *Archaeopteris* trunks have indicated that the architecture of these trees was greatly advanced and much closer in evolutionary terms to modern trees than that of the other sporophyte trees present in the early forests.

The stem of *Archaeopteris* was eustelic in structure and composed of a central pith surrounded by primary xylem. Outside of this layer was a thick secondary xylem (up to 1 m diameter in some examples) made up of tracheids and narrow vascular rays.

In some examples there is also evidence of growth rings. The morphology of this wood suggests that it was dense and it bears a close similarity to the trunks of extant conifers.

The underground root system of *Archaeopteris* was extensive with a main axis and numerous lateral roots. It is presumed that the rooting system looked rather similar to that of modern conifers, although it has been demonstrated that structurally they were very different. In particular, lateral roots were formed by branching of the main root axis.

Archaeopteris had both fertile (with sporangia) and sterile (leafed) branches, as well as some branches that contained both sterile leaves and sporangia.

The sporangia were spindle-shaped and up to 3.5 mm in length. There is evidence in the fossil record that *Archaeopteris* was probably heterosporous.

In comparison to the other tree types in the early forests, *Archaeopteris* had a combination of key morphological characteristics that it is argued would have conferred a competitive advantage. In particular, these included perennial lateral branches, much deeper rooting structures, and megaphyllous leaves.

These would all have enabled growth beyond the lowland swamps and probably contributed to the almost worldwide dominance of Archaeopteris trees in late Devonian floodplain environments.

Earliest Seed-producing Trees

Along with the spore-producing giant horsetails, lycopsids, filicopsids, and progymnosperms, two groups of early seed plants,

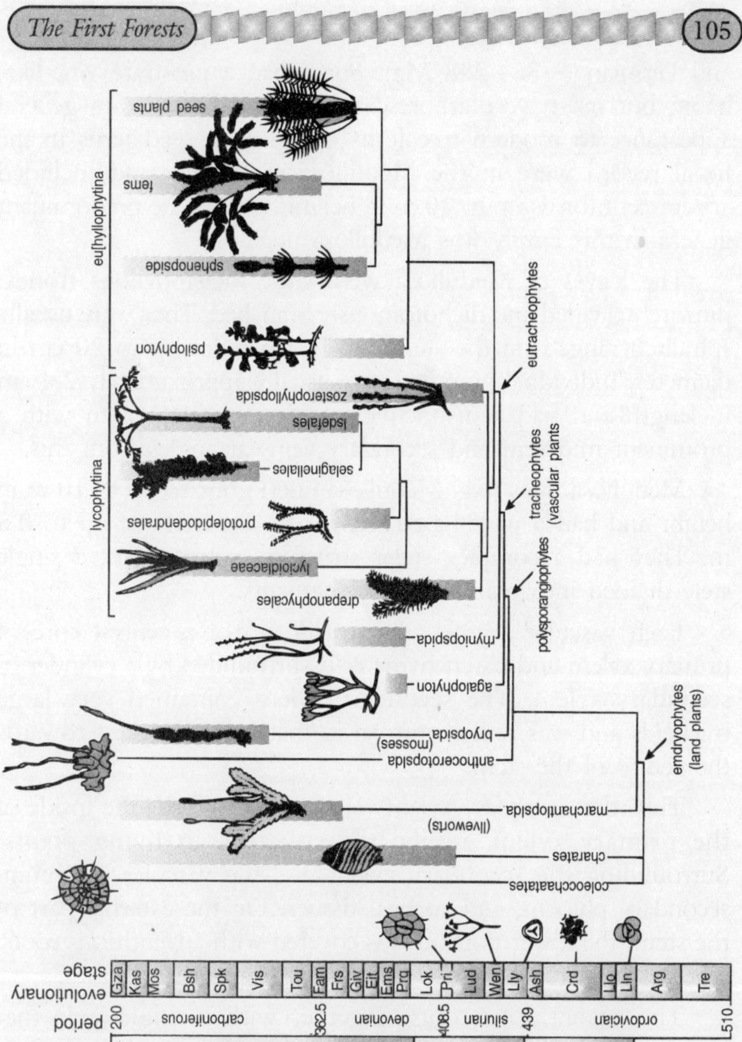

Figure 3.23: Phylogenetic relationship between extinct and extant early plants.

namely the pteridosperms and cordaites, were present in the forests of the early and late Carboniferous (~354-290 Ma).

Seed Ferns

The seed-ferns are so called because although they had fern-like foliage, they reproduced by seeds. There is fossil evidence for at least six families of seed ferns during the Carboniferous and Permian (~354-248 Ma). Some had a prostrate vine-like, habit, but most were arborescent forms and similar in general appearance to modern tree ferns. The largest seed ferns in the fossil record were in the Medullosaceae family and included arborescent forms up to 10 m in height. One of the predominant genera in this family was Medullosa noei.

The leaves of Medullosa were large megaphyllous fronds, pinnately divided and dichotomously branched. They were usually spirally arranged on the stem and had petioles up to 20 cm in diameter. Individual pinnules were usually approximately 2-4 cm in length and had a distinctive venation pattern, often with a prominent mid-vein and secondary veins at angles from this.

Medullosa trees (e.g. Medullosa noei) grew to up to 10 m in height and had a wide-based stem with diameters of up to 0.5 m. They had a complex stelar structure composed of a single stele divided into many vascular segments.

Each vascular segment was made up of a central core of primary xylem and parenchyma cells surrounded by a cylinder of secondary xylem. The secondary xylem contained very large tracheids and was rather unusual in that it was thickest towards the centre of the stem.

Thus the secondary xylem was formed towards the inside of the primary xylem, unlike the situation in living plants. Surrounding the secondary xylem was the vascular cambium, secondary phloem, and cortical tissues. On the external part of the stem, the lower portion was covered with adventitious roots, whereas higher up there were spirally arranged leaf bases.

The adventitious roots, together with a single stele that became divided at intervals along the trunk, provided support. Fossil evidence suggests that these roots could be up to 2.5 cm in diameter, and were abundant, with secondary tissues.

Medullosa ovules are common in the fossil record and at least 14 morphologically distinctive types have been recognized. They range in size between 1 and 11 cm and have a three-layered enclosed integument with a micropyle and simple pollen chamber.

These ovules share a close morphological similarity to cycad ovules, supporting the suggestion that the two are closely related.

Table 3.2: Plant biogeographical classification schemes.

Classification based on taxonomic criteria	*Classification based on ecological criteria*
Realm	***Realm***
Defined on the basis of the (palaeo) geographic distribution of distinctive suites of taxa. Each suite includes a significant proportion of endemic families	Defined on the basis of the (palaeo) geographic distribution of distinctive suites of taxa. Each suite includes a significant proportion of endemic families
Region	***Biome***
Defined on the basis of the (palaeo) geographic distribution of distinctive suites of taxa. Each suite includes a significant proportion of endemic genera and/or species	Social groupings on an intercontinental scale composed of a characteristic set of taxa and has a characteristic overall physiognomy (such as plant stature, habit, leaf size, shape) and taxonomic diversity
Area	***Biocenosis***
Defined by differences in the proportions of the taxa comprising the suite and by lesser differences in the proportions of endemic species and genera	Social groupings of taxa representing integrated functional systems. The taxa comprising a biocenosis require a narrowly constrained range of environmental and edaphic conditions
Association	***Community***
Defined on the basis of a consistent co-occurrence of specific taxa	A biocenosis composed of a specific suite of taxa

However, very few fossil *Medullosa* ovule specimens have been found attached to the fronds, and as such their phylogenetic position remains uncertain.

The prepollen grains of the *Medullosa* trees were located in pollen organs borne on fertile branches in clusters, or in place of

Early Carboniferous (354-342 Ma)

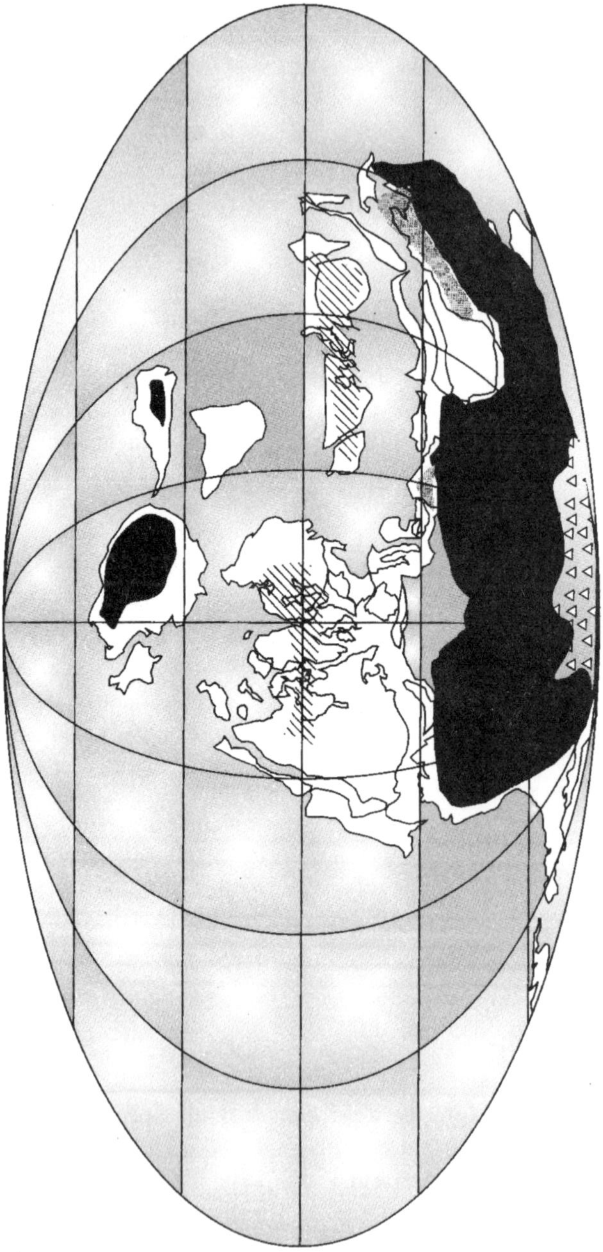

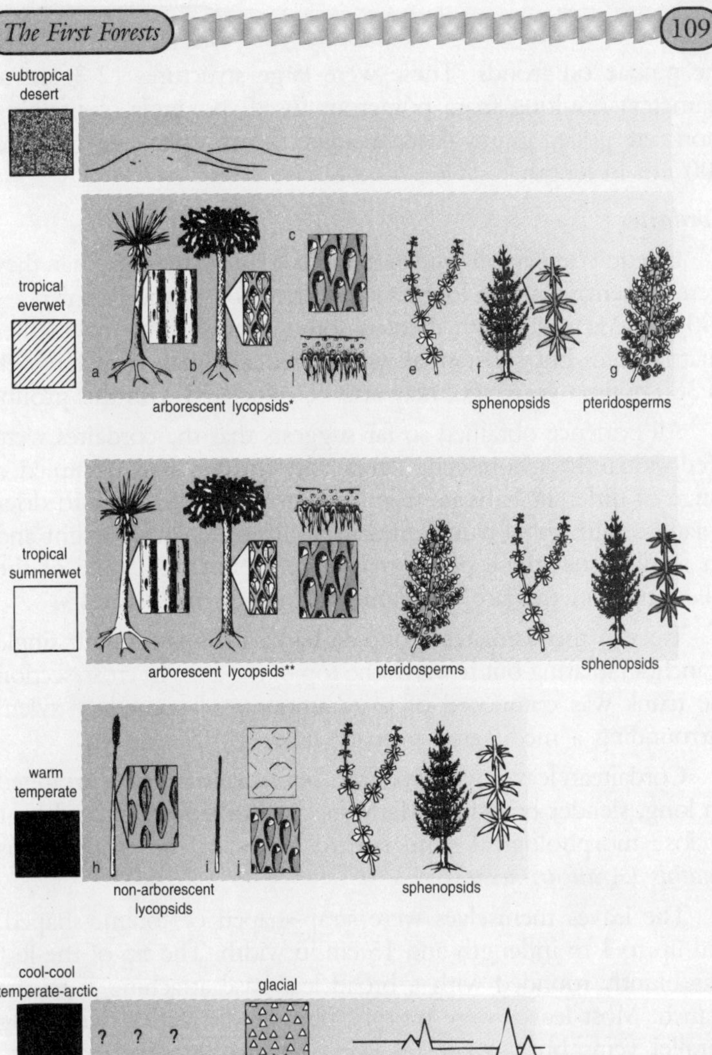

Figure 3.24: Suggested biomes for the early Carboniferous (354-342 Ma), with representatives of the most abundant and/or dominant fossil plant taxa shown. The biomes are superimposed on a global palaeogeographic reconstruction for the Visean (~340 Ma) (courtesy of C. R. Scotese and the PaleoMap Project). (a) Sigillaria tree with details of fossil bark; (b) Lepidodendron tree with details of fossil bark; (c) Stigmaria (lycopsid root); (d) details of fossil bark of Lepidodendropsis; (e) Sphenophyllum; (f) Calamites tree with details of leaves (Asterophyllites); (g) stylized pteridosperm frond; (h) Tomiodendron tree with details of fossil bark; (i) juvenile lycopsid; (j) Ursodendron bark.

the pinnae on fronds. These were large structures (2-3 cm in diameter) resulting from numerous fused sporangia, containing monolete pollen grains (with a single furrow) between 100 and 600 μm in length.

Cordaites

Unequivocal fossil evidence for cordaites suggests that they were present from the lower Carboniferous into the Permian (~ 330-250 Ma), although there is some discussion as to whether unattributed, but substantial, woody remains, dating as far back as 380 million years ago, may also be associated with this group.

All evidence obtained so far suggests that the cordaites were predominantly arborescent (trees and shrubs) and occupied a range of different habitats from mangrove-type habitats to drier uplands. With fossil trunks measuring up to 30 m in height and lm in diameter, these plants may have represented some of the tallest trees in the late Carboniferous and Permian forests.

Trees in the cordaites group all had a main stem with single branches radiating out towards the top of the axis. In cross-section the trunk was composed of large amounts of secondary xylem surrounding a medullated primary stele.

Cordaitean leaves were variable, but usually helically arranged on long, slender branches. Many species in the fossil record bear a close morphological similarity to leaves of the exant genus *Agathis* (*Araucari-aceae*).

The leaves themselves were strap-shaped or tongue-shaped, and up to 1 m in length and 15 cm in width. The tip of the leaf was bluntly rounded with a broad leaf base attaching it to the branch. Most leaves were morphologically distinctive, with long parallel veins but no central vein (midrib) running down its length.

However, some cordaitean leaves were more needle-like in appearance, with only a single vein running down each leaf. Rooting systems of the cordaites were variable in structure.

Fossil evidence suggests that some groups had extensive rooting systems, with lateral roots radiating from large branched primary roots, whereas others consisted of lateral roots forming in clusters on only one side of the main root.

This latter type is typical of extant plants that grow in mangrove swamps and possibly indicates the environmental conditions in which these trees grew.

Reproductive structures were borne on the same branches as the leaves. Male and female organs were separate but probably located on the same tree.

The male organs were located on shoots up to 1 cm long that contained a number of scales arranged around the shoot axis in a spiral, forming a structure similar to a conifer cone.

The lower scales were sterile but the upper scales terminated in cylindrical pollen sacs (up to 1 mm in length), which contained numerous monosaccate pollen grains, each between 45 and 65 μm in diameter.

The female reproductive organs were also located on the branches and bore some similarity to the male organs in that they were cone-shaped and composed of fertile and infertile scales.

However, in the female organs, the fertile scales terminated in ovules rather than pollen sacs. Each seed was surrounded by three integumentary layers, forming an enclosed seed coat with micropyle. The margin of the seed extended as a wing (platyspermic).

EARLIEST VASCULAR PLANTS TO TREES

Ever since the first plant fossils were discovered, theories have been put forward to provide an evolutionary link between the earliest land plants, such as *Cooksonia* and *Aglaophyton*, to later groups, such as the progymnosperms and sphenopsids, and to our extant flora.

Recent cladistic analyses based on both morphological and biomole-cular analyses of extant and extinct plant groups suggest that all vascular plants can be divided into two well-defined clades-the Rhyniopsida and Eutracheophytes.

Two basal lineages emerged from the Eutracheophytina-the Lycophytina and Euphyllophytina (fern-Equisetum-seed-plant Glade).

The Lycophytina

The Lycophytina share a number of characteristics (known as synapomorphies) including kidney-shaped sporangia which develop on short laterally inserted stalks and exarch xylem. The lineage split early on in evolutionary terms to form two major clades, the Zosterophyllopsida (zosterphyllophytes), which bore lateral sporangia direct on their leafless stems, and the Lycopsida (lycopsids) which have microphyll leaves, with sporangia in their axils:

1. The zosterophyllophytes include only extinct members (e.g. *Zosterophyllum*,) and no further evolution of this Glade is thought to have occurred beyond the Devonian (~360 Ma).
2. The lycopsids, in comparison, include both extinct and extant members and indicate a phylogenetic relationship between the earliest vascular plants, such as *Baragwanathia* and the *arborescent Lepidodendron*, and extant families such as Lycoppdiaceae and Selaginellaceae.

The Euphyllophytina

The Euphylophytina are all characterized by a helical arrangement of branches, tracheids with bordered pits in the form of a ladder and often by sperm which is multiflagellate.

The Euphyllophytina also split early in evolutionary terms to form two clades, one containing the extinct genus *Psilophyton dawsonii* and the other including the ferns (filicopsids), horsetails (sphenopsids), and seed plants (spermatophytes).

From these cladistic analyses it would also appear that the spermatophytes are a sister group to the sphenopsids and filicopsids, thus suggesting a close phylogenetic relationship between members of the Euphyllophytina.

BIOGEOGRAPHICAL DISTRIBUTION

The ecology, structure, and diversity of some of the earliest forests of the middle to late Devonian (380-360 Ma) are well defined. However, it is not until the early Carboniferous that there are enough fossil floras to get a detailed global picture of

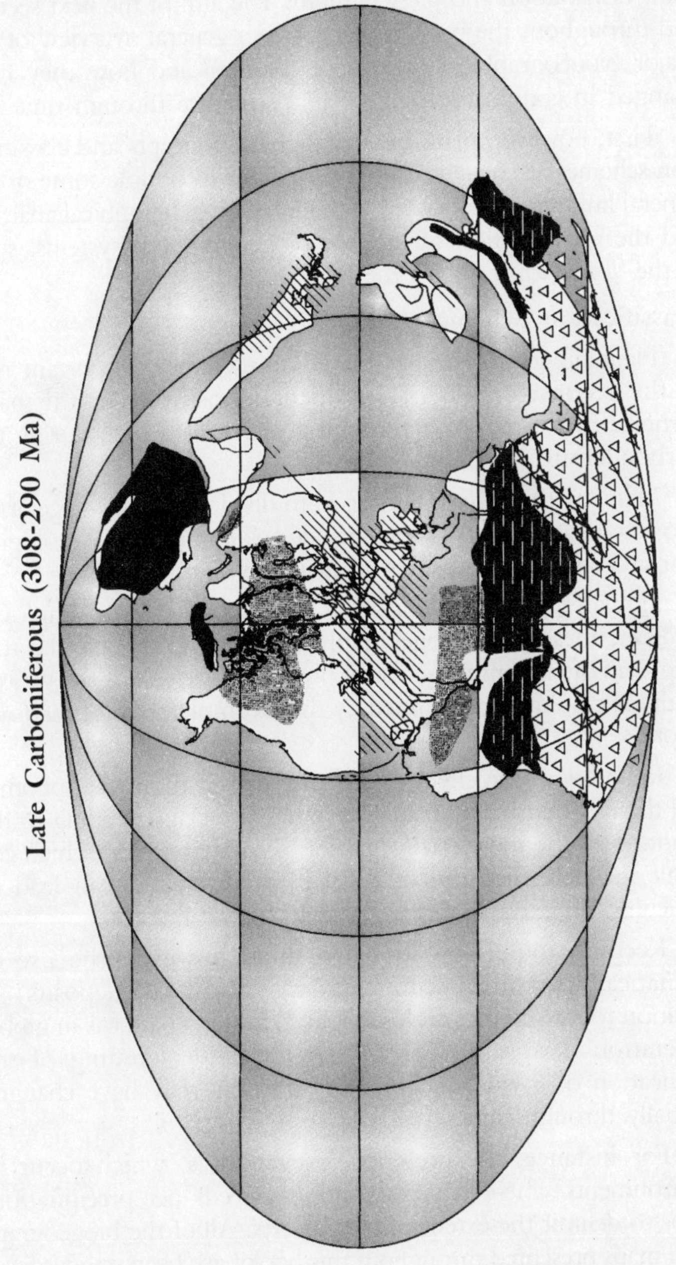
Late Carboniferous (308-290 Ma)

plant distribution and biogeography. The aim of the next section and throughout the book is to provide a general overview of the major biogeographical regions or 'biomes' and how they have changed in composition and spatial structure through time.

First, however, plant biogeographical concepts and classification schemes are reviewed briefly, in order to outline some of the general limitations associated with global biogeographical analysis, and the extrapolation of modern biogeographical systems, such as the '*biome*' concept, to the fossil record.

Classification Scheme

Plant biogeography has played an extremely important role in the reconstruction of continental positions in the past, particularly at times of high floral provincialism (e.g. during the Carboniferous).

Many methods have been used to divide up global vegetation into recognizable units. These include taxonomic and/or ecological characteristics and measures of plant diversity.

Similarly, many classific-ation schemes have been employed to define these plant biogeographical units and this has led to a long, and often confusing, list of nomenclature. All of the various methods employed are limited by the incompleteness of the fossil record.

In addition, the effect of differing preservation (taphonomy) and the fact that whole plants are rarely preserved, leading to the counting of the individual organs as separate species (which can result in overestimation of fossil plant diversity), can lead to difficulties in extrapolation of widely spaced floras.

Keeping these limitations in mind however, the use of 'climatically sensitive' sediments (e.g. coals, salt deposits) in addition to taxonomic, ecological, and diversity patterns in global vegetation have added greatly to our understanding of the delineation of fossil plant biomes and how they have changed spatially through time.

For instance, the presence of evaporites, which occur in environments where net evaporation exceeds net precipitation, helps to delimit the extent of past deserts. All of the biogeographical maps presented throughout this book have been standardized

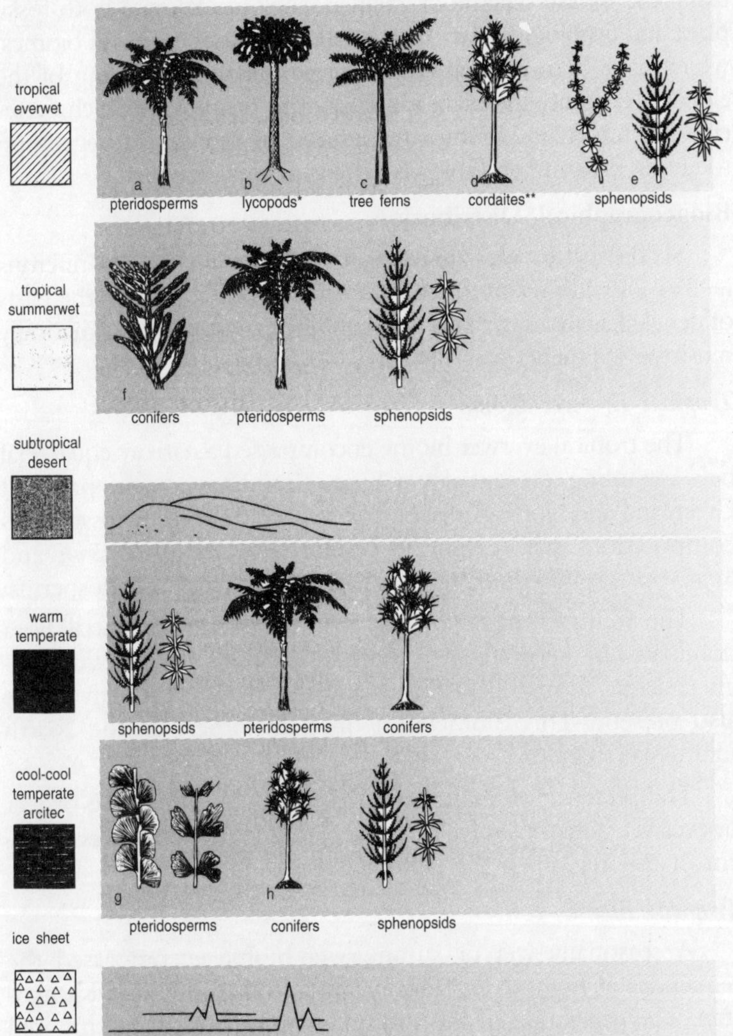

Figure 3.25: Suggested biomes for the late Carboniferous (300-286 Ma) with representatives of the most abundant and/or dominant fossil plant taxa shown. The biomes are superimposed on a global palaeogeographic reconstruction for the Wesphalian (~306 Ma). (a) Medullosa noei; (b) Lepidodendron tree; (c) Psaronius; (d) cordaites tree; (e) Calamites tree with details of leaves (Annularia); (f) fertile branch of Lebachia piniformis; (g) Botrychiopsis plantiana frond; (h) rhacopterid frond.

using the biome scheme of Ziegler. They incorporate both fossil plant and lithological data in the delimitation of the fossil biomes, which have been defined according to our understanding of the climatic, edaphic, and plant physiognomic features which characterize the ten major biomes recognized in our world vegetation today as laid out in Table elsewhere in this chapter.

Biogeographical Distribution

Six distinct biomes are recognized for the early Carboniferous (~354-342 Ma) using the biome scheme of Ziegler, on the basis of detailed analyses of fossil floras and from evidence of climatically sensitive sediments for this time.

Tropical Everwet Biome

The tropical everwet biome encompassed a narrow equatorial belt including present-day China, Scandinavia, and parts of Greenland and North America. It was characterized by fossil floras composed of arborescent lycopsids (e.g. *Lepidodendron* and *Stigmaria*), sphenopsids (e.g. *Sphenophyllum*), and pteridosperms.

The South China region had a similar 'broad equatorial' flora dominated by lycopsids with some sphenopsids and ferns, although endemic form-genera that made this region distinctive were also present. This biome is defined by others as the North Laurussian region.

The presence of abundant coals, which are indicative of wet or everwet climates, and a low palaeolatitude support the assignment of this region to the tropical everwet biome.

Tropical Biome

A seasonally wet or summerwet biome encompassed the remainder of Euramerica from palaeolatitude 5-30°, and Kazakhstan. The vegetation of the swamp environments was composed predominantly of arborescent lycopsids and pteridosperms, whereas sphenopsids were less abundant than in the tropical everwet biome.

The assignment of a summerwet biome to these areas is supported by evidence from palaeoecology for a seasonally wet climate. Tropicaldesert belts, indicated by the presence of evaporites, help to define the southerly limit of the summerwet biome.

The southern hemisphere portion of this biome is defined by others as the Acadian-Laurussian region. Kazakhstan, which was a separate continent was characterized by a flora composed of approximately 45% endemic form-genera, including species of lycopsids and seed ferns.

Although Wnuk (1996) attributes a warm temperate climate to the Kazakhstan region during the Tournaisian, the presence of evaporites, the general short stature of the vegetation, and lack of the rhizophorous rooting structures known as stigmaria indicate that this flora was also part of the seasonally wet biome.

Subtropical Desert Biome

The subtropical desert biome was very restricted during the Tournaisian, with evidence of evaporites indicating its presence in western Australia and northwestern Saudi Arabia. Fossil floras are absent from this biome.

Warm Temperate Biome

The higher palaeolatitudes between 30-70° make up the warm temperate biome. In Siberia the floras were dominated by small lycopsid trees, distinguishable by their shorter stature than those of the tropical everwet biome, and sphenopsids.

Fewer pteridosperms were present compared to the tropical everwet and summerwet biomes. This biome in the northern hemisphere is referred to by others as the Angaran region (Siberia and Kazakhstan).

In the southern hemisphere, classified as the Gondwanan region, the vegetation was dominated by arborescent lycopsids, sphenopsids, and early seed ferns.

Although the composition of the vegetation was very similar to that of the lower latitude biomes the diversity was considerably lower. Furthermore, the lycopsids of the Gondwanan region possessed similar morphological characteristic to those in the warm temperate biome of the northern hemisphere, in that they were shorter in stature and lacked stigmaria-type rooting structures, indicating cooler temperatures.

The morphological similarities of these highlatitude floras, together with their lower general diversity than those of the equatorial biome and the presence of coals, are indicative of warm, wet climates typical of the warm temperate biome.

Cool-cold Temperate, Arctic and Glacial Biomes

A gradation of climatic conditions and also biomes most likely existed between the warm temperature biome covering most of Gondwana and the glacial biome (ice sheet) to the south. However, as no fossil floras of early Carboniferous age are known south of 60° it is not possible, as yet, to indicate the limits of these biomes with confidence, or to document the composition of the vegetation that was present.

The northerly limits of the glacial biome are based on the presence of glacial deposits (tillites) and glacial pavement studies.

Distribution of Global Vegetation

By late Carboniferous time (~300-286 Ma) 6 to 8 biomes are recognized based on the same criteria as those used for the early Carboniferous and on biogeographical studies of Rowley *et al.* (1985), Ziegler *et al.* (1981), Cleal and Thomas (1991), and Wnuk (1996):

Tropical Everwet Biome

The tropical everwet biome encompassed present-day eastern North America, western Europe, China and north Africa. The vegetation of this biome was dominated by forests composed of pteridosperms, lycopsids, and tree ferns (filicopsids), as well as other early seed plants such as cordaites.

Lycopsid diversity and abundance in all of these low-latitude forests was greatly diminished (with the exception of those in the western Appalachian region of North America), compared to the dominant position they held in nearly all of the major biomes during the early Carboniferous.

Summerwet (tropical) Biome

The summerwet biome contained a higher proportion of more drought-resistant conifers, such as *Lebachia* and *Ernestiodendron*, with more reduced leaves compared to those of the tropical everwet biome. Sphenopsids such as *Phylotheca* were also present.

This biome covered a narrow band immediately to the north

and south of the tropical everwet biome. Cuneo (1989) suggests that floral differentiation was also apparent on the western coast of

South America, with a distinctive subtropical flora in what is now western Argentina at this time.

Subtropical Desert Biome

The frequent occurrence of evaporites (Ziegler, personal communication) and almost complete absence of fossil plants characterized this biome. It spanned an area including most of Greenland and Scandinavia and northern Canada in the northern hemisphere and parts of Brazil and western Africa in the southern hemisphere.

Warm Temperate Biome

By the late Carboniferous (~300 Ma) Kazakhstan had collided with Siberia, thereby increasing the aerial extent of the warm temperate biome (part of the Angaran biogeographical realm) in the northern hemisphere.

This biome spanned the entire area of present-day Kazakhstan and south-eastern Siberia (also known as the sub-Angaran realm) in the northern hemisphere and the north coastal fringes of Gondwana in the southern hemisphere.

Fossil floras of this biome were abundant, of high diversity, and well mixed. They were dominated by sphenopsids (including *Calamites*), pteridosperms, and cordaites.

Cool to Cold Temperate and Arctic Biomes

The cool/cold temperate biome in both hemispheres covered present-day north-eastern Siberia in the northern hemisphere and the entire Gondwana supercontinent with the exception of the coastal regions and those covered by ice.

It was characterized by significantly lower species diversity than that found in the warm temperate biome. The dominant vegetation included pteridosperms, cordaites, and significantly fewer sphenopsids.

In comparison to the wide diversity of taxa present in the warm temperate biome, vegetation became increasingly open, particularly in the southern hemisphere, by the late Carboniferous (300 Ma), and dominated by shrubby and herbaceous forms of lycopsids, sphenopsids, and the pteridosperm, *Botrychiopsis*.

The distinctly 'primitive' nature of the cold temperate floras of the southern hemisphere, compared with those of the tropical everwet and warm temperate biomes, have been interpreted by Retallack (1980) as a, 'tundra'-type vegetation.

It is possible therefore that an arctic biome existed between the cold temperate and glacial biomes, in areas close to the ice sheet. The assignment of these regions to the cool/cold temperate biomes is supported by the presence of both tillites and coals, which, when found in association, indicate cool temperate conditions.

Comparison of the composition of vegetation within each biome between the early and late Carboniferous reveals a number of striking differences, indicating major ecological turnover among a number of fossil plant groups.

In the tropical everwet biome, for instance, the lycopsid and sphenopsid composition of wetland swamps declined. In the tropical summerwet biome there was a coeval rise in the sporadic appearance of conifers.

Furthermore, the geographical extent of the subtropical desert biome expanded. All of these changes are thought to reflect a general aridification of late Carboniferous climates.

Chapter 4 WHAT IS A TREE?

From the earliest times plants have been classified as herbs, shrubs or trees. Thus, the concept of a tree is extremely familiar, even to small children. Ordinarily our image of a tree is that of a perennial plant, capable of attaining at least 6m (21ft), with a single woody self-supporting, trunk or stem which is usually unbranched for some distance above ground.

In brief, there are two components: a stem supporting, somewhere aloft, a crown of branches. Shrubs have a lower statu-re, the supporting trunk is less well defined and branching is evident at virtually ground level. Yet the borderline between the two categories is not always clear and on occasion tall shrubs and low trees may intergrade.

In any event, every tree must start life as a sapling, growing from a seed, or in the rarer instances of tree ferns, growing from a minute spore. The influence of Man should also be mentioned - many cultivars of true trees exist which only reach the stature of shrubs, while practices such as pruning will reduce a tree to the size and shape of a shrub,,

Trees as isolated specimens are a common enough sight in parks, gardens and, most notably, in large arboreta where the massing of many individuals of different species in a single collection allows comparison of the form (morphology) of one species with another.

In such circumstances it is easy to appreciate that each species is distinctive and often recognizable by a range of what the botanist calls morphological characters. Indeed, from an early age most people, in part unconsciously, make use of such characters in getting to know the common kinds of tree.

They include features of bark, leaves, buds and so on, in addition to the manner of branching which will give the tree its own distinctive shape. Notwithstanding the importance of single specimen trees—often there as the result of a deliberate planting policy—trees are very closely associated, in the minds of most people, with the notion of a forest or woodland.

To the botanist this embodies the science of plant sociology or of ecology—what might be called the gregariousness of trees. The first concept of a forest is again often derived from childhood experiences, the earliest notion normally being of a habitat that is uniform in character and somewhat dark within.

This simple picture in fact embodies two important botanical characteristics of so many forests in north temperate regions, namely the dominance of a single species (or sometimes of two or three) and, secondly, the canopy-forming capacity of trees massed together which so significantly reduces the amount of light available beneath them.

Thus, there is in a certain sense a general form, or morphology, both of the individual tree and of the forest. Although the former chiefly concerns us in the present context, it is worth noting in passing how very different from our own are the forests in most parts of the humid tropics—see later.

In northern regions it is customary to name the forest after a single species of dominant tree, as in oak (*Quercus* spp), beech (*Fagus spp*), pine (*Pinus spp*) or spruce (*Picea spp*) forests so widespread in Europe and North America. In the humid tropics, by contrast, scores of species of widely differing height, habit and type of foliage will commonly play approximately equal roles in the structure of the whole and the forest is a scene of bewildering diversity.

Nothing is more characteristic of such a forest than those tall individual trees, known as emergents, which protrude above the general level of the canopy in many tropical forests. Almost equally notable is the structural diversity of the trees themselves.

One of the most astonishing must surely be the Banyan Tree (*Ficus benghalensis*), an evergreen tree widespread in India. It can reach some 26m (85ft) in height and has long horizontally spreading branches, which put down aerial roots at intervals; these on reaching the ground act as pillars to support the branches.

These trees probably have the biggest crowns of any in the world and with their aerial pillar or prop roots, a single tree can make a small wood. The Banyan is sacred in India and an account of it was given as early as the 4th century BC during Alexander the Great's invasion of India at that time. Our concern is therefore with this structural diversity, as seen in simple botanical terms.

Yet, oak and beech, palm and pine, slender birch (*Betula spp*) and giant silkcotton trees (*Bombax* and *Ceiba spp*) all share something in common - the essential botany which makes them all trees. In short, they exhibit structural diversity within a common plan.

GENERAL FORMS OF TREES

To the public two general forms of tree are immediately recognizable—the spire—like 'fir' trees and the 'bushy-topped' deciduous trees. In general terms this division encompasses the conifers and broadleaves, respectively. Two other readily recognized, but less frequent, forms are the fastigiate types characterized by the Lombardy Poplar (*Populus nigra* 'Italica') and the classic palm tree form.

Botanists recognize many more forms. Indeed, one has only to look at deciduous trees in winter to see the highly distinctive pattern of branching of each species. Similarly in early summer a score of different tree species will display as many subtly different shades of green in their foliage.

Ultimately, all features of form and branching must be related to events in the growing shoot tips where the embryonic tissues are found. All these features follow in large measure a program laid down in the plant's heredity but modified by environmental influences.

However, they are always under precise physiological control. This brings us to the point where we recognize the first great uniformity in tree construction—that is the fact that within every tree, no matter what its species or where it is growing, there lies an organized assemblage of cells and tissues.

It is in terms of these cells and tissues that the anatomist will see the tree. Thus, to the trained eye, each species of tree has a characteristic form, or in botanical terms, gross morphology. This form is the outward expression of long-term events which, although physiological in character, must reveal themselves to the observer in anatomical terms.

In brief, just as each species of tree has its own external form, so it will be found to exhibit distinctive and sometimes unique features in its internal anatomy. This fact opens up for botanists the whole immense field of the comparative study of the microscopic anatomy of wood.

The general form of any species of tree is not something fixed and immutable, and even the most casual observer must have met with countless everyday examples of this. Certain features are constant enough but there is still a vast range of variation in general habit and stature to be found within the whole geographical range of a single species.

Nowhere is this more evident than in the Douglas Fir (*Pseudotsuga menziesii*) *as* seen in different parts of its vast North American range. Or again, one may contrast what we know as Lawson's (Cypress (*Chamaecyparis lawsoniana*), which in cultivation is a highly variable but commonly quite lowgrowing ornamental tree, with the forest giants 60m (200 ft) high found in western North America, where it is known as the Port Orford Cedat).

Among coniferous evergreens, such as the pines, spruces and silver firs, much of the distinctive general form, or silhouette against the skyline, of a particular species turns upon the behavior of the so-called leading shoot, and its growth in relation to that of the side shoots.

Marked dominance and extremely rapid growth of the leading shoot can give, over a period of years, the very elegant spire-like habit so characteristic of Engelmann Spruce (*Picea engelmannii*), as seen, for example, in the Rocky mountains.

A much reduced dominance of the leader can result in the comparatively bushy-topped growth habit of certain European species of pine, such as the Umbrella Pine (*Pinus pinea*). In the Scots Pine (*P. sylvestris*) it is possible to see the profound effect on overall habit of growing trees either in close stands, or as isolated individuals.

Finally, as the latitudinal or altitudinal limits of a given species are approached, increasingly severely stunted and often malformed specimens are seen, scarcely recognizable as belonging to the same species as the trees which grow farther south or lower down on a mountain.

It is easy to forget that some of these gnarled and stunted specimens may be of great antiquity—possibly hundreds of years old. Probably it is true to say that few trees continue to live in a healthy state beyond four to five hundred years—and this includes allegedly long-lived species such as the English Oak (*Quercus robur*), but a small group of species is well known to live for very much longer, for example the English Yew (*Taxus baccata*) is known to have reached i o0o years.

However, most notable are the Coast and Mountain Redwoods (*Sequoia sempervirens* and *Sequoiadendron giganteum*) of the Western United States and a few other conifers; also there are well authenticated long-lived individuals of the monocotyledonous Dragon Tree (*Dracaena draco*). In all of them a life span exceeding 4000 years is attained, with isolated examples of Dragon Tree and Bristle-cone Pine (*Pinus aristata*) achieving life spans in excess of 4000 years.

In practice many trees have their natural life span cut short by demands of forest management which call for regular felling and wood utilization and of urban amenity forestry where declining trees have to be felled because of the danger to the public.

TRUNK AND WOOD STRUCTURE

Ask a child to draw a tree and he will start with the trunk, then add a fan or brush of branches. In short, the trunk is integral to the popular concept of a tree, yet the prominence and size of that trunk can vary enormously.

In the tropics, trees with massive trunks and relatively little in the way of crown (because of restricted branching) are conveniently called '*pachycaulous*' (= thickstemmed) whilst trees with relatively *slende; stems* and a *generous bushy* crown from extensive branching, are known as 'leptocaulous' (= slender-stemmed).

In many low-growing trees, and even in some large, mature individuals of certain coniferous trees such as the English Yew and the Old World cedars (*Cedrus spp*), a single, well-defined trunk may not always be readily recognizable, yet in normal fullgrown specimens of most of our common deciduous trees, such as oaks, ashes and beeches, it is almost impossible to conceive of the tree without its trunk; and in the vast majority of conifers this is even more emphatically the case.

The existence and continuing prominence of the trunk springs from the fact that in early life there exists a radially organized central axis extending from the young shoot tip down into the root. At first, as in a beech seedling in the first year of life, the line of demarcation between stem and root in this slender axis may not always be readily apparent.

Yet their destinies are very different and it is the slender, already woody, stem of the sapling which is gradually transformed, over a period of years, into the trunk of the full-grown tree.

Growing trees in close-set stands can inhibit survival of lateral branches so that it is common to see such stands of pine or spruce composed of trees, perhaps thirty or forty years old, in which the trunks appear to rise unbranched to an impressive height.

To some extent the absence of lateral branches will have been encouraged by early '*brashing*' operations by foresters. Certainly, isolated individuals of the same species will present a very different picture. Many species of palm, including the Oil Palm of West Africa (*Elaeis guineensis*); Date Palm (*Phoenix dactylifera*) and Coconut Palm (*Cocos nucifera*) are structurally quite distinct in that the trunk is in a very strict sense an unbranched stem, surmounted only by a crown of enormous leaves.

Palms, moreover, it may be remarked, grow in an entirely different manner from either hardwood or conifer (softwood) trees, and their 'wood,' though chemically similar and extremely tough, is in its arrangement and disposition in the stem quite unlike wood as we ordinarily know it from hardwoods and softwoods.

In many tropical trees the trunks are sinuous to a degree not readily matched in the trees of north temperate forests. In a mature Baobab (*Adansonia digitata*) the trunk is characteristically of immense width. The anatomical arrangement of the cellular components of the trunk of a tree is basically similar in conifers and broadleaves, only the components themselves vary.

In simple terms a number of layers can be recognized - from the outside, the outer protective bark, the sugar conducting phloem (or inner bark) and the inner solid core of wood (xylem) through the younger elements of which water is conducted.

Between the phloem and wood there is a narrow band of actively dividing cells (vascular cambium) which produce secondary phloem to the outside and secondary xylem or wood to the inside.

To look at these layers in detail we will start with the wood which makes up the bulk of the trunk and is obviously the element of commercial importance. In socalled '*hardwoods*' or dicotyledonous (broadleaved) woody species the wood consists, in varying *proportions*, of five *principal components*.

Most characteristic are the vessels, which are made up of many tubular cells placed end to end with a free and open passageway between one vessel member and the next above or below it; these are the water-conducting pipelines of the plant.

Secondly, a high proportion of most hardwoods commonly consists of the fibrous component. This is made up of a great number of long, narrow cells (fibers) with thick walls and tapering ends, more or less closely bound together to form a strong matrix in which the vessels are interspersed.

The hardness of any particular wood will depend in considerable measure on the number of these cells and the thickness of their walls. Thirdly, most woods contain a certain proportion of living, fairly thin-walled cells (termed wood parenchyma), that are often loaded with storage starch.

They run in vertical sequences among the other, thicker-walled components. This living part of the whole is *physiologically* linked to the so-called '*rays*,' which are in effect walls consisting of a few vertically stacked layers of living (parenchymatous) cells, again commonly replete with storage starch.

In a severed trunk or branch (that is, as seen in transverse section) these rays form a series of radiating lines, the broadest of which are often easily visible to the naked eye. The, last of the five cellular components of wood are the tracheids.

They are not often very plentiful in hardwoods, but nevertheless they make up almost the entire 'woody cylinder' (apart from the rays) in all the softwoods (coniferous woods) and in a very small number of exceedingly primitive dicotyledons.

Tracheids are dual-purpose elements performing at one and the same time the conducting function of a vessel member and the strengthening role of a fiber. Parts of their longitudinal walls are very freely supplied with thin sites termed pits, and it is these which allow water transfer from cell to cell.

When young and living the walls of vessels, tracheids and fibers become impregnated with a substance called lignin. When they die this material remains so that the rigid cell shape is retained. Lignin is a generalized term given to a series of complex carbon compounds whose chemistry is imperfectly understood but it is clear there are a number of different kinds of lignin.

It is interesting to note that the lignins of conifers as a group are different from those of broadleaves. The important fact for us is that these cells and their lignin confer the properties of strength and rigidity—woodiness—so that the thicker the lignified wall, the more completely are these properties conferred.

Thus we come to see the wood of a trunk or branch as composed of a vast interlocking plexus of microscopic cells, some of which are heavily lignified and dead at the functional maturity of the organ; interlaced with these are others (composing wood parenchyma and rays) that are still alive and in varying degrees metabolically active.

All these cells originate from a cylinder of delicate, meristematic (that is recurrently dividing) cells termed the vascular cambium, which forms the boundary line between wood and bark. Needless to say, this vascular cambium, being a meristematic or formative tissue, is of critical importance not only in the development of the tree, but throughout its entire life.

The question may now be asked—how do the annual growth rings arise? The answer lies in the type and size of cells produced by the vascular cambium at different times of the year.

Annual rings are rendered more conspicuous in many cases on account of the first-formed vessels in spring being very much larger than those which are a component of the summer wood. English oak and ash both illustrate this feature well.

Such woods are known as 'ring-porous'; in many other woods, including beech, willow, apple and others, there is no marked difference in vessel diameter between spring and summer wood. Such woods are termed *'diffuseporous'* and in them the annual rings are often less clearly defined, although in many such examples summer wood is marked by the presence of other distinctive features apart from vessel size.

In a softwood such as that of Scots Pine the tracheids formed toward the end of the growth period, in summer, are of narrower bore and have much thicker walls than those formed in spring, and this fact forms the basis on which one can recognize annual growth rings in this otherwise rather uniform wood.

In the monocotyledonous angiosperms, such as palms, there is, in general, no such annual increase in girth resulting from a cylinder of vascular cambium; in other words, there is no comparable secondary thickening.

In very few cases of monocotyledonous angiosperms, however, there is a peculiar form of increase in girth quite different from that described above for the dicotyledons. A well-known' example occurs in the Dragon Tree.

Here cells in the general ground tissue become meristematic, that is, capable of division comparable with the cambial cells already described for dicotyledons (secondary meristem).

However, instead of cutting off phloem cells toward the outside of the stem and xylem cells toward the center, both types of cells, phloem and xylem, are cut off toward the stem center in such a way that the increments replicate the pattern of the vascular bundles seen in the primary stem.

The wood anatomist, wherever possible, likes to have at his disposal thin sections cut in three planes: the transverse, the radial longitudinal (as in quarter sawn wood)—in other words parallel with a radius or diameter—and the tangential longitudinal section (as in flat sawn wood)—that is at right angles to a radius or diameter. When examined microscopically these three preparations together give him all the information needed to identify the wood.

In most cases this is possible as far as the genus, sometimes even to species level. While a formidable array of characters becomes available through this procedure, it must not be forgotten that the wood of a tree has other attributes which are readily detectable without a microscope.

These include not only such features of the fine structure as will be visible under a hand lens or with the naked eye, but also such important general attributes as specific gravity and color. A consideration of color often has to take account of differences between the outer zone of living and often lighter colored sapwood and the central core of generally nonliving and darker hued heartwood.

It is the heartwood which is commercially valuable. To varying degrees this is impregnated with gums, resins and other deposits which act as a natural preservative. In a limited number of woods this heartwood is a notably distinctive color, as in several species of ebony (where it is black) and the leguminous Logwood Tree (*Haematoxylon campechianum*) where it is purple in hue.

Woods vary greatly in specific gravity and this important physical character is clearly linked with the uses to which particular species are put. Teak (*Tectona grandis*) *is* a particularly valuable timber, being a fairly heavy close-grained wood and exceptionally resistant to decay because of the deposition of resinous materials.

By contrast, American balsa wood (*Ochroma spp*) is an example of a wood valued for its exceptional lightness and the same is to some extent true of the wood of the widespread West African tree, *Triplochiton scleroxylon.*

In every case the usefulness of the wood is inseparably linked to its anatomical structure as revealed by a full microscopic examination. The importance of wood from an economic or utilitarian angle is discussed in a later chapter, as is the subject of its attack by fungi and insects.

We must turn now to the bark or rind, without which the living tree would be very incomplete. Botanically, bark is defined as 'all those tissues lying external to the vascular cambium,' and as such it includes a diversity of components.

In more detail bark may be divided into an 'inner bark' or 'bast' formed from the vascular cambium (already noted above) and an 'outer bark' formed largely from the *cork cambium*, which is discussed later. Formerly, *anatomists* sometimes distinguished two fractions of inner bark, namely '*hard*' bast which is composed of fibers and, secondly, the 'soft' bast or living elements of the phloem.

To the layman, 'bark' often means only these rough outer layers; yet the living phloem elements are indeed vital components of the tree since their function is to conduct sugars and other organic products of metabolism from one part of the plant to another. The outer bark is protective; it is also used in tree recognition.

It is not uncommon to see trees that have been the victims of browsing animals and have had their bark more or less stripped down to the wood. If this 'ringing' of the tree is complete (that is, a complete ring of phloem is removed) death will ensue because the conduction of organic products, from the leaves down to the roots, has been fatally impeded.

Phloem carries organic products about the plant with great speed and efficiency but even now the mechanism of this process is not fully understood. The phloem of a tree, however, is predominantly of secondary origin, that is, it has been formed, like the secondary wood (or xylem), from the activity of the vascular cambium.

Also, in trees, certain of the derivatives of the vascular cambium mature into fibers constituting the 'hard-bast' fraction of the inner bark, while yet others form ordinary living (parenchymatous) tissues. Thus, this secondary phloem is, like secondary xylem (or wood), a complex tissue and one that is renewed year after year.

The rays, too, extend out into the *phloem*, often expanding there so sharply as to present a characteristic *trumpet*—like form in transverse section. External to this elaborately constructed inner bark, in the early life of a woody stem or branch, lies the green cortex, bounded on the outside by the original '*skin tissue*' or *epidermis*.

Such an arrangement, however, cannot *accommodate* any marked expansion in girth unless a mechanism exists for the epidermis and cortex to keep pace by cell division or cell *expansion* (or both); and this is only rather rarely the case.

Normally, a special new growing zone, or secondary meristem has to arise; this is called the cork cambium or phellogen. Once formed, it can make provision for the entire protective-tissue requirement of trunk or branch and at the same time solve the girth problem.

The former it does by forming seriated layers of corky tissues interrupted only by scattered '*breathing pores*' termed *lenticels*. The girth problem is solved in various ways but often by *periodic* renewal of the cork cambium, in increasingly deep tissues.

When a young branch or sapling trunk which is green in its first season abruptly turns brown or grayish in hue, this color change is almost invariably correlated with the appearance of the first layers of cork.

Commonly, of course, the superficial cork amounts to only a thin skin but in rare cases, as in the Cork Oak (*Quercus suber*), much thicker layers are formed. Thus, bark is functionally very important to the tree, being both the locus of conduction (translocation) of organic substances (inner bark) and the provider of the tree's outer protective skin (outer bark).

Other components include nests of exceedingly hard, thick-walled cells aptly termed stone-cells. The bark in many instances is a commercial source of tannins and various crystalline deposits and in the Para Rubber Tree (*Hevea brasiliensis*) there are special vessels, the lacticifers, from which, when the bark is cut, a latex flows which is collected for conversion to (natural) rubber.

Perhaps the main interest of bark to the layman and structural botanist alike, lies in the variety and diagnostic value of its external features.

Even the most casual observer can see at a glance the differe-nces between the rugged, fissured bark of oaks, the fibrous '*stringy*' bark of false acacias (*Robinia spp*), the scaly bark of planes (*Platanus spp*) with their '*jig-saw puzzle*' surface pattern at some seasons of the year, and the almost papery texture of the silverwhite bark clothing the upper regions of trunk and branches in several species of birch (*Betula spp*).

Although most conifers have a bark that is in varying degrees scaly in texture, some are highly distinctive, such as the Mountain Redwood or Wellingtonia (*Sequoiadendron giganteum*) in which the texture is so softly spongy that it can be punched without detriment to the aggressive fist!

In this tree, native to western North America, the fissures and hollows in the bark have, incidentally, provided a favorite nesting site for the European Tree Creeper (*Certhia familiaris*). Observant people of many tropical countries have, down the centuries, come to know the marks of recognition in the barks of a great many species of tree, and botanists in recent times have seen the importance of pursuing this study further on a scientific basis.

THE ROOT SYSTEM

Absorption and anchorage are the two chief functions of a root system. Examination of a tree seedling of a broadleaf such as a beech will show two deep green cotyledons (seed leaves) raised well clear of ground level.

Below them the stem (hypocotylar) region passes almost imperceptibly into the crown of the young primary root or radicle which lies below ground level. Although at first a simple structure, '*programed*' to grow downward into the soil (*positively geotropic*), it soon becomes branched, through the origin of numerous lateral roots.

These arise at a deep level in the tissues of the parent root and well back from the apex. Immediately behind the apex most roots display a *'fur'* of *microscopically* small 'root hairs' which are the principal water absorbing components of the root.

At a remarkably early stage, in most tree species, the process of secondary thickening—wood and phloem production through cambial activity—will set in.

Thus, although the young root begins life with a different arrangement of vascular tissues from the stem, it will not be long before they bear a considerable resemblance to one another, at least when examined in transverse section—a central core of wood surrounded by the vascular cambium and bark.

These internal similarities, at tissue level, are however overshadowed by the differences in gross *morphology* which are evident for all to see. Roots never bear leaves and are not a normal site of bud production. Roots, moreover, are nongreen (in all typical cases) and, as already mentioned, branch in a manner peculiar to themselves.

The tip of a young root, as it makes its way through the soil, is protected by a root cap which is continually renewed from behind as it gets pushed off by the root's progress through the soil. This also has no parallel in the shoot apex.

Minute anatomical details, however, concern us less than a consideration of the tree's root system seen as a whole, its general character, depth and extent of spread in the soil. These are features which vary greatly from one tree species to another.

Many coniferous species, for example, are comparatively shallow rooted, hence easily storm-blown. It should be borne in mind, however, that an uprooted tree reveals only a small fraction of its total root system, the lateral spread of which may readily far exceed that of the leafy crown.

When one calculates the sum of the lengths of all the multiplicity of fine branch roots that go to make up an entire root system, prodigious overall figures are revealed. The *'free space'* beneath and around a tree is in a very full sense 'occupied' by its root system, and competition between root systems in a forest soil is intense and unrelenting.

The relationship between a tree's root system, the surrounding soil, and its varied microflora, is inevitably a complex one. Many factors— physical, chemical and biological—have to be taken into consideration.

The study of this so-called rhizosphere is probably even now only in its infancy. Sufficient is known, however, to make it clear that the relationship between a tree's roots and soil microorganisms can be both complex and important; and to some extent the same may hold for the root systems of adjacent trees.

Perhaps the best known and most fully investigated of these relationships is that between tree root and soil fungus which comes under the general heading of mycorrhiza. This relationship shows itself in the form of a mantle of fungal *threads* or *hyphae* (singular: hypha), collectively known as the mycelium, which encases many of the young rootlets and invades the intercellular space system of the root's cortex.

The rootlets, stimulated by the fungal invasion to branch freely, are often conspicuous for their coralloid form. Scots Pine and European Beech (*Fagus sylvatica*) are well-known examples, but the phenomenon is very widespread in tree root systems.

It seems that both fungus and host tree draw benefit, the latter especially through improved capacity for absorption of certain nutrients conferred by the presence of the mycorrhizal fungus. The roots of alders (*Alnus spp*) present another interesting association.

Here the root system has associated with it nitrogen-fixing microorganisms, the exact nature of which is not yet certain because, so far, it has not been possible to grow them in pure culture. At present there are several species referred to the genus *Frankia* and believed to be related to the filamentous bacteria sometimes known as ray fungi (actinomycetes).

A similar relationship is known in some other, quite unrelated trees. Perhaps the best-known root nodules are those on roots of the members of the pea family (Leguminosae or Fabaceae) where the microorganisms involved are bacterial species belonging to the genus *Rhizobium*. A number of distinct forms of modified roots occur in trees.

Around the bases of tropical trees surface roots are often extended vertically upward as plank—like triangles of wood serving as buttresses to the trunk. In other cases, for example, screw pines (*Pandanus spp*) and some mangrove species, roots arising from stems above the soil strike obliquely downward and form props or stilts; similar aerial roots occur in figs (*Ficus* spp) where they do not always reach the soil but hang below branches as aerial breathing roots. Tree roots originating underground can also assume respiratory functions as with the Swamp Cypress (*Taxodium distichum*).

LEAVES

The leaves of trees are almost infinitely diverse in size and form. Some, which are minute and scale—like, the layman might scarcely recognize as leaves at all. Examples are provided by the she-oaks (*Casuarina* spp) and some conifers.

The *botanist* sees them as leaves, for he recognizes a more or less constant relationship between stem, leaf, and the bud or branch in its axil. Seeking out the *axillary bud*, he designates as compound the leaves of walnuts (*Fuglans* spp), ashes (*Fraxinus spp*) and sumacs (*Rhus spp*) in all of which the leaf is composed of numerous leaflets, by contrast with such trees as *oaks*, *elms*, *beeches* and *limes* (*Tilia spp*) where the leaves are all '*simple*,' though differing in shape.

In short, there has arisen a considerable terminology in the descriptive morphology of leaves. The outcome is that, reading such a technical description, another botanist can form instantly in his mind a clear image of the precise shape and character of the leaf in question.

Some tropical trees bear extraordinarily large leaves, for example *Anthocleista spp*, a well-known genus of forest trees in tropical West Africa in which the leaves can exceed tm (3.3ft) in length and be proportionately broad.

The same holds good in many monocotyledons; one has only to think of bananas and the related plantains, and of course the compound leaves of palms.

More interesting than purely descriptive aspects, however, is the functional view of the leaves of a tree, namely their general structural features as seen in relation to their functioning as the primary food factories of the tree.

All normal leaves indeed show a remarkable compromise between the need, on the one hand, for maximum exposure of surface to the light and for freedom of entry of the carbon dioxide essential for carbon assimilation (photosynthesis) and on the other to include adequate safeguards against excessive water loss through the process of transpiration.

These considerations explain the broad expanse of leaf blade (lamina), the presence often of long leaf stalks or petioles allowing leaf blades to take up advantageous positions, the presence (most frequently on the under surface) of countless microscopic openings, the stomata and, finally, an adequate protective skin or cuticle.

The venation system provides both a skeleton and conducting tissues continuous with those of the stem. The basic anatomical plan of leaves is uniform although the variations on this plan are numerous. In all leaves the epidermis forms the outermost layer of living cells.

This is normally one cell thick and is bounded on the outside by the impermeable cuticle which is interrupted only by the actual pores of the stomata (referred to above). The internal tissues or mesophyll are the powerhouse of the leaf, each cell containing numerous green chloroplasts in which photosynthesis occurs.

In most leaves two types of mesophyll cell can be found. The upper or palisade mesophyll comprises columnar cells that are separated from one another by numerous narrow air channels. The lower or spongy mesophyll consists of irregularly shaped cells with large air spaces between them.

Most of the chloroplasts occur in the palisade cells. Each leaf of a tree can thus be seen as a delicately adjusted piece of machinery attuned to a functional life of immense importance—the synthesis of organic compounds such as sugars and starch from the simple raw materials, water and carbon dioxide.

In different climates very different stresses will be brought to bear on leaves. Thus, in the humid tropics there is less emphasis on the protective cuticle, whilst trees of semi-arid regions are often what are known as sclerophylls-the leaves stiff and hard in texture, limited in size and with a notably thick cuticle.

Even so, astonishing diversity can prevail even in a single climatic regime, as a glance at the composition of forests in the tropics will show. There the diversity is bewildering, but even in Europe trees presenting such diversified leaf morphology as holly (*Ilex* spp), *beech*, *ash* and *yew* can all be components of a single wood on downland.

We still know, indeed, far too little of the individual economies of different species of tree, but one widespread aspect familiar to all is that of leaf drop. A feature of fall in north temperate lands, it is also often related to the onset of a dry season in hot countries with a markedly seasonal climate.

It can be seen as a kind of economy measure, enabling a tree to shut down activity, and take a rest, in a particularly unfavorable season of any kind. Extremely widespread among dicotyledonous trees, it is rare in conifers, occurring in the larches (*Larix* spp) and swamp cypresses (*Taxodium* spp), for example.

So-called evergreens always display green foliage, but they too have their.times of leaf fall, though more unobtrusively. Individual leaves rarely last for more than a few seasons. It goes without saying that leaves supply a considerable range of characters usable by taxonomic botanists.

Indeed, although allowance has to be made for variation, seen for example in marked degree in mulberries (*Morus* spp), species can often be recognized by their leaves, especially if we take into account microscopic features of leaf anatomy, important among which is the hair covering or indumentum, when present.

Even so, one has always to be on one' guard, for striking examples can be found of the leaves of quite unrelated plants resembling one another very closely (maples (*Acer spp*) and true planes (*Platanus* spp) provide a case in point) whilst in the tropics trees of a great many quite unrelated species are alike in the possession of more or less ovate, smallish short-stalked leaves.

Only in rare cases, like the fanshaped leaves of the Maidenhair Tree (*Ginkgo biloba*) or the distinctively fourlobed leaves of the tulip trees (*Liriodendron* spp) is leaf form instantly diagnostic. Such examples are a boon to paleobotanists attempting to identify the trees of the past. The winter buds of deciduous species, like leaves, can lead to instant recognition.

Space does not permit us to make more than a passing reference to the foliage of trees as a habitat for other organisms. Clearly, they are the habitat of an almost limitless diversity of colonists and feeders, perhaps most notably in the world of the insects and the birds.

However, their utilization by other organisms is always to some extent bound up with their importance as a principal primary builder of the world's organic matter. Their all-round ecological significance, therefore, needs no further stressing.

FLOWERS AND FRUITS

Flowers are often described in botanical terms as consisting of 'essential organs,' surrounded by '*floral envelopes*.' The latter (petals and sepals) constitute the most conspicuous features of most flowers, including those of many trees. Numerous kinds of tree, however, including all the socalled catkin-bearing species, are without conspicuous floral envelopes, essential organs being associated only with relatively inconspicuous, scale-like structures termed bracts.

The most colorful feature of many flowers is the corolla (made up of the petals) but this is not necessarily so. Even the cones of coniferous trees constitute a type of flower, for in common with other flowers they are concerned with the transference of microspores (or pollen) to the receptive female parts.

In most cases, an initially soft female cone gives rise, eventually, to an ultimately hard-scaled cone as seen in the pines. Quite different are the 'berry-like' seeds found in junipers (*Juniperus spp*) and in the English Yew (*Taxus baccata*).

In conifers, the male cones (staminate flowers) in season produce myriads of tiny microspores (pollen) which in due course germinate by way of a pollen tube whence are finally released the microscopic sex cells or male gametes.

At the 'receiving end' of the wind-dispersed pollen grains are the familiar female cones (ovulate flowers) that are still young and soft, with scales open. Each such female cone represents one or more so-called 'naked ovules' set among scales.

Each ovule is a giant spore (megaspore) with protective 'wrappings' in the form of spore container and integuments, and concealed within it lies the female gamete—the egg cell (ovum). In due time the act of gametic union, or fertilization, takes place giving rise to a 'naked seed' (whence the term *gymnosperm* = *naked seed*). In some conifers fertilization is separated from pollination by as much as one year.

In flowering plants or angiosperms—in our context hardwood or broadleaved trees—we find more elaborately constructed and more varied flowers, most of which show the familiar components—*calyx* (*sepals*), *corolla* (*petals*) and internal to these the pollen-producing stamens and the ovary or ovaries which contain the ovules.

It is the ovary which characterizes the angiosperms, enclosing as it does, right from the beginning, the young and developing ovules and finally the seeds, so that they are at no time 'naked.' Because of this enclosing organ, a special receptive area (stigma) and conducting region (style) become essential adjuncts to the ovary.

Pollen is carried by wind, water, insect or other animals to the *stigma* where it germinates, producing a pollen tube which grows down through the style and eventually comes into close contact with the ovule via a minute opening termed the *micropyle*.

The pollen tube ruptures and two male gametes are discharged, one of which fuses with the egg, thus setting a seed. Again it has to be observed that pollination and fertilization are two distinct events, although the time between the two events is shorter than in conifers.

It looks as if the whole evolutionary history of flowers has been geared to pollen transference, or pollination, and the pollinating agency has profoundly modified floral form, in trees as in other flowering plants.

Thus, among tree species, we can recognize on sight as wind-pollinated the bulk of catkin-bearing trees, such as hazels (*Corylus* spp), birches (*Betula spp*) and poplars (*Populus* spp), for in all of them there is an abundance of loose pollen, no nectar, and no conspicuous insectattracting feature.

Willows (*Salix spp*), with their large nectaries, constitute an exception and are insect-pollinated. In marked contrast to the above stand those trees with large and colorful flowers—the only ones indeed which many laymen would recognize as '*flowering trees*' at all.

The great majority of these are adapted to a range of insect vectors of pollen, but quite numerous species, especially in the tropics, are adapted for pollination by birds.

These tend to have exceptionally strongly constructed, often scarlet or multi-colored flowers. A few trees, in various parts of the world, have batpollinated flowers.

Such flowers, which characteristically open in the evening, are often large, somber in color and capable of emitting characteristic musty odors. Examples are found in a number of families, including the *Leguminosae*, *Myrtaceae* and *Cactaceae*.

The expression '*flowering tree*' is apt to conjure up a picture in the mind of cherries and almonds (*Prunus spp*), crab apples (*Malus spp*) and others that are grown for their blossoms in park or garden. The reality is very different, for all broadleaf trees are potentially 'flowering' at some time in their lives, otherwise reproduction could not occur, except very locally by sucker growth.

The diversity of floral form cannot be encompassed in any short summary statement but will be apparent from the trees dealt with later in the book. Often in the humid tropics one meets a steady succession of flowers, of different species, throughout the year.

Each must be geared to the season of availability of its principal pollinator; but too little is known as yet about the precise range of pollinators utilized by many tropical trees. In north temperate lands, where spring and summer are the seasons of flowering, bees of various kinds must surely rank as the most important group of pollinating organisms.

Flowering is but the prelude to fruit production; and just as a fruit (botanically) is a ripened or mature ovary, so a seed is a matured fertilized ovule, carrying deep within it the embryo plant of the new generation. It is important to appreciate that if cross pollination has been achieved this new embryo will possess, in varying degree, a new genetic constitution.

This is of immense significance both for the evolutionary process and for the '*improvement*' of trees for use by mankind. It is possible to look at the fruits of trees from the angle of the botanist who classifies such structures in a manner that is convenient for descriptive purposes.

Thus, there are 'dry' fruits (*capsules*) which open (*dehisce*), thereby shedding their seeds; and there are 'fleshy' fruits of many kinds. Some, like Elderberry (*Sambucus nigra*) have their seeds lodged in compartments of a wholly fleshy fruit wall, whilst others, like plums and cherries, have a fruit wall (or *pericarp*) which is itself made up of an outer skin, a middle fleshy portion and an innermost stony layer.

The seed in such a case exists as the 'kernel' within the stone. Thus, the botanist distinguishes the berry from the stone fruit or drupe. This way of looking at fruits can be rewarding, if only because it encourages us to systematize our information.

Fruit structure, however, cannot be viewed in any complete way without reference to its important ecological implications, especially in connection with seed dispersal.

In this context we can contrast the dry, dehiscent capsules of willows which release their tiny seeds equipped with tufts of hairs to be dispersed by wind, with the great range of drupe and berry fruits which have in every case a built—in food store that will attract a dispersal agent, most often some species of bird.

Young Elder saplings lodged in unlikely places are sometimes eloquent testimony to the efficiency of a dispersal mechanism which allows the seeds to be voided in a viable state after the fleshy substance surrounding them has been digested.

Clearly, both the above mechanisms can lead readily to long-distance dispersal, an important consideration in the successful distribution of tree species in nature.

It is less easy to see how this can be achieved in the case of trees where both fruit and seed are bulky, as in the horse-chestnut (*Aesculus* spp), and not obviously attractive to animal dispersal agents. Even the ingenious winged fruitlets of the various species of *Acer* (sycamores and maples) seem unlikely to carry the new plantlet far from the parent tree and the same can almost certainly be said of the explosive fruits of the tropical American Sandbox Tree (*Hura crepitans*).

The light, winged fruitlets of ashes and pines, and the winged seeds which abound among the tree species of the tropical family Bignoniaceae, will surely fare better. The fruit of the Coconut Palm (*Cocos nucifera*) is exceptional among heavy fruits in that there is considerable evidence for its long-distance dispersal by ocean currents.

When the seed germinates and the new plant begins to grow, a range of controlling factors will immediately become operative. Soil reaction, available nutrients, moisture supply and temperature - all these must be right if it is to survive.

Most decisive of all, perhaps, is the inevitable factor, or complex of factors, entailed by the term competition. This relates not only to pressures exerted by countless other plants in the immediate vicinity but also to the influences exerted by various members of the animal kingdom, not least by human agency.

The first mowing of a lawn in spring is often the occasion for 'elimination by decapitation' of innumerable seedlings of sycamore or maple, and sometimes of other species.

Although all normal seeds carry, either free or within their cotyledons, a food reserve, it must frequently happen that this is exhausted before successful establishment has been achieved. Once established, in the face of all competitors, the young tree is free to grow.

GROWTH OF TREES

The growth of trees, our last topic in this brief botanical

introduction, is a big and complex subject, and only the barest essentials can be touched upon. Whole treatises have been written on the growth of many of the economically important trees and successful growth of his introduced species must always be a primary concern of the forester.

Often this entails fitting a particular exotic species into an environ-ment which especially suits it, as in the coastal plantings of Corsican Pine (*Pinus nigra* var *maritima*).

At other times successful growth has to be coaxed from a species by appropriate treatment of an essentially unfavorable environment, as with the vast plantations of Sitka Spruce (*Picea sitchensis*) on the peat moors of Northern Europe.

In natural forest communities it is probably safe to assume a strong correlation between the component species and the character of the substratum. We think of beech on the chalk, oak on heavy clays, pine and birch on nutrient—poor sands and gravels, alder along the banks of rivers or canals.

Thus, the successful growth of each appears linked to a given environment; yet the ecological amplitude of most of our common native trees is certainly wider than such a generalization would indicate. Competition is still operative.

Growth will tend at all times to be closely dependent on adequate water and nutrient supplies, and temperature—the latter often a limiting factor.

The seasonal character of tree growth in north temperate latitudes, although so familiar as to pass without comment, reflects this correlation with temperature, but it must not be forgotten that there are also important links with two aspects of the light factor—day length and absolute light intensity.

The student of growth phenomena in trees, as in other plants, is often faced with the difficult task of *elucidating* the relative significance of several quite distinct factors in the environment, each of which is known to be operative in a general way.

These he endeavors to study in relation to the demonstrable overall growth increment, as shown by suitable measurements, and resulting in a figure for '*net assimilation rate*,' or '*productivity*.'

The mechanisms by which trees achieve this are clearly beyond the scope of this brief introduction.

Suffice it to say that the reactivation of the cambium in spring is brought about through the production and mobilization of plant growth hormones (*auxins*) in the expanding buds. Meanwhile there is an upsurge of activity in the primary apical meristems in the course of which stored food is used up and energy released, sufficient to allow cell division and cell enlargement to go on apace.

The reactivated vascular cambium loses no time in forming new tissues (*xylem* and *phloem*) which will facilitate rapid transport of raw materials and mobilized storage products.

There is an intense level of chemical activity within the individual cells, and as this entails respiration, photosynthesis, protein-building, the fashioning of new cell walls and other processes it is easy to appreciate something of its hidden complexities. What the eye sees as a result of all this internal activity (at cellular level) is the burgeoning of new leaves on the trees in spring.

When we bear in mind that a single mature foliage leaf will commonly comprise some 15 million cells we begin to glimpse something of the unimaginable scale of cell production, each spring time, in a single forest tree.

Nevertheless, this particular manifestation of growth is there for all to see. Opening buds, new leaves, elongating twigs, these cannot pass unnoticed, but not so the scarcely perceptible increments in girth and stature of the older trees.

Fast-growing species of tree, for example birches, illustrate how rapidly height increases in the early years following successful establishment and how markedly it slows down later. Yet some increments will take place, however slight, in every spring for the duration of the tree's life.

With few exceptions, at least in temperate regions, the increase in girth of a tree at breast height (1.5m; 5ft) is very close to 2.5cm (1 in) a year. This is for trees growing under conditions such that their crowns are not inhibited from full development by overcrowding. This figure is useful for estimating a tree's age. Thus, with a breast height girth of 2.5m (8ft) the tree will be about too years old.

Some exceptions to this rule are:

Wellingtonia (*Sequoiadendron giganteum*),
Coast Redwood (*Sequoia sempervirens*),
Cedar of Lebanon (*Cedrus libani*),
Douglas Fir (*Pseudotsuga menziesii*),
Southern Beeches (*Nothofagus spp*),
Turkey Oak (*Quercus cerris*),
Tulip Tree (*Liriodendron tulipifera*),
London Plane (*Platanus acerifolia*)

which increase girth at 5-7.5cm (2-3in) a year, and

Scots Pine (*Pinus sylvestris*),
Horse Chestnut (*Aesculus hippocastanum*),
Common Lime (*Tilia x europaea*)

which increase girth at less than 2.5cm (1 in) a year.

In other climates very different conditions of growth prevail. In the humid tropics two years of more or less uninterrupted growth activity can easily result in a tree many metres high.

On the fringe of the great deserts of the world, notwithstanding the high temperatures, water shortage makes the trees of the specialized genera that grow there among the most slow-growing of all. In the high Arctic, temperature imposes comparably severe restrictions.

On wind-exposed coastal stations both wind velocity and salt spray can play a part in restricting the height and distorting the growth of trees. Even so, for certain species at least, life itself may be retained with tenacity, in the face of all obstacles.

Thus, the shock is the greater when a single virulent fungus such as *Ceratocystis ulmi* (which causes Dutch Elm Disease) can bring about the death of up to to million British elms in the course of a few seasons. Our knowledge of the botany of trees appears powerless to arrest this devastation.

It is equally powerless to check the havoc wreaked from time to time by forest fires on the tinder-dry, oil-rich, evergreen eucalyptus forests of Australia. Our remedy must be to grow more trees.

5

Chapter

FORESTS

Vegetation in which trees are important or dominant—forests and woodlands—occupies about 40 percent of the world's land surface, ranging from the tropics to high latitudes (about 70° in the Northern Hemisphere) and from sea level to about 3 Boom (12 500ft) in some mountain passes.

The structure of the forest, whether deciduous or evergreen, broadleaved or needleleaved, as well as the species present in it, varies considerably in response to the climate, topography, rocks, soils and past history of the different regions of the world. However, despite their diversity, forest ecosystems share certain features which make an overview possible.

When bare ground becomes available for colonization the first plants are relatively simple, often algae, mosses and lichens, which form rather simple communities.

Through the action of these plants on the substrate, and the accumulation of their dead remains, a soil begins to form which permits the development of more complex communities dominated by pioneer flowering plants, usually herbs.

These in their turn are succeeded by other more closed communities, increasingly rich in species and dominated by ever taller plant forms, until a stage is reached at which a relatively stable vegetation is produced.

This *climax* vegetation is the most complex that can be supported under the prevailing climatic and other environmental conditions of a region. The most complex climax vegetation is usually considered to be that dominated by trees and forest ecosystems normally develop where there is a reasonably long growing season in which mean temperatures do not fall much below 10°C (50°F), a reliable supply of ground moisture and protection from drying winds during the winter when moisture cannot be absorbed from the chilled soil.

Where regions are too dry, too wet, too cold or too exposed, forest gives way to ecosystems such as grassland, bogs, tundra or desert scrub, in which trees are of little or no importance. While forest ecosystems are able to develop because of the environmental conditions prevailing in a region they are also important in modifying these conditions to provide a series of microclimates which profoundly influence the occurrence of plants and animals in forest communities.

In forests the tree top canopy is often the densest part of the vegetation, reflecting or absorbing much of the sunlight, so that only i percent or less reaches the forest floor.

Winds are also greatly reduced by tree cover; in pine forest, for example, the wind speed at ground level is less than onequarter of that above a canopy 14m (45ft) high and there is proportionately greater reduction in taller forest. The soil, too, is modified by the dominant trees.

In addition to the moisture of forest soils their chemical and physical features are affected by the leaf-litter which falls on to them. Leaf-litter supplies the humus which sustains the clay-humus complex of forest soils and contains the reserves of soluble nutrients.

Leaves with abundant organic acids or very woody tissues are not easily eaten by the soil fauna and tend to decompose slowly by rotting to give a thin, leached, acid soil, as under beech, while leaves with less acid organic matter are quickly broken down to give the deeper, less acid soils, supporting abundant animal life, found under oak and holly.

Such differences can be seen over quite short distances in mixed oak/beech woodland, for example. The presence of myccorhiza (fungal threads which join the tree roots to the leaf-litter) can provide the tree with nutrients derived from the saprophytic fungi thus making the tree less dependent on the soil fertility.

In forest dominated by evergreens, or in the summer phase of deciduous forest, the reduced light and wind give cool, damp conditions which fluctuate much less through the day than in more open habitats. Plants and animals unable to withstand constantly changing conditions thus find a home in these forest habitats.

Forests, however, do not provide uniform conditions, as is shown by the vertical stratification of the vegetation they contain. The canopy of the forest is made up of trees which benefit from strong light at maturity.

In temperate mid-latitudes there is usually only one canopy, but in energyrich tropical rain forests there may be two or three canopy layers, often with strongly light-demanding plants such as palms protruding above them as emergents.

Beneath the canopy, shade-tolerant shrubs usually form another stratum while herb and ground layers (mosses etc) can often also be distinguished. The development of the two latter has been found to depend not only upon the available light but also upon the amount of litter, which probably has a shading effect.

It has been shown in British woods that the total mass of the herb and ground layers decreased proportionally with increasing amounts of litter and, furthermore, that certain plants, such as grasses and mosses, were more speedily eliminated than others, such as Bluebell (*Endymion non-scriptus*) and Yellow Deadnettle (*Galeobdolon luteum*).

In deciduous woodland the difference between conditions inside and outside the tree-dominated ecosystem decreases during the winter when the lack of leaves allows the increased penetration of both light and wind.

Many herbaceous communities of deciduous forests are adapted to these seasonal differences and we find in Hornbeam (*Carpinus betulus*) woodlands, for example, that the Wood Anemone (*Anemone nemorosa*), Dog's Mercury (*Mercurialis perennis*) and Celandine (*Ranunculus ficaria*) complete their flowering period and much of their leaf-production before the tree leaves expand.

Other species, such as the Bluebell and Ramsons (*Allium ursinum*), probably prolong their flowering under full shade because of the food stored in their bulbs. Because trees are relatively long-lived, opportunities for regeneration in virgin forest depend upon the death of individual trees or their destruction by winds, fire and other hazards.

The seeds of many forest trees are large and rich in food reserves which enable them to germinate and survive as seedlings under the low light levels and high competition of the forest floor. Many species are able to remain as small seedlings waiting for a break to occur in the canopy; oak shoots, for example, that were aged as six years by growth rings were growing from roots as much as 31 years older.

Herbivores (*rabbits*, *rodents*, *insects*) and fungi destroy enormous quantities of seeds and seedlings so that successful establishment only occurs in years of high seed production. When a suitable break appears in the canopy this is colonized by light-demanding plants.

The tree seedlings have to compete with these initially and then, as a scrub of tree species emerges, the saplings compete with each other until, finally, one of these rises above the others to fill the gap as a mature tree.

The forest ecosystem, then, comprises a series of habitats, supporting a myriad plants and animals, dependent upon the microclimatic conditions resulting from the dominant trees, which themselves individually provide support for climbers (honeysuckles, lianes etc) and epiphytes, such as ferns, mosses and various flowering plants, and partial nutrition for parasites such as mistletoes.

The forest is one of the most complex ecosystems known and its food chains are consequently long and interrelated. Most of the nutrients in a forest are present in the bodies of the plants, animals and other organisms that make up the various communities.

In virgin forest the level of nutrients is maintained relatively constant by the recycling through food chains and the importance of trees is shown by the fact that 82 percent of the total mass of land plant tissues is locked up in forests, although they cover only about 4o percent of the land area.

The removal of forest interrupts this cycle and the nutrients are dissipated. In consequence, the destruction of forest by Man has not only removed the myriad habitats that depend upon tree cover but has also greatly reduced the fertility levels of many regions, which largely explains the current preoccupation with the conservation of existing forests.

FORESTS OF THE WORLD

Forests are the climax vegetation over about 40 percent (4500 million hectares or 11115 million acres) of the world's land surface, although Man has substantially altered them or entirely removed them from vast areas—from much of Western Europe, for example.

Different types of forest are found in different climates, and there are striking convergences in forest structure and general appearance between areas with the same climate in different continents where the same type of forest occurs although composed of different species.

The explanation of this similarity of appearance, or epharmony as it is called, is still largely unexplained, although physiological causes such as response to water stress or mineral deficiency are clearly involved.

Tropical Rain Forests

In the tropics and subtropics evergreen tropical rain forests occupy about i o0o million hectares (2 500 million acres) in the wettest climates. They occur in three great blocks centered on Amazonia, the Guinea-Congo region of Africa and the Malay archipelago, the latter extending from the Western Ghats of India to the wet, high islands of the Pacific.

There is also an isolated small zone in east Madagascar and the Mascarenes. There are 13 major categories or formations of tropical rain forest. Three of these (lower montane, upper montane and sub-alpine forest) occur at progressively higher altitudes.

Beach, mangrove forest and brackish water forest are coastal. Two formations, peatswamp and freshwater swamp forest occur on inundated ground inland, three on extreme substrata (limestone, ultrabasics and nutrient-poor sands) and two on dry lowland mesic sites in continuously humid and mildly seasonal climates respectively.

These last two formations include the most complex and species-rich plant communities in the world. They occur in the best conditions for plant life, with no dry or cold season to interrupt growth. The biggest trees average 30-45m (100-150 ft) in height, although some reach 60 m (200 ft) or more.

Beneath them grows a dense profusion of smaller trees. The tallest trees commonly occur as isolated emergents standing head and shoulders above a continuous canopy. Shrubs and herbs are rare, the undergrowth plants consisting mostly of small trees. Different tree species reach different heights at maturity, and characterize different strata in the canopy.

The emergent and tallest canopy trees usually have broad, sympodial crowns, composed of numerous small rather dense subcrowns. Smaller trees commonly have crowns taller than broad, and these are frequently of monopodial construction, that is having a single main axis.

Buttresses, which may reach rom (33ft) or more up the trunk, are an important feature of many types of rain forest, and in some types stilt roots are common. Leaves are principally of mesophyll size and may have the apex extended as a prolonged drip tip. Climbers (lianes) and epiphytes are common in a great diversity of form and species. Stranglers, which start life as epiphytes but send down roots and ultimately engulf and kill the host tree, are prominent.

Saprophytes and parasites occur (including in the East *Rafflesia*, which produces the largest flower in the world). The trees provide a complex framework for these other plant forms, and an intricate set of niches for animals.

Both flora and fauna are exceedingly rich. For example, the rain forests of the Malay peninsula occupy an area equal to England and Wales, containing some a 500 tree species and a total flora of about 8 000 species of vascular plants. Many botanists believe that flowering plants evolved in tropical rain forests.

Today they certainly contain the greatest concentration of primitive groups. Small areas of forest in southeast Asia are richer than in Latin America. The African forests are much poorer, for example as many species of palm are found on Singapore island as on the entire continent of Africa.

Structure becomes simpler and species become fewer away from the optimum, northward and southward where tropical forests merge into equivalent subtropical formations, for instance in Indochina and south China.

There is a similar trend to simplification within the tropics to the other rain forest formations listed above. One of the most strikingly distinctive lowland rain-forest types is so-called heath forest (caatinga and campos in South America) which is, however, virtually absent from Africa.

This develops on soils which even by tropical standards are impoverished, are mostly coarse, freely draining siliceous sands, and become podozolized. Heath forest is of low stature, microphyllous and very dense, with a uniform canopy top of high albedo. Its physiognomy is an adaptation to periodic water stress and to mineral deficiency.

In the eastern tropics this structure and physiognomy is also found in upper montane rain forest (*cloud forest*) and several species occur in both.

Upper Montane or Cloud Forest

Upper Montane or Cloud Forest is rain forest which occurs above the cloud level on tropical mountains. Its lower limit is quite sharply at the cloud line. Cloud forest characteristically has a low, dense canopy of small trees with thick, gnarled crowns of tiny, leathery leaves and high reflective power. Trees and ground are thickly swathed in epiphytes, mainly filmy ferns, but including bryophytes and flowering plants. *Sphagnum* (bog moss) often occurs in open places.

In very humid climates peat accumulates. The soil is

waterlogged for all or much of the time. Much of the precipitation is derived by the fog (ground-level cloud) condensing on the vegetation. Cloud forest occurs as low as 600m (1970 ft) in Malaysia, and at 3000-3300m (9250-10830 ft) in the main cordillera of New Guinea.

On the very highest mountains subalpine forest occurs above cloud forest up to the tree line; it is of low stature with very tiny leaves of nanophyll size. Lower montane rain forest occurs between upper montane and lowland forest.

It has a general resemblance to the latter and merges through a broad ecotone but differs in species composition and several structural features which taken together are diagnostic, and include lower canopy with fewer, smaller emergents, smaller buttresses and absence of big woody climbers.

Mangrove

Mangrove is a type of forest associated with muddy shores of a belt surrounding the equator. This belt reaches latitude 32°N, and as far south as Auckland in New Zealand and South Australia. Mangroves develop on sheltered muddy shores of deltas and estuaries exposed to the tide.

They vary in width, some reaching up to several kilometres. The trees are evergreen, with the thick leathery leaves frequently associated with plants of saline soils and other physiological adaptations to live in salt water. Many species have viviparous seeds, which develop into seedlings on the parent tree and on being shed stick into the mud, when roots develop very quickly.

Various types of prop and aerial root are another characteristic of these trees. Breathing roots enable the root system to respire in the anaerobic mud. The vegetation is almost entirely woody, varying from low scrub to forest 30m (100ft) high.

Mangrove swamps are one of the most unpleasant types of vegetation for the human visitor: the aerial roots make progress very difficult, and the deep mud releases unpleasant fetid gases which accumulate in the anaerobic conditions. The myriad biting insects are yet another disincentive.

There is a zonation of vegetation in mangrove swamps associated with the degree of immersion. Different species have different competitive powers according to their tolerances of salinity.

Monsoon and Savanna Forests (Dry Tropical Forests)

Rain forests change with increasing length of dry season to semi-evergreen and deciduous types. Initially species composition alters although the genera and families present remain much the same and only the taller trees are deciduous.

Leaf shedding and flowering become synchronized and correlated with climatic seasonality. In the strongly seasonal dry tropics, forests of much simpler structure and with fewer woody species occur and ultimately closed forest is replaced by open woodland and savanna.

In all climates with a marked dry season fire is an important factor controlling structure and species composition of the vegetation. In progressively drier climates, total amount of moisture becomes more important than length of dry season.

Characteristically these so-called monsoon and savanna forests form a mosaic pattern. Closed moisture-loving, more nearly evergreen, so-called gallery forests occur along water courses. These seasonally dry tropical forests are extensive in all three continents.

The flora is rich, with many fire-resistant herbs (including bulbous types) and grasses in the drier and more open types. There is a rich fauna, notably the spectacular group of ungulates in east Africa.

Sclerophyllous Forests

Sclerophyllous Forests, with winter rain, occur around the Medit-erranean and in the other parts of the world with similar climate. The summers are hot and dry, the winters warm and wet due to cyclonic rain. Annual rainfall is 500-1000mm (20-40in) but irregular, and there are prolonged periods of low relative humidity.

There is no really cold season. Spring is the main growing and flowering season. The Mediterranean basin has been the center of civilizations from ancient times and *deforestation*, *cultivation*, *grazing* and *soil erosion* have destroyed most of the original forest so that only variously degraded communities now remain.

The original zonal vegetation was forest dominated by a canopy of the Holm Oak (*Quercus ilex*), 15-18m (50-60ft) tall, with shrubs and herbs beneath. Where the trees are cut about every 20 years it is replaced by a dense *shrub vegetation* called maquis.

This is very rich in species including many geophytes, but is subject to periodic fires and becomes degraded by excessive grazing and burning to form open *garigue*. All the best sites are now occupied by vineyards and other agriculture.

Many species are adapted to Mediterranean climatic conditions by the possession of small, leathery, evergreen leaves which minimize water loss in dry periods. Similar vegetation occurs in central and southern California.

Here evergreen forests occur to the north, but southward, with decreasing rainfall, are replaced by a scrub called chaparral which is comparable to maquis except that it is the natural zonal vegetation with lightning-induced fires as a natural controlling factor.

In the *Southern Hemisphere*, *sclerophyll forests* occur in a tiny area of Chile (only relicts remain), the Cape of South Africa, where the flora is fantastically rich especially with members of the heath family (*Ericaceae*) and the southwest tip of Australia, where the general appearance differs due to the predominance of members of the families Epacridaceae and Proteaceae and the genus *Eucalyptus*.

The area occupied by dry forest and woodlands of all kinds (Mediterranean sclerophyll type, plus the monsoon and savanna tropical and subtropical forests) is 1400 million hectares (3500 million acres).

Warm Temperate Evergreen Forests

There are two groups of warm temperate forests. They total 100 million hectares (247 million acres) in area. The first kind is an extension of sclerophyll forest in conditions where there is no summer drought.

In California north of 36°, the coastal strip is moist from summer fogs which result from cool onshore ocean currents. Forests of the Giant Redwood (*Sequoia sempervirens*) occur. This is the tallest tree in the world, attaining loom (330ft) and more.

Farther north on the same coast there are magnificent temperate rain forests of *Tsuga heterophylla* (Western Hemlock), *Thuja plicata* (Western Red Cedar) and *Pseudotsuga menziesii* (Douglas Fir). There is a comparable forest in South America, the Valdivian forest of Chile, but none in Africa.

In Australia, the Karri (*Eucalyptus diversicolor*) forest abuts the summer-dry sclerophyll forest zone. This also is a tall forest. Like the North American examples it is an important timber resource.

In the Mediterranean region, this type of vegetation occurs around the Black Sea, east as far as the shores of the Caspian, and includes the species-rich Tertiary-relict Colchic forest of Transcaucasia, which lies in a region where the summers are mild and wet enough for tea cultivation to have replaced most of the zonal forest.

The main warm temperate forests are found on the eastern seaboards of the continents, exposed to monsoon or trade winds. Rainfall is plentiful, 150-300cm (60-120in), and well distributed throughout the year. In southeast Asia (*Thailand*, *Indochina*, *China*, *Korea* and *southern Japan*), eastern Australia and southern Brazil there is a continuous gradation with increasing latitude from wet tropical to subtropical to warm temperate conditions.

It is very difficult to distinguish zones in these evergreen forests. Characteristically penetration is difficult; they are rich in tree species including some conifers, and in epiphytes and climbers, but less so than the tropics. Plank buttresses are absent.

Some trees are deciduous, giving marked seasonal differences in appearance. Mosses, liverworts and ferns are abundant on the ground and tree-trunks. Bamboos are common in some types, as are tree ferns. There are strong similarities in structure and physiognomy with montane tropical forests and at the family level also in the flora.

The climate, however, has a marked annual rhythm, whereas"

the montane tropics have a greater diurnal than annual climatic range. General appearance varies with different regions and there is a complete change in flora from low to high latitudes.

In Australia, it has been shown that tropical types extend farthest south on the best soils and moistest sites. The main temperate type is the *Nothofagus* forest of Tasmania and Victoria, whose boundaries are determined by frequency of fire.

In Africa, only the Drakensburg mountains have suitably moist sites for this type of forest, and it is of limited extent. In North America it is also poorly defined because cold air masses move south as far as the Gulf of Mexico, but it is found near the coast from Louisiana, Florida and Georgia to North Carolina.

The tree flora is rich including evergreen oaks (*Quercus spp*), a few palms and some climbers. Bald Cypress (*Taxodium distichum*) swamps occur in wet areas and fireclimax pine (*Pinus spp*) forests are found on dry sands.

Most of the forests of New Zealand fall into this class; dominant trees include *Nothofagus*, mixed conifers, and a kauri pine (*Agathis* australis)-subtropicalbroadleaved species mixture, depending on locality, soil and past history.

Temperate Deciduous Forests

Temperate Deciduous Forests are perhaps the most familiar type in the world. The total area is Boo million hectares (2000 million acres). They formerly covered most of Western Europe and are still extensive in North America.

They are virtually restricted to the Northern Hemisphere (apart from an area in Patagonia, southern Chile and Tierra del Fuego). Leaf fall is an adaptation to the marked but not very prolonged cold season when water is unavailable or restricted (by contrast with the tropics where it is simply an adaptation to drought).

Annual rainfall is 70-150cm (28-60in). Evergreen broadleaved trees cannot withstand cold or winter drought and in Western Europe *Ivy* (*Hedera helix*) and Holly (*Ilex aquifolium*) are both Atlantic species absent farther east where winters are more severe.

Rhododendron and *Vaccinium* species, also evergreen, by

contrast, survive winter cold below a snow covering. These forests are found on the eastern coasts of North America and Asia between the warm temperate forests and cold or arid temperate regions.

In North America, they extend north to the Great Lakes and upper reaches of the Gulf of St. Lawrence, and west of the Mississippi. In Asia, they occur in northern Japan and on the adjacent part of the continent.

They are also found on the western edge of Eurasia in Europe, north of the Mediterranean zone, and where the Gulf Stream causes winter rains to be replaced by evenly distributed rainfall or rain with a summer maximum, and where the cold season is relatively short. Here they range east to the Urals as a wedge between the steppes and the boreal coniferous forests.

Deciduous trees occur where there are four to six months with adequate rain and this forest is absent from extreme maritime climates of the western seaboard as well as extreme continental climates.

The temperate deciduous forest zone of Western Europe is one of the most populous regions of the world because the climatic conditions also favor prosperous agriculture and grazing, and only tiny fragments of the forest remain with virtually none in virgin condition.

Floristically the Western-European forests are poorer than the others due to extinction in the Pleistocene ice ages. Beeches (*Fagus spp*), oaks (*Quercus spp*), limes (*Tilia spp*) and ashes (*Fraxinus spp*), are locally dominant in the single tree layer.

In wet places alders (*Alnus spp*) and willows (*Salix spp*) become common. There is a single shrub layer in which hazels (*Corylus spp*), Field Maple (*Acer campestre*) and hawthorns (*Crataegus* spp) are common, and a herb layer. There are few climbers and only cryptogamic epiphytes.

The trees flower early, commonly before the leaves open, and most are wind-pollinated; this allows a long period for fruits to form and ripen before the onset of winter.

In early spring before the canopy becomes leafy the forest floor herbs flower, creating carpets of blossom; especially of

Bluebell (*Endymion non-scriptus*), Primrose (*Primula vulgaris* and Oxlip (*Primula elatior*), which are one of the glories of these forests, equalled only by the spectacular yellow, orange and red tints of the dying foliage in the fall.

The early spring temporal niche is succeeded by a spring one, occupied by other herbs, for example Wood Sorrel (*Oxalis acetosella*), which flower at the time of leaf flush. In Asia and North America there are more genera and species in both tree and shrub layers, including magnolias, numerous maples (*Acer spp*), Tulip Tree (*Liriodendron tulipifera*), buckeyes (*Aesculus* spp) and hickories (*Carya* spp), as well as temperate outliers of mainly tropical families.

The Boreal Region

The Boreal Region encircles the globe at and beyond the northern limit of forests and covers major portions of North America and Eurasia as well as the islands of Newfoundland, Sakhalin and Iceland.

It abuts southward on the temperate deciduous forest but the winters are colder and longer. Part of the region, between 45° and 70°N is occupied by the very extensive boreal coniferous forest, which covers 1500 million hectares (3700 million acres).

In addition there are big areas of bog, peatland and swamp, known as muskeg, and in oceanic regions, such as Iceland, dwarf shrub vegetation known as heath. The main forest dominants are conifers with xeromorphic needle leaves, more resistant to winter cold and drought than broadleaved trees.

Such trees can commence photosynthesis immediately conditions permit in the spring, so are better adapted to exploit regions where the growing season is short. Deciduous trees need about 120 days per year with mean temperature over 10°C, conifers can manage with 30 days, though there are differences between species.

The narrow, conical, monopodial tree form with drooping branches is adaptive to regions of high snow fall. These forests have only a poorly developed shrub and herb layer: shade is greater, decay of falling leaves is slow so that undecomposed litter covers much of the surface, and the climate is worse.

Spruces (*Picea* spp) with Norway Spruce (*P. abies*) merging eastward with Siberian Spruce (*P. obovata*) in Eurasia and White Spruce (*P. glauca*) in the New World, firs (*Abies* spp), pines (*Pinus* spp) and larches (*Larix* spp) dominate in different places.

At its northern limit the boreal conifer forest merges into open parkland with scattered groves of trees, taiga. The northernmost forest in the world is in eastern Siberia at 72° 50°N, 105°E and is dominated by a larch *Larix gmelinii* (*L. dahurica*), which is highly productive in the very short summer, but one of the few deciduous conifers, losing its needles each winter.

The ground layer of boreal forests is predominantly of dwarf shrubs, for example bilberries and cranberries (*Vaccinium* spp), Leatherleaf (*Chamaedaphne calyculata*) and Labrador Tea (*Ledum palustre*), and is also richly mossy.

Drier pine forests typically have herbs like *Linnaea borealis*, *Trientalis europaea* and the wintergreens (*Pyrola spp*) *as* well as saprophytes such as the orchids *Goodyera repens* and *Corallorhiza trifida*.

There is no comparable belt of coniferous forest in the Southern Hemisphere, where indeed there is no land mass at the appropriate latitudes.

On north temperate mountains south of the boreal zone a conifer forest zone commonly occurs above the deciduous broadleaved forest, reaching up to the tree line. Resemblance extends to the herbs - several species are shared with boreal latitudes.

Trees, though of the same genera, are mostly different species, for example the European Larch (*Larix decidua*) and in the Appalachians the Red Spruce (*Picea rubens*) and Fraser Fir (*Abies fraser:*).

Forest Dynamics

As we have seen, the species composition of a forest is dependent at the grossest scale on plant geography and within any region there is variation due to habitat, for example between swamp and dry land, and with different soil types.

A further important variation arises from the complex

structure of a forest community. At maturity a closed forest canopy casts dense shade. Plants can only grow up under the canopy which are able to succeed in conditions of low light and high root competition.

In temperate deciduous forest many herbs to some extent avoid these limitations by making much or all of their growth (including flowering) before the trees come into leaf.

Only certain tree species have seedlings which can grow up under a closed canopy. These are often called shade bearers. Sometimes gaps form in a closed forest canopy. A storm may blow down isolated trees or fell a swathe, fire may sweep through.

A second group of tree species has seeds efficiently dispersed and (in the tropics) continually available, and these soon colonize such gaps. The seedlings are adapted to grow and succeed in the brightly lit, sometimes desiccating, conditions of gaps.

These species are often known as light demanders. The seedlings cannot grow up in shade, so the trees cannot replace themselves *in situ*. They always colonize gaps and are also sometimes referred to as pioneer species.

The forests of pioneers are always seral. Familiar English examples are Scots Pine and birch. In fact there is a spectrum of types from obligate shade bearers to strict pioneers, especially in regions with a rich flora, and most markedly in the humid tropics.

In the temperate deciduous forest of North America the pioneers *Pinus strobus*, *Quercus* spp and *Castanea spp* tend to be replaced in the absence of catastrophic forest destruction by the shade bearers *Acer spp*, *Tsuga* spp and *Fagus* spp.

The two oaks native to England (*Quercus petraea* and *Q. robur*) are also both light-demanding species. In West Africa present-day extensive tall speciesrich rain forest containing much valuable timber in the form of several species of Meliaceae (African mahogany) is being replaced by a lower forest with fewer species of less commercial value.

The principal timber species of Malaysia, the Philippines and Indonesia, light-wooded meranti (*Shorea* spp), are near-pioneers, favored by mild but not total forest disturbance. This dynamic aspect of forest composition, with different species adapted to different temporal niches in the canopy growth cycle, therefore has important ecological and commercial implications.

The science of *silviculture* is based on understanding and manipulating it. Trees have long lives, and rare catastrophes leave their mark on forest composition for a century or more. 'Pioneers come up in large gaps as even-age stands and a rather coarse mosaic of large patches of different age develops.

Shade bearers succeed the pioneers, replacing each other or themselves on smaller areas so that ultimately a mixed-age stand develops with a fine-scale mosaic pattern of gap, building phase and high mature forest.

But it is doubtful if there is ever an equilibrium state, or constant species composition; a catastrophe, or indeed secular climatic change, sooner or later intervenes to cause gross alteration.

In Western Europe Man's interference with the forests has been prolonged and profound and influences present-day structure and species composition. The dominance of light-demanding oak over much of England reflects its conscious selection by silviculture not its ecology.

TREES AND MAN

As we have seen forests occupy over onethird of the earth's land surface. They are of immense variety, ranging from the dwarf trees with imperceptible growth in the Arctic regions, to the tropical rain forests, rich in species and varied in structure; from the vast areas of closely stocked coniferous forest in the North American continent, and in northern Europe, to the open savanna with a low stocking of trees which covers extensive areas in the tropics and subtropics.

The growing stock of trees is estimated to be 350 000 million cubic metres (1.24 million cubic feet) of which two-thirds is hardwood and one-third softwood. Total annual removals are of the order of 2 500 million cubic metres (88 000 million cubic feet) of which 45 percent is coniferous.

Seventy percent of the hardwood removals are used for fuel. For millennia the immense resource that these forests represent has been exploited by Man, whose activities have reduced their area to about half their greatest extent.

Since ancient times the forest has been cleared for agriculture, for protection against wild beasts or human enemies, and to obtain its products. The main instruments of destruction have been fire and the grazing of domestic stock, supplemented at times by the deliberate introduction and release of nonindigenous species of herbivorous animals.

It is reasonable to suppose that the net area of forest in the world is still decreasing by several million hectares per annum owing to continuing destruction and degradation chiefly by shifting cultivation in South America, Africa and parts of Asia.

Only in modern times has there arisen a concept of management of forests for the perpetuation of the renewable resource they represent and only in very recent times has the full scope and range of that resource begun to be realized. Forests have always been exploited for the wood they provide for innumerable purposes through the ages—fuel, implements, shelter and housing, furniture and fencing.

Today's industrial needs generate an increasing range of uses, often involving the breakdown of the structure of raw wood, and its reconstitution into paper or board, or its combination with plastics into new forms of material.

With the predicted rise in world population from the present 4 000 million to 6 ooo million by the end of the 20th century and an assumed annual increase in world consumption of wood of 2 percent, the need for management is evident; a continual increase in the supply of wood is required from a dwindling area of forest.

In addition to the production of wood it is now recognized that forests fulfill a wide variety of functions essential to Man's well-being. They protect the soil and so counter erosion and reduce flooding; they shelter and protect agriculture and influence local climatic extremes; they ensure clear water supplies and prevent pollution; they provide a habitat for a vast array of flora and fauna, a resource in itself.

Forests, woodlands and trees are essential components of attractive landscapes and are becoming increasingly important for the recreational facilities they can provide for the urban populations of industrial countries. The modern forester is therefore faced with a dilemma: the necessity to increase the sustained supply of wood from the forests as rapidly and as economically as possible and the need to protect the forest ecosystem to maintain all the other benefits, often not quantifiable in economic terms, which derive from the forest.

This challenge must be met within the framework of his government's economic planning. Their approach is now to select practical patterns of action, supported by scientific findings, on both biological and mathematical grounds, in order to achieve a balance between efficient production and safeguarding the environment.

Silviculture is the art of creating and tending a forest. It involves the application of detailed knowledge of the life history and general characteristics of trees, with particular reference to *environmental* factors. Each tree species differs in its requirements and its reactions to site conditions, in its pattern of growth, and in its ability to withstand extremes of climate or *terrain*.

It is by understanding these factors for all the trees within the climatic range that the silviculturalist controls the development of the forests under his care. Some trees, such as pines (*Pinus spp*) and birches (*Betula spp*), can be used as pioneers on exposed and infertile sites, while others, such as oaks (*Quercus spp*) and ashes (*Fraxinus spp*) grow best in more sheltered places and on rich deep soils.

Species such as larches (*Larix spp*) and oaks need full light all around their crowns for optimum growth; others such as beeches (*Fagus spp*) and silver firs (*Abies spp*), are shade bearers and can remain growing slowly in the understorey till eventually freed to grow into the upper canopy of the forest.

Once a forest has been established it needs continuous tending to maturity, with periodical thinning to give more room for the best stems, which are selected to remain. As maturity approaches consideration must be given to the next generation.

Measures taken to achieve the desired result include natural seeding, replanting after clearing with the same or another species or planting under the shelter of the existing stand. Various silvicultural systems have been evolved to secure the regeneration of forests in different conditions; the more diverse the structure, the more complex the system.

The simplest system (though not necessarily the best) is clearcutting followed by replanting. The most complicated selection system is that in which single scattered mature trees are removed periodically to encourage continuous natural regeneration and the maintenance of a permanent uneven-aged structure, normally of mixed species. This system is often used in mountain regions to prevent erosion.

Afforestation is the creation of new areas of forest or woodland on sites that have been without tree cover for a long period, often hundreds of years or even since prehistoric times.

Such sites may have been used for agriculture and allowed to deteriorate or they have changed because of climatic factors, as in the case of sand-dune invasion or as a result of industrial dereliction such as slag heaps in a mining area.

In nearly all cases afforestation is in fact restoration of tree cover after a long interval and in conditions totally different from those when the forest was there before.

The purpose of afforestation is often to satisfy the growing demand for industrial wood but other objectives, such as flood control, shelter, prevention of erosion or the amelioration of the climate (particularly in arid countries) are also important.

It is estimated that there are about too million hectares (250 million acres) of newly-created forest in the world and that this figure will be doubled by the end of the 2oth century.

Large programs of afforestation have been carried out in many countries; the Tennessee Valley scheme restored the '*dust-bowl*' to fertility in the 193o's and in the EEC countries it is proposed to afforest 5 million hectares (12 million acres) of `surplus' agricultural land. But it is in the USSR and China that really massive programs of afforestation for timber production and shelter are now taking place.

The techniques required for afforestation often differ considerably from those used in the regeneration of existing forests. The conditions are nearly always harsh, the soil impoveri-shed, exposure to wind or sun severe, and the risk of damage by animals and pests much greater than in the more stable forest ecosystem.

In wet uplands the land must be drained and impacted soils must be broken up by some form of cultivation to enable the small tree roots to penetrate. On the arid slopes of hills in hot climates terracing may be necessary to conserve any rain that may fall and in rocky terrain it is sometimes essential to import soil to enable the newlyplanted trees to make a start.

Fertilization of the soil, particularly with phosphates, is nearly always necessary. The species of tree selected for afforestation are not necessarily the same as those of the indigenous forests of the region. Fastgrowing species are needed to satisfy industrial needs and they must also be hardy to withstand the rigorous conditions as pioneers.

This normally means that conifers will form the bulk of the crop that is planted and these are often exotic species not present in the natural forests of the country. Thus Sitka Spruce (*Picea sitchensis*) from North America is the principal species used in afforesting the wet uplands in Britain.

The Monterey, Pine (*Pinus radiata*) from California is the main species used in New Zealand and Australia and the Cuban Pine (*Pinus caribaea*) from the southeastern United States is extensively used in South Africa.

In some countries where conditions permit, broadleaved trees such as oaks, poplars (*Populus* spp), *Eucalyptus,* alder (*Alnus* spp) and birches are included in the initial planting; the more rigorous the conditions, however, the less chance there is for the successful establishment of a diverse crop in the original planting.

Normally afforestation must be regarded as the pioneer stage in the restoration of a forest ecosystem which may take 50 or ioo years to re-establish. Nevertheless, even a monoculture of a pioneer coniferous species brings a great environmental gain to the site.

Protection from grazing and disturbance, from wind and erosion, and the conservation of moisture, start the chain of events in the ecological development of the site from a plantation to a forest with its diversity of composition and structure and flora and fauna.

Improvement of Existing Forests

The need to conserve natural forest systems for their environmental value, rather than replace them with man-made forest, and at' the same time increase their potential production of utilizable wood, has been receiving increasing attention from foresters.

The tropical rain forests, threatened by exploitation for their valuable timbers and by destruction through shifting cultivation, pose many silvicultural problems. Management to increase the productivity of useful species without destroying the primeval ecosystem is a complex matter.

Natural regeneration is difficult to ensure and the introduction of exotic species involves the progressive destruction of the ecosystem. Only if foresters and biologists can work together with substantial research facilities at their command, can a solution be found before it is too late.

In the past the need for a country to formulate a national policy has been mainly dependent on the need for a sustained or increased yield from its forests to supply established wood-using industries. Underdeveloped countries have tended simply to exploit the forest to obtain capital for other purposes or land for agriculture.

Today the situation is different; the energy crisis, combined with a dwindling forest area and rapidly rising population, demands a purposeful statement of forestry policy for the sake of Man's economic and social well-being.

There are a number of essential components required for a national forestry policy in this context. Efficiency of production and harvesting the raw materials of the forest must be balanced against safeguards for the environment. For example, modern chemical sprays give the forester a powerful yet destructive weapon if not controlled.

The dominant use in multipleuse forests must be defined. This may be protective rather than productive, as in the Alps. There is a need to define how the forest is to fulfill the national aims and there must be an input of investment in trained experts and money to gain a continuing output in raw materials.

More research is needed and this is paramount if the joint problems of increased supply of wood is to be combined with conservation of the environment. Genetic research is particularly important in order to achieve better growth in each region.

It has been calculated that improvements in this field could raise the potential global yield to more than ten times the present figure without depleting the growing stock. One side effect would be greater scope for conservation within the forest.

Forest managers at all levels must be trained in the scientific basis for the application of forestry techniques, which will result in greater yields of wood without damaging the environment.

Governments must also recognize the long-term nature of forestry and maintain policies that ensure continuity.

FOREST PRODUCTS

Forests provide one of the most important renewable resources in the world. The forests themselves are the habitat of many plants and animals and the home of many people of many races, who depend on these plants and animals for food, clothes, building materials, fuel and other supplies.

In many parts of the world they serve as a source of a wide range of raw materials for major forest industries and for minor forest products. Many forests provide a source of recreation for the local population, particularly for those living in large cities and their associated conurbations.

From the many statistics associated with forestry and forest products, perhaps the most remarkable fact to emerge is that about half the world's annual forest crop is used as fuel (either as firewood or as charcoal) and that 90 percent of the population in the developing countries depend on wood as their only source of fuel.

The major forest industries are concerned with timber and timber products, plywood, wood chips, wood pulp and paper. The so-called minor forest products include: vegetable products, such as leaf fodder and litter; bark for use as cork or tanstuffs; ornamental trees and shrubs; medicinal plants; edible fruits, seed and other plant parts; naval stores; *oils*, *fats*, *resins*, *turpentine*, *gums*, *latex*, *dyestuffs* and *sap sugar*; *fibers*, *yarns* and *flosses*; *osiers*, *canes*, *bamboos*, *reeds*, *rushes* and thatching materials. Plants have also given rise to mineral products in the form of peat, lignite and coal.

Wood and Timber

The major forest industries are based on the utilization of part or all of the forest tree. Mature trees are felled, the branches removed and the trunk (or stem) cut into logs from which solid timber components are cut. In the early 1970's the annual world consumption of wood was estimated at 2300 million cubic metres (81000 million cubic feet) of which some 1100 million cubic metres (39000 million cubic feet) were used as fuel.

The rest was processed for industrial purposes of which sawn timber accounted for two-thirds, paper nearly a quarter and panel products (plywood and other boards) about a tenth.

About two-thirds of all the sawn timber or about 44 percent of all industrial wood was used for building construction. Of the paper over half was used for wrapping and packaging papers and about a quarter for writing and printing papers while about 17 percent went for newspapers.

The rates of increase in the manufacture of paper and panel products (especially particle board) over the previous ten years had been much higher than for sawn timber but sawn timber still retains its position as the largest single product of industrial wood and will do so for a considerable time to come.

The annual rate of increase in the use of industrial wood over the previous decade had been about 3.5 percent per annum (simple interest on the 1964-1973 decade). Taking the total known area of the world's forests and calculating the quantity of wood which could, at present rates of growth, be added per year, gives an increment which amounts to about twice what is at present being removed.

This calculation, however, ignores the fact that large areas of forest (16 million hectares—40 million acres) in many countries are being turned over to agriculture each year and many of the present exporters of timber are aiming to meet not more than their own needs in the long-term future.

Moreover, much of the world's forest area is situated in very remote areas and its utilization is likely to become increasingly costly. Planted forest to date only amounts to about 3-5 percent of the total exploitable forest area, so the vast majority of the wood cut at present is being '*mined*' from forests not planted by Man and in which little or no capital has been invested before the harvesting operation.

There is a strong likelihood, therefore, that wood, along with many other raw materials, will become increasingly scarce and costly. There is also evidence to suggest that it will be the higher quality timber necessary for joinery, furniture and other uses, where it has to pass exacting specifications, which will rise in cost faster than the lower quality wood.

It takes longer to produce and requires more care in growing than, for example, wood grown to produce paper. Wood for fuel is easier still to grow.

The suitability of the wood of a particular species of tree for a particular use depends both on the properties of the wood imparted to it by the mixture and nature of the different tissues of which it is composed and on the requirements of that use.

Ebony is no more used for making model airplanes than balsa wood is used for high-class carving. Wood 'quality' is something that can be judged only in terms of the product to be made from it.

If a wood is to realize its full potential and to be utilized in an optimum fashion, it needs to find the highest value use for which there is a market and to be manufactured into the finished article with a minimum of waste and in such a way as to render the finished articles as durable as possible in order to make replacement necessary as infrequently as possible.

Appearance becomes more important as the value of the end product increases and, for such things as carvings, veneers, paneling and high-grade furniture, it is paramount in importance.

Appearance is not a single property but a combination of many; the difference between wood and its substitutes is primarily that no two pieces of wood are identical. Color is determined partly by the quantity of cell wall in relation to cell lumen but also by the colors of various substances contained in the cells, normally of the heartwood.

Changes in color are provided by growth rings and the patterns produced can be varied by cutting the wood in different ways. Oak, for instance, is normally more attractive quarter-sawn and elm flat-sawn. Strong differences in color patterns are often found in softwoods with a large contrast between early wood and late wood.

Douglas Fir, when flat-sawn or peeled as a veneer, for example, shows prominent 'contour' patterns. Some woods have dark and light patches within the wood, for example olive wood.

Grain is a collective term describing the appearance of the patterns of cells and tissues in the wood. The patterns of vessels, rays and parenchyma give rise to the prominent rings in ash and elm (vessels), the fleck in beech (rays) and the pattern of light-color wood around vessels in *Iroko* (parenchyma). Changes in grain direction result in waves in the grain and in an interlocked grain which, on quartercut timber, is shown up as the well-known stripe in such timbers as mahogany.

About a quarter of all wood used industrially is made into furniture and joinery. Not all needs to be of good appearance and high quality but a good proportion must be so. About another quarter of all industrial wood is used structurally in building where strength is an important property.

Here the wood must be used in its natural form to make use of its peculiar property of being strong in resisting forces at right angles to the grain direction.

It is unlikely that reconstituted wood will ever improve on solid wood, used structurally, because its alignment in the tree is as near ideal as it is possible to get.

Wood density is closely related to strength and since it is easy to measure can be used to predict strength; but there are variations in the strength/ density ratio and some trees have more efficient wood than others. Shrinkage and movement are particularly important where wood components need to fit closely together as in such uses as furniture, joinery and flooring.

Wood is also a good insulator, electrically, thermally and against sound. In this respect, provided it is well treated against rot, it has considerable advantages over metal for such uses as window and door frames.

There are, therefore, good reasons for preferring wood for so many things. It is common, renewable and infinitely variable. What is sometimes forgotten is that, although it does 'grow on trees,' it takes a very long time to do so and there is by no means an inexhaustible supply.

Minor Forest Products

The relative importance of minor forest products has changed over the years due to the effects of industrialization and the development of technology. Naval stores provide a good example.

The term first appears in England in the 16th century and covers the very important group of shipbuilding materials, that is pitch, tar and timber, all derived from species of pine. These commodities have always been of vital importance for the building and caulking of wooden ships and waterproofing their associated ropes, rigging and cordage.

Much of the naval strategy of the seafaring nations from the 16th to the 19th centuries was based on a regular and reliable supply of these materials. Naval stores today are generally one of three types, known as gum, wood and sulfate naval stores.

Gum naval stores are produced by tapping or wounding certain resinous species of pine, collecting the oleoresin and treating it to produce rosin and turpentine.

Wood naval stores arise from the slow burning (or destructive distillation) of pine species under carefully controlled conditions to produce turpentine, pine oil, rosin and pitch or tar.

Sulfate naval stores form a by-product of the 'Kraft' process for the chemical production of wood pulp. The material produced is known as tall oil and contains resin acids and fatty acids.

The greater portion of tall oil undergoes further processing to produce rosin and fatty acids. Naval stores now form part of what has been called the silvichemical industry, which is concerned with the production of chemicals from trees.

The industry covers a wide range of materials, such as *lignin derivatives*, *vanillin*, *essential oils*, *maple syrup*, *oleoresins*, *alkaloids*, *tannins*, *rubber*, *true gums*, *ethanol*, *acetic acid*, *vitamins* and *waxes*.

Many plants growing in forests produce extracts that have important medicinal properties. In the tropical forests *Cinchona* spp are a source of quinine; *Carapa spp* growing in America and Africa provide medicinal materials from both bark and seeds; *Strychnos* spp give rise to a number of alkaloids, which combine medicinal properties with deadly poisons, such as strychnine, brucine and curarine (the active principle of curare).

Of the forest plants that are edible or produce edible fruits and seeds cocoa, coconut, coffee, tea, bananas and spices are all important examples. Latex and rubber are tapped both from the forest tree and from plantation-grown crops.

Chicle, the basis of chewing gum, is a natural product from a forest tree and is obtained by tapping the tree every five years to collect the exudate. Dyestuffs such as indigo and logwood are important locally, although synthetic dyes have largely taken over the world market.

The products of the forest are many and varied and have served to provide for many of the needs of Man since earliest recorded times.

Great areas of forest have already been destroyed but the importance of this renewable resource underlines the necessity for the conservation and plantation of forests for the benefit of future generations. It is a matter which cannot afford to be overlooked.

AMENITY OR URBAN FORESTRY

At the onset of the Iron Age the greater part of Western Europe was covered with forest—spruces, pines and birches in Scandinavia, pines, firs, beeches and oaks in central Europe and the oaks, birches and firs in the British Isles.

Early man feared the forest, not only for its darkness and wild animals, but also for the outlaws who frequented its vastness. Nevertheless, he took such timber, vines and stakes as he needed to satisfy his simple domestic requirements and cleared away the trees for pastures and crop production.

From earliest times trees have been venerated, used in religious symbolism and for aesthetic purposes. The *yggdrasil* of Norse mythology, a huge spreading ash tree, was the very pillar of the world, binding together earth, heaven and hell.

Trees and groves were sacred to the Greeks, often being associated with particular deities: the Oak with Zeus, the Olive with Athena, the Laurel with Apollo. Such veneration did not prevent trees being felled but when virgin forest was cleared individual trees or clumps would be left as holy relics—a custom worthy of resurrection today. Transplanting of trees is known to have been practised as early as 1500 BC in Egypt and in classical times Theophrastus and Pliny recorded methods of tree care—probably the first records of arboricultural practise.

The regard that society has had for trees is reflected in the countless place names which owe their origin to the trees which grew in the vicinity, while in poetry, prose and song, tree imagery is to be found in every language.

With the increasing sophistication of society in the Middle Ages the demands on the forest estates of the developing countries of the world increased to provide the raw materials for manufacturing industry.

The extent of the forest clearing since early days can be seen from the accompanying table in which the area of woodland is given as a percentage of the total area of land in 1968—for most of these countries the 'natural' forest cover should be over 80 percent.

USA	30.00	Belgium	18.20
Great		Norway	23.80
Britain	6.10	Denmark	9.30
Germany	26.80	Netherlands	6.10
France	19.10	Ireland	3.10

Up to the 13th and 14th centuries, the administration and exploitation of natural forests was often controlled by royal authority. However, this patronage waned concurrently with an increased demand for forest resources in the form of naval stores and fuel for the early iron-smelting industries.

The 'gaps' produced by such exploitation were soon filled by increasingly sophisticated agricultural demands and practises. The result was the loss throughout Europe of vast tracts of natural forest that were never replaced. Concern over the depletion of European forests was constantly being voiced.

For example, legislation was enacted in 1581 to try to control the destruction of the oak forests to the south of London which were being exploited for the production of charcoal for the iron-smelting industry.

From the view of amenity forestry there was, however, one clear benefit from this age. The period from the 15th to the 19th century was a time of naval powers, colonization and exploration—all made possible because of the forest resources of the homelands.

With the opening up of new lands, thousands of new and curious plants were discovered, many of which were trees. This supply of unusual plants was further stimulated by their becoming fashionable among the new upper classes.

The age of the landscape garden in which trees formed a primary part had started. Specimen tree collections in the form of arboreta and artificial landscapes began to appear in earnest during the 18th century, especially around the family residences of estates in Great Britain and in France, for example the work of Alphand in Paris.

It reached its peak in the 19th century and even today we owe many of our landscape gardens to the endeavors of estate foresters a century or more ago. The earliest manual on tree care both for their timber and their fruit was John Evelyn's *Sylva—a Discourse of Forest Trees and the Propagation of Timber* (1664), in which reference to previous work is made and detailed directions are given on the care of trees.

Following the ravages of two world wars the landscape of Europe needed to be rejuvenated and towns and cities rebuilt. At this time there was an increasing awareness of the contribution that trees make to the quality of life so that many government authorities at local and central level made resources available for the planting and maintenance of trees in both urban and rural areas.

Many new towns also sprung up in which provision was made for new plantings while at the same time preserving the existing tree population, especially where they formed essential features of the landscape. Professional associations lobbied legislatures to enact regulations to provide for due consideration to the preservation and conservation of treed landscapes which were threatened by development.

Fragile areas were given special status, for example the designation in Great Britain of Areas of Outstanding Natural Beauty and Sites of Special Scientific Interest, and the provision of Tree Preservation Orders. Tree planting grants to private individuals and organizations were made available from government-sponsored agencies such as the Countryside Commission in Great Britain.

A further reflection of the growing interest in trees and the demand for instruction is to be found in the significant increase in the number of volumes that can be found in any bookshop.

Despite this increased public awareness and the protective legislation, the destruction of trees still continues, and this does not include just those forests and woodlands which are deliberately cropped for the timber that they produce.

The systematic management of trees for the production of a raw material is just as essential for any society as the cropping of a field of grain, as both instances are examples of plants being used in the service of Man. The thoughtless parking of cars has been responsible for the loss of many elegant city and town trees.

Vandalism in major cities contributes to pointless casualties, especially in new landscapes. Many authorities prefer to record their tree planting progress by the number of trees planted instead of those which become successfully established.

In far too many cases new trees end up merely as supports for their stakes because there are not sufficient funds to allow for aftercare. Discouraging as these disappointments are, far greater loss and mutilation of trees occur in the name of progress, perpetrated by sections of the community who should know better.

Those involved with the development or use of land must carry a large share of the blame. Modern society requires houses, factories and roads and, except in a limited number of cases, rural areas and the parklands landscaped during past centuries are lost to urban and industrial demands.

It is only when loud local protests have been mounted that, for example, motorway planners have been forced to realign routes which initially were carved through irreplaceable trees and wooded areas. An awareness of the damage to the landscape that motorway construction can cause has resulted in many fine planting schemes financed by central government.

Trees are not necessarily just ornamental additions to our environ-ment; trees lining a trunk road give protection from wind turbulence, thereby increasing highway safety. Other benefits include reduction in noise levels (in so far as tree noises, for example the rustle of leaves, mask traffic roar) and the alleviation of glare caused by buildings.

Housing development consumes large numbers of trees despite the conditions placed by planning authorities on their retention and protection. The alteration of the water table following disruption of the soil during building operations, the laying down of hard surfaces—concrete and tarmacadam—and the excavation and filling which alter the configuration of the land, deprive existing trees of their sources of moisture to the extent that they are placed under stress during a time when they are attempting to adjust to the changed environment they find themselves in.

In this respect it is as well to remember that a tree has no option but to die when its environment changes for the worse. The provision of utility services involves digging trenches to lay down pipes for gas and electricity and when major roots are cut to allow their passage not only is the stability and nutrient source of the tree in jeopardy but fungal pathogens such as *Ganoderma applanatum* can gain entry into the cut surfaces.

The resulting incipient growth goes unnoticed until spectacular bracketshaped fruiting bodies appear as a precursor to the complete collapse of the tree. Badly-laid gas pipes which leak can kill trees in a very short time as has been found in Holland. The tree can often be cited as a villain when this is far from the truth.

The drought of 1976 in Western Europe caused clay soils to shrink which in turn caused structural failure of buildings. Because it has been shown that trees reduce the moisture content of soil, trees were blamed for the structural failures.

Attempts were therefore made to limit tree growth to a distance from buildings equivalent to 1 2 times their mature height which, if enforced, would result in a treeless suburbia. While there is no denying the fact that trees in proximity to houses which have been built on shrinkable clays can be associated with structural failure during periods of dry weather, inadequate foundations are equally to blame.

Planners and local government agencies are often torn between the demands for housing and the demands for an acceptable living area. Local conservation groups are seen as interfering busybodies and the voices of protest have great difficulty in countering the economic or political arguments (spurious or real) which are presented for the destruction of trees.

A compromise solution is usually arrived at when conflicting interests meet but these solutions are often overtaken by events. For example, trees may be retained so near to a new structure that their removal is necessitated within a twelve-month period of the completion of the building because they have deteriorated to such an extent, due to damage during construction, that they become a danger.

Individual owners of trees must also take a share of the blame for the mutilation of trees and their destruction. Many owners resort to the practise of lopping or pollarding in the mistaken idea that the pruning reduces the thickness of the branches or will stop, for example, the drip of honeydew from limes and sycamores which ruins the protective paint of cars.

This practise of lopping to remove a '*nuisance*' only alleviates the problem for a short time, as the rejuvenating processes produce a proliferation of branches which in a few years forms a denser growth than before and once again lopping is necessary. The cut ends or pollarding points develop areas of rot due to fungal infection of the cut surfaces and this rot slowly eats its way down the trunk.

In the end a hideous tree looking like a hatstand in the winter and a lavatory brush in the summer is formed. Correct pruning procedures and skillful thinning of the canopy can alleviate the supposed nuisances without disfiguring the tree. In such instances it is essential to consult a professional tree surgeon if the best results are to be obtained.

On new developments the correct choice of trees to enhance a property prevents the problem of trees overtaking the limited space available. The average suburban property is not large enough to support a tree of forest proportions and therefore it is wiser to plant the smaller type tree—birches (*Betula spp*) or rowans (*Sorbus* spp), for example, or some of the smaller maples, for example, *Acer griseum* or *A. hersii,* rather than the beeches, oaks, or monkey puzzles, which are best incorporated in special areas in the form of spinneys or copses.

In rural areas, hedgerows have been the traditional site for trees since the loss of the true forest cover and are, in effect, linear nature reserves. The effects of diseases, such as Dutch Elm Disease, and the reduction of hedges are continuing to alter the landscape. The arable farmer complains of trees reducing his cropping areas or of the damage the roots of trees can cause to expensive machinery.

He is justified in making these complaints but in every farm there are areas which cannot be cropped and where groups of trees could be planted to form spinneys and copses. Stock requires shade—protection in the summer and in the winter—and therefore good cattle husbandry includes the provision of trees in pastures.

Having provided protection and shelter these same trees can produce timber for use in the estate or farm in the centuries to come. With the greater mobility of city populations of the Western world, their demand for recreational areas has introduced the concept of amenity woodlands—areas of trees set aside for their aesthetic and recreational value as opposed to their timber production potential.

The proximity of these woodlands to population centers dictates the frequency with which the woodlands are used. Their management, usually the responsibility of local authorities, has to take into account the pressures which visitors place on the delicate balance of a woodland ecosystem.

That local authorities should be expected to look after recreational woodlands would seem an obvious step when the organizational skills in the maintenance of public parks and street trees already exist. The concept of so-called '*urban forestry*' has been with us for two decades and in the first instance this revealed the gulf in understanding between the management practises required for individual urban trees and the silvicultural practises required to manage a forest or woodland.

Urban forestry, which was first developed in Canada, has been defined as a practise that 'does not deal entirely with city trees or with single tree management but rather with tree management in the entire area influenced and utilized by the urban population.'

By definition, a forest or plantation managed for the production of timber comes within the above definition of the urban forest.Government forest departments have now realized the recreational value of the commercial forest.

In Holland, forests are opened for recreational purposes once the initial establishment stage has been completed and in Great Britain forest walks are now to be found in all the large afforested areas. Even private forests have recently been opened to the public by provision of, for example, nature trails. In North America and Scandinavia vast tracts of forest are open to the public for recreation purposes.

Amenity woodlands and commercial forests therefore require the same approach. Because the landscape of Europe has been manipulated by Man to the extent that natural forest is virtually nonexistent and is confined to the more remote areas, management of woodlands for amenity is essential. The forester aims at what is termed a sustained yield and hence income.

For the amenity forester the value of woodlands is expressed in terms of social benefit, which means that external finance is required. However, there is no reason why woodland areas cannot be managed at two levels—the income from the true forestry used to subsidize the amenity facilities.

In an amenity woodland, trees have to be replaced, and therefore silvicultural practises are demanded just as they are in the commercial forest. Trees have been referred to as the furniture of the landscape and for their survival all members of society must take their share of responsibility.

It is irresponsible for the public to demand both conservation measures from the public authorities and unrestricted access to woodlands. The compaction of the soil by many feet and the dumping of litter caused by open access, for example, will only hinder conservation measures.

The task of maintaining a national heritage such as the country's rural and urban landscape is enormous and initiative rests with all, not just a few, if the inheritance is to be passed on to future generations.

DISEASES AND PESTS OF TREES

From early times trees have played an important part in Man's technological development. This readily available natural resource was used for tools, fuel, shade, shelter and food. Much later, when Man came to raise trees under the less natural conditions of productive forestry, a need arose to concern himself yvith their diseases and pests.

The early work on tree diseases was carried out in Germany by Robert Hartig in the late 19th century. Since that time science has provided a far greater understanding of both the tree and its disorders, and has often helped to minimize losses.

Occasionally this has been achieved by direct control measures, but more often through disease avoidance. Parasitic organisms causing disease (pathogens) are a legacy from the ancient natural forest. There they played an important role in a balanced ecosystem by assisting in the death and destruction of the old and the weaker trees, thus providing space and soil enrichment for the survivors.

To a large extent Man has now taken over the role of natural selection by choosing his species and the individuals that he wishes to survive, but the pathogens remain, and are a potential threat to his trees.

Trees can outlive all other plants; they have achieved this unique longevity by evolving highly efficient defenses against the entry of those organisms which seek to use them as a source of nutrition. A tree presents a veritable larder of food for those organisms that can overcome its defensive barriers or bypass them through wounds. Most pathogenic microorganisms attempt to gain entry by using a form of chemical and physical warfare. The tree's defense operates in a similar way, mostly employing complex chemicals which interfere with, or present a barrier to, the growth of the invader.

In any disease syndrome, three major factors are involved: the pathogen, the tree and the environment. These are constantly interacting and in any disease investigation no single factor should be considered in isolation.

Different strains of a pathogen may vary in their aggressiveness, and individual trees of the same species can vary in their inherent ability to resist infection. Many pathogens have very specialized requirements, often having a very limited host range, and may flourish only under certain environmental conditions.

Adverse environmental factors such as drought, water-excess, soil compaction and pollution can cause stress, sometimes weakening some part of the trees' defenses. Many fungal pathogens and insect pests can be quick to take advantage of weakened 'stressed' trees and their presence may cause sufficient further stress for the survival of the trees to be in jeopardy.

However, a return to more favorable conditions for growth may enable a tree to overcome the pathogen or pest and recover, with the loss perhaps of only a small part of the tree. Financial losses from diseases, pests and other adverse agents in the forest are enormous.

It is estimated that around half these losses are caused by diseases (which cause mortalities, growth reduction and decay); the remaining losses are due to insect pests, fire, and other factors, in more or less equal proportions.

However, in any locality at a particular time, any one of these agents can be of prime importance. Amenity trees grown for ornament-ation or shade are normally less prone than forest trees to large-scale losses.

This is mainly because the diversity of species used and their sporadic distribution make it more difficult for a pathogen to become widely established.

However, the loss of a single tree growing in an important

position can be as disastrous to the urban arborist as a hundred or more trees to the forester.

Control

Wherever possible the control of pests and diseases of trees should be achieved through good management rather than by employing more intensive chemical methods. This is because the longevity of trees may necessitate the repeated application of chemical treatments over long periods of time to give lasting protection.

This could be uneconomic and may be damaging to the environment. Biological control methods, utilizing natural enemies or antagonists of pests and disease agents, have attracted much attention in recent years, especially with regard to insect pests, since they are cheap, nonpolluting and may he self-perpetuating.

There are still, however, relatively few instances where such methods are used, although the use of insect pathogens, especially viruses, is now being assessed. With some insect pests, however, there may be no practical alternative to chemicals.

More intensive control methods become worthwhile for high value amenity trees. Such trees, growing along roads and in small gardens in towns, can experience a wide variety of stress factors. Frequently the arborist can only minimize physical damage and ensure an adequate supply of water, nutrients and air to the roots, so that the natural defense mechanisms can function effectively.

To avoid disease problems it is important to select the most suitable species or variety of tree and to apply stringent regulations on the importation of plant material or timber, which may carry a foreign disease or pest into a country.

Diseases

Although the spore-bearing structures (sporophores) such as '*toadst-ools*' and '*brackets*' are conspicuous, the principal part of a fungus consists of a network of fine strands (hyphae) which individually are invisible to the eye.

These hyphae ramify through the soil or other substrate, absorbing and transporting nutrients. Not all fungi produce such obvious sporophores; in some species they are microscopic, in others they appear as tiny pustules on leaves or twigs. Fungi are classified on the form these structures take. Most types of fungi rely on wind to transport their spores, but rain, insects and other animals may also facilitate their spread. Normally spores are produced in vast numbers, as only a small number ever reach their goal and initiate a new infection.

When a spore reaches a suitable substrate it germinates, producing a hypha which attempts to penetrate the cells of the host. If the cells are susceptible, the fungus may continue to grow and thus establish a new infection.

Most trees are, however, resistant to attack by most fungi. If a spore alights on a resistant plant, as is frequently the case, fungal development is prevented at an early stage.

As well as dispersal by spores some fungi, in particular those infecting roots, may spread locally by means of extensive hyphal growth. Diseases caused by microorganisms can be broadly characterized according to the parts of the tree where the infection occurs, although the more obvious symptoms of the disease may be manifested elsewhere.

In particular, the first symptoms of root diseases often become apparent in the crown. This is well illustrated by the diseases caused by *Phytophthora cinnamomi,* a fungus of very wide host range and the agent of Littleleaf Disease of pines and the Jarrah Dieback of *Eucalyptus* in Australia.

These diseases are seen as a slowing of growth or as death of parts of the crown, but the fungus infects and destroys the fine feeder roots of the tree. This fungus has motile spores which are actively attracted to suitable host roots. It is favoured by wet soils, through which these spores readily move.

In contrast, other root-infecting fungi may attack the woody roots of their hosts. Such a pathogen is the Honey (or Shoestring) Fungus (*Armillariella mellea* = *Armillaria mellea*) which is very common throughout the world, attacking a wide range of trees and shrubs.

The Honey Fungus can spread from a well-colonized root system for several metres through the soil by means of rhizomorphs. These are black shoestring-like strands of aggregated hyphae which are well suited to survive the rigors of the soil environment. On contacting a suitable host these rhizomorphs penetrate the bark of the roots and the hyphae grow through both bark and wood, killing and decaying the infected roots. As the proportion of infected roots gradually increases, crown symptoms may appear in the form of sparse or pale foliage.

Large trees, however, often tolerate considerable amounts of root infection without noticeable symptoms, and succumb to lethal levels of invasion only after being weakened by an additional stress factor such as drought.

The honey-colored toadstools of the fungus are often produced in clusters around the base of killed trees or old stumps, but the spores they produce rarely initiate new infections. The best means of control is the removal of infected stumps and roots from which the rhizomorphs are produced.

Heterobasidion annosum (*Fomes annosus*), another root-decaying fungus, can be particularly detrimental to many managed coniferous forests. Unlike the Honey Fungus, the spores of *Heterobasidion* are important in its spread. New centers ofinfection are initiated when spores colonize the stumps of recently-felled trees.

The fungus then spreads down into the roots of the colonized stump, infecting neighboring living trees via root contacts, which occur frequently in forest plantations. In Britain the spread of this fungus has been greatly reduced by applying chemicals to the stumps to prevent the initial establishment of the pathogen.

In the case of pines, which are frequently killed by the fungus, a biological control method is used; spores of a harmless saprophytic fungus are applied to the stumps. This fungus grows rapidly in the stumps and prevents establishment of the pathogen.

Both *Heterobasidion annosum* and the Honey Fungus can also spread into the bole of infected trees and cause decay. Some other decay-causing fungi, including *Poria weirii* and *Polyporus tomentosus,* both of which can cause extensive loss of timber in North America, also spread from tree to tree via root contacts.

There are numerous other fungi which cause decay in standing trees. Many of these are incapable of attacking the living tissues of their hosts, but grow actively in the dead inner wood of trees. Such fungi usually require some form of wound to establish infection.

Suitable wounds may be produced when branches die or break off, or may be made by humans either inadvertently, or deliberately in the process of pruning. Various fungi, such as *Ganoderma applanatum,* frequently cause decay in old ornamental trees, rendering them unsafe, while others like *Phellinus pini* can cause considerable loss of timber.

Such fungi do not affect the vigor of the tree, which may show no obvious outward sign that decay is present. The presence of sporophores of these fungi is, however, a sure indication of decay.

Other types of fungi can attack the living tissues of the bark, some giving rise to cankers. These may spread rapidly, girdling and killing the infected stem, or may attack only a more restricted area, sometimes persisting for many years.

Endothia parasitica, which causes Chestnut Blight, is a pathogen of the former, more aggressive type. It also provides an example of the damage a pathogen can do when introduced by Man to a new, highly susceptible host. The disease was first noticed in the United States in 1904 and is believed to have been imported with chestnuts from Asia.

Once established it rapidly spread through the highly susceptible native population of American Chestnut (*Castanea dentata*), leaving few mature survivors. Attempts to eradicate the Chestnut Blight came too late, when the disease was already well established.

Chestnut Blight has now reached southern Europe, but its effects there have been less severe than in North America. In contrast to the more aggressive bark pathogens, the canker on hardwoods caused by *Nectria galligena* has less overall effect on the vigor of infected trees, although small branches may be killed.

The area of infected tissue extends slowly when the tree is inactive in winter, but in summer the tree puts on healing growth. These cankers may persist for many years. Many of the rust fungi cause cankers.

These fungi are specialized parasites, having a complex life-cycle, usually involving two different hosts. The most destructive is the White Pine Blister Rust (Cronartium ribicola) which causes spreading cankers and can kill susceptible pines.

The spores produced on infected pines cannot directly reinfect pines, they must first infect currant plants (Ribes spp) on which spores are produced which can then infect other pines. In theory the eradication of Ribes in the vicinity of susceptible trees should control the disease, but this has proved impractical, and rust-resistant varieties of pine are being developed by plant breeders.

Some fungal pathogens may thrive in the conducting vessels of the tree, through which they can spread very rapidly. These diseases are called vascular wilts, and are seen as a more or less rapid wilting of the foliage, followed by death of the infected branches.

These symptoms are caused by an interruption in the supply of water to the crown owing to the diseased condition of the vessels. Dutch Elm Disease, which, like the Chestnut Blight, has been inadvertently spread by Man, is a typical vascular wilt disease.

The fungus (Cerato(ystis ulmi) is spread from tree to tree by Elm Bark Beetles (Scolytus scolytus). These vectors become contaminated with spores of the fungus as they emerge from their breeding galleries in the bark of infected trees. Before breeding again, the beetles feed on young elm twigs, and frequently introduce the spores into feeding-wounds.

From these wounds the fungus rapidly spreads through the vessels to colonize the entire tree. Oak Wilt, caused by the fungus Ceratocystis fagacearum, is a very similar disease principally damaging red oaks. It too is spread by vectors, but these are less efficient than those of Dutch Elm Disease.

Both Dutch Elm Disease and Oak Wilt can also spread on a local basis between the root systems of adjacent trees where root grafts may occur naturally. Oak Wilt is currently restricted to certain parts of the United States and stringent quarantine measures are in operation in an attempt to prevent the introduction of.this disease into Europe.

Sanitation felling and removal of diseased trees has been used to slow the spread of both these diseases and locally this has met with some success. Injection of fungicides to protect specimen trees has also been tried but generally success has been rather limited.

The symptoms of Elm Phloem Necrosis are not readily distinguished from those of Dutch Elm Disease, but are probably caused by a mycoplasma—like organism which appears to be a specialized type of bacterium. This disease is also currently restricted to the United States.

In contrast to diseases of roots and stems, the diseases of leaves of trees are of relatively minor importance, except on very young trees. Many species of fungi can infect leaves, causing local areas of discoloration or death.

One of the most striking is Tar Spot of maples (Acer spp) and the European Sycamore (Acer pseudoplatanus), which produces large black spots in the leaves in late summer. These are resting structures, enabling the fungus (Rhytisma acerinum) to overwinter on fallen leaves before producing its spores in spring to infect the new foliage.

Overwintering is a major problem for fungi that infect the leaves of deciduous trees: most species overwinter on fallen leaves in this manner, but some may survive in the buds of their hosts. Infection of ornamental trees can often be reduced by the simple expedient of removing infected fallen leaves in winter.

On conifers leaf diseases tend to be more serious as the needles are normally functional for several years. Although broadleaved trees can withstand quite extensive defoliation or leaf damage, loss of foliage in the case of conifers tends to be accompanied by a corresponding reduction in vigor.

Some diseases of leaves can also infect young shoots, killing them, though this progressive dying of twigs from their tips, commonly termed '*dieback*,' can also be a secondary symptom of many other tree disorders.

Gnomonia veneta causes a disfiguring dieback on plane (*Platanus spp*) trees, and *Scleroderris lagerbergii* can be damaging on certain conifers. The latter fungus typically only causes serious damage on weakened trees, and is unimportant on vigorous, healthy specimens. Bacteria are very small single-celled microorganisms, typically a few thousandths of a millimetre long. They reproduce by dividing into two identical cells and these vegetative cells serve also for their dissemination, which is usually by rain splash or animal vectors.

Bacteria are much less important than fungi as a cause of disease in trees, although a few notable exceptions exist, such as Fire-Blight, caused by Erminia amylovora, and a canker on poplars (*Populus spp*) caused by Xanthomonas populi (*Aplanobacter populi*).

This may be because their unicellular growth habit is less well adapted to colonizing solid substrates than the hyphae of fungi. Viruses, which can also cause disease in trees, are as yet rather poorly understood, but it seems likely that they are of only minor importance.

They are submicroscopic pathogens which require living host cells in order to reproduce. Virus spread usually requires vectors such as sap-sucking insects or nematodes, although they may also spread from place to place in seed and from tree to tree in pollen.

Viruses normally cause only mild disfigurement of the foliage in the form of yellow mottling but may also reduce growth, sometimes without causing leaf symptoms. Although virus spread may be reduced by removing infected trees and killing the vectors, infections cannot readily be cured, so healthy planting stock should always be used.

Pests

Trees may also be damaged by many insects, mites and eelworms (nematodes), which use trees as sources of food. Plant material is not very nutritious and these pests need to eat large quantities to survive, thus causing serious damage to trees.

Most insects with a potential for causing such damage are kept in check by climate, the tree's defenses (for example leaf toughness and toxic chemicals), predators, parasites, and competition for food and space.

If the balance of these factors is upset, for example by uniform planting of a single species (*monoculture*) which provides an extensive food supply, pest outbreaks may ensue. Similarly, insecticide usage may result in the breakdown of regulation by natural predators.

Often the most obvious insects to a casual observer are those which feed by chewing leaves, the defoliators. Many groups of insects, such as the larvae of moths (*order Lepidoptera*) and sawflies (*order Hymenoptera*) live in this way. Some beetles (*order Coleoptera*) and, in warmer climates, grasshoppers (order Orthoptera) and stick insects (*order Phasmida*) can also become pests.

The Gypsy Moth (*Lymantria dispar = Porthetria dispar*) *is* arguably the most serious defoliator of broadleaved trees in North America. First introduced from Europe in 1869, the Gypsy Moth has spread to become a pest over 520000 square kilometres (200000 square miles); it has had few natural enemies to stop it and no problems of food shortage as the caterpillars feed on a large variety of both broadleaved and coni-ferous trees.

Complete removal of the leaves each season results in death after two or three years. Some insects feed directly on sap and have piercing or sucking mouthparts. These include *capsid bugs*, *leaf hoppers*, *aphids*, *mealybugs* and *scale insects* (*order Hemiptera*).

One of the most common tree aphids in Western Europe is *Elatobium abietinum* (*Neomyzophis abietina*) the Green Spruce Aphid. Its effects are typical of many *herbivorous Hemiptera* : the leaf becomes discolored around the site of feeding. This discoloration may spread to produce large blotches, sometimes followed by total browning and leaf fall.

Aphids rarely cause tree death, though growth may be diminished. Scale insects, as adults, live under protective layers of waxy wool or under hard shells. Some species feed on the stems instead of the leaves, as in the case of the Felted Beech *Coccus* (*Cryptococcus fagi*).

This feeds on the bark of beech trees, covering the infected areas with a white 'wool.' The combined effect of the damage caused by this feeding, and the fungus *Nectria sp,* which may subsequently enter, often kills areas of the bark in a syndrome known as Beech Bark Disease, which may kill the tree.

Despite the environmental damage that may result from the use of chemicals, it is often necessary to control severe outbreaks of both '*chewing*' and '*sucking*' insect pests if extensive destruction of trees is to be avoided.

Currently, research is progressing into breeding trees resistant to herbivores, as well as into biological methods for their control. The larvae of certain small moths (*order Lepidoptera*) and flies (*order Diptera*) burrow within leaves, feeding on the internal tissues and leaving visible tunnels. Nearly every holly bush in Britain shows the effects of the Holly Leaf Miner (*Phytomyza ilicis*).

Galls are structures developed by the plant in response to feeding by certain insects and mites. Sycamores and maples frequently have their leaf surfaces covered with small bright red swellings, produced by mites of the genus *Eriophyes.*

Although unsightly, leaf miners and galls rarely cause much economic damage. Some insects live in shoots, bark and/or wood. Caterpillars of the Pine Shoot Moth (*Rhyaciona buoliana*) burrow into the buds and leading shoots of pines, killing the tips or distorting them.

This species and its relatives are particularly troublesome in young plantations in Europe and North America. The pests considered so far infest more or less healthy trees; however, bark and wood borers rely in the main on trees with reduced vigor.

Bark beetles (family Scolytidae) have been mentioned previously. The wood-boring larvae of woodwasps, moths, and especially beetles venture farther into the wood, although initially they may live just under the bark.

In Europe and North America, one of the largest wood-boring beetle families is the Cerambycidae, the longhorn beetles. External signs of attack vary; when main trunks are infested no evidence is found until the bark begins to fall off, or adult exit holes appear in it.

In those species which burrow into thinner stems, localized swellings and bark splittings can occur, as in the case of *Saperda populnea,* the Poplar Longhorn, a widespread pest over much of Europe, Asia and North America. The best control methods for bark and wood borers center around the removal of dead or unhealthy, including felled, timber before it can be used for breeding.

Logs which cannot be processed in time can be protected with persistent insecticides. Most species of tree benefit greatly from symbiotic relationships between their roots and fungi. Some nematodes, for example *Aphelenchus sp* feed on these mycorrhizal fungi.

In forest nurseries, nematodes such as *Pratylenchus* feed as parasites on the roots of conifer seedlings, resulting in stunted, sickly or dead plants. The roots of mature trees can also be attacked by nematodes, although the actual damage caused has rarely been assessed. Soilinhabiting nematodes can be controlled by use of soil fumigants.

In addition to predisposing trees to diseases and insect pests, nonliving (abiotic) factors can alone cause considerable damage to trees. Droughts or excesses of water, extremes of temperature, wind, snow, fire and nutrient deficiencies can all weaken or damage trees.

In the case of urban trees additional factors such as pollution, soil compaction and vandalism may be involved. Many of these can lead to the ingress of wood-decaying fungi.

Additionally, trees weakened by root disease or decay may be more severely damaged by these environmental factors. Despite the numerous pests and diseases that can attack trees, the majority survive to maturity and fulfill the purpose for which they were grown.

It is only in exceptional circumstances, as, for example, with Dutch Elm Disease, that pests or diseases endanger the survival of whole tree populations. Such instances are generally attributable to the activities of Man upsetting the balance of natural systems.

MONOCOTYLEDON TREES

M*onocotyledon trees* are a kind of plant quite beyond the experience of persons brought up in temperate countries Jand contribute strongly to the overwhelming impression of strangeness and luxuriance of the vegetation felt on entering the tropics for the first time.

All monocotyledonous trees have a certain similarity of appearance which reflects their underlying common characteristics and sets them apart ftom dicotyledonous (broadleaved) trees. They occur in several different Orders, mainly the *Arecales*, *Pandanales*, *Zingiberales* and *Liliales*.

The stem structure with numerous scattered closed vascular bundles (that is without cambium) is fundamentally different from that of dicotyledons (see chapter What is a Tree?). With few exceptions they lack a secondary *cambium*. This means that no extra conducting tissue is formed as the stem ages, and so the size of the crown and number of leaves it can bear is restricted.

Moreover, stem thickness does not increase. Leaves usually have sheathing bases and are formed one at a time; this secures them an ample *vascular* supply. Roots cannot increase in size so increase in water and nutrient supply to the stem depends on an increase in their number; thus *monocotyledonous* trees characteristically have numerous, often fibrous, roots.

Each node bears but one bud. The trunks of many monocotyledonous trees are unbranched, although some are sparsely branched and then the branching is usually dichotomous or apparently so. Most have big leaves, rather few in number. A minority of monocotyledonous trees of the Liliales (for example *Cordyline*, *Dracaena*, some *Aloe*, *Yucca*, some *Vellozia* species) and *Nivenia* species (Iridaceae) have a special kind of secondary thickening. A cylindrical cambium forms around the inner cortex and this develops closed vascular bundles and secondary çortex.

These trees have the same limitations to the development of an extensive root system and vascular supply to the leaves and they resemble in appearance other monocotyledonous trees.

THE PALMS

The palms (family Palmae or Arecaceae) are one of nature's greatest gifts to tropical Man, with a myriad uses. They form the biggest single group of monocotyledonous trees, with over 200 genera and nearly 3 000 species. Their occurrence is strongly centered in the tropics with some subtropical and a few temperate outliers.

As a group they are easy to recognize from all other *monocotyledonous* trees although they share the same basic characteristics. They produce a few large leaves that are borne one at a time and clustered at the stem tip; they are erect and sword-like in the crown center when young.

Leaf construction is more complex than in other monocotyledons. The blade is folded and usually split at the folds which are either displayed along an extended axis, as in the feather palms, or else arise crowded from a short central rib, as in the fan palms.

A few species have no splits, and these entire-leaved palms are spectacular ornamentals. Aerial branching of the stem is rare; clump forming is common. The biggest genus of palms, *Calamus*, some of its 'allies and a few unrelated palms are climbers, adapted to scrambling through forest by spines borne on leaves, leaf sheaths and the inflorescence.

The stem of many commonly reaches 30m (100 ft); the longest ever recorded was 17 gm (556ft) and it is claimed that another which was considerably longer was torn up by elephants before it could be measured.

There is great diversity in inflorescence from the huge terminal panicle of the Talipot (*Corypha umbraculifera*), reaching 6m (20ft) tall by 9-12m (30-40ft) across and containing several hundred thousand flowers, to tiny spikes (for example *Pinanga spp*).

Most palms have the inflorescences borne laterally but in a few they are terminal: in these the stem accumulates starch which is expended in a single giant reproductive burst of flowering and fruiting, after which the tree dies.

The flowers are small and basically have parts in threes but with much variation. Pollination is by insects or in a few cases (*Cocos*, *Elaeis*, *Phoenix spp*) by wind. Fruits are one or few-seeded and also vary greatly in size, from the Double Coconut (*Lodoicea maldivica*), biggest seed in the world, 45 cm (18in) long and weighing 14-23kg (30-50lb), down to pea-sized.

They are nearly all indehiscent and many are fleshy. The greatest number of palms occur in the Asian tropics; Singapore, an island the size of the Isle of Wight, has more kinds than the whole of Africa. Latin America is the region with the second greatest number, including the highest concentration of primitive palms.

Colombia probably has the richest palm flora of any single country. In Europe there are only two native palms, both Mediterranean, a species of Date Palm (*Phoenix theophrastii*) on Crete and the Dwarf Fan Palm (*Chamaerops humilis*), very familiar as an ornamental. In Asia the windmill palms (*Trachycarpus*) reach as far north as the southern Himalaya.

The Chusan or Windmill Palm (*T. fortunei*) is unusual in withstanding frost and snow and is often cultivated in temperate areas. At the southern limit New Zealand has a single species of palm. Few palms occur wild on more than one continent; exceptions include raffia and the oil palms (*Raphia*, *Elaeis spp*) which span the Atlantic and four genera common to Africa and Asia (*Borassus*, *Calamus*, *Hyphaene* and *Phoenix*) and both the Coconut (*Cocos nucifera*) and date palms (*Phoenix* spp).

Palms reach their greatest diversity and abundance in the humid tropics; for example Malaya has about 34 genera and 220 species. They are found from sea level to high in the mountains in all sorts of forest.

Species of wax palm (*Ceroxylon*) reach over 4000m (13000ft) elevation in the Andes, above the tree line, and *Ceroxylon alpinum*, found to 3000m (10,000ft) in Colombia, is one of the world's tallest trees, attaining 6om (200ft)—a splendid, eerie sight, towering over the dwarf mountain scrub.

Palms occur in swamps, for example *Raphia* species in Africa, and a few in mangrove forests, namely *Nypa fruticans* and the Mangrove Date Palm (*Phoenix paludosa*) of Asia and *P. reclinata* of West Africa. Some palms are restricted to semi-deserts, most famous amongst these being the true Date Palm (*Phoenix dactylif ra*). Palms are a well-defined group of plants and are commonly classified as a single family, but this conceals the great diversity of the group, and in fact five separate natural lines can now be recognized, which have each evolved separate distinctive characteristics.

The first group contains nearly all the fan palms (Coryphoid line) and many splendid ornamentals, for example *Acoelorraphe*, *Borassus*, *Corypha*, *Latania*, *Sabal*, *Washingtonia*. The second group has scaly fruits (Lepidocaryoid line) and contains most of the climbers (the rattans), raffia and the sago palms.

The third group contains the single species *Nypa fruticans*. This is a very remarkable plant. It is one of the seven earliest flowering plants in the fossil record (dating back 100-110 million years to the Cenomanian) yet has extremely advanced characters of flower and inflorescence.

It is now found only from the Bay of Bengal to. the Solomon Islands but once grew along the shores of the Tethys sea and to West Africa and America; it is common in the Eocene London Clay flora. The fourth line contains the bipinnate fishtail palms *Caryota* and *Arenga*—the sugar palm genus.

Finally, the fifth and most advanced line are the arecoid palms, a huge alliance of nine separate groups including the cocosoid group (Coconut, oil palms, Cohune Nut and a few climbing palms), the vegetable ivory palms (*Phytelephas* spp) of Latin America and the betel nut group (*Areca* spp).

Many arecoid palms have the trunk topped by a crown shaft, formed of the erect sheathing bases of the leaves and several are as a consequence of this superbly ornamental, witness the Sealing Wax Palm (*Cyrtostachys lakka*) in which the crown shaft is scarlet and the stately royal palms (the genus *Roystonea*) which grace many a tropical avenue.

Several groups of the arecoid line have evolved diminutive palms of the forest undergrowth and some of which make fine house plants; familiar amongst them are members of the small genus *Howeia* of Lord Howe Island and species of the very big Amazonian genus *Chamaedorea*.

Many towns of the tropics and subtropics are graced by ornamental palms but relatively few species are widely grown and the full diversity remains to be exploited.

There is great interest in the warmer parts of North America where the flourishing Palm Society is based; their journal *Principes*, devoted entirely to this one plant family, is a continuous source of infor-mation on all aspects of palms.

The uses of palms by Man stretches back into antiquity and is closely woven into the folklore of the countries where they occur. They provide many of the necessities of life, as well as the refinements of leisure—poles, planks, fruits, oils, fats, waxes, starch, sugar, wine, charcoal, medicines, magic, ritual and totem objects, perfumes, poisons, alcohol, fiber, rattan canes, vegetable ivory, drinking vessels, dragon's blood, beads—the list is endless.

Temperate Man has long imported palm products, for example the trade between the Malay archipelago and China is of great age, and during the last century or so has also stimulated the development of great plantations of a few species, mainly Coconut and oil palms; also the Carnauba Wax Palm (*Copernicia prunifera*) is cultivated in Brazil as a source of wax mainly for use in floor polish.

Several other palms have potential for large-scale commerce and are likely to become economic as the price of energy from fossil-fuels increases in the future. The production of sugar and alcohol will probably be the first to become economically viable. Fibers are another possibility.

Palms are the pre-eminent source of thatch for tropical Man, and thatch from some species, for example sago palms (*Metroxylon spp*) and *Nypa fruticans* though not of Coconut, is durable for approaching io years. Palms also provide poles and planks and the cord to tie them together so that a completely palm-built house is commonplace.

Palms are an important tropical source of sugar, prepared by bruising and cutting the young inflorescence then tapping the exuded fluid which continues to flow for many weeks and can be boiled to yield many pounds of sugar, or fermented to produce palm wine or toddy, which by distillation gives a truly potent spirit.

The Sugar Palm (*Arenga pinnata*) is a principal source; like so many economic plants its native area has never been located and it is only known in cultivation. Lontar or Tal (*Borassus flabellifer*), Coconut and *Nypa fruticans* are also extensively tapped.

The palms which flower just once accumulate starch in their trunks, and from many species this is extracted for human or animal food. The best-known is the Sago Palm (*Metroxylon sagu*) which is native to the Moluccas and New Guinea but now cultivated throughout the eastern tropics.

Nowadays palm starch is for most peoples a famine food but in Borneo nomadic jungle dwellers still subsist on the sago of *Eugeissona utilis*. In South America some Indian tribes fell such palms, and return to them some months later to harvest insect grubs which develop in the decaying trunk—several pounds per tree. Millionaires' cabbage, palmito or heart of palm, are names applied to the edible apex of some palms; it is a crunchy, green-white vegetable reminiscent of celery.

Harvesting destroys the stem, hence its name. This vegetable is especially eaten in South America where species of *Euterpe* are the main source. In a few palms this 'cabbage' is poisonous, for example *Orania* species, or irritant, for example *Caryota* species, but many can provide food for benighted jungle travelers.

Oils and fats can be obtained from the fruits of some palms, pre-eminently Oil Palm and Coconut. Many palms have edible fruits though rather few are widely cultivated for this product, amongst them Salac (*Salacca edulis*) of southeast Asia; the Peach Palm (*Bactris gasipaes*) of tropical America, which is excellent when boiled (this is another palm which has never been found wild), and the Doum Palm (*Hyphaene thebaica*) of Africa and west Asia, which is unusual in its truly dichotomizing trunks and whose fruits taste of gingerbread.

Rattans, the climbing palms of the alliance of *Calamus*, are immensely important throughout the eastern tropics for a host of purposes—rope, furniture, baskets, mats, hammocks, cradles, blow pipes and dragon's blood resin (used in lacquer and medicine).

They enter world trade and there is a steady market at high prices; commercial cultivation is only now commencing, as the source diminishes with continuing conversion of their rain forest habitat to agriculture.

Palm fibers important in world trade are piassaba (*Attalea funifera and Leopoldinia piassaba*) of South America and raffia (*Raphia spp*) from Africa. The latter has the distinction of possessing the world's longest leaf, 23m (75ft) long.

Walking sticks are provided by Malacca Cane (*Calamus scipionum*), the ornamental small lady palms of the genus *Rhapis*, for example the China or Partridge Cane (*Rhapis excelsa*), and Penang lawyers, comprising the larger Malayan species of the genus *Licuala*.

Vegetable ivory, once important for button manufacture, is produced from the hard endosperm of palm seeds, important sources being the South American genus *Phytelephas* and Asian *Metroxylon* (the Melanesian pidgin name Hebe Nut is a corruption of Ivory Nut).

All these items of international commerce are produced from palms cultivated by villagers or gathered from wild jungle palms. Organized large-scale agriculture is based mainly on the Coconut which provides from its endosperm copra, which is a source of hard vegetable oil and cattle food, from the hard endocarp a very high-grade charcoal used in medicine and the food industries, and from the fibrous mesocarp, coir fiber for rope and matting. More recently Oil Palm has come to be very extensively cultivated, and in Malaya palm oil now vies with rubber in value as an export commodity.

The earlier cultivation and breeding work was in West Africa, mainly in small village plantations. The palms as a group truly then deserve their scientific group name, *Principes*—the princes of the plant kingdom—or in another idiom appealing to the adventurous plantsman 'palms are the big game amongst plants.'

OTHER MONOCOTYLEDONOUS TREES

As we have seen the palms are the largest group of monocotyledonous trees, but there are in addition dendroid groups in several other Orders of monocotyledons.

These and the palms have certain important basic features of construction in common which is reflected in a general similarity of appearance, based on their simple stems or crowns with only one or a few orders of branching and rather few large leaves with sheathing bases.

The pandans or screwpines are an entirely tropical genus (*Pandanus*) with 600 species found throughout the Old World tropics. The scientific name comes from the Malay vernacular, and the English name refers both to the compound fruit, reminiscent of a pineapple, and the conspicuously spirally inserted leaves, stiff, leathery, pointed straps with toothed margins borne tightly at the branch tips.

Several species have edible fruits and in the New Guinea highlands and some Micronesian islands have until recently been staple food items; there has been massive selection and very many different clones (forms) exist.

Pandans are also important as a source of fibers for weaving and basketry and one (*Pandanus odorus*) has delicately fragrant leaves used extensively in Malay and Indonesian cooking. *Sararanga* is a related genus, with leaves in four ranks and small, simple fruits in big panicles.

The joshua trees (*Yucca spp*) and dragon trees (*Dracaena* spp) are probably the most familiar monocotyledon trees to inhabit temperate countries because they are cultivated outdoors in Mediterranean and other warm temperate climates, where winter frosts are slight or unknown.

Their trunks reach large girth and the crown is formed of a

dense mass of clusters of strap-like simple leaves on a few, rather stout dichotomizing branches. Yuccas are native to the southern United States, Central America and the West Indies and have developed a complex symbiosis with a moth which pollinates them and hatches its caterpillars within the ovary. Not all the species are trees. Dracaenas come from northern Africa and the Mascarenes.

The famous specimen of the Dragon Tree of Tenerife (*Dracaena draco*) was blown down in 1868 when it was ztm (loft) tall and 14m (45ft) in girth and supposedly 6000 years old. Dragon's blood, a red resin from the trunk, was known to the Greeks and Romans, and for long believed to come from an animal.

These two genera have secondary thickened stems as do *Cordyline* and the few tree species of *Aloe.* Some *Cordyline* have purplish or striped leaves and are familiar as ornamentals and house plants; in New Guinea they are totem plants. Most aloes are rosette plants and a few are trees; the genus is confined to the drier parts of southern Africa.

The leaves are very fleshy and contain a bitter substance. The grass trees of Australia (*Xanthorrhoea spp*) have numerous grass-like leaves arising from a trunk which is made up of the fibrous leaf-bases gummed together with a yellow resin which dries hard.

They occur in fire-swept scrub and are sometimes called 'black boys' in allusion to the charred, blackened stem. The inflorescences are long terminal spikes. A few species of *Vellozia* reach tree size while others are low barely dendroid shrubs or herbs. The flowers are lilylike, on pendulous racemes.

The great Order of the gingers (*Zingiberales*) which includes the canna lilies and bananas, has a few tree members. The Traveller's Palm (*Ravenala madagascariensis*) is the most spectacular. Its leaves are banana-like and are displayed like a gigantic fan which is set apically on a stout trunk.

The inflorescences are pendulous and few in number but large in size and borne in the leaf-axils. The name comes from the water trapped in the ensheathing leaf-bases—solace for the thirsty traveler.

Ravenala is effective as a large-sized foil for a public building but planted in groups has the snag that as the tree grows and new leaves form the plane of the fan slowly rotates, so that an initial effect of formality eventually becomes disarrayed as individual trees develop at differing rates.

Ravenala comes from Madagascar where it forms huge thickets after felling of moist tropical forest. A very similar genus of two species, *Phenakospermum*, occurs in northern South America. A few species of *Strelitzia* develop trunks. This is a big African genus of mainly herbaceous species, also with banana-like leaves, whose showy flowers are subtended by equally showy bracts, and have copious watery nectar.

The yellow, orange and blue colors are typical of bird-pollinated flowers. They are much grown as ornamentals in the tropics. Most strelitzias are herbs, as are the true bananas (*Musa* spp). The apparent stem of a banana plant is in fact the tightly enwrapped leaf-bases, held erect solely by turgor pressure.

Eventually a flower stalk pushes its way up the center and produces the familiar terminal inflorescence that develops into a bunch of bananas. One member of the pineapple family (Bromeliaceae) reaches tree-dimensions.

This is *Puya raimondii* of the high equatorial Andes which develops the pineapple-like tuft of leaves apically on a stout stem and ultimately throws up a huge vertical inflorescence spike taller than a man. Also in South America occurs the only dendroid member of the great arum lily family Araceae.

This is a swamp plant, *Montrichardia*, and grows in dense thickets at least 3m (tuft) tall, fringing water courses in the Amazon basin rain forests. Finally we should mention the bamboos which have hard, woody, hollow stems and one of which reaches 18m (60ft) tall and 1m (3ft) girth.

They are vitally important in the economy of the seasonally dry tropical countries where they are most abundant. Traditionally they provide building materials, conduits and food vessels, although nowadays there is a growing utilization of bamboos as a source of fibers and cellulose for modern industry including paper manufacture.

8

Chapter

TREES OF THE TROPICS

The tropics have a far richer diversity of trees than anywhere else on earth. Tropical trees have for centuries provided many fine cabinet woods and today provide most of the world's hardwood timber. They also provide many spices, gums, resins, latexes, fruits and medicines whose importance will increase in the future as fossil fuels become scarcer.

Numerous tropical trees have spectacular flowers and are widely cultivated for ornament, many of them pantropically. No botanist can consider his education complete without acquaintance with the tropics. Violets and milkweeds grow on trees.

The spurges are represented by hundreds of species and dozens of genera. Malaya has over 80 oaks, and whole families occur which are totally absent from the colder parts of the globe. In the following sections we discuss the important economic and ornamental species from tropical Asia, Africa and America.

Important species that are now grown pantropically will be mentioned in the context of their area of origin. The majority of species included are broadleaves; the other main group of monocotyledon trees, including the palms, has been covered earlier.

TREES OF TROPICAL ASIA

Teak (*Tectona grandis*) one of the most famous and valuable of world timbers, grows wild in the monsoon forests of India, Burma, Thailand and Indochina and has for centuries been exploited, so much so that the more accessible forests have been exhausted. It is also planted there as well as in Java, to which island it was introduced over a millennium ago.

Teak needs a climate with an annual dry season and will not grow in rain forests. These in Asia are currently one of the world's main sources of hardwood timbers, meranti or Philippine mahogony (*Parashorea spp*, *Shorea* spp), keruing or opitong (*Dipterocarpus* spp) and kapur (*Dryobalanops* spp) being prominent.

These are all members of the single family Dipterocarpaceae, which is dominant in the western Malay archipelago. Export is largely to Korea and Japan for processing to plywood, which is then re-exported to the industrialized West. The monsoon forest tree Sal (*Shorea robusta*) of India, Pakistan and Bangladesh, is second to teak as an important timber in southern Asia.

The rain forests too provide many other timbers, including one of the world's lightest (47-77kg/m^3 - 3-5lb/ft^3) which comes from *Alstonia spathulata*, and was once used in the manufacture of 'pith' helmets, and fine cabinet woods, for example ebonies (*Diospyros* spp) and rosewood (*Dalbergia spp*) as well as many general purpose light hardwoods.

From the peat swamp forests of Borneo comes ramin (*Gonystylus bancanus*) which is used for mouldings. Nowadays, large areas of rain forest are being cut down and there is an increasing interest in plantations of trees to replace the natural source in the future as this becomes inadequate. Relatively few species are used for this purpose.

Some are unfamiliar to the layman, although widely utilized in the tropics, for example *Gmelina arborea.* Others have familiar relatives, for example there are several species of pine tree in monsoon tropical Asia (*Pinus kesiya*, *P. merkusii*, *P. roxburghii*, *P. wallichiana*), and these are well-suited to be grown in infertile, seasonally dry places in the tropics and subtropics.

From the rain forests have been selected two relatives of the Monkey Puzzle, the Hoop Pine (*Araucaria cunninghamii*) and Klinki Pine (*A. hunsteinii*) in the New Guinea forests, and another conifer genus, *Agathis*, a relative of New Zealand's famous Kauri Pine.

In plantation all of these grow fast into well-formed tall trees and produce valuable pale, closegrained, knot-free timber. Many of the world's spices come from Asia and mostly from trees. Indeed, outside interest in the Malay archipelago began with the spice trade, and led eventually to the Colonial era as European nations attempted to secure and monopolize the source of supply.

Cloves (*Eugenia caryophyllus*) originate here, but are now mainly grown in East Africa, especially Zanzibar (though Indonesia is the principal market, for flavoring the distinctive local cigarettes). Nutmegs (*Myristica fragrans*) came from the Moluccas and the Dutch, having achieved a monopoly there, forbade export of live material only to find the fruits were transported elsewhere by the group of pigeons which are specialist feeders on the family.

The wall of the nutmeg fruit provides the spice known as mace. Cinnamon is the peeled, dried and rolled bark of a few species of lauraceous trees of genus *Cinnamomum*, marketed as small cylinders known as quills. Production is greatest in Sri Lanka, from whence the highest grades come.

The Seychelles is an important subsidiary center. Western medicine has never exploited the full range of native Asian drug plants and few feature widely in trade but reserpine, from *Rauvolfia serpentina* is important in treating high blood pressure, producing very few side effects.

Derris comes from the roots of climbers and trees of the leguminous genus *Derris*, its use as an insecticide being first discovered by a surgeon in Singapore. Strychnine is obtained from several species of *Strychnos*, a genus of trees and woody forest climbers; *Strychnos nux vomica* is the main source.

There has been more extensive exploitation of resins, gums, waxes and latex for the industrial world, currently at a low ebb with the advent of plastics based on petrochemicals, but with signs of renewed interest. Jelutong, a latex from the giant trees of the genus *Dyera*, is tapped in Malaysia and Indonesia, and is the principal component of bubblegum.

Gutta percha is produced from latex, mainly of members of the family Sapotaceae. *Palaquium gutta* is the best source arid the latex is extracted either from the leaves with hot water or from the bark. The only remaining use of gutta percha is for temporary dental fillings. Until recently it was used in submarine telegraph cables.

It is a better insulant of heat and electricity than rubber. Resin from members of the Dipterocarpaceae and Burseraceae (Damar) and *Agathis* species (Manila copal) still has a small market for a few specialpurpose varnishes and paints.

In Indonesia pine plantations are used to produce turpentine. The dye gamboge yellow comes from resin produced by trees of the genus *Garcinia* and gives its name to the country Cambodia. Asia abounds in fruit trees. Some are now cultivated throughout the tropics, for example the Mango (*Mangifera indica*) of India to Thailand.

Others are well-known throughout the region, for example the Rambutan and Pulasan (*Nephelium lappaceum*), Mangosteen (*Garcinia mangostana*) and Durian (*Durio zibethinus*). The last has achieved notoriety from its very strong flavor, likened by some to onionflavored custard, and from its nauseating smell reminiscent of a malfunctioning sewerage works, but many would agree with A. R. Wallace that 'it is worth a trip to the East to sample a durian.'

These fleshy fruits of the western end of the Malay archipelago are replaced eastward in New Guinea and the islands of the western Pacific by a group of nut-trees which are little-known outside their homelands, species of *Barringtonia* and *Terminalia* and of *Canarium* for oil as well as whole kernels.

Kenari (*Canarium commune*) *is* also cultivated for its edible fruit wall in western Indonesia and traded to China. Breadfruit (*Artocarpus altilis*) is indigenous to the eastern Malay archipelago, and Bligh was in the process of introducing it to the New World at the time of the *Bounty* mutiny.

A later attempt was successful. Its edible relatives are several and include the giant Jackfruit (*A. scortechinii*) of which an individual can weigh 25kg (551b); these latter species are all fleshy and eaten fresh for their flavor rather than as a source of storable starch.

Other tree fruits of the Asian rain forests are less wellknown elsewhere, they include, to name only a few, Mata Kuching ('Cats' Eyes') (another *Nephelium*, *N. malaiense*), Rambai and Tampoi (*Baccaurea griffithii*, *B. motleyana*), Langsat and Duku (*Lansium domesticum*), Sentol (*Sandoricum koetjape*) and Petal (*Parkia speciosa*).

Ornamental tree species from Asia include a few grown nowadays as houseplants, such as the India Rubber (*Ficus elastica*) and *F. benjamina*, which in the wild is a banyan, and the crotons (*Codiaeum spp*).

Some of the loveliest tropical flowering trees originate in Asia. Pride of Burma (*Amherstia nobilis*) is often claimed the most beautiful of all. It was discovered in a Burmese temple garden in 1826 and soon became world famous.

It has proved difficult to propagate and cultivate so remains rare. The flowers hang in racemes 0.6 0.9m (2-3ft) long; each is vermilion and yellow, and averages 20cm (8in) long by locm (¢in) across. The tree has handsome pinnate leaves 0.9m (3ft) long, and the young leaves hang in brownish-pink tassels.

Shower of Gold (*Cassia fistula*) is another beautiful leguminous tree of tropical Asian origin. This is easily grown from seed and is now very commonly cultivated. It bears its big panicles of golden yellow flowers once or twice a year.

The Apple Blossom Cassia (*C. javanica*) is equally lovely with a foaming mass of big pink-white flowers. Yet another legume, deservedly widely cultivated, is the Yellow Flame (*Peltophorum pterocarpum*) with rusty twigs and flower buds and erect yellow panicles later bearing purple-brown pods.

This species is native on the coasts. Finally, *Lagerstroemia speciosa*, a tree member of Lythraceae, must receive mention for its lovely copiously-flowered mauve to pinkish panicles; the timber of this genus is highly prized for boatbuilding. The most famous curiosities amongst Asian trees are the Upas or Ipoh (*Arrtiaris toxicaria*) and the strangling and banyan figs.

The former is, with strychnine, the main constituent of arrow poisons and knowledge of it was long withheld from Europeans; to forestall enquiry the myth was propagated that it killed all that came near it, a fantasy which gained extensive currency in Europe. It has a wide range throughout tropical Asia and in many forests is rare, but it is never found in the forest without tapping scars.

TREES OF TROPICAL AFRICA

African hardwoods have been the most important of tropical timbers imported into Britain and much of Europe in the last quarter century. Most buildings built since the Second World War have some on show as doors, paneling or stairs. Important kinds are African mahogany (*Khaya* spp), sapele and utile (*Entandophragma* spp) *and Guarea* species.

These are all members of the mahogany family (Meliaceae) and come from the rain forests of West Africa. Other rain forest timbers important in international trade are obeche (*Triplochiton scleroxylon*, family Sterculiaceae), gaboon (*Aucoumea klainiana*, family Burseraceae) and *Afzelia* species (family Leguminosae).

In addition afrormosia, the timber of *Pericopsis* (formerly *Afrormosia*) *elata*, another legume, has proved a fine substitute for teak for such purposes as laboratory benches, and iroko (*Chlorophora excelsa*, family Moraceae) is also used instead of teak, for example for garden furniture.

Many of these timbers are used as facing veneers for plywood in which form their attractive grain and color is well-displayed. Some countries have already passed the peak of their supply, for example Ivory Coast, and in Nigeria the internal market now absorbs a high proportion of production.

As the natural rain forests have rapidly become depleted, plantations are being established or alternatively young trees are being planted in lines in logged out forest.

Species which need full light and grow fast are used for these purposes and these include several indigenous African species amongst which several *Terminalia* species (idigbo, afara, limba) and *Nauclea diderrichii* (opepe) are important as well, recently, as obeche.

In the future these names will become increasingly familiar in the European timber trade. Tropical Africa has no indigenous species of pine tree and species from subtropical Asia and America are extensively planted as well as teak and the Asian *Gmelina arborea*.

Tropical Africa also entirely lacks another important family of trees, the Fagaceae, which contains the oaks, beeches and sweet chestnuts.

The African equivalent of South American Balsa is the Umbrella Tree (*Musanga cecropioides*), a fast grower which comes up gregariously in big forest clearings and produces pale light timber. Like Balsa the timber is used for rafts and many village purposes, but it does not enter commerce.

Africa is a useful source of ebony, from some of the many species of the pantropical genus *Diospyros* which occur there (see separate entry). Flame of the Forest or Flamboyant (*Delonix regia*), rivals the Asian tree *Amherstia nobilis* as the tropic's most glorious flowering tree. Both are members of the Leguminosae.

Delonix originates in Madagascar and is reputed to have entered cultivation from a single village tree discovered by a missionary. It is now common everywhere in the tropics and subtropics. The flowers are produced once a year.

They are vivid scarlet and borne copiously all over the shallow, domed crown. The foliage is finely feathery and briefly deciduous in seasonal climates. The pods are huge, flat and woody, im (3.3ft) or more long, borne in pendulous clusters and contain numerous seeds.

The African Tulip Tree (*Spathodea campanulata*, family Bignoniaceae) is the other big African ornamental species which is now a common sight throughout the tropics. The flowers are also bright red, but are tubular and with copious watery nectar. They are borne on the outside of the dark green crown and pollination is by bats.

The leaves are large, pinnate and opposite. *Spathodea* flowers more or less continuously and this redeems the rather ungainly appearance of its illshaped, dense crown. The common red garden Hibiscus (*Hibiscus rosa-sinensis*), a small bushy tree found now in all tropical countries, is believed to have originated in east tropical Africa, but like many cultivated plants it has never been found truly wild.

The most important world tree crop of African origin is coffee. Both *Coffea arabica* and *C. liberica* are indigenous, to the mountain forests of Ethiopia and lowland forests of West Africa respectively; there are also several other species. Coffee is a small tree or shrub, found wild as a component of the forest undergrowth.

The Horseradish Tree (*Moringa oleifera*), native from north-east Africa to India, is now widely grown as a village tree throughout the tropics. The roots, like true Horseradish, are a stimulant to digestion. The seeds contain a saponin as well as up to 38 percent of an oil (Ben Oil) extracted locally for culinary purposes and once used for oiling clocks and watches.

It is scentless, does not go rancid, is an excellent salad oil and makes a good soap. A common small tree of open savanna woodland is the Shea Butter Tree (*Butyrospermum parkii*, family Sapotaceae). The kernels are collected and from them an edible oil extracted which is widely used for cooking. It is a good substitute for lard and can be used for candle- and soap-making.

The oil occurs at 45-55 percent by weight of the seeds. The bark of *Butyrospermum* yields a reddish gum, gutta shea. The Miraculous Berry (*Synsepalum dulcificum*) is another small tree or shrub of the Sapotaceae, native to West Africa where it is also commonly planted on farms and around villages.

The sweet-acid pulp surrounding the seeds has a curious, powerful, lingering after-effect of sweetness. It has greater effect in sweetening acidity, such as sour fruits than in countering bitterness. Nevertheless even substances so bitter as quinine taste sweet if taken as much as an hour or two after it, hence the common name.

Synsepalum has been investigated by Western chemists, although interest in sugar substitutes is now directed elsewhere, for example to the monocotyledon herb *Thaumatococcus daniellii* (Marantaceae) which is also from West Africa.

The Sausage Tree (*Kigelia africana*, family Bignoniaceae) has a wide range in tropical Africa and is now sometimes cultivated elsewhere in the tropics. The big, hanging, sausage-like fruits and other parts have various medicinal uses. The Kapok Tree (*Ceiba pentandra*, family Bombacaceae) is very common in tropical Africa and has many uses.

It is in fact one of the largest trees of the continent, reaching 49m (t6oft) tall and 2m (6.5ft) or more in diameter. It now grows wild as well as being cultivated, but was in fact introduced from America, probably by the Portuguese.

Finally, Africa, like the other tropical continents, has its contingent of curious and fantastic trees. In the Dark Continent many are weird by virtue of possessing huge, grossly swollen trunks. The most famous is undoubtedly the Baobab (*Adansonia digitata*) native to seasonally dry Africa and famous for four things.

Firstly, Baobabs live to an enormous age; over iooo years has been measured by radio carbon dating and much greater ages by less precise methods. Secondly, the diameter of the trunk, which often reaches 9m (3oft) is out of all proportion to the height of only about 12M (40ft).

Thirdly, Baobabs do not continue to grow in size year by year, and big trees may even shrink. This is attributed to periodic droughts. Finally, all parts of the plant are extremely useful, providing timber, fibers, leaves as a vegetable and acid seeds as an important source of vitamin C.

The Cucumber Tree of Socotra (*Dendrosicyos socotrana*, only tree member of the cucumber family, Cucurbitaceae) is another weird and littleknown 'bottle tree.' A species of *Adenium*, related to the Frangipani of America, also occurs on Socotra and it produces similar beautiful and fragrant flowers and poisonous white sap.

There are about 10 species of *Adenium* in total, all African and all have swollen trunks. In the savanna woodlands of central Africa a number of groups of trees have evolved with their trunks below ground and the leafy crown arising only a little above ground level.

This example of convergent evolution in unrelated species is presumably an adaptation to periodic fires; the effect is of an underground forest. The drier parts of Africa also house big dendroid species of the spurge genus *Euphorbia*, with swollen, fleshy, sparsely branched stems, sometimes candelabroid in appearance.

This is another example of convergent evolution, in this case the resemblance is to the New World cacti and is a response to aridity of the habitat. But euphorbias have white sap and thorns in pairs rather than clusters. Finally, the African mountains are famous for two kinds of extraordinary trees, the tree heaths (*Philippia* spp and *Erica arborea*), which form a belt above the rain forests, high on the slopes of the big East African mountains, and which have no equivalent anywhere in the world.

These mountains also have the giant groundsels and lobelias (*Senecio* spp and *Lobelia* spp) found above the level of continuous forest and which do have an equivalent in the Andes. Massive stems, big, terminally tufted leaves and lack of branching give these dicotyledonous trees belonging to highly advanced families a resemblance to the dendroid monocotyledons.

Some aspects of their form can probably be regarded as a response to the extremely harsh climate they inhabit, although they have sometimes been reckoned primitive relics—hulks of the past history of flowering plant evolution.

TREES OF TROPICAL AMERICA

The true or South American Mahogany (*Swietenia macrophylla*) comes from the rain forests of tropical Central and South America where it is of widespread but usually scattered occurrence. Undoubtedly the most famous timber of the region, it has been sought out ever since the discovery of the New World.

The logs are dragged down to a water course and then floated down river for export. Due to nearly five centuries of exploitation *Swietenia* is nowadays a rare tree in much of its range and its cultivation in plantations is seriously hampered by a shoot boring insect *Hypsipyla*.

A second genus of the same family, Meliaceae, is of almost equal fame; this is *Cedrela* or the South American cedars, used amongst other things for cigar boxes. A few other fine tropical American timbers enter world trade.

Lignum vitae (*Guaiacum* species mainly *G. officinale*) provides the heaviest of all commercial woods (1250kg/m^3—80lb/ft^3) and is also extremely strong and tough. It is used for bowling balls, pestles, mortars, pulleys and mallet heads.

It is resinous and one of its most important uses is for the bushing of the stern tubes of ships' propellor shafts, as it combines the requisite strength with self-lubrication. Lignum vitae was once considered an important medicine. Rosewood comes from species of the legume genus *Dalbergia*.

The very light wood balsa (*Ochroma lagopus*), weighing only 150kg/m^3 (101b/ft^3) is the most important of all pale, light tropical timbers, finding a use in model making and formerly also in airplane construction.

There has not yet been such widescale felling of the forests of Latin America for the world timber trade as has taken place in Africa and Asia and this is because many of the tree species have dense, siliceous timbers and rather short, fluted or twisted trunks.

It is still the case that only about 25 species out of the many hundreds which occur make up the bulk of the lumber coTipg from the whole Amazon rain forest, and of these about half comes from a nutmeg-relative *Virola*.

Another fairly important Amazonian timber is jacareuba, from *Calophyllum brasiliense*, which is also exploited in Central America, under the name of santa maria. Wallaba (*Eperua Jalcata*) and greenheart (*Ocotea rodiaei*) are other very heavy timbers which enter world trade.

Trees which are beginning to become important for timber plantations are jequitiba (*Cariniana*), *Cordia* and *Leucaena* species (especially *Cordia alliodora and Leucaena leucocephala*) and probably much will be heard of them in the near future.

But it is the Central American and West Indian pines, mainly *Pinus caribaea* and *P. oocarpa*, which have stolen the scene so far. These species of periodically burned savanna forests are now planted on a huge scale throughout the tropics and subtropics to provide fibers and cellulose, mainly for paper, and on a short rotation of less than 20 years.

Central America is the headquarters of the world's oaks (*Quercus* spp) but although many species occur and there are extensive mountain forests they are unimportant in world trade.

Several world famous fruit trees come from tropical America. The Brazil Nut (*Bertholletia excelsa*) is a common, widespread tree of the Amazonian rain forest, regenerating after disturbance of the forest canopy. The individual nuts are borne in clusters inside a hard, woody case like a cannon ball.

This species has the, curious property of concentrating strontium in the endosperm storage tissues of the nuts, and for a time during the sixties the fruits were perceptibly radioactive due to the accumulation of part of the fallout from aerial atomic explosions.

The nuts are collected wild from jungle trees for both local use and export. Avocado Pear (*Persea americana*) is another South American tree now widely grown and highly esteemed. *Theobroma* is a small genus of undergrowth trees of the western Amazon rain forests and one species, Cacao (*Theobroma cacao*) is now extensively cultivated, mainly in West Africa.

Others are grown locally in South America either for cocoa or for their comestible fruits. The range of *T. cocoa* was extended in pre-Colombian times, for it was an important crop for the Central American civilizations, and chocolate, from *chocolatl*, is one of the few Aztec derived words in the English language.

Papaya or Pawpaw is the rather bland fruit of *Carica papaya*, a sparsely-branched treelet with a terminal tuft of large palmately-divided leaves. Like so many crops its exact place of origin is unknown but all its wild relatives are tropical American.

All parts have a white latex which contains the proteolytic enzyme papain, an important article of commerce, able to digest 35 times its own weight of lean meat. The Cashew Nut, fruit of *Anacardium occidentale*, originates from the West Indies and is also now cultivated pantropically.

The kidney shaped nut is borne on a swollen fleshy receptacle, the Cashew Apple, which is red or yellow and juicy when ripe. The shell contains a highly irritant oil and the nuts are heated before extraction of the kernel to render this less caustic.

Para Rubber (*Hevea brasiliensis*) is of Brazilian origin. The story has been told many times how, in the mid 19th century, Wickham sent seeds to Kew where they were germinated and a few seedlings sent out to Malaya. Of the second consignment a few survived and on them the great rubber plantation industry of the Far East was founded.

Recently, new introductions have been made to increase the genetic diversity for crop breeding and other species of the small genus *Hevea* have been studied, although none so far has such promise. Rubber cannot be grown as a pure crop in plantations in the New World because of a devastating leaf blight fungus.

A huge prewar plantation company, which involved foundation of the town Fordlandia, failed; but very recently resistant races of tree have been bred.

In the late 19th century a major industry grew up within the Amazon based on collecting rubber latex from wild trees, great fortunes were made and the wealthy merchants built elaborate mansions and a great baroque opera house in Manaus, the city of the central Amazon, to which leading European musical companies came on tour.

The rubber boom collapsed once the Asian industry got started. Its traces can still be seen in the old part of Manaus and other Amazonian settlements. Minor forest products from tropical America include the dye haemotoxylin from the wood of a leguminous tree, *Haemotoxylon campechianum;* curare, a powerful nerve poison, from the indigenous *Strychnos* species; and chewing gum from the resinous latex (chicle gum) of *Manilkara* (*Achras*) *zapota*.

This last is a tree of disturbed forest and is particularly common in Central America on the sites of Mayan and Aztec ruins, having established itself after these habitations were abandoned. *Manilkara zapota* produces an edible fruit, known as the Sapodilla Plum, and is nowadays cultivated throughout the tropics.

Fruits of local importance within the region include two palms, the Babassu (*Orbignya speciosa*) and Peach Palm (*Gulielma gassipaes*). Allspice, native to and cultivated in the West Indies, is the rapidly dried unripe fruit of the small tree *Pimenta officinalis*.

Tropical America vies with Asia in the number of superb ornamental flowering trees which originate there. It is the home of some 50 species of the *genus Jacaranda* which have lilac flowers and feathery foliage, of several coral trees (*Erythrina* spp) with their big robust, red or yellow bird-pollinated flowers and of the lovely leguminous tree 'Rose of Venezuela' (*Brownea grandiceps*) with its spectacular heads of deep pink to red blossoms, tightly packed as in a *Rhododendron*, and showy hanging tassels of young pink leaves.

The Sandbox Tree (*Hura crepitans*) a relative of the Brazil Nut, is a curiosity of many tropical botanic gardens, with its massive, fleshy, asymmetric flowers crowded on trunk-borne racemes. Napoleon's Button (*Napoleons heudottii*) is another lesserknown relative, as is the Cannon Ball Tree (*Couroupita guianensis*).

The Brazil Nut family (Lecythidaceae) is in fact concentrated in the New World tropics. The Buttercup Tree (*Cochlospermum vitifolium*) is aptly named, its brilliant yellow flowers, borne on the bare crown, are each ioII.5cm (4-4.5in) across.

The leaves are deeply palmately lobed and covered below with stellate hairs and the capsule contains numerous small seeds covered with a long white cotton-like floss. But perhaps the most lovely of all tropical American ornamental trees are the frangipani trees (*Plumieria alba* and *P. rubra*).

These are small open-crowned trees bearing masses of white or red blossoms of an exquisite, heavy fragrance and are now found planted everywhere in the tropics. In the East they have become associated with temples and burial grounds. Broken parts of the plant exude a copious white latex to which medicinal properties have been attributed.

Other useful trees now planted throughout the tropics are *Gliricidia sepium*, a small, short-holed leguminous species with pale lilac flowers, valuable as a shade tree and for enriching the soil by nitrogen fixation, and the Rain Tree (*Samaneu saman*), one of the most useful of tropica shade trees and one which also produces dark, heavy, stable wood in great demanc for turnery.

The dried leaves have the heavy, new mown hay scent of

coumarin The name derives from 'to kill a dormouse and alludes to the use of scented hay to mask the flavor of rodent poison.

The Kapok Tree (*Ceiba pentandra*) is native to the Amazon region, and is indeed the tallest tree of the hylaean forest, often seen from the rivers as a giant emergent standing head and shoulders above the main forest canopy.

It has now become wild in tropical Africa and is widely planted in Asia. The big leathery capsules contain kapok as a covering to the seeds. To South America goes the distinction of having the tree that grows at the highest altitude—*Polylepis* forms low forests close to the snowline in the equatorial Andes, though these have now been largely removed for firewood and replaced by paramo steppe.

In the paramo occurs the giant *Puya raimondii* (see Other Monocotyledonous Trees). Elsewhere in the high Andean paramo occur *Espeletia*, sparsely branching tree composites, the New World counterpart of the African giant groundsels. Weird trees of the mountain and lowland forests are *Clusia*, many of whose species are stranglers like the figs of Asia.

Perhaps the most curious tree of all, however, is the Cow Tree of Venezuela (*Brosimum galactodendron*) which is a member of the fig family (Moraceae) and .exudes a milky latex in considerable quantity from the cut bark, which has the taste of ordinary milk and is used for just the same purposes.

Chapter 9

TREES OF EVERY KIND

Three main types of trees are popularly recognized in terms of a single character—the leaf. They are the conifers with basically needle- and scale-like leaves, the *broadleaves* which primarily have flattened simple or compound leaves that are generally smaller than those of the third group, the *monocotyledon trees* such as the palms, in which they are also flattened but mainly fan-like or fern-like in appearance.

Today there is no doubt that the broadleaves are the dominant natural tree-form throughout the world, except in the more extreme cooler climates where conifers still prevail.

In temperate and warm temperate areas in particular, forestry policy is often to replace natural broadleaved forest or grassland with conifer monoculture under which conditions these trees thrive.

The palms are mainly tropical with only a few of the 2 Boo species occurring in the subtropics and temperate regions. They are an ancient group and there is some evidence that their distribution was once wider even in the tropics, for example more species in Africa.

Today, the conifers are the only gymnosperms that occur in any quantity. Their history extends back some 300 million years but today they only dominate the cooler and cold areas of the world, such as the vast Boreal Region of the Northern Hemisphere and mountain habitats throughout the world.

Their continuing success compared with other gymnosperm

groups is probably due in part to the evolution of drought resistant features such as the needle- and scale-like leaves. Other gymnosperms with a tree-form are represented by two quite differing groupsthe cycads and the Maidenhair Tree (*Ginkgo biloba*).

Both these are the barest relicts of a flora that dominated the world during Mesozoic times, 225 to about 64 million years ago, although their evolutionary history extends back at least as far as that of the conifers.

The only other primitive tree-like forms found today are the so-called *tree-ferns* which represent only a small proportion of the 12 o00 species of all ferns and although the fossil record of tree-ferns extends back only about 19o million years the record of all ferns goes back 350 million years.

It is interesting to observe the similarity in gross form between treeferns, cycads and palms, all groups that have evolved at quite different times and along vastly different lines, not the least in forms of reproduction.

The last group of tree-like species to be considered are the so-called '*tree cacti*,' which are highly specialized plants adapted to harsh desert climates.

In purely botanical terms they could be considered broadleaves, since they are dicotyledonous angiosperms, but because the majority lack true leaves, having spines instead, and because, at least in the young stage, mechanical support is given by the water storage tissue of the photosynthetic tissues not the wood, these plants bear little resemblance to the conventional broadleaved tree.

Here we therefore give them separate treatment. In this chapter 'Trees of Every Kind' we treat all these groups. Conifers, broadleaves and monocotyledon trees clearly take up to greatest space but tree ferns, cycads, the Maidenhair Tree and 'tree cacti' all have comprehensive coverage for their size.

In the conifers section all genera found throughout the world have been included, despite the fact that many of the Asian and Southern Hemisphere genera only occur in temperate Northern Hemisphere cultivation as shrubs, rockery or alpine subjects.

The dominant status, and consequent great variety, of the

broadleaves makes it impossible to cover all genera to the same detail. Therefore in this chapter we have restricted our coverage to those broadleaved genera native to or cultivated in the cool, temperate and warm-temperate (Mediterranean-type) climates; broadleaved trees of the tropics are covered in the chapter 'Trees of the Tropics.' Selection of genera to be included is difficult since there are many which comprise mostly shrubs but which include some trees. We have included such genera when they contain important trees even if the majority are shrubs or smaller.

Once selected, coverage of species is comprehensive in that *all* important species are dealt with, whether trees or not. Thus, for example, under the entry '*Willows*,' as well as the well-known trees, we also include the shrubby sallows and osiers and even the Arctic Willow which only grows to a height of a few centimetres.

A general account of monocotyledon trees, including the palms, is also given, highlighting their distribution, ecological and economic importance. The text in 'Trees of Every Kind' falls into two groups: main text and concise tables. All entries have a discursive main text that gives details of number of species, distribution, diagnostic features of the genus, general horticultural and economic importance and diseases and pests where relevant, plus any specific interesting information relevant to that genus.

About 70 genera also have concise tables which, where possible, list all the species of the genus, for example the beeches (*Fagus*) with 8-10 species, or for the larger genera, for example *Rhododendron*, list the main species.

The majority of these tables are accompanied by an artwork panel of representative species plus a map of native distribution, green for conifers, orange for broadleaves. The table entries give concise facts on common names, distribution and diagnostic features for each species, plus extra details of horticultural or economic importance where relevant.

Wherever possible the species in each table are divided into natural divisions (*Subgenus*, *Section*, *Series* etc) but, where there is no such natural division available, but the species can be grouped, the general terms *Group I*, *II*, *III*... have been used. In some cases an entire table or parts of it have been constructed in the form of a key, coded by letters of the alphabet.

Thus the first keyed entries will be under A, with the alternative AA and even AAA. Further keyed items work through the alphabet *B*, *BB;* C, CC etc.

In the main text, dimensions are given in metric measurements with Imperial measures in parentheses, but for conciseness only metric dimensions are used in the tables. When giving dimensions of, for example, a leaf it is often necessary to show both the normal parameters and extreme limits that may be found reasonably often; thus (to)12-15(17)cm long indicates normal dimensions of 12-15cm but with common extremes of as little as iocm or as much as 17cm.

Most trees have a number of popular or common names and here we have given as many alternatives as possible. With regard to the scientific name or binomial there *should* of course be just one correct name. However, it is often not as simple as this since historically several names have been applied to a single species.

Here we have always used the *currently* accepted scientific name, as far as is possible, throughout an entry but at first mention we have also given other synonyms either in parentheses or by using an = sign.

Throughout this work, scientific terminology has been kept to a minimum, but inevitably some has had to be used for the sake of conciseness. For this reason a comprehensive illustrated Glossary has been provided at the end of the book and the chapter 'What is a Tree?' should be consulted for an account of the structure, reproduction and growth of trees.

TREE-FERNS

Unlike the other tree species mentioned in this book, tree-ferns are true ferns of the Class Filicopsida, related to the common Male Fern (*Dryopteris filix-mas*) and Bracken (*Pteridium aquilinum*). In most ferns, however, the stem is reduced to a compact rootstock, as in the Male Fern, or elongated, as in the rhizome of Bracken.

In both cases the aerial foliage, both sterile and fertile leaves (or fronds as they are often called in ferns), arises, even in Bracken, at ground level direct from that stem. 'Tree-fern' is the name given to members of the family Cyatheaceae in which the rhizome is erect and stout and forming a trunk, with a crown of leaves at its apex.

This arborescent growth is also developed in *Sadleria*, a genus of the Blechnaceae, and occasionally in other *Blechnum* species, for example *Blechnum braziliense*. It is only in the Cyatheaceae, however, that the plants reach any large size and ecological importance and the account below will be confined to those species.

Fossil tree-ferns have been found as far back as the Jurassic and that called *Coniopteris hymenophylloides* is most like *Dicksonia.* The gross morphology of the tree-fern stem differs considerably from that of the angiosperm tree trunk.

First, the tree-fern rarely branches; when it does, the stem divides dichotomously into two equal branches. Occasionally side branches may form, for example in *Cyathea mexicana*, from adventitious buds at the base of old petioles. Second, the tree-fern is without a true bark layer (periderm) although its outer surface is roughened by leaf-stalk remains and often covered with lichens, mosses and other epiphytes as in other trees of the tropical forest.

Third, there is no massive root system as in true trees; the lower part of the stem has many adventitious roots which become entangled and form a tough covering often doubling the thickness of the trunk, thus supporting it.

Tree-ferns may reach up to 25m (82ft) but at this height they are usually supported by surrounding vegetation. The internal organization of tissues of the tree-fern is similarly less advanced although, at the cellular level, xylem (water-transporting cells) and phloem (sugar-transporting cells) are present and function as they do in higher plants but, unlike conifers and broadleaved trees, there is no secondary tissue and the fern trunk cannot increase in girth.

The xylem and phloem are associated in vascular bundles (*meristeles*) which are embedded in an often corrugated cylinder of lignified fibers (*sclerenchyma*) collectively called a *dictyostele.* The leaves are arranged in a spiral arrangement around the stem and form a rosette at its apex which is protected by scales or hairs. The number of mature leaves in the crown varies with the species, being from five or six, as in *Cyathea contaminans*, to as many as 40, as in *Cyathea atrox.*

In some species the leaf falls upon dying through the action of a rapid abcission layer leaving a characteristic scar on the trunk surface; in others, the petiole remains as a persistent covering for many years, for example *Dicksonia antarctica* and *Cyathea pseudomuelleri.* The leafarchitecture is that of a typical fern, usually being twice to four times divided.

The midrib (*rhachis*) and petiole (or *stipe*) may be covered in scales or thorns (as in *Cyathea*) or stiff bristles (as in *Dicksonia*). The leaf blade tissue is similar in anatomy to angiosperms but there is less ecological variation in thickness or adaption to drought.

Along each side of the petiole are peg-like outgrowths called *pneumathodes;* on the young leaf they act as respiratory or water-control organs. Like most other ferns reproduction is by spores formed on the backs of normal green leaves. In some species, such as *Cyathea lurida*, the fertile leaves are morphologically distinct, being reduced in area.

The spores are produced in *sporangia* growing in clusters called *sori*, which are protected when young, or in some species until the spores ripen, by a membranous flap or cover called an *indusium.* Spores give rise to the sexual generation, which is a small wedge-shaped platelet of green cells (*gametophyte*), embedded in which are the sexual organs. On the fertilization of the female egg-cell by the motile male sperm a new tree-fern (*sporophyte*) plant develops, which may not reach maturity for t o to 15 years.

The Cyatheaceae is divided into four subfamilies : *Dicksonia* and *Cyathea* are placed in the Cyatheoideae which also includes *Cnemidaria* and *Lophosoria*, two nonarborescent tropical American genera. Other genera in the family are *Cystodium* (closely related to *Dicksonia*), *Culcita*, *Thyrsopteris*, *Cibotium* and *Metaxya;* all are nonarborescent. The main differences between *Cyathea* and *Dicksonia* can be summarized as follows. *Cyathea* has scales on its stem apex, petiole, midrib and veins; its sori are in the middle rather than the edge of the leaf; they may lack indusia or more likely have a saucer- or cup-like one which may, in some species, enclose an entire sorus.

Dicksonia, on the other hand, has stiff hairs or bristles and sori on the edges of the leaf which are protected by thin flap-like indusia on their inner face and the reflexed margin of the leaf on the outside.

Dicksonia comprises some 25 species distributed in the Southern Hemisphere. In New Zealand they grow from sea level to boom (2 oooft) in the *Nothofagus-Podocarpus-Dacrydium* forests.

In the southernmost latitudes *D. squarrosa* regularly withstands frost. In southeast Australia and Tasmania, *D. antarctica* is an important constituent in the *Nothofagus* forest where it forms a 3m (ioft)-high stratum beneath the dense canopy, young treeferns being able to grow even when receiving only 1 percent of the total light.

If the forest is burnt dicksonias survive, their growing tips protected by dense hairs. *Dicksonia* spreads into the tropical areas of New Guinea and the Malesian archipelago reaching Sumatra and Luzon (*D. blumei*) where they grow in mid-montane rain forest. Eight species are found in the Americas reaching as far north as Mexico (*D. cicutaria*).

The genus is not found in Africa but one endemic species (*D. arborescens*) is found on the island of St. Helena. *Cyathea* contains over 700 species, spread throughout the tropics, north to the Himalaya and North Honshu (*C. spinulosa*), south to Tasmania (*C. australis*) and the southern tip of New Zealand, where *C. smithii* grows in the *Metrosideros lucida* forest within a few metres of the ice of Franz Josef glacier.

Elsewhere in south and southeast Asia tree-ferns are common throughout the everwet rain forest becoming a significant component in the mid- and upper-montane forest particularly where clouds regularly rest.

Treeferns are a conspicuous member of open grassland above

the tree line, about 3 000m (10000ft) in New Guinea, Sumatra and Sulawesi.

Surprisingly, although each plant must produce many grams of spores, germination or dispersal is low and species are not wide ranging, and almost each mountain range will have its endemics, for example *C. pseudomuelleri* of Mount Wilhelmina.

A few species are widespread and common in secondary forest and near rivers throughout southeast Asia and islands, for example *C. contaminans.* The genus is less dominant in Africa and there *C. dregei*, a savanna species, can withstand periodic burning.

In America the genus has its center of speciation in tropical South America, again mainly as a forest species, reaching Mexico in the north and Paraguay in the south.

Dicksonia fibrosa, called '*Whekiponga*' by the Maoris of New Zealand, is used in the building of their huts and fences since the trunks last well in the ground and there is a belief that rats cannot gnaw their way through such tough material.

It is also used both structurally and decoratively in ceremonial houses (runaga-houses) where the outer surface is shaved off to accentuate the gray and black pattern left by the leafscars.

Cyathea species are used for house building by native peoples throughout its range and living trees are often left for this purpose when forest is cleared for gardens. Maoris make jugs and vases from *C. dealbata* (called Ponga—hence Ponga ware) and other New Zealand species.

When shaved the vascular tissue and leafgaps make an attractive pattern. The Maoris also use the pith from the upper part of the trunk as a type of sago and they, as do natives in New Guinea, Borneo, Indonesia and elsewhere, eat the young unfurling fronds as a vegetable. Dried fronds are also used for bedding by Maoris.

In Sabah, hollowed tree-fern stems are used as bee-hives. The masses of adventitious roots at the bases of *Cyathea* trunks are used in orchid culture, either as sawn solid slabs or broken in potting mixtures. The trade in all species of *Dicksonia* and *Cyathea is* prohibited, without special license, by the Trade in Endangered Species Convention.

Tree-ferns are cultivated as ornamentals in parks in warm temperate and tropical areas, for example several *Dicksonia* species and *Cyathea medullaris.* Once established they require very little management; propagation from spores is slow and germination rate low. *Dicksonia antarctica* is grown in conservatories in Europe and is often established outside in the more oceanic areas. The slowness of growth is a deterrent to short-term landscapers.

CYCADS

The cycads, comprising nine or perhaps ten living genera, are a group of very primitive woody plants which look like palms, although they are not at all closely related to this group. They represent the second largest order of living gymnosperms.

They are distinguished from the conifers by a number of important characters, most conspicuously by their palmlike habit and large pinnately-compound leaves, but also by quite numerous structural and reproductive characters.

Perhaps more than any other group of plants, except *Ginkgo biloba* (Maidenhair Tree), the cycads deserve to be called 'living fossils,' for the group reached its climax of evolutionary development in the Mesozoic era (about 200 million years ago) and since then has apparently declined without undergoing any appreciable evolutionary change.

The earliest fossil cycads are now known from the Permian period of the late Paleozoic (about 240 million years ago) and these, in the form of their seedbearing organs and in other characters, were very like the living genus *Cycas.*

In the succeeding Triassic and Jurassic periods, cycads enjoyed a widespread distribution and, judging from the abundance of fossilized leaves in many deltaic sediments laid down during these periods, the plants were often abundant.

As fossil plants are nearly always preserved in a dismembered state—and cycads are no exception - few of these Mesozoic forms have yet been reconstructed, but those that have showed surprisingly little difference from some of the living representatives.

The geographical distribution of the living genera is interesting, suggesting that they are of ancient origin. *Cycas*, with about ao species, is distributed most widely: it extends from Polynesia to Madagascar and northward to Japan; *Stangeria*, with only a single species, is confined to South Africa and *Encephalartos* (about 30 species) is more widely distributed in tropical and southern Africa.

Bowenia, with only two species, is in northern Australia and *Macrozamia* (14 species), with *Lepidozamia* (two species), which is sometimes distinguished from *Macrozamia* as a separate genus, are also Australian.

Ceratozamia (four species) and *Dioon* (three to five species) are found in Mexico and Central America. *Microcycas* (one species only) is confined to Cuba and *Zamia* (30-40 species) is more widely distributed in tropical America.

This pattern of distribution is usually interpreted as meaning that the cycad genera are relict and happen to have survived in these relatively confined areas. As cycads are very ancient plants it is not surprising that they exhibit many peculiar features, some of which may be of a truly primitive nature.

In habit most are rather palm-like with an unbranched erect stem bearing a crown of leaves. It is not known if this is a truly primitive condition or whether it may represent a reduction from something more elaborate.

It is difficult to ascertain the habit of the fossil forms. *Macrozamia hopei*, a native of Queensland, is reputed to be the tallest of the cycads, reaching a height of about 2om (65ft). Some living cycads have only a short subterranean stem; this is likely to be a modified and reduced condition.

They are extremely slow-growing and longlived plants. It has been estimated that some living specimens may be over 1000 years old. They produce new leaves at rather prolonged intervals and may some times enter a dormant phase when no new growth occurs for several years.

Like all other known gymnosperms, cycads are woody plants but their wood is peculiarly spongy. The leaflets of the pinnately-compound leaves in most cycads have a system of forking veins running more or less parallel but in *Cycas* there is only a single mid-vein and in *Stangeria* the leaflets have a fern-like venation with a mid-vein and forking laterals.

The root system is not without peculiarities. Some roots grow up to the soil surface and these branch profusely to form coralloid masses. These roots contain a microscopical plant, a blue-green alga, in a special layer of cells in the outer tissues.

The cvcad is believed to benefit by the fixing of atmospheric nitrogen by the alga. All cycads have separate male and female plants. In all except the female plants of *Cycas*, the reproductive structures are borne in massive cones (usually terminally on the stem), growth of the stem then being continued from a bud near the cone base.

In the female of *Cycas* there are no cones; instead the seed-bearing megasporophylls, which resemble the vegetative leaves to some extent, are borne in place of ordinary leaves and the stem therefore goes on growing and producing new leaves beyond.

There are a number of exceptional characteristics of the reproductive process but perhaps the most interesting of all is the production of swimming male sex cells (sperms). Two are produced in each germinated pollen grain after pollination of the ovules (young seeds).

In only one other seed plant—the Maidenhair Tree—are motile sperms produced. Cycads are of enormous scientific interest but of little economic value. They are sometimes called sago palms because the soft, starch-rich tissues of the stem in some species, for example *Cycas circinalis* and *C. revoluta*, can be used to prepare a kind of sago.

The large seed kernels can also be eaten but it is said that cycad tissues may be poisonous unless prepared in a certain way. Cycads, especially *Cycas species*, *are* cultivated as greenhouse ornamentals in *temperate countries or outdoors* in *tropical gardens.* The one most commonly grown as an ornamental is *Cycas revoluta.*

THE MAIDENHAIR TREE

The Maidenhair Tree (*Ginkgo biloba*) is the only living representative of a large ancient Order of conifer-like trees. The name

Ginkgo is derived from the Japanese name for the plant or its nuts, the latter being regarded as a delicacy in the East.

The Maidenhair Tree is sacred according to the Buddhist religion and has been cultivated for many centuries in both China and Japan, especially in the grounds of temples.

It became known to Western science in the 18th century when the first specimens were planted in Europe. For some time it was believed that the species may have been saved from extinction only by cultivation in the Far East but there is now good evidence for believing that it occurs in a truly wild state at the borders of Chekiang and Anhwei provinces in eastern China.

Within the last aoo years the tree has been planted widely and has been grown successfully under many different conditions of soil and climate. It is also remarkably free of disease and resistant to pests and air pollution.

The Order Ginkgoales flourished mainly during the Mesozoic era, especially during the Jurassic period (about 150 million years ago) when the great dinosaurs dominated the fauna. The genus *Ginkgo* itself probably extends back to this period but the group was very rich in species and some of them certainly represent distinct genera. *Ginkgo* enjoyed a worl d-wide distribution and the species were no doubt important constituents of the flora.

Fossil leaf remains are often found abundantly in deltaic sediments laid down during Mesozoic times. Toward the end of the Mesozoic era *Ginkgo* declined and this continued during the Tertiary until today only the one species remains.

Ginkgo forms a massive tree and old specimens—some are believed to be more than 1000 years old—attain a very large size. In the young tree there is usually a strong leader which forms the main trunk. The branches are somewhat straggly and these give the tree its rather distinctive appearance in the winter leafless condition.

The leaves are especially interesting, with a wedge-shaped leafblade borne on a long stalk (petiole); the venation is an open forking system without any vein fusions. It is the delicate fern-like foliage and the shape of the lamina that account for the tree's popular English name of Maidenhair Tree.

In the fall the foliage turns a brilliant shade of yellow. There are separate male and female trees. It appears that most of the earlier specimens planted in Europe were male, the first female one being recorded near Geneva in 1814.

Some trees in cultivation have had branches of the opposite sex grafted onto them. The pollen-bearing cones are not especially distinctive, being similar in a general way to the male cones of conifers. The seeds are borne usually in pairs but sometimes on stalks which appear to be equivalent *morphologically* to the male cones.

Both are carried on leafy dwarf-shoots. Thus, there is no female cone in *Ginkgo* comparable with that in conifers. One of the most remarkable features of the reproductive cycle in *Ginkgo is* the presence of swimming male cells (sperms) similar to those found in cycads.

Indeed, there are several features of seed development which are similar in cycads and *Ginkgo.* It is believed that these do not indicate any close relationship but rather that they are primitive features which have been retained by these extraordinary ancient and primitive plants.

Ginkgoes grow well in most temperate regions except the cold northern regions. They seem impartial to soil type so long as it is fertile. They grow best in sunny positions. They make imposing specimen trees but are also often planted in avenues; they are tolerant of pollution and so are useful trees for industrial areas.

Cultivars available include '*Fastigiata*,' a columnar form with semierect branches, 'Pendula' with weeping branches and 'Tremonia' which has a conical form.

The mature seed has a soft outer fleshy layer which has the unpleasant odor of rancid butter. For this reason male trees are usually preferred for avenue planting. In the Orient the white seed kernel is regarded as a delicacy.

CONIFERS

The living conifers and taxads (yews) comprise some 50 genera divided among seven families. They are the only numerically and economically important groups of gymnosperms, the other groups containing tree forms being the cycads and Maidenhair Tree (*Ginkgo biloba*) already dealt with.

Conifers are an ancient group, their fossil history extending back to the late Carboniferous period (300 million years ago). Several families are represented only by fossils. The living families themselves are mostly ancient.

Thus, the monkey puzzle family (Araucariaceae) and redwood family (Taxodiaceae) extend back to the Jurassic period (195 million years ago) and the pine family (Pinaceae) at least to the Lower Cretaceous (135 million years ago).

Conifers are sharply divided into the Northern Hemisphere group and the Southern Hemisphere group. Although this general pattern of distribution probably has extremely ancient origins and may be related to the period in the past when there were two major land masses separated by the east-west running Tethys sea.

Certainly other factors are involved. For example, there has undoubtedly been much extinction. There is good evidence that in the Jurassic and Cretaceous periods members of the Araucariaceae grew in Europe and other areas of the Northern Hemisphere.

Many conifer genera now confined to relatively small areas once enjoyed a very much wider distribution. Thus, to give one example, *Sequoia sempervirens* (Coast Redwood), now confined to western North America, was in earlier geological times widely distributed in the Northern Hemisphere.

There are several Far Eastern genera which were once widely distributed. The Pleistocene glaciations (2 million years ago) pushed many genera to the south, a contraction from which not all have fully recovered.

Most conifers are trees of cooler climates (either high latitude or high altitudes). Few occur in tropical or subtropical lowlands. Large areas in higher latitudes are still naturally dominated by conifer forest, although the virgin forests have largely been exploited for timber.

Many conifers of particular value as timber trees have been planted extensively well beyond their areas of natural distribution.

Pinus radiata (Monterey Pine) which is confined as a native to a limited area of California, has been planted in many areas of Australia, New Zealand and South Africa and has become a very important timber tree.

The '*softwoods*' of commerce are by definition the timbers produced by conifers. The term is not altogether appropriate, for the softest woods known are in fact obtained from broadleaved trees (*dicotyledons*), and some conifer woods are fairly hard, for example Yew (*Taxus baccata*).

Softwoods, however, have a greater homogeneity than hardwoods (that is broadleaf tree woods) because they lack the same differentiation of their elements (see chapter What is a Tree?).

Softwoods are used not only as an important constructional material, but also in various manufacturing industries (paper, textiles, synthetic board and packing materials, chemicals etc). Resins produced by conifers are important as the source of turpentine and various other substances used in the paint, pharmaceutical and perfumery industries.

As a source of food, conifers are of little value. The seed kernels of a number of pines are eaten, especially the Stone Pine or Umbrella Pine (*Pinus pinea*)—the 'pignons' of Mediterranean regions.

Another use of increasing importance is in horticulture. There are very numerous horticultural varieties of many conifers which have been selected for their special ornamental value.

Some members of the cypress and pine families (*Cupressaceae* and *Pinaceae*) are particularly rich in named horticultural varieties, many of them of dwarf form and prized for 'alpine' gardens.

The only known intergeneric hybrids among conifers (*x Cupressoc-yparis*) have arisen in cultivation. The best-known hybrid is *x C. leylandii*, *a* cross between *Chamaecyparis nootkatensis* and *Cupressus macrocarpa*.

This hybrid species is remarkably vigorous and is now widely grown as a hedge plant and screenforming tree. The conifers are generally considered to represent an Order Coniferales (= Coniferae) within the Class Coniferopsida. Living conifers (including the yews) comprise seven families, which are given in the accompanying table together with the genera belonging to them. Here the Taxaceae is included within the conifers, but some botanists would regard these as representing a separate Order.

One reason for this is that their seeds do not seem to be borne in cones in the manner of typical conifers, for example *Pinus*.

In this, the Taxaceae is not alone—typical cones are not formed in the southern pine family (*Podocarpaceae*) and the cow's tail pine family (Cephalotaxaceae).

These three families, because of the absence of typical (female) cones, are commonly and conveniently referred to as 'taxoids' to distinguish them from the remaining four families which have recognizable cones and are correspondingly known as 'pinoids.'

The case of the junipers (*Juniperus*—Cupressaceae) may, at first glance, seem exceptional as a 'pinoid'; the fruiting cone is fleshy and commonly known as a 'berry.' Closer examination, however, soon reveals the characteristic cone structure and it is merely the fleshy scales which are misleading.

Some modern texts refer to the '*taxoids*' as having 'imperfect cones' and the '*pinoids*' as having 'perfect cones.' This raises the question of the term to be used for the female reproductive structure. The term cone is quite acceptable for the 'pinoids' but not for the 'taxoids' (for the reason already given).

Traditionally the term 'female flower' has been used for both 'pinoids' and 'taxoids' and this is still used by some distinguished taxonomists, but others, equally distinguished, would restrict the term 'flower' to the Angiosperms (flowering plants) only, although even here the word has to be severely stretched to cover all cases.

In this book, the practice has been adopted to use the words male cone for the male reproductive structures of both 'pinoids' and 'taxoids' and female cone for the female reproductive structures of the 'pinoids'; 'female cone' (within inverted commas) has been adopted for the female structures of the 'taxoids.'

In other words, cone = perfect cone, 'cone' = imperfect cone, to use the other current expressions for the female structures. In biological terms, this distinction between 'pinoids' and 'taxoids' is significant because the former group is adapted to wind dispersal of its seeds (except *Juniperus*) and the latter (including *Juniperus*) to animal dispersal.

DIAGNOSTIC FEATURES OF THE CONIFER FAMILIES

Pionids

Pinaceae—the Pine Family

Leaves needle-like and, like the 'cone-scales, spirally arranged but sometimes, by twisting, appearing two-ranked; buds scaly; male and female cones on the same plant (monoecious); cone-scales of two kinds - bract-scales and ovuliferous-scales, the latter separate from and borne in the axils of the bract-scales and bearing two inverted ovules on the upper surface, these giving rise to a distinctive type of seed with a membranous wing extending from the base; microsporophylls (stamens) of male cone with two pollen sacs; pollen grains with two bladderlike wings except in *Larix*, *Pseudotsuga* and *Tsuga*.

Widespread in the Northern Hemisphere. Ten genera: *Abies* (firs), *Cathaya*, *Cedrus* (true cedars), *Keteleeria*, *Larix* (larches), *Picea* (spruces), *Pinus* (pines), *Pseudolarix* (Japanese Golden Larch), *Pseudotsuga* (Douglas firs), *Tsuga* (hemlocks or hemlock spruces). (*Cathaya* is a Chinese genus but as yet no material or data is available in the West.)

Taxodiaceae—the Redwood Family

Leaves linear to awl-shaped and, like the cone-scales, spirally arranged (except *Metasequoia*, where they are opposite), buds not scaly; monoecious; cone-scales not distinct as bract- and ovuliferous-scales, these, allegedly, being almost completely united to form a virtually single structure and each bearing two or more erect or inverted ovules which give rise to seeds which, in some genera, have marginal wings.

Microsporophylls with two to nine pollen sacs; pollen without wings. Nine genera, eight in Northern Hemisphere, but *Arthrotaxis* is Southern Hemisphere: *Arthrotaxis* (Tasmanian cedars), *Cunninghamia*, *Glyptostrobus*, *Metasequoia* (Dawn Redwood), *Sciadopitys* (Japanese Umbrella Pine), *Sequoia* (Coast Redwood), *Sequoiadendron* (Big Tree, Giant Sequoia or Sierra Redwood), *Taiwania*, *Taxodium* (swamp cypresses).

Araucariaceae—the Monkey Puzzle Family

Leaves narrow to broad with parallel veins, and, as also the cone-scales, spirally arranged; monoecious or dioecious (sexes on separate plants); bract- and ovuliferous-scales not distinct, but allegedly, fused into a single structure and each bearing a single ovule, the subsequent seed being shed with the cone-scale. Male cone relatively large; microsporophylls with up to about 12 pollen sacs, pollen without wings. Two genera, mainly Southern Hemisphere: *Agathis* (kauri or kauri pines), *Araucaria* (monkey puzzles).

Cupressaceae—the Cypress Family

Adult leaves mostly small and scale-like (juvenile leaves sometimes needle-like) typically in opposite pairs, rarely in whorls of three; monoecious or dioecious; cones more or less globose, small, 2-3cm (0.8-1.2in) diameter, the scales in pairs and *either* peltate or flattened and imbricate, at least finally more or less woody (berry-like in *Juniperus*), the fertile scales with one to numerous erect ovules; seeds winged or not.

In *Juniperus* the (ovulate) cone is much reduced to a single pair (or whorl of three to eight) fertile scales which coalesce and become fleshy. In the typical cone of this family the scale is commonly interpreted as resulting from the complete fusion of a bract- and an ovuliferousscale.

Seventeen genera: *Callitris*, *Calocedrus*, *Chamaecyparis* (false cypresses), *x Cupressocyparis*, *Cupressus* (cypresses), *Diselma*, *Fitzroya*, *Fokienia*, *Juniperus* (junipers), *Libocedrus*, *Neocallitropsis*, *Papuacedrus*, *Pilgerodendron*, *Tetraclinis*, *Thuja* (arborvitae), *Thujopsis*, *Widdringtonia*.

Taxoids

Podocarpaceae—the Southern Pine Family

Leaves spirally arranged in all except *Microcachrys* and scale-like or needle-like but in *Phyllocladus* the leaves are extremely reduced, their photosynthetic function being taken over by flattened stems (cladodes); monoecious or dioecious; cones much reduced to a few scales and maturing to contain only one seed (from an inverted ovule), which may be surrounded or embedded in a fleshy structure known as the epimatium—of doubtful homology, but commonly interpreted as an ovuliferous-scale; cones may be borne on a fleshy stalk or 'foot' (hence 'podocarp'); pollen grains mostly winged. The family is virtually confined to the Southern Hemisphere, only a few species extending north of the Equator. Seven genera. *Acmopyle*, *Dacrydium*, *Microcachrys*, *Microstrobus*, *Phyllocladus*, *Podocarpus* (podocarps), *Saxegothaea*.

Cephalotaxaceae—Cow's Tail Pine Family

Leaves spirally arranged on main shoots, but appearing as in two opposite ranks on laterals; pollen sacs three to five; usually dioecious; cones much reduced comprising a few decussate pairs of simple bracts each subtending two ovules, but there is generally only one seed in the whole cone when it reaches maturity; the nature 'cone' is relatively large, protrudes beyond the original cones, and has an outer fleshy layer (aril) with a thin inner woody layer. *Cephalotaxus* is the only genus, the four to seven species being natives of the Northern Hemisphere.

PINES (GENUS PINUS)

The true pines (genus *Pinus*) are a group of 70-100 species of evergreen conifers found almost exclusively in the north temperate zones of the Old and New Worlds. They range from just south of the equator in the Malay Archipelago, northward to the limit of the northern coniferous forests on the edge of the Arctic Circle.

Pines are predominantly trees of pyramidal habit but a few shrubs occur. The leaves in adult plants are of two types: bracts and adult leaves. The bracts are scale-like and are borne spirally, usually on lower parts of young shoots (long shoots).

They are normally deciduous and bear in their axils so-called undeveloped or '*short shoots*.' On these short shoots arise the adult leaves (needles) which are borne in clusters of two to five (usually two, three or five but at times up to eight or reduced to one). The needles spring from a basal sheath of 8-12 bud scales.

These adult leaves persist for up to five years or more. The male and female cones are separate but on the same tree. The male cones are short and cylindric, and are catkin-like.

The female cones have a central axis bearing spirally arranged bract-scales, in the axils of which eventually arise the conescales (ovuliferous or fertile scales) each bearing two ovules on the lower surface.

The apex of these cone-scales becomes enlarged and this enlargement (apophysis) may bear a more or less central spine or prickle. Part of the apophysis may be raised and differentiated to form what is called an umbo and this may bear a spine or prickle.

The cones may be erect, inclined or pendulous. Pollination is by wind and pollen is often so abundantly produced that it may become visible. Dispersal of pollen is aided by each grain having two bladder-like wings.

At least a year elapses between pollination in the spring and fertilization, during which time the female cone remains small. After fertilization it grows rapidly to adult size, at first green becoming brown, and seeds are commonly ripe by about the following fall. Some species, however, require an extra year.

The seeds in most species are winged, the wing almost always being longer than the seed. The Bristle-cone Pine (*Pinus aristata*) is one of the most remarkable species. It giows in the Rocky mountains of Colorado, Utah, Nevada and Arizona.

In these high-altitude conditions it grows extremely slowly, becoming gnarled and stunted with much dead wood. Some specimens are reckoned to be the oldest living things on earth today, reaching ages of up to 6000 years. Pines are subject to a number of fungus diseases, especially on acid soils with poor drainage.

Amongst the rust fungi are: *Cronartium flaccidum* which causes blisters on the branches of the Weymouth Pine (*P. strobus*) and other five-needle pines. The alternate hosts are species of *Ribes* (currants). The disease is serious, causing stunting of the trees.

Another rust disease is caused by *Coleosporium senecionis* on the Scots Pine (*P. sylvestris*) and produces similar blisters, but only on the needles. The alternate hosts are groundsels (*Senecio* spp). Amongst the larger parasitic fungi of pines are the bracket fungi *Heterobasidion annosum* and *Phaeolus schweinitzii*, both serious agents of disease in forests and plantations.

There are also many insect pests, including pine shoot beetles (*Myelophilus* spp), Pine Shoot Moth (*Rhyacionia buoliana*) and the Pine Weevil (*Hylobius abietis*), which is particularly destructive.

The timber of pines is the most important of all the softwoods. The most widely planted forest species are the Scots Pine (*P. sylvestris*), Monterey Pine (*P. radiata*) and Corsican Pine (*P. nigra* var *maritima*). The timber is utilized in every kind of constructional work and carpentry.

The resin helps to preserve the wood considerably and when coated with creosote it is ideal for outdoor use as telegraph poles, railroad sleepers and road blocks. The wood of the Scots Pine is known as yellow deal; its resin, obtained by tapping the trees, is distilled to give turpentine and rosin.

Destructive distillation in closed (air-absent) vessels yields tar and pitch. Pine oils are obtained by distillation of leaves and shoots. Pines are also planted extensively for ornament, either singly or in groups for landscaping, and as shelter trees. Notable tall ornamental pines are Lodgepole Pine (*P. contorta* var *latifolia*), Cluster Pine (*P. pinaster*), Stone Pine (*P. pinea*) and Weymouth Pine (*P. strobus*). Dwarf forms include the Lacebark Pine (*P. bungeana*), the Dwarf Mountain Pine (*P. mugo* var *pumilo*) *and P. sylvestris* 'Beuvronensis.'

The Monterey Pine (*P. radiata*) is outstanding as a windbreak, especially on sea coasts; these trees also remove salt from the atmosphere. It is very extensively planted in New Zealand especially on poor soils.

Propagation is usually from seed in the spring and is timed so as to avoid frost damage to the young seedlings. Cultivars are grafted. Young seedlings are transplanted about every two years to stimulate development of abundant fibrous roots.

Most species are tolerant of a wide range of soils, provided they are well-drained, but some species are more or less calcicole, that is requiring a distinctly lime-rich soil. Stone Pine seeds, which are large and soon lose their vestigial wing, are eaten as a delicacy in the Mediterranean region where they are known as 'pignons.'

Some Plants having the Common Name 'PINE'

Common Name	*Species*	*Family*
Black Pine	*Callitris calcarata*	Cupressaceae
Bluegrass Pine	*Poa scabrella*	Gramineae
Brazilian Pine	*Araucaria brasiliensis*	Araucariaceae
Bush Pine	*Hakea leucoptera*	Proteaceae
Celery Pine	*Phyllocladus trichomanoides*	Podocarpaceae
Chile Pine	*Araucaria araucana*	Araucariaceae
Cypress Pine	*Callitris* spp	Cupressaceae
Ground Pine	*Ajuga chamaepitys*	Labiatae
Hoop Pine	*Araucaria cunninghamii*	Araucariaceae
Huon Pine	*Dacrydium franklinii*	Podocarpaceae
Japanese Umbrella Pine	*Sciadopitys verticillata*	Taxodiaceae
Kauri Pine	*Agathis spp* (especially *A. australis*)	Araucariaceae
King William Pine	*Athrotaxis selaginoides*	Taxodiaceae
Moreton Bay Pine	*Araucaria cunninghamii*	Araucariaceae
Murray Pine	*Callitris* spp	Cupressaceae
Needle Pine	*Hakea leucoptera*	Proteaceae
Norfolk Island Pine	*Araucaria heterophylla*	Araucariaceae
Parana Pine	*Araucaria angustifolia*	Araucariaceae
Parasol Pine	*Sciadopitys verticillata*	Taxodiaceae
Red Pine	*Dacrydium cupressinum*	Podocarpaceae
Rubber Pine	*Landolphia kirkii*	Apocynaceae
Screw Pine	*Pandanus spp*	Pandanaceae
She Pine	*Podocarpus elatus*	Podocarpaceae
Westland Pine	*Dacrydium westlandicum*	Podocarpaceae
White Cypress Pine	*Callitris glauca*	Cupressaceae
White Pine	*Podocarpus elatus*	Podocarpaceae

The common name 'pine' has been applied to many pine-like trees which do not belong to the genus *Pinus*—indeed some are not even conifers. The accompanying table gives some examples.

THE MAIN SPECIES OF PINUS

Subgenus Strobus—The Soft Pines

Leaves with one vascular bundle. Sheaths of short shoots (those bearing leaf clusters) deciduous. Base of scale leaves not decurrent. The wood contains little resin and the timber is soft.

A Leaves in clusters of 5.

B Margin of leaves (lens) serrulate.

P. cembra Swiss Stone Pine, Arolla Pine. Alps of C Europe, NE USSR and America. Tree 10-25(40)m. Shoots tomentose with thick brown hairs. Leaves dark green, 5-12cm long, lacking conspicuous white lines on the back. Mature cones 5-8cm long with unarmed terminal umbo; seeds without wings.

'Aureovariegata' A form with yellowtinged leaves.

'Stricta' A columnar form with ascending branches.

P. lambertiana Sugar Pine. N America. Tree 50-100m. Shoots tomentose. Leaves 710cm long with conspicuous white lines on back. Mature cones (25)30-50cm long, seeds with wings longer than themselves.

P. peuce Macedonian Pine. Balkan mountains. Tree 10-20m. Shoots greenish, hairless and without bloom. Leaves 712cm long. Mature cones more or less cylindric, 8-1 5cm long; apophysis much swollen, seeds 8-10mm with longer wings.

P. strobus Weymouth Pine, White Pine.

N America. Tree 25-50m. Shoots hairless, without bloom. Leaves 6-14cm long, soft and flexible. Mature cones often curved, 8-20cm long with flat apophysis; seeds mottled. 6-7mm long with longer wings.

'Compacta' A slow-growing dwarf form with a dense habit.

"Contorta' A form with twisted branches and leaves.

'Fastigiata' A form with erect branches and columnar habit.

'Prostrata' A prostrate form with flat or slightly ascending branches.

P. wallichiana (*P. griffithii*, *P. excelsa*) Himalayan or Bhutan Pine. Himalaya and westward to Afghanistan. Tree usually about

35m, but sometimes 50m. Shoots hairless with evident bloom. Leaves 1220cm long. Mature cones 1 5-25cm long with convex apophysis, its umbo touching the scale below, seeds 8-9mm with longer wings.

BB Margin of leaves (lens) entire.

P. aristata Hickory or Bristle-cone Pine. SW USA. Usually a bushy tree reaching 15m. Shoots pale orange, soon hairless. Leaves 2-4cm long. Mature cones 4-9cm long, the terminal umbo with a slender curved spine 6-8mm long.

AA Leaves in clusters of 1-4.

P. bungeana Lace-bark Pine. NW China. Tree 20-30m. Shoots hairless. Leaves 5-10cm long with entire (smooth) margins (lens); in clusters of 3. Mature cones 5-7cm long; apophysis with an umbo bearing a broadbased recurved spine; seeds 8-12mm long with short wings. The popular name derives from the exfoliating bark exposing striking multicolored areas of bare trunk.

P. cembroides Mexican Stone Pine. Arizona to Mexico. Tree 6-7m. Shoots dark orange, soon hairless. Leaves 2-5cm long with serrulate margin (lens), in clusters of 1-4. Mature cones almost globose, 2.5-5cm long with a broad umbo; seeds 15-30mm long with unusually narrow wings.

Subgenus Pinus—the Hard Pines

Leaves with two vascular bundles. Sheaths of short shoots persisting. Base of scale-leaves decurrent. The wood contains significant amounts of resin and the timber is comparatively hard.

C. Leaves in clusters of 3 (exceptionally otherwise, eg P. halepensis, P. radiata, leaves in 2's).

D. Leaves not exceeding 15cm in length.

P. ha/epensis Aleppo Pine. Mediterranean region and W Asia. Tree 10-1 5m. Leaves 6-15cm long, sometimes in clusters of 2. Mature cones 8-1 2cm long, the apophysis more or less flattened, the umbo obtuse and unarmed (ie with no prickle or spine).

P. radiata Monterey Pine. California. Tree 25-30m. Leaves 10-15cm long, occasionally in clusters of 2. Mature cones 7-14cm long, stout, asymmetric, sessile and reflexed, the apophysis rounded with a minute prickle. *P. rigida* Pitch Pine, Easter Pine. E USA. Tree 10-1 5(25)m. Leaves firm, 7-14cm long. Mature cones symmetrical 3-7cm long, umbo prominent with a sharp, slender recurved prickle.

DD. Leaves more than 15cm long.

P. coulteri Coulter or Big-cone Pine. S California and S Mexico. Tree to 25m. Shoots with bloom. Leaves 1 5-30cm long. Mature cones massive, 25-35cm long, the raised apophysis with a large umbo forming a stout, curved spine; wings thick and twice the length of the seeds.

P. palustris Longleaf or Pitch Pine. E USA. Tree to 40m. Bud scales white fringed. Shoots not bloomed. Leaves 20-45cm long. Mature cones 1 5-20cm long, almost without stalk, the umbo with a short reflexed prickle; seed wings membranous, about twice the length of seeds.

P. ponderosa Western Yellow Pine. W N America. Tree 50-75m. Shoots without bloom. Leaves (12)15-26cm long. Leaf clusters sometimes 2, 4 or 5. Mature cones yellowish-green, almost without stalks, 8-15cm long, the umbo with a stout recurved prickle.

P. jeffreyi Jeffrey's Pine. W N America. Tree similar to *P. ponderosa* but shoots with bloom. Mature cones larger and resin with a characteristic citronella-like smell.

P. taeda Loblolly Pine. E and SE USA. Tree 20-30(50)m. Shoots without bloom. Leaves (12)15-25cm long, bright bluegreen. Mature cones sessile, 6-12cm long, the umbo projected as a stout triangular somewhat recurved spine; seeds 6-7mm long with wings about 25mm long.

CC. Leaves in clusters of 2.

E. Leaves not exceeding 8cm.

P. sylvestris Scots Pine, Scotch Fir. N and C Europe and W Asia. Tree 20-40m. Upper part of the trunk smooth and reddish. Leaves 2-7cm long, blue-green, often twisted. Mature cones 3-7cm long, the umbo almost symmetrical with a minute prickle. The subspecies *scotica* is broadtopped and native only in the highlands of N England and Scotland.

P. mugo Mountain Pine. Mountains of

C Europe. Very similar to *P. sylvestris* but usually a shrub with leaves a brighter green. Very variable.

P. contorta Shore Pine. Coastal areas of W N America. Tree to 1 Om. Leaves 3-5cm long, firm and twisted. Mature cones very oblique, 2-5cm long; prickles of the umbo prominent but fragile. The *var/atifolia* (Lodgepole Pine) is the inland representative.

EE. Leaves predominantly more than 8cm long.

P. pinea Stone Pine, Umbrella Pine. Mediterranean region. Mushroom-shaped tree 1 5-25m. Leaves 10-20cm long. Mature cones almost globular, 6-9cm long. The species is known by its seeds, which are 12-18mm long, the wing only 6-7mm long and quickly falling off.

P. halepensis Aleppo Pine. Leaves also in 3's—see earlier description, under leaves in 3's.

P. radiata Monterey Pine. Leaves mainly in 3's—see earlier description, under leaves in 3's.

P. thunbergii Japanese Black Pine. Japan. Tree to 30m. Winter buds grayish-white, not resinous, with fimbriate scales free at the tips. Leaves (6) 8-11 cm long, the basal leaf-sheath terminated by two long filaments. Mature cones 4-6cm long, the umbo with a prickle or not.

P. pinaster Cluster Pine. W Mediterranean region. Tree to 30m. Winter buds not resinous. Leaves 10-20cm long, firm; basal leaf-sheath without terminal filaments. Mature cones symmetrical, in clusters, 9-18cm long, the umbo with a prominent prickle.

P. nigra Austrian or Black Pine. Austria and eastward to the Balkan Peninsula. Tree 20-40(50)m. Bark characteristically dark gray and fissured into scaly plates. Leaves 9-1 6cm long and firm. Mature cones symmetrical, 5-8cm long, the umbo usually with a short prickle. The var *maritima* is the Corsican Pine, with lighter green, twisted leaves 12-18cm long.

SPRUCES (GENUS PICEA)

The genus *Picea* comprises some 40-60 species of evergreen

trees and is widely distributed over the cooler areas of the Northern Hemisphere of both the Old and New Worlds, from the Arctic Circle to the high mountains of the more southerly warm temperate latitudes of the Tropic of Cancer.

They form trees of more or less conical outline with irregularly branched horizontal to pendulous branches and reddishbrown furrowed bark. The branchlets are characterized by woody peg-like decurrent leaf bases, which are continuous with the cushion-like structures (pulvini) surrounding the shoots, separated from each other by grooves.

Winter buds may be resinous or not. The leaves are needlelike, appearing either more or less radially arranged around the lateral shoots (leading shoots are less constant) or somewhat parted beneath to pectinate, that is the lower ranks of leaves, at least, are in two horizontal rows, one row on each side of the shoot.

The leaves are of two types diamond-shaped quadrangular with the width about equal to the height, or flattened with the width much greater than the height, so that there are essentially only two sides-an upper and a lower. Each leaf has typically two marginal resin ducts, sometimes one or rarely none.

Male and female cones are borne separately on the same tree, the male axillary in yellow or crimson catkin-like clusters, the female terminal. The young female cones are green or purple, each cone with numerous scales and each scale with two ovules at the base on the underside.

Once fertilized, the cones ripen within the year and are pendulous and do not break up when ripe. The seeds are winged and more or less compressed. Most species of *Picea* succeed in wet and cold soils, although in shallow soils they may not withstand much wind; otherwise they tolerate a lot of exposure and when firmly rooted can serve as windbreaks.

Propagation is usually by seed. For ornamental purposes the seedlings are transplanted every two years until final transplant-ation to the permanent position, which should be not later than when they are about 1m (3.3ft) high. For forestry purposes, it is usual to transplant at a height of about 30-40cm (10-15in). Young shoots are liable to late spring frost damage.

Spruces are susceptible to attacks by the rust fungus *Chrysomyxa rhododendri*, with the aecidial stage on *Picea abies* and *P. pungens*, the alternate host being *Rhododendron*. The imperfect fungus *Ascochyta biniperda will* attack two- to three-year-old species, especially of *P. abies*, as well as adult and old trees, causing defoliation.

Bracket fungi, such as *Phaeolus schweinitzii*, *Phellinus pini* and others, also cause serious damage. *Phellinus pini is* particularly destructive, attacking mature trees, especially *Picea sitchensis*, causing Red-ring Rot.

The spruce aphid *Elatobium abietinum* causes defoliation in a number of spruces, including *P. sitchensis.* Plant lice also attack many spruce species forming so-called pineapple galls. Species of the genus *Adelges* are involved and have a complex life history requiring more than one coniferous host.

However, spruce are always the primary hosts and the ones bearing the galls. These are unsightly but do little harm to the tree. Three North American species are of great economic importance—Red Spruce (*P. rubens*), Black Spruce (*P. mariana*) and White Spruce (*P. glauca*) - being widely used for paper pulp.

In Norway and the United Kingdom the Norway Spruce (*P. abies*) is widely planted for afforestation, as also is the Sitka Spruce (*P. sitchensis*), the latter being particularly successful on a very wide range of soils from sandy to cold, wet and boggy.

Each species occupies not far short of 10 percent of the total productive forest in these countries. Spruce wood is soft and without odor, is easy to work and takes a good finish. It is used in general carpentry, for propping poles, packing cases and sounding boards and also for stringed instruments.

The timber is also extensively turned into wood pulp for use in the manufacture of paper and rayon. The resin of the Norway Spruce is purified to yield Burgundy pitch and the leaves and shoots are distilled to give Swiss turpentine.

Extracts of shoots and leaves (also of *P. abies*) mixed with various sugary substances, can be fermented to make spruce beer. The bark of *P. abies* is also used commercially in the tanning of leather.

Although various conifers may be sold as Christmas trees, the Norway Spruce is the most commonly chosen. Other spruces are extensively planted as ornamentals, notably cultivars of *P. pungens* (Colorado Spruce) and *P. engelmannii* (Engelmann Spruce).

Dwarf spruces popular for planting in rock gardens include *P. glauca* 'Albertina Conica' and *P. abies* '*Clan*brassiliana,' 'Nidiformis' and 'Pumila.'

THE MAIN SPECIES OF PICEA

Group I: Leaves flattened (showing virtually only 2 surfaces) with 2 white stomatic bands on the apparent lower surface (facing downward on horizontal branches), the apparent upper surface green, rarely with a broken stomatic line.

A. First-year lateral shoots hairy.

P. omorika Serbian Spruce. Europe, especiall' Yugoslavia. Tree to 30m. Leaves on horizontal branches more or less parted below and exposing shoot (ie pectinate), thin, keeled on both surfaces, (8)1218 × 2mm; abruptly pointed. Mature cones 3-6cm long, ovoid-oblong.

P. brewerana Brewer's or Siskiyou Spruce. W USA. Tree to 40m. Leaves radially spreading on pendulous shoots, 2-2.5 (3.0) cm long, slightly convex on both surfaces, apex pointed. Mature cones 6-12cm long, cylindric-oblong; conescales entire.

AA First- year lateral shoots hairless. Leaves pectinate on lower surface of shoot. Cone scale with jagged margin.

P. jezoensis Yeddo Spruce. NE Asia, Japan. Tree to 50m. Leaves 1-2cm long, the apex pointed but not horny and pricking. Mature cones 4-8cm long, cylindric-oblong. Variety *hondoensis*, with shorter leaves, often does better when cultivated than the type.

P. sitchensis Sitka Spruce. W coastal regions of USA from Alaska to California. Tree to 60m. Leaves 1 .5-2.5cm long with sharp, horny, pricking apical point; convex and slightly keeled on both surfaces. Mature cones 6-10cm long, cylindric-oblong.

Group II: Leaves 4-sided and quadrangular diamond-shaped in cross-section, the width equal to or slightly less than the height;

each side with (2)3-5(6) white (not banded) stomatic lines.

B. First-year lateral shoots hairless (sometimes hairy in P. abies and P. asperata) and at least the upper ranks of leaves bent forward over the shoot.

C. Lower ranks of leaves parted laterally into 2 more or less horizontal sets (ie pectinate), those above overlapping.

P. abies (*P. excelsa*) Norway or Common Spruce. C and N Europe. Tree to 50m.

Leaves 1-2(2.5)cm long, green. Mature cones cylindric, 10-1 5cm long. Occasionally has faint pubescence on shoots. About 150 cultivars including many named dwarf forms.

P. glauca White Spruce. Alaska, Canada, N USA. Tree to 30m. Leaves 8-18mm, blue-green, glaucous, with a rank smell when bruised. Mature cones cylindricoblong, 3.5-5cm long.

CC. Lower ranks of leaves not parted beneath but more or less pointed downward (ie radially arranged).

P. smithiana Himalayan Spruce. The Himalaya. Tree 30-50m. Winter buds more or less resinous. Leaves 2-4(5) × 1 mm; apex acute. Mature cones 12-15(18)cm long, cylindric.

P. asperata Chinese or Dragon Spruce.

W China. Tree to 25m. Winter buds more or less resinous. Shoots yellowish-brown sometimes hairy. Leaves subradially arranged, 1-1.8cm long, sometimes curved; apex acute. Mature cones 8-10cm long, cylindric-oblong.

P. schrenkiana Schrenk's Spruce. C Asia. Tree to 35m. Winter buds not resinous. Shoots gray. Leaves radially arranged, 2-3.5cm long, sometimes curved; apex pointed. Mature cones 7-10cm long, cylindric-oblong; cone-scales entire.

BB. First-year lateral shoots hairless but all ranks of leaves more or less spreading outward, radially or subradially at 45° to almost 90", the upper ranks not bent forward over the shoot. Mature cones more than 5cm long.

P. polita Tiger-tail Spruce. Japan. Tree to 40m. Leaves 1.5-2cm long, curved, very rigid and with sharp pricking point; shining deep green. Mature cones 8-10cm long.

P. pungens (glaucous cultivars) Colorado Spruce. SW USA. Tree to 50m with horizontal branches. Leaves 1.5-2.5cm, somewhat incurved, glaucous on all sides with waxy bloom obscuring the stomatic lines, rigid and stiff with sharp, prickly point, more leaves on upper than lower half of shoot. Mature cones 6-i0cm long, cylindric-oblong.

The above description covers the cultivars 'Glauca' (Blue Spruce) with horizontal branches and 'Kosteriana' with pendulous branches, both of which are commonly planted.

BBB. First- year lateral shoots hairy and lowei leaves parted laterally into two horizontal sets (ie pectinate), those above overlapping. (In P. asperata and P. mariana the leaves are more or less radially arranged.) D Terminal bud with basal ring of awlshaped (acicular) scales; cones less than 5cm long.

P. mariana Black Spruce. NW N America. Tree 20-30m. Young shoots glandular, hairy. Leaves 7-1 5mm long, somewhat glaucous with more stomatic lines on the sides next to the shoot; apex blunt. Mature cones ovoid.

P. rubens Red Spruce. Canada and southward to N Carolina. Leaves 1-1.5cm long, abruptly acute, deep to bright green, with about twice as many stomatic lines on the side next to the shoot. Mature cones 3-4(5)cm long, oblong.

DD Terminal bud without basal ring of awlshaped (acicular) scales. Cones more than 5cm long.

P. engelmannii Engelmann Spruce. W N America. Tree 20-50m. First-year shoots yellowish-gray with glandular pubescence. Leaves 1.5-2.5cm long with acute apex, upper ranks bent forward over shoot; rank smell on bruising. Mature cones up to 8cm long. Rare in cultivation.

P. obovata Siberian Spruce. N Europe. N Asia. Tree to 50m. First-year shoots brown, pubescence fine. Leaves 1-1.8cm long, apex acute. Mature cones 6-8cm long, cylindric-ovoid; scales entire.

P. orientalis Oriental Spruce. Asia Minor and Caucasus. Leaves dark green, shining, 6-8mm (occasionally 12mm) long, with blunt apex. Mature cones 6-9cm long, cylindric-ovoid.

Group III: Leaves pectinately arranged and quadrangular but somewhat compressed from above downward so that, in cross-section, the width is greater than the height, with twice as many stomatal lines on the 2 sides next to the shoot (upper side) as on the other 2 (lower) sides (lens). Cones more than 5cm long.

P. bicolor Alcock Spruce. Japan. Tree to 25m. Primary shoots hairy, lateral ones not so; terminal bud without awl-shaped (acicular) scales at base. Leaves 1-2cm long, with 5-6 stomatic lines on each upper side and 2 on each lower side. Mature cones 6-12cm long, cylindricoblong.

P. glehnii Sakhalin Spruce. Japan. Tree to 40m. Shoots reddish-brown, terminal bud with awl-shaped (acicular) scales at the base. Leaves 6-12mm long with 2 white stomatal bands above and 1-2 broken lines on each lower side; apex obtuse or acute. Mature cones 5-8cm long. cylindricoblong.

P. likiangensis Likiany Spruce. W China. Tree to 30m. Shoots grayish-yellow. Upper 2 ranks of leaves imbricate and bent forward more or less parallel with the shoot. Leaves 8-1 5mm long, with 2 white bands above and 1-2(3, 4) broken stomatal lines on each lower side: apex acute, horny pointed. Mature cones 5-8cm long, cylindricoblong.

FIRS (GENUS *ABIES*)

Abies is a genus of evergreen trees comprising some 40-50 species widely distributed in the mountainous regions of the Northern Hemisphere: in central and southern Europe (southern Spain and the opposite region of North Africa), in Asia northward from, and including the Himalaya, as well as Japan and extensive areas of North America.

The generic name occurs in classical Latin, referring to some kind of fir tree, although not necessarily a species of *Abies*. However, in the English language the word 'fir' is now restricted to species of this genus, except that Douglas Fir is the traditional name for species of the genus *Pseudotsuga* and Scotch Fir is a name traditionally given to the Scots Pine (*Pinus sylvestris*).

Some authorities use the name silver firs for members of the genus *Abies* to distinguish them from other firs. It is not difficult to distinguish the genus *Abies.* The erect cone, breaking up at maturity, the needles occurring singly, the rounded disk-like needle scar which is not raised above the level of the bark, thus giving a virtually smooth branchlet—this combination of characters readily identifies a conifer as a member of the genus *Abies.*

Some 30 species are planted outside their native regions but more for their fine and lofty appearance than as a commercial undertaking. The Common Silver Fir (*Abies alba*), Grand Fir (*A. grandis*), Noble Fir (*A. procera*) *and* Caucasian Fir (*A. nordmanniana*) are the commonest firs grown for ornament in parks and gardens, the first three also having some value on a limited scale as plantation trees.

They require a moist, preferably deep soil and a moist climate and clean air, their susceptibility to atmospheric pollution rendering them unsuitable in or near industrial areas. Fraser's Balsam Fir (*A. frasert*) and the Balsam Fir (*A. balsamea*) are used as Christmas trees in America and Canada.

Propagation is by seed usually in nursery beds, sometimes in a cold frame or propagating cabinet. Hybrids and varieties need to be grafted.

Firs are subject to attack by insects, aphid species of the genus *Adelges* being particularly serious. The extent of injury varies with the region. Thus, *Adelges picae* has little more than nuisance value in Europe, but in Canada it can kill trees of *Abies balsamea* at all stages.

'Silver Fir Dieback,' caused by *Adelges nuesslini*, is so serious in the United Kingdom on the Common Silver Fir that extensive planting of this tree has been abandoned. In general, treatment with an aphicide is only effective with young plants still at the nursery stage. No treatment is effective for badly affected trees.

Such trees may be recognized by the development of gout-like swellings on the branches and the presence of the insects covered by a white, protective exudate.

Abies alba is sometimes disfigured by small so-called 'witches-broom'—a dense tuft of weak branches. Some of these appear to arise spontaneously but others are a response to attack by the rust fungus *Melampsorella caryophyllacearum*, whose alternate hosts are various species of the family Caryophyllaceae.

Abies wood is sold as (white) deal and varies from white to yellowish or reddishbrown with no obvious distinction between heartwood and sapwood. Resin canals are normally absent. This soft wood is easily worked, yielding a good surface, which readily accepts paint and polish.

Its main use is for indoor work, but treated with a preservative it has been used out doors, for example for telegraph poles. As the wood has no noticeable smell it has also been used for crating grocery and dairy products that might otherwise become tainted.

In certain American firs, the bark of young trees bears 'resin blisters' from which resin is obtained. Resins are nonvolatile mixtures, insoluble in water, but soluble in organic solvents.

Steam distillation removes turpentine, the residual solid being rosin, which is used in the manufacture of products such as plastics, soaps and varnishes. Canada balsam, extensively used as a permanent mounting medium in microscopical preparations, and in pharmacy, is obtained from the Balsam Fir and other North American species.

THE MAIN SPECIES OF ABIES

Group 1: Needles all arranged in one plane or at least some of them widely parted above (pectinate) Needles flat unless otherwise indicated.

A. alba (*A. pectinata*) Common Silver Fir. Mountains of C and S Europe. Tree to 50m. Branchlets hairy, not grooved; winter buds not resinous. Leaves 1.5-3cm long, notched at apex with two white stomatal bands on lower surface. Resin canals lateral.

A. balsamea Balsam Fir. Balm of Gilead. Common and widespread in N America, extending to Arctic Circle. A source of the resin Canada Balsam. Tree to 25m. Branchlets hairy, not grooved; winter buds resinous. Leaves 1.5-2.5cm long, notched at apex with 4-9 lines of whitish stomatal bands on lower surface only. Resin canals median.

A. concolor Colorado or White Fir. Mountains of Colorado to S California, New Mexico, Arizona and Mexico. Tree to 40m.

Branchlets minutely hairy or hairless; winter buds resinous. Leaves 4-6cm long with white stomatal lines on both surfaces; not notched at apex. Resin canals lateral.

A. grandis Giant Fir. W N America. Tree to 100m; does well in cultivation, but then reaches only some 50m. Practically free from injury by disease or insect attacks and resistant to frost. Branchlets olive-greenish, minutely hairy to almost hairless; winter buds resinous. Leaves 3-6cm long, notched at apex; white stomatal bands only on lower surface. Resin canals lateral.

A. magnifica Red Fir. Oregon to California. Tree to 70m. Branchlets minutely rusty pubescent; winter buds resinous. Leaves 2.5-4cm long, quadrangular in section, not notched at apex; stomatal bands on all sides. Resin canals lateral.

A. procera (*A. nobi/is*) Noble Fir. Cascade mountains, Washington to N California. Tree to 80m. Commonly planted under forestry conditions where it may reach 50m, but sometimes suffers serious attacks *by Adelges.* Branchlets minutely rusty pubescent; winter buds resinous. Leaves 2.5-3.5cm long, flat or grooved above, not or slightly notched at apex; stomatal bands on both surfaces. Resin canals lateral.

A. spectabilis Himalayan Fir. NW Himalayan mountains. Tree to 50m. Branchlets reddish-brown with pubescence in grooves; winter buds resinous. Leaves 2.5-6cm long, notched at apex; stomatal bands only on lower surface. Resin canals lateral.

Group II: Needles not pectinate as in Group I, but densely overlap-ping above. Branchlets hairy. Needles flat. *A. amabilis* Red Silver Fir. Mountains of British Columbia, Alberta and Oregon to Washington. Tree to 80m, but only about 30m in cultivation and subject to aphis attack; winter buds resinous. Leaves 2-3cm long, truncate or notched at apex; stomatal bands white, only on lower surface. Resin canals lateral.

A. cilicica Cilician Fir. Mountains of Asia Minor, N Syria and Antitaurus. Tree to 30m. Winter buds with a few scales free at the tips, not or only slightly resinous. Leaves 2-3cm long, slightly notched at apex; stomatal bands whitish, only on lower surface. Resin canals lateral. Cone with hidden bracts.

A. nordmanniana Nordmann or Caucasian Fir. N Caucasus,

Asia Minor. Tree to 50m. Very similar to preceding, but winter bud scales not free and cone with exserted and reflexed bracts.

Group III: Needles neither overlapping nor pectinate but directed upward and outward; flat.

A. koreana Korean Fir. Korea. Tree to 18m sometimes shrubby in cultivation. Winter buds slightly resinous. Leaves 1-2cm long, usually tapering downward with whitish stomatal bands only on lower surface. Resin canals median.

Group IV: Needles radially arranged around branch lets.

A. cephalonica Greek Fir. Mountains of Greece. Tree to 30m. Winter buds resinous. Leaves flattened, 2-3cm long, apex sharply pointed; white stomatal bands on lower surface only. Resin canals lateral.

A. pinsapo Spanish Fir, Hedgehog Fir. S Spain. Tree to 25m. Tolerant of lime. Winter buds resinous. Leaves 1.5-2cm long, thick rigid, apex not sharp pointed. Resin canals median.

HEMLOCKS OR HEMLOCK SPRUCES (GENUS TSUGA)

Tsuga is a genus of about to species of evergreen trees (sometimes bushes) native to North America, Japan, China, Taiwan and the Himalaya. In habit they arc broadly pyramidal, the branches being horizontal to somewhat pendulous.

The leaves are flat, short-stalked (petiolate) and spirally inserted but appearing in twc horizontal ranks by twisting of the petiole: the stalk is borne on a projecting decurrent leaf-base. The leaves persist for several years, finally falling off to leave a semicircular scar on the projecting leaf-base.

The spruces (*Picea*) are distinguished from *Tsuga* by the leaves being sessile (without stalks), with more prominent roughly diamond-shaped leaf-scars and the cones more than 2.5cm (tin) long. except that *Tsuga mertensiana* and the closely related supposed hybrid *Tijefreyi* have cones to 7cm (2.8in) long.

The male cones are minute, up to 5mm (0.2in), yellowish-white, but more often a shade of red. The female cones are characteristically small, rarely exceeding 2.5cm (tin) long. They are pendulous and ripen in the first year but persist several years after shedding their seeds, which are small and winged, two occurring under each cone-scale.

Hemlocks like a good, fairly welldrained soil. Propagation is usually by seed, the varieties and forms by shoot cuttings or by grafting. In addition to the numerous varieties and forms, mostly of the species *T. canadensis* (Common or Canada Hemlock), there are a number of intergeneric hybrids, namely *Tsuga* × *Picea* (= *Tsugo-Picea*); *Picea* × (*TsugoPicea*); *Tsuga* × (*Tsugo-Picea*); *Keteleeria* × *Tsuga.*

The wood of the Common Hemlock is used for building construction generally and for ladder making. The resin is also useful and is known commercially as Canada Pitch. The bark contains tannin which is extracted for tanning leather etc.

The Western Hemlock (*T. heterophylla*) and Mountain Hemlock (*T. mertensiana*) are the species most frequently cultivated as ornamentals, the Western Hemlock also being found in forestry plantations particularly under hardwood crops.

THE MAIN SPECIES OF TSUGA

Group I: Leaves spirally arranged around branches, more or less rounded above or only slightly grooved. Cones 5-7.5cm long.

T. mertensiana Mountain Hemlock. W N America. Tree usually to about 30m, but up to 50m in its native habitat. Specific name formerly used for what is now known as *T. heterophylla*. Cones sprucelike in clusters on shoot tip, 7 × 3.5cm, green when young, turning deep redbrown when mature. Bark brownishorange with fine vertical fissures.

Group II: Leaves essentially in one plane (= pectinate), flat above and grooved. Cones 2-3cm long.

***T. sieboldii* Japanese Hemlock. S Japan.**

Tree to 30m in its native habitat, about half as high in Europe, where it is often little more than a large bush. Branchlets hairless (glabrous), leaves notched, margin entire. Cones pendulous, ovoid, 2.3 × 1.3cm, with flat topped scales and dark brown when mature. Bark pink-gray, at first smooth with horizontal folds, later cracking into squares and becoming flaky. *T. canadensis* Common or Canada Hemlock. E N America. Tree 25-30m. Branchlets covered in fine hairs (pubescent). Leaves with serrulate margins, distinct stomatal lines beneath and with distinct green edges.

Cones numerous on side shoots, ovoid, 2 × 1 cm, coffee-brown when ripe. Bark orange-brown on young trees, dark purplish gray-brown when mature. Many forms and varieties in cultivation.

TT heterophylla Western Hemlock. Coastal regions of W N America. Tree 30-60m. Branchlets pubescent. Leaves with serrulate margins, indistinct stomatal lines beneath and edges not obviously different.

Cones pendulous and numerous on side shoots, blunt, ovoid, 2-3cm long, green to purplish when young, becoming light brown. Bark gray-green and smooth when young, russet-brown and narrowly fissured when mature.

T. diversifolia Northern Japanese Hemlock. Japan. Tree to 25m in its natural habitat, but often a large shrub in cultivation. Branchlets pubescent all round. Leaves with entire margins, 8-1 5mm long, notched at apex. Cone cylindrical ovoid, 2-2.8cm, dark shiny brown. Bark orange-brown with pink fissures.

T. chinensis Chinese Hemlock. W China. Tree to 50m. Branchlets pubescent. Leaves with entire margins, up to 25mm long, notched at apex sometimes with a few marginal serrulations. Cone long-ovoid, 3 × 1.3cm, green turning to red-brown. Bark with curving patterns of dark graygreen scales becoming very flaky and fissured dark brown and gray.

T. caroliniana Carolina Hemlock. Mountains of SE USA. Tree to 1 5m occasionally to 25m. Branchlets pubescent. Leaves with entire margins, 8-18mm long, not or scarcely notched at apex with conspicuously white stomatal bands below. Cone long-ovoid, 2.5 × 1.5cm, orangebrown. Bark dark red-brown with yellow pores, becoming fissured and purple-gray.

DOUGLAS FIRS (GENUS PSEUDOTSUGA)

Some zo types of Douglas fir have been described but only

five or six are recognized as 'good' species. They are *natives* of western North America, China, Japan and Taiwan and succeed on a wide range of soils but flourish in a damp climate on a moist, well-drained soil.

Douglas firs are evergreen trees, generally pyramidal in the early stages, finally somewhat widely spreading. The winter buds are characteristically spindle-shaped, not unlike those of the beech. The branchlets have slightly raised oval leaf-scars and the leaves are needle-like, grooved above, and spirally arranged.

They have two white stomatic lines on the lower side and appear to be in one plane because the leafbase is twisted (except in *Pseudotsuga japonica*). Each leaf has two marginal resin canals and one vascular strand. The male and female cones are separate but borne on the same tree.

The male cones are short and catkin-like comprising numerous pollen sacs; the females are terminal, consisting of numerous persistent cone-scales, each scale with two ovules beneath. The mature cone is pendulous with the bractscale prominently exserted (protruding), its apex being three-lobed. The seeds are winged.

The generic name *Pseutotsuga* (literally 'false hemlock') suggests a relationship with *Tsuga*, but the Douglas firs are easily distinguished by the plainly visible trifid exserted bract-scales of the mature cones and by the leaf-bases being not, or scarcely decurrent.

The genus *Abies*, in which the Douglas firs were once placed, is distinct in its erect mature cones whose scales fall away from a persistent axis. In *Abies*, moreover, there is no exserted trifid bractscale and the leaf-scars are circular and flat and level with the branchlet surface.

Douglas firs are susceptible to a number of fungus diseases. The gray mold fungus *Botrytis cinerea* affects seedlings and is able to flourish because of excessive damp and overcrowding. In older trees, *Rhabdoclyne pseudotsugae* causes brown patches on the leaves of *Pseudotsuga menziesii* (Oregon or Gray Douglas Fir) and its variety *glauca* (Blue Douglas Fir).

More serious is canker and dieback caused by *Phomopsis pseudotsugae*. The main insect pest is the aphid *Adelges cooleyi;* the

Douglas fir acts as the secondary host, the primary (sexual stage) host being various species of *Picea.*

The timber of *P. menziesii* is in great demand and is the premier wood of North America. Although constituting half the standing timber of the western forests, its exploitation without replacement is leading to concern.

Individual trees provide an immense quantity of timber which is, however, very variable in strength and grain, and requires careful grading to ensure reasonable uniformity. It is used for practically every type of constructional work—houses, bridges and boats, for general carpentry, rolling stock and all kinds of poles and posts including commemorative flagstaffs.

A mature Douglas fir is also a fine sight as an ornamental tree, especially when cleared of the lower and dead branches. Single subjects are therefore extensively planted in rural areas and parks, while some dense stands can be found in forested areas.

THE MAIN SPECIES OF PSEUDOTSUGA

Group 1: Leaf apices acutely pointed, or if somewhat blunt, then not broadly rounded or notched. Cones 5-1 8cm long.

P. menziesii (*P. douglasii*, *P. taxifolla*) Oregon or Gray Douglas Fir. W N America extending to N Mexico. Tree to 100m.

Branchlets pubescent, rarely glabrous. Leaves 2-3cm, acute or blunt, dark green or bluish-green above. Cones 5-10cm, the trifid bract-scales usually erect, occasionally reflexed. The crushed leaves have a characteristic pleasant citronella-like smell. *var,glauca* E Rocky mountains from Montana to Mexico. Tree to about 40m. Leaves shorter and thicker than the type, bluntly pointed, glaucous, smelling of turpentine when crushed.

Cones 6-7.5cm, the bracts usually with reflexed tips. Typical specimens are distinctive and known as Colorado Douglas Fir but a continuous chain of intermediates connects it with the type. More susceptible to fungus attack by *Rhabdocline pseudotsugae* than the type but more resistant to the aphid *Adelges cooleyi.* It is planted for its decorative value and has no commercial potential.

P. macrocarpa Large-coned Douglas Fir. SW California. Tree

12-16(25)m. Leaves 2.5-3.5cm, light green. Cones 10-1 8cm, the bract-scales less exserted than in *P. menziesii*. The cone size at once distinguishes this species from all others.

Group 11: Leaf apices broadly rounded or notched. Cones 3-6cm.

P. japonica Japanese Douglas Fir. SE Japan. Tree 1 5-30m. Branchlets glabrous. Leaves notched, directed forward but spreading in all directions, not obviously arranged in one plane, pale grayish-green. Cones 3-5cm, few-scaled (15-20).

P. sinensis Chinese Douglas Fir. W China. Tree about 20m. Branchlets hairy, reddishbrown. Leaves 2.5-3cm, arranged in one plane. Cones 5-6cm.

P. wilsoniana Taiwan and Mekong valley. Tree 20-30m. Branchlets at first reddishbrown becoming grayish, glabrous or sparsely and minutely hairy. Leaves to 5cm, arranged in one plane. Cones 5-6cm, the bract-scales with long reflexed central prong.

LARCHES (GENUS LARIX)

Larix is a genus of about 12 species of deciduous, commonly fast-growing trees, native to the cooler mountainous regions of the Northern Hemisphere - central and northern Europe, North America and Asia from the Himalaya to Siberia and Japan.

Larches are more or less pyramidal trees with spreading irregularly whorled branches. The leaves are borne spirally on the long shoots, but are most conspicuous as dense clusters on the very short shoots. The female cones are finally erect and are very attractive when young, with crimson bract-scales ('larch noses').

The cones mature within a year, becoming pale brown, but persist after the shedding of seeds. There are two seeds under each ovuliferous- or cone-scale, each seed having a thin well-developed wing. Mature cones are essential for species determination.

In the young cone and at the time of pollination the bract-scale much exceeds the ovuliferous-scale, but at maturity the bract-scale may or may not be hidden by the ovuliferous-scale.

Larches do best on well-drained light or gravelly loams and

are intolerant of lowlying areas where water is liable to accumulate and which are subject to frost. Propagation is by seed; varieties are sometimes grafted.

Larch wood is strong and durable and used for posts, pit-props, barges etc. The relatively rapid rate of growth of most species is also an advantage when a quick return on investment is being sought.

A disadvantage of larch cultivation, however, is that many are susceptible to a number of diseases. *Larix decidua* (European Larch) and *L. occidentalis* (Western Larch) suffer especially from Larch Canker or Blister caused by the ascomycete fungus *Trichoscyphella willkommii*, which flourishes where the trees are overcrowded or on poorly-drained soil.

Infected trees are useless for timber and may be killed outright. Larch Chermes, a species of *Adelges* (related to aphids but much smaller) cause serious shoot damage thus retarding growth. The larch is the secondary host for these insects, the primary host being species of *Picea* (spruce).

The bark has been used for tanning and dyeing and has medicinal properties and is mainly used in veterinary practise. Venice or Larch Turpentine, obtained by tapping, is so used. In summer months the leaves exude a whitish and sweet substance known as briancon larch manna which was also once used in medicine. It contains the unusual trisaccharide sugar melecitose.

THE MAIN SPECIES OF LARIX

Unless otherwise stated all species below have an almost concealed bract-scale which does not project beyond the cone-scale (= ovuliferous-scale).

Group I: Leaves with two distinct white or greenish-white bands on under side.

L. kaempferi (*L. leptolepis*) Japanese Larch. Japan. Tree to 30m. Leaves 2-3.6cm, each white band beneath comprising five rows of stomata. Cones up to 3.5cm with tips of cone-scales recurved, reddish-brown and scaly sometimes with flakes that break away. Makes rapid growth and is much planted.

L. griffithiana Sikkim Larch. E Nepal, Sikkim, Tibet. Tree to

20m. Leaves 3-4cm with greenish-white bands beneath. Cones erect, cylindric, abundant, purple-brown 6-11 cm; bract-scales protruding as fine points, some depressed against cone. Bark reddish-brown with scales. Grows best in mild climates.

Group 11: Leaves without white bands beneath.

L. laricina Tamarack, Eastern Larch. N America. Tree to 20m. Leaves 3cm. Branchlets hairless (glabrous). Cones

1.5 × 1 cm with 12-15(16) scales, glabrous on outside and shining, with erect or slightly incurved tips. Bark dull pink or pinkish-brown, finely flaking but with no fissures. Tolerates wet peaty soils.

L. gmelini Dahurian Larch. NE Asia. Tree to 30m. Leaves 3cm. Branchlets usually covered in fine hairs. Cones 2-2.5cm with 20-40(50) scales, glabrous on outside and shining, with erect or slightly incurved tips. Bark reddish-brown and scaly.

L. decidua (*L. europaea*) European Larch.

N and C Europe and Siberia. Tree to 35m. Leaves 2-3cm. Cone-scales 40-50 straight not incurved at apex and pubescent to shortly downy (tomentose) outside; bractscales about half length of cone-scales. Bark greenish gray-brown and smooth when young later becoming fissured vertically.

L. russica (*L. sibirica*) Siberian Larch

E Russia and Siberia. Tree to 30m. Leaves 1.5-3cm. Cone-scales slightly incurved at apex and pubescent to shortly tomentose outside; bract-scales about one-third length of cone-scales.

L. × *eurolepis* Dunkeld Larch. This is a vigorous natural hybrid between *L. decidua* and *L. kaempferi*, pollen being supplied by the first species. What might be called typical specimens are intermediate between the parents, but seedlings from the hybrid itself show a wide range of variation between the original parents. Bark reddish brown. Shows greater resistance to insect and fungal pests than other species.

L. occidentalis Western Larch. N America - British Columbia, Oregon, Washington, Idaho. Tree 43-55m high. Leaves 3-5cm. Cones tall ovoid, 3-5cm, purple-brown when ripe; bract-scales protrude as long spreading or down-curved points. Bark purplish-gray with deep wide fissures with flaky edges.

GOLDEN LARCH (GENUS PSEUDOLARIX)

The Golden Larch (*Pseudolarix amabilis* = *P. kaempferi*) *is* a splendid tree, the leaves turning a rich, golden yellow toward the end of the season whence the Chinese name 'chin-lo-sung' = Golden Deciduous Pine is derived.

Pseudolarix amabilis is the only confirmed species of the genus and is native to east China (Chekiang and Kiangsi provinces). A second species *P. pourteli* from central China has been proposed but this is known only from vegetative material; it has small quantitative differences from *P. amabilis* and may be the juvenile state of this species.

Pseudolarix is a deciduous tree reaching 4om (z Soft). Its leaves are needle-like, about 4-6.5cm (1.6-2.6in) × 2-3mm (0.08-0.12in); they are produced either singly and spirally arranged on long shoots which are rough with persistent bases of shed leaves or in almost umbrella-like clusters on short shoots which are characteristically club-shaped and curved with persistent scales and distinct close-set, annual rings separated by constrictions.

The cones are not unlike those of *Larix*, the males clustered in catkins about 2.5cm (iin) across, the females on the same tree about 5 × 1cm (2 × 0.4in) comprising thick, acuminate, woody scales which break up at maturity, releasing the seeds.

The Golden Larch differs from *Larix* (in which genus it was once placed) in the more robust leaves, the curved short shoots, the more or less pointed conescales (not blunt-rounded) and the cone breaking up at maturity (remaining intact in *Larix*).

The Golden Larch is quite hardy in the warmer parts of temperate regions but slow growing. It requires a good, deep, well-drained soil but is intolerant of lime. Propagation is best from seed which is often abundantly set in some cultivated areas, for example Italy.

CEDARS (GENUS CEDRUS)

Cedrus is a genus of stately evergreens commonly regarded as comprising four species *Cedrus atlantica*, *C. brevifolia*, *C. deodara* and *C. libani*. Some authorities consider them all to be geographical infraspecific taxa of a single species. This is probably true, but long-standing horticultural practise and convenience keeps them at the species level. They have a wide but discontinuous distribution in the Old World.

All species have long and short shoots, the latter with clusters of needle-like leaves, 0.5-5cm (0.25-2in) long according to species. Male cones are erect, ovoid or conic, up to 5cm (2in), opening September to November. Female cones are erect, up to 1cm (0.4 in) borne terminally on short shoots.

The fruiting cones, which take two or three years to mature, are oval to oblong, rounded at the apex and about 5-10cm (2-4in) long; the numerous flattened scales are finally deciduous from a central axis. On average, trees do not bear cones until they are *40* or 50 years old.

Cedars grow best in a well-drained rich loam or sandy clay. Propagation is from seed. Mature cones should be gathered in the spring and kept in a warm place. The cone-scales break away and free the seeds, which are then ready for germination; the seedlings are planted out in the following spring.

Apart from *C. brevifolia*, which is little cultivated, all the species have numerous forms. Probably the best-known is the Blue Cedar (*C. atlantica* var *glauca*), which is prized for specimen planting and is probably the best colored of all 'blue' forms of conifer.

The wood of *Cedrus* is soft but durable and is widely used in building construction and for furniture. The resin has been used for embalming.

THE SPECIES OF CEDRUS

C. at/antica Atlas or Atlantic Cedar. N Africa (Algeria). A pyramidal tree up to 40m with an upright leading shoot and lateral branches ascending, but not becoming horizontal. Needles 2.5cm long. Cones 5-7cm × 4cm, with a flat or slightly depressed apex. Variety *g/auca* (Blue Cedar) has light blue or waxy leaves.

C. brevifolia Cyprus Cedar. Mountains of Cyprus. A broad dome-shaped tree up to 1 2m with spreading to recurved leading shoots. Needles 5-6mm long. Cones 7 × 4cm, with a depressed apex and short umbo.

C. deodara Himalayan or Indian Cedar, Deodar. W Himalaya. A pyramidal tree when young, although irregular when rriature, growing up to 60m with a pendulous leading shoot and slightly drooping lateral branches with pendulous tips. Needles are 2.5-5cm with an apical spine. Cones 7-10cm x 5-6cm, barrelshaped with a rounded apex.

C. libani Cedar of Lebanon. Lebanon, Taurus mountains, Syria. A dome-shaped tree up to 40m with an upright to spreading leading shoot and characteristic tiers of lateral branches ascending for a few metres then becoming horizontal. Needles 2.53cm. Cones 8-10cm × 4.6cm with a flat or depressed apex.

Some Trees having the Common Name 'Cedar'

Common Name	*Species*
African Cedar	*juniperus procera*
Alaska Cedar nootkatensis	*Chamaecyparis*
Atlantic or Atlas Cedar	*Cedrus atlantica*
Australian Red Cedar	*Toona spp*
Bastard Cedar	*Soymida febrifuga*
Bermuda Cedar bermudiana	*juniperus*
Black Cedar	*Nectandra pisi*
California Incense Cedar	*Libocedrus decurrens*
Cedar Elm	*Ulmus crassifolia.*
Cedar of Goa	*Cupressus lusitanica*
Cedar of Lebanon	*Cedrus libani*
Cyprus Cedar	*Cedrus brevifolia*
Eastern Red	*juniperus*
Cedar	*virginiana*
Himalayan Black Cedar	*Alnus nitida*
Himalayan Cedar	*Cedrus deodara*
Himalayan Pencil Cedar	*Juniperus macrocarpa*
Incense Cedar	*Calocedrus decurrens*
Indian Cedar •	*Cedaus deodara*
Japanese Cedar	*Cryptomeriaspp*

Mahogany Cedar	*Entandrophragma candolei, E. cylindricum*
Manado Cedar	*Cedrela celebica*
Mlanje Cedar	*Widdringtonia whytei*
Oregon Cedar	*Chamaecyparis lawsoniana*
Pencil Cedar	*Juniperus spp (especially J. virginiana)*
Prickly Cedar	*Cyathodes acerosa*
Red Cedar	*juniperus spp (especially J. virginiana)*
Sharp Cedar	*Acacia oxycedrus, Jniperus, oxycedrus*
Siberian Cedar	*Pinus cembra*
Stinking Cedar	*Torreya taxifolia*
Western Red Cedar	*Thuja plicata*
Western White Cedar	*Thuja plicata*
West Indian Cedar	*Cedrela spp*
White Cedar	*Chamaecyparis spp, Chickrassia, Melia azedarach*
Yellow Cedar	*Chamaecyparis spp*

KETELEERIA

The genus *Keteleeria* contains about four 'good' species but segregates from these, by some authorities, raise this number to nine. Like *Abies* in its upright (not pendulous or reflexed) cones it differs mainly by the cone falling in one piece, whereas in *Abies* the cone-scales are deciduous from their axis.

In *Keteleeria* the leaves are keeled above and (mostly) below, the under surface is pale yellowish-green as in yews (*Taxus* spp) and there are no whitish stomatal bands on the under surface, as there are in *Abies*. Keteleerias are evergreen trees native to southeast, central and western China extending to Indochina and Taiwan (Formosa).

In form they are pyramidal to finally more or less dome-shaped with spreading branches in whorls. The leaves are needle-like, linear to slightly tapering, solitary, spirally inserted but are mostly twisted so as to lie in one plane (pectinate).

The mature cones are large, upright and ripen in the first year. Each cone consists of numerous persistent broad woody scales, each in the axil of a forked bract-scale about half the cone-scale length. The seeds are winged and similar to those in *Abies* - two are produced for each conescale.

Keteleerias are only marginally hardy in temperate regions and thus distinctly rare in cultivation and even then only two of the species are represented: *K. davidiana* (central and west China, Taiwan) and *K. fortunei* (east China). The former is the most hardy of this generally 'unhardy' genus but the latter has survived in cultivation in Italy.

REDWOODS (GENERA METASEQUOIA, SEQUOIADENDRON, SEQUOIA)

The redwoods comprise three genera of living coniferous trees : *Metasequoia* (one living species; some to fossil representatives), *Sequoia* and *Sequoiadendron*, each with a single living species. Usually placed in the family Taxodiaceae, some Chinese authorities have suggested that all the *Metasequoia* species should be separated out as a separate family Metasequoiaceae.

Metasequoia is unusual in that it is deciduous, shedding its leafy dwarf-shoots in the fall. The Dawn Redwood (*Metasequoia glyptostro-boides*) was originally described from fossil material in 1941 and appears to have been widely distributed in the Northern Hemisphere back to the Cretaceous period (136 million years ago) and extending through to the early and middle parts of the Tertiary period (down to about 26 million years ago).

The living tree was described in 1945 from Hupeh and Szechuan provinces of China. It was introduced into cultivation in 1948 from seed received at the Arnold Arboretum and is now widely grown in temperate regions. It has proved quite hardy. In the British Isles trees have already exceeded tom (65ft) tall and although female cones are produced they do not appear to set seed, possibly because of failure of male cones to produce fertile pollen.

Its possibility as a forestry tree is being considered as it is a fast grower—1m (3.3ft) a year in the first to years, but then slowing down. In cultivation, it favors welldrained sloping ground but is equally at home on moist land near a lake or stream or even in an average garden soil.

Propagation is readily effected by cuttings, halfripe ones being struck in the summer months; a cold frame is adequate for hardwood cuttings. In general appearance and especially its deciduous habit, the Dawn Redwood resembles the Swamp Cypress (*Taxodium distichum*) but the Dawn Redwood has the leaves and shoots opposite (not alternate).

Diseases and pests are not yet established. The Sierra Redwood (*Sequoiadendron giganteum*), also known as Big Tree, Giant Sequoia, Mammoth Tree or Wellingtonia, is a native of the western slopes of the Sierra Nevada, California.

It was formerly placed in the genus *Sequoia* along with *S. sempervirens* with which it shares the characteristic thick, spongy bark which can be 'punched' without injury to the fist. It is sometimes confused with the Japanese Red Cedar (*Cryptomeriajaponica*) but this has leaves 1-1.5cm (0.4-0.6in) long with incurved points, whereas the leaves of *Sequoiadendron* are less than 1cm (0.4in) long, awl-shaped, with straight tips.

The Redwoods

Single sex coniferous trees with woody cones of spirally-arranged compound scales (the bract-scale is not distinct, but fused with the ovuliferous scale). Leaves arise singly or in pairs and are either evergreen, needle or awl shaped and alternately (spirally) arranged or deciduous, needle-shaped, opposite (as also are the shoots) and in the same plane.

Metasequoia glyptostroboides Dawn Redwood. Hupeh and Szechwan Provinces, China. Tree, in its native habitat, to about 40m tall; in cultivation, since its introduction, to more than 20m. Crown conical. Young bark orange-brown, flaking; older bark more brownish and somewhat furrowed Leaves deciduous yellowishgreen, all in one plane (pectinate) in opposite pairs along the shoots, flat and linear, 2—4 × 2mm. Male cones in small ovoid clusters, 2-5 at base of leaves; female cones more or less cylindric to 2.5cm on stalk to 5cm, each of about 12 green scales, somewhat swollen at the tips, seeds winged.

Sequoiadendron giganteum Sierra Redwood, Big Tree. Giant Sequoia, Mammoth Tree, Wellingtonia. California. Tree to 100m. Crown conical. Bark light brown, thick, soft, fibrous, deeply furrowed. Leaves evergreen, alternate, of one sort, ovate to lanceolate, 3-7mm long, sometimes to 12mm. Male cones sessile, 4-8mm long, yellow when mature in spring; female cones ellipsoidal, 5-8 × 4-5.5cm, very woody, finally pendulous, the scales flattened, diamond-shaped, each with 3-9 seeds and with slender spine when young; ripening second year. Seeds 3-6mm long, pale brown, winged.

Sequoia sempervirens Coast Redwood. S. California. Tree to 120m. Crown conical. Bark brown, thick, soft, fibrous, furrowed. Leaves evergreen, dark green, alternate, of two sorts (dimorphic). on leading shoots more or less spirally arranged, ovate-oblong to 6mm long, tip incurved, while on lateral shoots more or less in two ranks, needlelike and often falcate, 6-1 8mm long. Male cones minute to 1.5mm long; female cones ovoid to 2.5cm long, finally pendulous, scales slightly flattened obliquely, ridged, often deciduous, each scale bearing 2-5 winged seeds.

Propagation is best from imported seeds, but cuttings can be used toward the end of summer. Erect shoots are best, but if side shoots are used, these should, after rooting, be cut back when dormant buds will be stimulated to give leading shoots.

Cuttings can be struck in sandy soil and should root by spring. Adult trees and certain specimens have so captured the American imagination that they have been assigned personal individual names. The General Sherman Tree, for example, which stands in the Sequoia National Park, is alleged to be more than 3000 years old and is claimed, at 2000 tonnes, to be the most massive (though not the tallest) tree in the world.

Sequoiadendron is relatively free from disease and pests but young trees and seedlings are susceptible to the common gray mold fungus *Botrytis cinerea.* Gray mold has a grayish-brown appearance and attacks many conifers, causing the shoots to curl and wither. Supplies of timber are limited but when used it is mainly for farm buildings, posts and stakes since the wood is durable, especially in contact with soil. Although straight-grained, light and soft, the wood is not particularly easy to work.

This vigorous and long-lived tree is much grown in parks and gardens, either as specimen trees or, particularly imposing, lining roads and avenues. 'Aureum' is a slower-growing cultivar with a dense upswept crown and pale gold young foliage; 'Pendulum' has a weeping form with downswept side branches.

The Coast Redwood (*Sequoia sempervirens*) is now the only member of the genus *Sequoia*, the Sierra Redwood having been transferred to a separate genus *Sequoiadendron*. Native specimens of *Sequoia sempervirens* are immense and stately, more or less columnar, evergreen trees, found wild only on a narrow coastal belt—the 'fog belt'—on the Pacific coast of North America from southwestern Oregon through northern and central California to south of Monterey.

It rarely extends inland for more than about 4okm (25mi) and will not grow at an altitude of more than 1000 m (3500 ft). Trees of this species are probably the tallest in the world, the maximum height being about 120M (400ft); the diameter of the trunk at ground level may reach tom (30ft). The Coast Redwood may live for nearly 1000 years, the average range being 400-800 years.

The tree is at its best on a good, moist but well-aerated soil with considerable atmospheric moisture. In California it has successfully grown under such conditions to form pure forest with the huge trunks unusually close to one another.

It can also grow (but less impressively) in thin soil on rocky slopes. It is unusual amongst conifers in that it suckers freely and thus can readily regenerate by sprouts from the bases of felled trees.

This is important because, although seeds are readily formed, the successful germination rate is low and, moreover, the seedlings are intolerant of shade.

The wood of *Sequoia* is in great demand being soft, fine-grained and easy to work. Long lengths are obtainable of up to

2m (6ft) wide without defects. It is used in building construction and carpentry generally, also for paneling, railway sleepers, telegraph poles, road blocks, fence poles etc.

It takes a good polish. Excessive demand has denuded many of the original forests but some have been preserved by conservation efforts. As with the Giant Sequoia, the Coast Redwood is an outstanding tree for single specimen planting in parks and large gardens. 'Adpressa' is a smaller-leaved cultivar which has creamy-white young foliage.

SWAMP CYPRESSES (GENUS TAXODIUM)

Taxodium is a genus of three closely related species of deciduous or more or less evergreen trees, all of which are popularly known as swamp cypresses. They are natives of southern and southeastern United States and Mexico.

The shoots (branchlets) are either persistent with axillary buds near the end of each year's growth or deciduous without buds and falling within the current year or at irregular intervals. The leaves are pale green, flattened or awl-shaped, arranged essentially in one plane on the deciduous shoots or radially on the persistent shoots.

The male and female cones are present on the same plants, the male in pendulous panicles. The female cones ripen in one year and when mature are globular, a5mm (iin) in diameter, comprising numerous peltate scales, which are irregularly foursided on the outside. Each scale bears two angular three-winged seeds.

The most commonly cultivated species, *Taxodium distichum* (Swamp or Bald Cypress), is a tall handsome tree whose pale green foliage gives it a surprisingly delicate feathery appearance. It usually favors swamps and streams, but will grow equally well on drained soil.

Under swamp conditions the roots will produce upright protuberances or 'knees,' which rise above the level of the water and so assist in root aeration. These 'knees' are comparable to the specialized roots (pneumatophores) of the mangroves and other tropical swamp inhabitants.

Taxodium ascendens (Pond Cypress or sometimes also Bald Cypress) and *T. mucronatum* (Montezuma or Mexican Cypress) are both less hardy than *T. distichum* and so are not cultivated so much.

Taxodium mucronatum is evergreen in its native Mexico but becomes deciduous in cooler climates. One particular specimen, in the Mexican village of Santa Maria del Tule near the city of Oaxaca, is named *El Gigante*.

It has become a historic landmark and is viewed locally with great pride. The Spanish conquistador Hernan Cortes wrote about this same tree which he saw during his expedition of the 1520'S. For a long time this tree was believed to have the thickest trunk in the world until it was revealed that its massive size was the result of three trees having grown and fused together.

The timber most commonly used is from *T. distichum;* the wood is soft and does not shrink, is resistant to insect attack and is little affected by damp conditions. These qualities make it a suitable packaging material and useful for piping, ventilators, fencing and garden furniture.

THE SPECIES OF TAXODIUM

T. distichum Swamp or Bald Cypress. SE USA and westward to Illinois and Missouri; Arizona. Tree to 30-50m. Branches more or less horizontal, conical at first becoming round-headed at maturity.

Leaves spreading, a characteristically delicate pale green, 8-18mm long, spirally arranged but twisted at the base and, as a result, appearing in one plane; reddish-brown at the end of the season and falling separately or with the deciduous branchlets.

In wet ground roots produce upright 'knees' to assist in root aeration. *T. ascendens* Pond Cypress, Upland Cypress or Bald Cypress. SE USA and westward to Alabama. Tree rather similar to *T. distichum*, but smaller, reaching about 25m, the trunk swollen at the base, the branches spreading, but the ultimate branchlets more or less erect.

Leaves awl-shaped, not in 2 ranks but arranged all around the shoots, adpressed. 5-10mm long, bright green, turning to a rich brown in the fall. *TT mucronatum* Montezuma or Mexican Cypress. Mexico. Tree much the same size as *T. distichum* but not well-known outside its native Mexico. It differs from T. *distichum* in being half-evergreen to evergreen with longer male cones, the pollen sacs opening in the fall and not in spring as in the other species.

CHINESE FIRS (GENUS CUNNINGHAMIA)

Cunninghamia (Chinese or China firs) is a genus of two, perhaps three, species native to China and Taiwan. The Chinese Fir (*Cunninghamia lanceolata*) *is* infrequently found in cultivation but in its native China it is an important timber tree.

They are evergreen trees with spreading branches. The leaves are stiff, decurrent, linear-lanceolate with serrulate margins, white-banded beneath and spread in two ranks, but arise spirally. Male cones are oblong, borne in terminal clusters.

Females occur on the same tree as the males and are subglobose, comprising rather thin, leathery, overlapping, serrate, pointed scales without distinct bractscales. There are three inverted ovules per scale, each maturing to a narrowly-winged seed.

Chinese firs are not particularly hardy except in the milder/warmer parts of temperate regions, hence are not often seen in cultivation, and then only in sheltered positions on a good soil. They will regenerate from stool shoots of felled trees.

Propagation is best from seed, but cuttings from erect shoots may be used. Two species have been positively identified. *Cunninghamia lanceolata* (south and west China) grows to 25m (82ft) and has leaves 3-6cm × 2-6mm (1.2-2.4 × 0.080.2in) with two broad, white stomatal lines beneath. The mature cones are 2.5-5.ocm (1-tin) long.

The timber is much used for coffins. *Cunninghamia konishii* (Taiwan) reaches 25m (82ft) or more and differs from the previous species by having smaller and narrower leaves, 1.8-2.8cm × 2mm (0.7-1.1 × o.o8in); stomatal bands are absent or not clearly marked.

The mature cones are up to 2.5cm (tin) long. The doubtful species is *C. kawkamii* also from Taiwan, which is intermediate in form between the two previous species and is probably a variety of *C. konishii*.

JAPANESE UMBRELLA PINE (GENUS *SCIADOPITYS*)

The Japanese Umbrella Pine or Parasol Pine (*Sciadopitys verticillata*) is an ever green pyramidal tree reaching 40m (130ft) in its native habitat of central Japan, where it sometimes forms forests up to an altitude of 1000m (3300ft). The bark is almost smooth but separates into thin shreds. The leaves are of two types. The main ones are in whorls of (10)20-30 paired leaves 8-12 × 0.2-0.3cm (3-5 × 0.08-0.12in), each pair united along their whole length by their sides; stomata are found only over a small area in the groove on the lower surface.

The appearance of each whorl is very much like that of the 'stays' of an open umbrella. Along the internodes between these whorls are triangular, somewhat overlapping, scale-like leaves which are green at first, becoming brown in the second year. Male cones are in terminal clusters, each cone with spirally-arranged pollen sacs. The female cones are solitary, on same tree as the males, each comprising numerous (ovuliferous) scales, which, in the young state, are much smaller than, the subtending bract-scales, but greatly exceed them in the mature cone when they become woody and more or less wedge- or fan-shaped.

Each scale bears seven to nine seeds in the second year, the cone then ovoid and 8-12 × 3.5-5.0cm (3-5 × 1.4-2in), the upper margin of each scale being slightly recurved. Seeds are compressed ovoid, 12mm (o.48in) long and narrowly winged. This species is a slow grower and hardy in temperate regions where it readily produces seed by which it is propagated. However, it is uncommon in cultivation and grown only for its unique appearance - quite unlike any other conifer.

The wood is durable and water resistant which makes it useful for boatbuilding.

TASMANIAN CEDARS (GENUS *ATHROTAXIS*)

Athrotaxis comprises three species of evergreen trees or shrubs all from the mountains of Tasmania. The leaves are spirally arranged and scale-like or awl-like. Cones are unisexual, the females finally woody, ripe within one year, more or less globose and comprising 5-20(25) spirally-arranged scales, each subtending a bract which is fused with its scale except at the tip.

The scales are swollen at their free (outer) end, tapering to the base at the point of attachment. The seeds are winged. The Smooth Tasmanian Cedar (*Athrotaxis cupressoides*) is a tree to 6-12m (204oft) in its native habitat of the mountains of central and western Tasmania where it grows at altitudes in excess of 1000m (3300ft), but it reaches about half this height in cultivation.

The branchlets are rounded and concealed by the denselypacked adpressed, decussate scale-like leaves, about 3mm (0.12in) long, which are rhombic in outline, with a translucent, finely serrate margin. The leaf bases overlap and on larger branches the leaves are larger.

Female cones are finally about 12mm (0.48in) across, comprising five or six scales, the free tip of each bract-scale projecting as a short, spiny point. It is distinguished from the other two species by the scale-leaves being closely adpressed along all their length to the branchlets and the absence of stomatal bands on the ventral surface.

The King William Pine (*A. selaginoides*) tops 33m (108ft) in its native habitat of western Tasmania. The leaves are 7-12mm (o.28-0.48in) long, lanceolate to awlshaped, curved toward but free of the branchlet, pointing forward at about a 30° angle.

They are much less densely arranged than in the previous species from which it is also distinct in having two stomatal bands on the ventral surface of the leaf and lacking translucent margins.

The Summit Cedar (*A. laxifolia*) is intermediate in form between the previous species, growing to a height of iom (33ft) in the western mountains of Tasmania. Its leaves are slightly spreading, 4-6mm (o. t6-o.24in) long, the margin translucent and entire; two stomatal bands are present on the upper (ventral) surface.

The wood of Tasmanian cedars has some value in cabinet-making and lighter types of carpentry. All three species are marginally hardy in temperate zones.

JAPANESE RED CEDAR (GENUS CRYPTOMERIA)

The Japanese Red Cedar (*Cryptomeria japonica*) *is* the only member of its genus but exists in two distinct, geographically isolated varieties. The one seen most frequently in cultivation is var *japonica* from Japan, while var *sinensis is* native to China. Cryptomerias are evergreen trees with reddish-brown bark which detaches in longish shreds.

The leaves are spirally arranged in five ranks and more or less awl-shaped, 6-12mm (0.24-0.48in) long, the base decurrent on the shoot. Male and female cones occur on the same branch, the male in short spike-like clusters each with numerous pollen sacs, the female solitary and maturing in one year into a woody, erect, stalked cone 2-3cm (o.8t.2in) across comprising 20-30 wedgeshaped composite scales.

The outer edge of each of the composite scales (conescales) appears disc-like and has a more or less central recurved spine with the upper margin bearing three to five short rigid processes.

Variety *japonica* is of more compact appearance, the branches more spreading and the leaves stouter; the female cones comprise some 30 scales, each fertile scale maturing to bear five seeds. In var *sinensis* the habit is more open with the ultimate branchlets tending to droop; the female cones rarely have more than 20 scales, each fertile scale maturing to bear two seeds.

Variety *japonica* is commonly favored as an ornamental forming a bright green narrowly conical crown with a rounded apex. It is fully hardy, growing best in coo, damp areas with good deep alluvial soil. Propagation is by seeds or cuttings.

There are numerous cultivars; 'Elegans' is often planted but despite its name is sometimes an untidy sight. Its leaves are 2-3cm (0.8-1.2in) long and of the juvenile type; they are of a fine green color in summer changing to reddish-bronze as winter approaches. Cones are rarely produced in this cultivar.

In Japan about one-third of the area under afforestation is

devoted to var *japonica.* It is also planted by temples and at the sides of many celebrated avenues to which it has contributed much of their fame. The wood is durable, easy to work and resistant to insects. It is much used in building construction and for furniture and the bark is valuable as a roofing material.

CHINESE SWAMP CYPRESS (GENUS GLYPTOSTROBUS)

The Chinese Swamp Cypress or Chinese Water Pine (*Glyptostrobus lineatus* = *G. pensilis*) is a small deciduous tree native to south China. Like the Swamp Cypress (*Taxodium distichum*) it is characteristic of damp places in its native China where it appears to be mainly a cultivated tree, possibly because it is believed to bring luck to the home and rice crops.

Glyptostrobus is closely related to *Taxodium*, differing in its pear-shaped, stalked female cones comprising thin, elongated nonpeltate scales which are coarselytoothed at their apices; the seeds are oval to oblong with a single wing and not, as in *Taxodium*, three-angled and appearing as if with three thick wings.

The Chinese Swamp Cypress is scarcely hardy in temperate regions and is hence rarely seen in cultivation. The shoots are hairless and of two types: either persistent (usually terminal) and spirally arranged with axillary buds, or deciduous, falling with leaves in the fall and without axillary buds.

The leaves on persistent shoots are scale-like, 2-3mm (0.08-0.12in) long, spirally arranged and overlapping while those on deciduous shoots are more or less needle-like, 8-12mm (0.32-0.48in) long and about 1 mm (0.04in) wide and arranged in the same plane, one row on each side of the shoot (pectinate) and falling with the shoot in the fall.

The sexes are separate but on the same tree, the male cones in hanging clusters, the females finally about I8mm (0.7in) long on a 12-18mm (0.50.7in) long stalk.

TAIWANIA

The genus *Taiwania* comprises three very closely related species of evergreen trees, which may in fact be geographical subspecies of a single species, namely *Taiwania cryptomerioides*. They are native to north Burma, southwest China, Taiwan and Manchuria.

Taiwania cryptomerioides is a tree to about 6om (195ft) but rarely reaches more than 15-16m (49-52ft) in cultivation. Its leaves are of two types; on juvenile and sterile shoots they are awl-shaped, 1218mm (0.5-0.8in) long, curved and much like those of *Cryptomeria* with a broad glaucous stomatal band on each surface; leaves on adult and fertile shoots are scalelike, smaller to about 6mm (0.2in) long, triangular and overlapping with stomatal lines on all surfaces.

Female cones are sub-globose, 10-II(15)mm (0.4-0.45(0.6) in) long, comprising numerous rounded and mucronate scales. Each scale bears two ovules which mature into winged seeds. *Taiwania* is related to *Cunninghamia* but this has three ovules per scale.

Taiwania cryptomerioides is scarcely hardy in temperate regions, but has survived with winter shelter.

MONKEY PUZZLE (GENUS ARAUCARIA)

Araucaria is a genus of evergreen coniferous trees comprising some 18 species all confined to the Southern Hemisphere, notably in South America, Australasia and the islands of the South Pacific. The genus includes the well-known Monkey Puzzle Tree or Chile Pine (*Araucaria araucana* = *A. imbricata*), the Norfolk Island Pine (*A. heterophylla* = *A. excelsa*) and the Parana Pine or Candelabra Tree (*A. angustifolia*).

Members of *Araucaria* are tall imposing trees with branches in regular whorls. The bark of the old trees is ridged with the remains of old leaf-bases or rough and peeling off.

The leaves persist for many years and are flat and broad or awl-shaped (acicular) and curved; some species have awl-shaped juvenile leaves. Male and female cones are usually borne on different trees but sometimes on separate branches of the same tree.

The male cones grow in large cylindric terminal or subterminal clusters, each with numerous pollen sacs. The females mature in two to three years, often as very large globose or ovoid cones of woody overlapping scales, which break up when the seeds are ripe.

There is one seed on each scale and adherent to it, with a marginal wing on all edges, in most species. The genus is very closely related to the kauri pines (*Agathis*) but an essential difference is that the seeds are free from the cone-scale in this genus and not adherent as in *Araucaria*.

Propagation is mainly by seed but cuttings of terminal shoots from well-established plants can also be used.

The wood of *Araucaria* is resinous, straight-grained and easy to work. *Araucaria araucana*, *A. bidmillii* (Bunya-Bunya) and *A. cunninghamii* (Moreton Bay Pine or Hoop Pine) are the most important timber trees although the latter is susceptible to serious attack from the Hoop Pine Borer, a species of *Calymmaduus.*

The timber is mainly used for general indoor joinery and carpentry and for boxes and masts as well as pulp for papermaking. For all practical purposes it can be used as a substitute for the Scots Pine (*Pinus silvestris*).

The striking appearance of the Monkey Puzzle Tree has made it a popular subject for cultivation in parks and gardens. It was most popular during the late 19th century and is not frequently planted these days.

The tree was introduced to Britain by Archibald Menzies in 1795, who removed some of the edible seeds when dining with the Viceroy of Chile. It became popular after a good supply of seed was sent back by William Lobb in 1844.

Its fascination led to much planting in highly unsuitable places, especially suburban gardens where it rarely does well, looks out of place, and generally bedraggled and unhappy through loss of the lower branches at an early stage—a response to poor soils and atmospheric pollution. It does best on moist but adequately drained soils in a humid and clean atmosphere. It is, and looks at its best in arboreta and parks especially when in pure stands rather than randomly distributed amongst other trees.

In addition to *A. araucana*, the seeds of *A. bidmillii* are an important article of diet of Australian aborigines and for this reason there are government restrictions on felling in certain areas.

The Norfolk Island Pine is, amongst others, commonly grown as an indoor plant and does well when planted in a large tub with a good fibrous loam—leaf mold and sand mixture.

There is, however, one fine specimen of this plant growing outdoors in the famous subtropical gardens at Tresco, one of the Isles of Scilly, about 5okm (30mi) west of Land's End in Cornwall, England.

THE MAIN SPECIES OF ARAUCARIA

Group I: Leaves broad and flat, about 1.5cm long. Cone-scales without or with only vestigial wings.

A. araucana (*A. imbricata*) Chile Pine or Monkey Puzzle Tree. Chile and W Argentina. Tree 30-50m with spreading, stout, upwardly curved branches of striking appearance. Leaves 2.5-5 × 2.5cm, densely imbricated, ovate-lanceolate but with a broad base, firm and with a sharp, pointed apex. Male cones in catkin-like clusters, cylindric, 8-1 2cm long, mature cones more or less globose up to 1 5(20)cm across; seeds somewhat compressed, 2.5-3.5cm long, adnate to scale, each with recurved apical appendage.

A. bidwillii Bunya-Bunya. Coastal district of Queensland, Australia. Tree to 50m and fast-growing. The main branches horizontal, younger branchlets pendulous. Leaves on sterile shoots 18-25 × 4.5-11 mm, lanceolate, with a narrow base, the apex tapering to a long stiff point, leaves on fertile shoots (and the upper branches) stiffer and incurved, 1 5-25mm long.

Sexes usually on separate plants (dioecious), the male cones in clusters 1 5-1 8 × 1 .3cm, cylindrical and catkin-like; mature cones elliptical, up to 30 × 23cm and weighing up to 5kg; scales large with a long recurved point; seeds large and pear-shaped up to about 6.5 × 2.5cin with a rudimentary wing.

A. angustifolia Parana Pine or Candelabra Tree. Brazil and Argentina. Tree to 35m with a flat crown, the branches in whorls of 4-8. Leaves with long points, stiff and leathery, the stomata on lower surface, leaves of sterile branches 3-6 × 0.6cm and appearing opposite, those of fertile branches shorter and arranged spirally.

Cones 17cm across, 12cm high, each scale with a recurved, stiff appendage; seeds 5 × 2cm, light brown. Allied to *A. araucana* but differs in the leaves being softer and less crowded. The wood is soft and commercially valuable.

Group II: Leaves either more or less awl shaped to broadly ovate or less than 1 cm long. Cone-scales obviously winged.

A. heterophylla (*A. excelsa*) Norfolk Island Pine. Restricted to Norfolk Island in the South Pacific. Handsome tree to 70m, main branches horizontal, lateral branches sometimes pendulous.

Leaves on young lateral and sterile shoots 8-13(15)mm long, spreading, not crowded and those on older and fertile shoots incurved, crowded and overlapping, 6-7mm long with incurved horny point, the midrib hardly visible Male cones in clusters, 3.5-5cm long and catkinlike; mature cones more or less globose about 10-12cm across, seeds with welldeveloped wings, the adherent scales each with a flat triangular incurved spine. Much cultivated in the Mediterranean area and places of similar climate as an ornamental tree. Many cultivars.

A. cunninghamii Moreton Bay Pine or Hoop Pine. Mainly in New South Wales and Queensland, Australia and also in New Guinea. Tree 60-70m. Bark characteristically cracking into horizontal hoops or bands, peeling. Branches horizontal, the branchlets mostly concentrated at the ends.

Leaves on sterile lateral branches and young trees in general lanceolate 8-15(19)mm long, straight and spreading with a sharp, pointed apex; on older trees and fertile branches, leaves more crowded, shorter, incurved with a short pointed apex.

Male cones in clusters, 5-7.5cm long and catkinlike; mature cones broadly ellipsoidal about 10 × 7.5cm with exserted (protruding) stiff, recurved apices of the cone-scales; seeds with narrow membranous wings.

A. columnaris New Caledonian Pine. New Caledonia and Polynesia. Tree closely allied to A. *heterophylla* under which name it often appears. Fertile and older branch lets with densely overlapping, incurved leaves, each with a distinct midrib, giving a characteristic and distinctive whip-cord appearance; leaves on sterile and young branchlets triangular or lanceolate.

A. balansae New Caledonia. Tree 12-1 8m, the branches more or less horizontal and turning down at the ends. Leaves densely crowded, broadly awl-shaped about 3mm long with stomata on inner surface. Mature cones at the apex of short shoots, oval, 6-7 5 × 5-6.5cm, each scale with a hard bristle 8mm long. Close to *A. columnaris* which has larger leaves. Of little or no commercial value.

KAURI PINES (GENUS AGATHIS)

The kauri or kauri pines (genus *Agathis*) are the most tropical genus of all the conifers. Some 20 species have been described but five (or more) may be, at most, subspecies.

Representatives are found in the wettest tropical rain forests of the Malay archipelago, Sumatra, the Philippines and Fiji, with oufliers in the subtropical forests of Queensland in Australia and northernmost New Zealand.

They are imposing evergreen trees with massive columnar trunks and large spreading crowns. Male and female cones are borne on separate trees.

Kauri pines differ from *Araucaria* by the seed being free from the (ovuliferous) scale and not adnate to it, the larger leaves which are broad and flat rather than more or less awl-shaped or lanceolate and the seeds being mostly unequally winged whereas in *Araucaria* they are wingless or about equally winged.

Agathis timber is one of the most valuable softwoods in the world and is highly prized for boatbuilding, as a decorative veneer and for household utensils and drawing boards.

The wood of most species is strong, durable and of excellent quality and because of the shedding of lower branches in young specimens, is remarkably free from knots.

All parts contain a resin (kauri gum) and in several species it exudes spontaneously and from injuries, accumulating on branches, trunks and at the base of trees.

It has been extensively used in the manufacture of varnishes, linoleum and paints, being also known as an anime and more specifically as copal, damar or dammar, these last two a reference to *Agathis dammara* formerly known as *Dammara alba* and *A. alba*.

Other sources are from *A. robusta* and the very important *A. australis*, the Kauri (or Cowdie) Pine from the North Island of New Zealand. In addition to the freshly-exuded resin, there are large quantities of fossil resin preserved in peat bogs where kauri pines no longer grow.

This supply is even more esteemed, sought after and commercially exploited. The preserving peat has also been distilled to yield a petroleum spirit and turpentine. Kauri pines have been so over-exploited for their products that Government action was required to conserve them.

Most *Agathis* timber now comes from small groves or isolated trees scattered through primary forest but the plantations on Java promise to be a major timber source when the virgin rain forests have disappeared.

CYPRESSES (GENUS CUPRESSUS)

Cupressus—the true cypresses—is a genus comprising, as now understood, about 20 species. Cypresses are widely distributed in the New and Old Worlds, from Oregon to Mexico in North America, the Mediterranean area, western Asia, the western Himalaya and China.

They are evergreen trees, rarely shrubs; the branchlets are densely clothed with small overlapping scale-like decussate leaves with minute denticulate-fringed margins (lens). On older branches the leaves are more awl-shaped (acicalar), larger and spreading.

Male and female cones are terminal and solitary on separate branches of the same tree. Mature female cones are globose to broadly elliptic, mostly more than 1cm (0.4in) across, with 6-12 finally woody, peltate scales, each bearing 6-12 (sometimes as many as 20) more or less winged seeds, which may be smooth or beset with a few resinous tubercles.

The cone requires 18 months to mature. The limits of the modern genus have been reduced by the transfer of a number of species to *Chamaecyparis* known as false cypresses. In almost all cases trees and shrubs of both genera are easily distinguished. In *Chamaecyparis* the ultimate branchlets are usually flattened in one plane and these flattened foliar-like sprays (phyllomorphs) are commonly horizontally (sometimes more or less vertically) disposed. In *Cupressus* the ultimate branchlets are not generally so flattened but diverge in various directions so no phyllomorphs are evident.

It is also interesting to note that, generally speaking, the species of *Chamaecyparis* are much more hardy than those of *Cupressus*, which, in much of northern Europe at least, are regarded as 'semi-tender.' There is no doubt that the two genera are closely related and this is borne out by the existence of the inter generic hybrid × *Cupressocyparis*.

In suitable climatic conditions, including reasonably clean air, cypresses are not particular as to soil type, succeeding on light to heavy loams and even on a highly sandy soil, provided adequate moisture is maintained. This is true of *C. macrocarpa* (Monterey Cypress), the most commonly planted species in the United Kingdom, which does well by the sea in the southwest, where the high relative humidity no doubt significantly reduces transpiration and thus equally the demand for water.

Propagation of species is mainly by seeds and the cultivars by cuttings and sometimes by grafts on the appropriate stock. Cypresses are susceptible to bacterial and fungal diseases, notably *Bacterium tumifaciens*, which can cause galls on the stem and root, especially near soil level, and stem canker caused by species of the imperfect fungus *Pestalotia* (*Pestalozzia*).

Amongst insect pests, the aphid *Cinara* (*Cupressobium*) *cupressi* can weaken trees of *C. macrocarpa* by feeding in vast numbers on the sap. It also excretes 'honeydew' on which disfiguring growths of sooty molds can occur.

The Conifer Spinning Mite (*Oligonychus ununguis*) also attacks the genus, causing, amongst other things, an unsightly chlorosis. The wood of many cypresses is valuable, being durable and easily worked. It is used in general building construction, carpentry and for posts and poles of all sorts, but not for packing cases since the often spicy odor of the wood may contaminate susceptible contents. The most commonly used timbers are those of *C. macrocarpa* and *C. sempervirens.* These two species are also widely planted as ornamentals but their 'semi-tenderness' restricts them to the mildest areas and they are likely to suffer in anything approaching a severe frost. In more subtropical areas of the world, plantations, especially of *C. macrocarpa*, have been established. This species is also increasing in popularity as a screening or hedging plant.

THE MAIN SPECIES OF CUPRESSUS

Group 1: Leaves conspicuously resinous and glandular on the back, the ultimate branchlets typically diverging at all angles and not flattened into one plane as phyllomorphs.

C. macnabiana Macnab Cypress. Mainly N California. Shrub or small tree to about 12m Branchlets compressed dorsiventrally, leaves rich green or glaucous, about 1 mm long, densely set, the apices enlarged and blunt. Mature cones 12-19mm across with 6-8 scales

C. arizonica Rough-barked Arizona Cypress. Arizona, Mexico and New Mexico Tree 1 5-25m. Bark rough reddish-brown, graying, not exfoliating. Branchlets not compressed, leaves acute, deep green to grayish-green about 2mm long, the margin (lens) finely toothed. Mature cones 1 2-25mm across with 6-8 scales.

C. glabra Smooth Arizona Cypress. C Arizona. Tree 7-18m. Bark cherry-red. smooth and exfoliating each year. Branchlets not compressed. Leaves 152mm, long, white-spotted with resin, acute, finely toothed margin (lens), gray to grayish-green, keeled. Mature cones 20-26mm across, with usually 8(5-10) scales, each with a prominent umbo Tolerates calcareous soils and is drought resistant.

Group II: Leaves not conspicuously resinous or glandular on the back, but sometimes with a faint nonresinous 'slit' or pit, and then ultimate branchlets flattened in one plane

A Ultimate branchlets flattened in one plane (phyllomorphs), more or less horizontally disposed. Cones subglobose, 8-16mm across.

C. lusitanica vat *benthamii* Mexican Cypress, Cedar of Goa. Mexico Tree to about 33m. Leaves shining, dark green, with central dorsal 'pit' and acute apex. Mature cones about 12-1 5mm across with 6-8 scales, each scale with a prominent umbo, slightly, or not reflexed, seeds smooth.

C. torulosa Bhutan or Himalayan Cypress. W Himalaya and Szechwan, China. Tree to 50m Ultimate branches more or less flattened, curved and characteristically whip-like Leaves about 1.5mm long, somewhat blunt at the apex, usually with a dorsal, central pit. Mature cones about 11 (12)mm across with 8-10 scales, seeds relatively few, 6-8 per scale with tubercles.

AA *Ultimate branchlets not flattened in one plane*, *but diverging at all angles. Cones 1-4cm wide or long.*

C. macrocarpa Monterey Cypress. California Tree to about 25m, at first pyramidal, finally with a broad crown. Leaves 1-2.5mm gong, densely packed, apices adpressed, rather blunt; bruised foliage with citronella like smell. Mature cones subglobose, 2.5-4 × 1.75-2.5cm, with 8-12(14) scales, each with a short, stout and blunt umbo, seeds minutely tubercled Distinguished by its large cones from al other commonly cultivated species except *C. sempervirens*, which has smaller leaves and smooth seeds Useful as a windbreak in exposed places by the sea.

C. sempervarens Italian Cypress. Mediterranean Cypress, Funeral Cypress The classical cypress of the ancients Mediterranean area including Crete, Cyprus and Sicily Switzerland, USSR and the mountains of N Iran l ree usually 20-30m, out up to bUm in the Mediterranean area Branches either spreading (vat *hortzontalis;* or Last grate (vat *sempervirens;*. Leaves dark green, 1 mm long, diamond-shaped but apices bluntish; bruised foliage with, little of no smell Mature cones subglobose to broadly elliptical, 2 5-3 × 2cm with 8-14 scales, the central umbo inconspicuous, seeds smooth.

The type is vat *sempervirens* and is very striking with its erect, fastigiate branches, the whole tree being lanceolate to narrowly pyramidal in outline This variety is also known as 'Stricta'.

C. goveniarra Gowen Cypress. California Shrub or small tree to 20rn Leaves 1-2mm long, sometimes with a pit,' gray to blackish green, bruised foliage with distinct, pleasant, resinous smell; shoots purplish brown. Mature cones globose, 10—1 bmni across with 6-10 scales, each with a low blunt umbo; seeds smoth.

CC lusitanica Mexican Cypress, Cedar of Goa. Mexico, extending to the mountains of Guatemala l ree reaching 30m but variable. Branches commonly spreading and pendulous at the ends, ultimate branchlets not flattened in one plane but diverging at all angles (compare with *C. lusitanica* var *benthamo* above).

Leaves acute, glaucous to gray green, the tips spreading, 1.5-2mm long, bruised foliage with little or no smell, shoots pinkish brown. Mature cones subglobose, 12-16mm across with 6-8 scales, the umbo pointed and often hooked, seeds smooth, the wing sometimes little developed

HYBRID CYPRESSES (GENUS CUPRESSOCYPARIS)

The genus × *Cupressocyparis* (hybrid cypress) is a natural bigeneric hybrid × *Cupressocyparis leylandii*—between *Cupressus macrocarpa* (Monterey Cypress) from California and *Chamaecyparis nootkatensis* (Nootka Cypress or Yellow Cypress) from the Pacific coast of northwestern America.

× *Cupressocyparis* is thought to have arisen in cultivation in England at Leighton Hall, Welshpool, Shropshire in 1888 when a number of seedlings of the Nootka Cypress were being raised from seed. A Monterey Cypress was growing in the same garden.

In 1911 further seedlings were raised at Leighton Hall, this time from seed taken from *Cupressus macrocarpa.* From these original seedlings a number of clones have now been established numbering some io or 11, with some differences in growth habit, color and texture.

The hybrid cypress only really began to attract widespread attention in the 1950's for fast-growing shelter belts and hedges; by the 196o's demand began to outstrip limited supplies largely due to this hybrid needing to be propagated vegetatively from cuttings.

Today × *Cupressocyparis leylandii* is widely planted as a very fastgrowing, hardy and adaptable conifer. A tree planted in 1916 is now over 33m (110ft) high with a girth of 2.5m (8ft). From a distance it resembles the Nootka rather than the Monterey Cypress in general appearance but is usually far more columnar and erect in habit.

However, the leaves and branches are less flattened than Nootka and resemble more the filiform shape of Monterey. Cones are produced on more mature trees and they are somewhere between the cone structures of the two parents, with tubercles on the cone-scales.

The hybrid cypress seems to inherit its hardiness from the Nootka parent and its fast growth from the Monterey. It with stands clipping and can be made into a dense hedge from zm (6.6ft) in height but it is not suitable for dwarf hedging. In the last ten years or so, research and further selection of the original seedlings from Leighton Hall and also from others found elsewhere, have produced the following clones:

'Green Spire' (Clone 1). Dense and narrow with bright green foliage.

'Haggerston Gray' (Clone 2). Probably the commonest clone; green foliage but slightly grayer than 'Green Spire.'

'Leighton Green.' Another widely grown clone.

'Naylor's Blue.' A narrow column tree with gray-green foliage.

'Stapehill.' This has a more flattened type of green foliage.

Two other *Cupressocyparis* hybrids have also emerged: *x C. notabilis* (*Chamaecyparis nootkatensis x Cupressus glabra*) (Arizona Cypress) and × *C. ovensii* (*Chamaecyparis nootkatensis x Cupressus lusitanica*) (Mexican Cypress).

The timber of the Leyland Cypress is of good quality and since the tree can be readily grown under forestry conditions it is likely to become widely planted.

FALSE CYPRESSES (GENUS CHAMAECYPARIS)

The false cypresses comprise seven species of evergreen conifers of the Northern Hemisphere. They are found mainly in the western and southeastern coastal regions of North America and in Japan and Taiwan. In cultivation, they are not particular as to soil provided it is not too calcareous and is moist without being waterlogged.

The false cypresses are hardy, mostly pyramidal trees with a habit very similar to that of the true cypresses (*Cupressus*) except that the young shoot systems or sprays (phyllomorphs) are flattened and in one plane, a characteristic they share with species of the genus *Thuja* (arbor-vitae).

The leaves are scale-like, opposite and decussate, but the juvenile leaves are sometimes awl-shaped. The two sexes are found on the same tree but on separate branches. The female cones are globose and very small—up to icm (0.4in) across.

They mature in a year except in *Chamaecyparis nootkatensis* (Nootka Cypress), which requires about 18 months. The seeds are somewhat compressed, each with a thin broad wing.

The timber of most of the species of *Chamaecyparis* is of high quality, being generally light, durable, easily worked and resistant to fungus decay and insect attacks. The wood of most species has its own pleasant distinctive odor and color.

Chamaecyparis fhrmosensis is one of the most valued timber trees in Taiwan where it grows at an altitude of 2000-3000m (6500-10000ft). Specimens can reach 50m (165ft) high and some are estimated to be about 3000 years old.

This is one of the woods without a distinctive odor. The wood of *C. lawsoniana* is no less useful and has an odor that can be described as 'spicy.' It is used for general building, for floors, furniture and fence posts, railway sleepers and in boatbuilding.

The wood of *C. nootkatensis* is also of excellent quality and is used in much the same way. It is known in the trade as 'yellow cypress,' though this popular name is also used for the wood of the Swamp Cypress (*Taxodium distichum*).

The excellent wood of *C. obtusa is* much prized in its native country of Japan and is probably unsurpassed for the highest quality work in all kinds of construction. It is very straight, evenly grained and often beautifully marked. *Chamae cyparis pisifera*, another Japanese species, is perhaps the least exploited of the false cypresses but is nevertheless extensively used for less ornamental kinds of carpentry.

Outside their native habitats, several species of *Chamaecyparis* and their numerous cultivars are planted for ornamental purposes, including *C. pisifera*, *C. obtusa* and *C. nootkatensis.* As well as being popular ornamentals for parks and large gardens, there are many dwarf cultivars of these species suitable for growing in small gardens and rock gardens.

However, the best-known cultivated species is the Lawson Cypress (*C. lawsoniana*) from southwestern Oregon and northwestern California. The number of cultivars is in excess of 200, ranging from dwarf shrubs grown in rock gardens to tall, columnar trees with many different color forms. It also makes an excellent hedging or screening subject and will grow in a wide range of conditions, including shaded or exposed sites.

THE MAIN SPECIES OF CHAMAECYPARIS

Group I: Underside of phyllomorphs partially whitish or at least glaucous, especially on leaf margins (lens). Lateral leaves significantly larger (twice as long) than facial ones and all closely adpressed-except *C. pisifera* where leaves ate about the same size (and length) with acute more or less spreading tips

C. formosensis Formosa Cypress. Taiwan. Tree reach ng 65m with a girth of 24m in its native habitat- Lateral and facial leaves of equal length, about 15mm, keeled or with glandular pit, dull green. bronzetinged, often whitish beneath, smelling of totter seaweed when crushed. Mature cones 8-9mm across but ellipsoidal, with 10-11 scales, the outer surfaces more or ess wrinkled; seeds 2 per scale, oval with narrow wings and conspicuous resin tubercles.

The species is close to *C. pisitera* but differing in color, shape and the smell of the crushed leaves. It forms pure forests in Taiwan on Mount Morrison at 2300-3300m in association with *C. obtusa.* It is a valuable timber tree in its native land (the wood is resistant to insect attack and decay) but it is in danger of extinction through over felling.

C. lawsoniana Lawson Cypress. Extreme W USA Tree 25-

50m, spire-like with spreading branches, pendulous at the tips. Lateral leaves of ultimate branchlets 2.5-3mm long, facial leaves about half as long, all acute and with glandular dots appearing conspicuously translucent when examinec under lens against light.

Male cones characteristically crimson. Mature cones about 8mm across with usually 8 scales, each with 2-4 seeds Much planted and with 200 or more named cultivars.

C. obtusa Hinoki Cypress. Japan, with var *formosana* in Taiwan. Tree to 40m, pyramidal. Leaves distinctly obtuse, without glands, the white markings beneath somewhat Y-shaped; lateral leaves about twice as long as the facial ones. Mature cones 8-10mm across with 8-(10) scales, each with up to 5 seeds. Numerous cultivars. Intolerant of lime and a dry climate.

C. pisifera Sawara Cypress. Japan. Tree to 50m. Leaves with spreading acute tips, the facial and lateral leaves about the same size and obscurely glandular. Mature cones 6(8)mm across with 10(12) scales, each scale with 1-2 seeds. Numerous cultivars.

Group II: Underside of phyllomorphs the same color as the upper side or slightly paler, without whitish or glaucous marking.

Lateral leaves about the same size as the facial leaves or only a little longer.

C. thyoides White Cedar (sometimes also known as White Cypress). E N America. Tree to 25m. Branchlets distinctly compressed and phyllomorphs less uniformly disposed in the horizontal plane. Leaves bluish-green on both sides, conspicuously glandular. Mature cones 6(7)mm across.

C. nootkatensis Nootka or Yellow Cypress. W N America. Tree 30-40m, more or less conical with spreading branches, pendulous at the tips. Phyllomorphs horizontal and characteristi-cally drooping at the sides, giving the appearance of a short circle segment, branchlets not obviously compressed; leaves green above, paler beneath, virtually without glands. Mature cones 10(1 2)mm across with 4-6 scales and 2-4 seeds on each scale.

ARBOR-VITAE (GENUS THUJA)

There are six species (some with numerous varieties) in the genus *Thuja*, and all are generally known as arbor-vitae. They are evergreen trees and shrubs from China, Japan, Taiwan and North America. The trees are usually of pyramidal habit and the young shoots (phyllomorphs) are characteristically flattened in one plane and bear scale-like decussate leaves.

Male and female cones are borne on the same plant. The male cones are very small and borne terminally on the smallest shoots. The female cones are erect, solitary with imbricate cone-scales; only the middle two or three pairs of scales are fertile and each bears two seeds on the lower surface.

Arbor-vitae are often grown as ornamentals, growing well on well-drained loams, also on light moist sandy soils and in peat. Propagation is by seeds or cuttings, the cultivars by cuttings rather than by grafting.

The large cultivars, such as those of the White Cedar (*Thuja occidentalis*), the Chinese Arbor-vitae (*T. orientalis*) and the Western Red Cedar (*T. plicata*) make excellent single specimen trees for large gardens, and are finding some use as hedging, particularly the latter which withstands clipping well although *T. occidentalis* does better in cold climates. The numerous slow-growing, dwarf cultivars are particularly suitable for some gardens and rock gardens.

Scale insects are about the only serious pest and are controlled by spraying every eight days for six weeks with a soft-soap and paraffin wash.

The wood, which is light, easy to work and without resin canals, is used for general building, furniture, telegraph poles etc. The outer bark makes a useful roofing material.

There is an inner, more fibrous bark which serves as a stuffing for upholstery. In the United States timber of the Western Red Cedar (*Thuja plicata*) *is* used for roofing tiles.

This same species has also proved a successful timber tree in Scotland but in the warmer, southern parts of England it is unsatisfactory, mainly because of extensive shrinkage during the seasoning process, which causes significant gaps to occur between the annual rings.

Trunks of the Western Red Cedar were those most frequently used by the North-American Indians as totempoles.

THE MAIN SPECIES OF THUJA

Subgenus *Biota*

Shoots (phyllomorphs) predominantly in vertical planes and green on both sides. Cone-scales thick, recurved at the apices; seeds without wings. This subgenus is sometimes regarded as a separate genus.

T. orientalis Chinese or Oriental Arbor-vitae. N and W China. Tree 5-1 Om, sometimes more or less shrubby. Leaves with small gland on the back. Mature cones 1 .5-2.5cm long, usually with 6 scales. Easily recognized by the subgeneric characters. Numerous named varieties.

Subgenus *Thuje*

Phyllomorphs predominantly in horizontal planes and often white-streaked on underside of leaves. Cone-scales thin, the apices not recurved; seeds winged.

T. occidentalis American or White Cedar.

E N America. Tree to 20m. Underside leaves of phyllomorphs without white streaks or markings, usually yellowish or bluish-green, each leaf at least of main axis with conspicuous glandular dot on the back (lens). Cones 8-12mm with 8-10 scales, only half of them fertile. Numerous named varieties.

T. plicata Western Red Cedar. W N America. Tree 30-60m. Underside leaves with more or less X-shaped white streaks and any glands inconspicuous; bruised foliage strongly aromatic. Mature cones about 12mm long with 10-12 scales, each with a small spine; about half the scales fertile. Numerous named varieties.

T. standishii Japanese Arbor-vitae. Japan. Tree to 18m. Phyllomorphs not obviously flattened; leaves without glands, the underside ones with more or less triangular white markings; bruised foliage not aromatic. Mature cones with 8-10 scales, only the middle 4 fertile.

T. koraiensis Korean Arbor-vitae. Korea. Usually a somewhat sprawling shrub, but sometimes a slender conical tree to 9m. Phyllomorphs much flattened; leaves with conspicuous glands, dark green on the upper surface of the phyllomorphs, contrasting with the almost white lower surface; bruised foliage not aromatic. Mature cones 8-10mm with 4 pairs of scales, the middle 2 pairs fertile. *T. sutchuenensis*, from NE Szechwan in C China, is little known and is not yet in cultivation.

A broadly-conical specimen of the Hiba Arbor-vitae or Japanese Hiba (*Thujo psis dolobrata*) native to Japan contrasts well with the golden-yellow foliage of the English Yew, *Taxus baccata* 'Aurea,' in the left background.

HIBA (GENUS THUJOPSIS)

This genus has been separated from *Thuja* to accommodate the single species *Thujopsis dolobrata* (Japan) which differs from *Thuja* in having much more flattened branchlets and each fertile cone-scale maturing three to five seeds and not just two.

The Hiba Arbor-vitae is a pyramidal tree to 15m (soft) but it is often shrubby in cultivation. The scale leaves are decussate, 4-6mm (0.16-0.24in) long, the lateral more or less spreading and acute, the facial obtuse, both virtually white beneath except for a thin green margin.

Female cones are broadly ovoid to 15mm (0.6in) long, comprising six to eight scales each with a subapical boss or mucro on the outside; the upper pair of scales are sterile and bear winged seeds. In cultivation the Hiba is hardy in temperate regions where it thrives on welldrained soils.

It is much planted for its handsome and pleasing appearance, differing at a glance from typical species of *Thuja* by its broader branchlets, often much denser habit toward the base, much tore rounded cones and thicker cone-scales. Several cultivars have been developed including the golden-yellow-leaved 'Aurea,' variegated 'Variegata' and dwarf 'Nana.'

The soft, durable wood is used locally in Japan for general construction work and the bark for caulking boards.

SOUTHERN INCENSE CEDARS (GENUS LIBOCEDRUS)

As now understood, the genus *Libocedrus* (*sensu restricto*) comprises five species, two native to New Zealand and three to New Caledonia. They are evergreen trees and shrubs with the branchlets flattened into spraylike phyllomorphs.

The juvenile leaves,are short and needle-like, the adult ones scalelike, arranged in decussate pairs and mostly dimorphic. Male and female cones occur on the same trees. Mature cones comprise two pairs of decussate, woody, valvate scales but only the upper pair are fertile.

Each scale is more or less dorsally spined, the fertile scales producing one or two unequally winged seeds. Only two species are found in cultivation and then only rarely. Pahautea (*Libocedrus bidwillii*) comes from New Zealand, where it grows at altitudes of up to 2 ooom (6 5ooft) and reaches a height of 25m (82ft).

Its ultimate branchlets are flattened and the juvenile leaves markedly dimorphic—the facial about 1 mm (0.04in) long, the lateral about 3mm (0.12in). Adult leaves are scale-like, adpressed, triangular and all about 2mm (0.08in) long.

Female cones are ovoid, about iomm (0.4in) long, the four scales each with a spine-like horn and the two fertile scales each maturing a single seed. Kawaka (*L. plumosa* = *L. doniana*) also from New Zealand, reaches a height of 33m (110ft).

Its branchlets are distinctly flattened and the juvenile leaves very dimorphic—the laterals to 5mm (0.2in) long, the facial barely 1mm (0.04in). The adult scale leaves overlap and are adpressed, subequal, the laterals about 3mm (o.12in) long, the facial just over imm (0.04in).

Female cones are ovoid, finally 10-15mm (0.4-0.6in) long, each of the four scales with a curved dorsal spine. One seed is produced on each fertile scale. Both these species are only marginally hardy in temperate areas. The wood is of some economic value, fragrant and durable.

The following species remain in the genus *Libocedrus* (*sensu restricto*) : *L. austrocaledonica*, *L. bidmillii*, *L. chevalieri*, *L. plumosa*, *L. yateensis*. Changes to new genera are as follows:

L. arfakensis becomes Papuacedrus arfakensis

L. papuana becomes *P. papuana*

L. toricellensis becomes *P. toricellensis*

L. chilensis becomes *Austrocedrus chilensis*

L. decurrens becomes *Calocedrus decurrens*

L. formosana becomes *C. formosana*

L. macrolepis becomes *C. macrolepis*

L. uvifera becomes *Pilgerodendron uviferum*

NORTHERN INCENSE CEDARS (GENUS CALOCEDRUS)

Calocedrus comprises three species respectively from the Pacific coast of North America, China and Taiwan. They are evergreen trees with their ultimate branchlets (sprays or phyllomorphs) flattened.

The leaves are scale-like, flattened, decussately arranged, with the edges of the lateral ones overlapping and virtually equal in length to the facial ones; both sets are adpressed except at their slightly recurved pointed apices.

The cones are unisexual and typically on different branches of the same tree, rarely on separate trees. The male cone is oblong comprising 6-16 decussate pollen sacs. The female cone is elliptic-oblong comprising three pairs of finally woody, imbricate scales, each scale with a subapical recurved thorn-like process.

Only the middle pair of scales are fertile each bearing two ovules; the innermost pair of scales are fused together, and the outermost (lowest) pair much shorter and recurved. The cone matures in one year, each seed with two very unequal wings.

The three species were formerly included under *Libocedrus* (*sensu lato*), one character separating them out being that the facial and lateral scale leaves are nearly equal in length.

The Incense Cedar (*Calocedrus decurrens*) (formerly *Libocedrus decurrens*) grows to 45m (148ft) in its native habitat and has an elongated conical canopy in the wild state. Its bark is deeply furrowed and reddish-brown.

The leaves are long decurrent, those on the ultimate lateral branches about 3mm (0.12in) long, but up to 12mm (0.48in) on the main branches with juvenile leaves even longer. Male cones are 6mm (0.24in) long, the females ovate, 18-25mm (0.71-0.98in) long, pendulous, fleshy at first, finally woody.

It is native to Oregon and western Nevada to lower California, growing at altitudes between 1000 and 2750m (3280 and 9020ft). The Incense Cedar is by far the best known of the species and is widely planted in temperate regions, being fully hardy.

There are some four cultivars, but 'Columnaris' with its narrow columnar canopy is the commonest in cultivation. It is not particular as to soil, but flourishes best in a moist, well-drained loam away from atmospheric pollution. Propagation is best from seeds, but cuttings may be taken.

The wood is light, resistant to decay and fragrant. It is used for pencils and general carpentry, boxes, fence posts etc. *Calocedrus macrolepis* is a tree to 35m (115ft) which differs from the previous species by its larger leaves on the ultimate lateral branchlets—6-8mm (0.24-0.32in) long—and only one seed is usually produced on each fertile scale.

It is rare in its native habitat of south China to the Burmese border and not really hardy in cultivation, but may be grown in warmer parts of temperate regions.

Calocedrus formosana is very close to *C. macrolepis* in form but its leaves are only 2mm (0.08in) long, with two stomatal lines on the lateral leaves, whereas there are typically four in *C. macrolepis.* It is native to the broadleaved forests of Taiwan ascending to altitudes of nearly 2000m (6560ft) and it is little known in cultivation.

CHILEAN INCENSE CEDAR (GENUS *AUSTROCEDRUS*)

Austrocedrus is a genus of one species, the Chilean Incense Cedar (*Austrocedrus chilensis*) native to Chile and Argentina; it was formerly included under *Libocedrus.*

It differs from this genus in having scale leaves that are much more strongly dimorphic—the facial ones being onequarter (or less) the length of the lateral ones (one-half in *Libocedrus*)—blunter and rhombic to ovate as against triangular, and cones comprising four valvate scales, only two of which are fertile, each with one or two unequally winged seeds.

It is an evergreen tree to about 25m (82ft) in its native habitat, but little more than 15m (soft) when cultivated in temperate regions.

The shoots are compressed, frond-like (phyllomorphs) with the leaves arranged in decussate pairs, the lateral ones 2-4.5mm (0.08-0.18in) long, the facial (upper and lower) ones rarely more than a quarter of this length.

The male cones are about 3mm (0.12in) long, and comprise numerous pollen sacs. The female cones are solitary and finally woody, each of the four valvate scales with a minute subterminal dorsal tubercle.

Only the upper two scales are fertile, these being about 8-12mm (0.32-0.48in) long and therefore much longer than the lower two sterile scales. The Chilean Incense Cedar is reasonably hardy in temperate regions, where it favors moist but well-drained soils.

However, since it has few attractive qualities, it is not much planted outside botanical collections. Propagation is usually by cuttings, but seeds can be used. The wood is scented and durable and has been used for general carpentry purposes.

PAPUACEDRUS

The three doubtfully distinct species of this genus of evergreen trees from the Moluccan Islands and New Guinea were formerly placed in *Libocedrus* (*sensu lato*) but they differ from *Libocedrus* (*sensu restricto*) in leaf form and anatomy and cone structure.

Male cones comprise numerous whorled bracts that are not decussately arranged. Female cones have four valvate scales each with a dorsal, short, stumpy spine; only the upper, much larger pair of scales is fertile and these mature four very equally winged seeds.

The main species is *Papuacedrus arfakensis* from the Arfak mountains of New Guinea where it grows up to an altitude of 1000m (3300ft). It is a tree up to 35m (115ft) with a more or less pyramidal form and red, scaly bark.

The juvenile leaves are up to 2cm (0.8in) long, almost herbaceous, with a slender spreading point. The facial pair are more or less overlapped by the lateral pair, both pairs tapering downward; the greatest width of about iomm (0.4in) occurs just below the spreading point.

The adult leaves are smaller, darker green, widening upward to an erect blunt apex. Female and male cones occur on different branches of the same tree.

The two upper (inner) fertile scales are narrowly ovate, each about 12 × 8mm (0.48 × 0.32in). None of the species is extensively cultivated.

PILGERODENDRON

Pilgerodendron contains a single evergreen species which was formerly placed under *Libocedrus* from which it differs in leaf form and arrangement, and cone structure. *Pilgerodendron uviferum* is restricted to the Andes of southern Chile and Argentina including Patagonia and Tierra del Fuego.

It is a tree to 25m (82ft), rarely a shrub. The branchlets are quadr-angular in outline. Leaves are scale-like, boat-shaped, 3-8mm (0.12-0.32in) long, opposite and decussate.

They are all essentially similar in size, overlapping and adpressed to the shoots except at the somewhat spreading bluntish, slightly incurved tips to which they taper from a broad base.

The cones are 8-12mm (0.32-0.48in) long, ovoid and comprise two pairs of woody, valvate scales, each scale with a subapical curved, dorsal spine.

Only the upper pair of scales are fertile, each scale with one, rarely two, ovules; the lower sterile pair are much smaller.

The seeds have very unequal wings. *Pilgerodendron uviferum* is sometimes mistaken for *Fitzroya cupressoides*, which has leaves wider above, narrowing to a decurrent base and the cones have three pairs of scales.

This species only occasionally survives in temperate regions and is thus rare in cultivation. The timber is extensively used in its native area.

CYPRESS PINES (GENUS *CALLITRIS*)

Callitris is a genus of some 14-16 species which are native to Australia, Tasmania and New Caledonia, particularly dry and and regions. They are evergreen trees or shrubs with sexes on the same plant. The adult leaves are scale-like, arranged in alternating whorls of three and adpressed, except at the tips; the juvenile leaves are 6-12mm (0.24-0.48in) long arranged in whorls of four.

Male cones are either solitary or clustered, small and cylindrical to oblong. Female cones are mostly 2-3cm (o.8-r.2in) long, globular to narrowly pyramidal, solitary or clustered and comprising six to eight thick, woody, often pointed, unequal valvate scales that are grossly warted, veined or smooth on the back.

Two to nine seeds are produced per scale, each with one to three wings. *Tetraclinis* and *Widdringtonia* are closely related genera and in both the cones are normally composed of not more than four scales. *Tetraclinis* also has the leaves in fours whilst in *Widdringtonia* they are arranged alternately in opposite pairs.

In north temperate zones, for example Europe, cypress pines require a cool greenhouse except in the warmest parts, such as southwest England and Ireland and southern France. Propagation is by seed or cuttings.

The most frequently cultivated cypress pines include the following species. The Murray River Pine or White Cypress Pine (*Callitris columellaris* = *C. arenosa*) from New South Wales and the southern coast of Queensland, is a shrub or slowgrowing tree to 25m (82ft).

Its wood is very fragrant, insect resistant and is much used for panels and cabinet-making. The Black or Red Cypress Pine (*C. endlicheri*) from New South Wales, northeastern Victoria and Queensland, is a tree to some 25m (82ft). Its polished wood is finely figured and hence much used for paneling.

The Rottnest Island Pine or Common Cypress Pine (*C. preissii* = *C. robusta*) from southern and western Australia, is a low shrub or tree to 30m (iooft). The Oyster Bay Pine or Port Jackson Pine (*C. rhomboidea*) is a tree to 10-15m (33-50ft).

It is widely distributed in Australia but only locally frequent; it is also naturalized in New Zealand. The Tasmanian Cypress Pine (*C. oblonga*) from Tasmania is a bush or small tree to 8m (26ft).

In general cypress pine wood is closegrained, hard, fragrant, and takes a good polish, the grain patterns often being quite striking. The presence of natural preservatives no doubt adds to its resistance to insect and fungal attack. It is used for building purposes, furniture, turnery and general carpentry. The bark can be slashed for resin and is also an economic source of tannins, whilst the cones, leaves and shoots can be distilled for the fragrant principles they contain.

JUNIPERS (GENUS JUNIPERUS)

There are about 60 species of evergreen trees and shrubs in the genus *Juniperus*, commonly known as junipers. They are widely distributed throughout the Northern Hemisphere, from the mountains of the tropics as far south as the equator and ranging as far north as the Arctic.

The Common Juniper (*Juniperus communis*) *is* extremely widely spread in temperate regions, forming dominant scrub on chalk, limestone and slate. Junipers have leaves of two kinds: the normal adult leaves are small, scale-like and decussate, closely pressed to the shoot, crowded and overlapping; the juvenile leaves are larger and awl-shaped (acicular), growing in three's or opposite pairs at a node.

In a number of species the awlshaped, juvenile leaves are the only ones present. They do not always connect smoothly with the stem (on which, in some species, they are decurrent) but sometimes there may be some kind of constriction at the junction with the stem, as in *J. communis*, where the leaf base is swollen, the swollen tissue being virtually free of the stem. There is thus a constriction between the swollen leaf-base and the stem, the actual connection between the two being much narrower. Such leaves are referred to as 'jointed.'

The scale-like leaf margin (lens) is denticulate in some species but smooth (entire) in others. Cones are unisexual, borne either on different plants or separately on the same plant. The male cones are solitary or in more or less crowded catkins; the female cones consist of three to eight fleshy, pointed scales which coalesce and finally form a more or less globular body or 'berry.'

This so-called juniper berry is often coated and bloomed, with subtending scaly bracts; it matures in the second or third year. There are between one and 12 seeds according to species. Propagation is readily effected from seed but germination may be delayed up to about one year.

Cultivars and varieties are increased by cuttings from the current year's shoot or by grafting on the appropriate stocks. The most serious fungus disease that junipers are likely to suffer is from the rust *Gymnosporangium*, which forms large unsightly gelatinous yellow patches around the stems.

These rusts are heteroecious, ie two hosts are required to complete the life history. Eradication of the alternate hosts—members of the rose family (Rosaceae)—is the best control measure. Insect pests include the juniper Webber (*Dichomeris marginella*), so-called because it spins foliage together which subsequently turns brown and dies.

The Juniper Scale Insect (*Caralaspis spp*) and the Conifer Spinning Mite (*Oligonychus ununguis*) also do serious damage. Juniper wood is generally durable and easy to work; the presence of oils is probably responsible for the juniper's resistance to many insect attacks.

The timber is used in general building, for roof shingles, furniture, posts and fences. In Burma *J. recurva* var *coxii* is the favored wood for coffins. *3uniperus virginiana*, generally known as the Pencil Cedar, is extensively used in the manufacture of pencils.

Cedar wood oil is obtained from a distillation of the sawdust, shavings etc and, until recently, was the main 'immersion oil' used in the highest power light microscopy. *Juniperus oxycedrus* (Prickly Juniper) yields Oil of Cade (Oleum cadinum) or juniper tar by distillation of the wood.

This oil has been used as a treatment for skin diseases, especially psoriasis, but is now largely replaced by coal-tar products, which prove more effective. It is also used in the perfumery industry. Oil of juniper is distilled from the fully grown but unripe berries of *3. communis* and is responsible for the characteristic flavor of gin.

It is either added to the rectified spirit obtained after fermentation of the mixed grain mash or the spirit is redistilled to gether with the berries. The word 'gin' is a corruption of Geneva, derived from the French word*genevrier*, meaning juniper, and has nothing to do with the famous Swiss town.

Oil of Savin, from *I. sabina*, is obtained by distilling fresh leaves and shoots. It is a powerful diuretic and has been used as an abortifacient. Junipers are slow-growing and hardy and a number of species are frequently grown as ornamentals in parks, large gardens and often in graveyards.

The most popular species are the Chinese Juniper (*J. chinensis*) and Pencil Cedar. Dwarf and prostrate forms suitable for ground cover and in rock gardens include the Creeping Juniper (*J. horizontalis*), the Procumbent Juniper (*J. procumbens*) and dwarf cultivars of the Common juniper, for example 'Compressa' and 'Stricta.'

THE MAIN SPECIES OF JUNIPERUS

Group I: *Caryocedrus* Leaves always awlshaped (acicular) and spreading, in 3's, jointed at base and decurrent on the shoot; white-banded (from stomata) on upper surface. Cones axillary, sexes on separate plants; seeds usually 3.

J, drupacea Syrian Juniper. Greece, Asia Minor, Syria. Tree 10-12m, usually narrowly pyramidal, Leaves decurrent on stem, narrowly lanceolate, 15-25 × 3-4mm, with 2 white bands on upper side, separated by green midrib, except sometimes at apex. Berries globose to broadly ovoid, 1.5-2.5cm long.

Group II: *Oxycedrus* Leaves always awl shaped (acicular), in 3 s and jointed at base but not decurrent on the shoot, white-banded (from stomata) on upper surface.

J. comrnunis Common Juniper. Cosmopolitan Shrub or tree to about 1 2m. Leaves more or less awl-shaped, hardpointed and skin piercing, 10-15 × 1-2mm, the upper surface with a single white band, broader than the green margins but divided at the extreme base by the midrib. Berries globose to broadly ovoid, 5-6mm long, bluishblack

Hibernica (Stricta), the Irish Juniper, has very dense foliage and short branches bending outward so that the upper surface, in the mass, presents a deep bluegreen appearance. *montana* (var *nana*, *J. sibirica*) *is* the Mountain Juniper, a prostrate shrub about 30cm high, the leaves scarcely prickly, it is characteristic of windswept areas-roughly arctic alpine Europe.

Note: A number of other very closely related species have been described but are now regarded as geographical variations, eg var *depressa* from E N America and var *hemisphaerica* from S Europe.

J. rigida Needle Juniper. Japan, Korea, Manchuria Tree to 13m, sometimes a shruo, with pendulous branches. Leaves narrowly awl shaped, 13-25 × 1 mm, sharply pointed, deeply grooved on upper surface with the single white band narrower than the green margins; keeled below Berries globose, about 6-8mm across, brownish-black.

J. oxycedrus Prickly Juniper. Spain, N Africa through Syria to the Caucasus. Shrub or small tree to 10m. Leaves linear-lanceolate, 12–1 × 8 × 1–1.5mm, apex piercing sharp, the upper surfaces with 2 white bands separated by a narrow green midrib and surrounded by a narrow green marginal band. Berries globose, 6-12mm in diameter distinctly reddish brown.

Group III: *Sabina* Leaves predominantly scale like, at least on adult plants, but sometimes wholly awl-shaped (acicular); awl-shaped leaves, when present, always decurrent on the shoot and in opposite pairs or 3 s. Cones terminal.

J. recurva Drooping Juniper. Burma, SW China, E Himalaya. Shrub or small tree to 10m, with spreading, pendulous branches. Leaves only awl-shaped and in 3's at a node, crowded and overlapping.

3-6 × 1 mm, sharp-pointed, white-banded above without a green midrib; not jointed at base. Berries ovoid, 8-10mm long, dark purplish-brown to black.

coxii (Coffin Juniper) is a large tree with larger, less crowded leaves, about 1 cm long, the upper surface of each leaf with 2 whitish bands on upper surface. It is sometimes considered a distinct species but, when typical, is probably only an extreme form of a variable species; there are intermediates.

J. Phoenicia Phoenician Juniper. Mediterranean region including Algeria, Canary Islands. Shrub or tree to 6m. Leaves predominantly scale-like, imbricate and closely adpressed, in 3's or opposite pairs, 1 mm long, blunt-tipped, the margin denticulate; awl-shaped leaves (rarely present) about 6mm long, 3 at a node. Berries more or less globose, about 8mm across, brown or reddish-brown.

Note: Specimens on the Canary Islands reach an exceptional size and may be 1000 years old. They have been described as a separate species (*J. canariensis*), but this is not generally accepted.

J. thurifera Spanish Juniper. SW Europe, N Africa, Asia Minor and the Caucasus. Tree to 12m. Scale leaves more or less diamond-shaped, opposite and decussate, imbricate and closely adpressed, sometimes in 3's on leading shoots; awl-shaped leaves in opposite pairs, 5-6mm long with 2 whitish bands on each upper surface; margin denticulate. Berries globose, about 8mm in diameter, blue or bluish; seeds about 4.

J. chinensis Chinese Juniper. The Himalaya, China, Mongolia, Japan. Tree to 20m, sometimes a low shrub. Leaves either wholly scale-like, diamond-shaped, crowded, imbricate and closely adpressed, 1.5mm long with blunt tip, or with a few awl-shaped leaves 8-1 2mm long, 3 at a node (less often in opposite pairs), with 2 white bands on upper surface, separated by a green midrib; margin entire; apex spiny and skin-piercing. Berries more or less globose, 6-8mm across, brown. A variable species with numerous cultivars.

J. sabina Savin. C Europe. Shrub to 5m, the bruised foliage having an unpleasant smell and a bitter taste. Leaves predominantly scale-like, diamond-shaped, imbricate and closely adpressed, about 1 mm long with a dorsal gland; awl-shaped leaves 4mm long, sharply pointed, each with a glaucous upper surface and prominent green midrib; margin entire. Berries globose to ovoid, 5-6mm across, brownish or bluish-black, pendulous. Numerous cultivars. *J. virginiana* Red or Pencil Cedar. E and C USA. Tree to 30m, with ascending or spreading branches, ultimate branchlets not reaching more than 1 mm thick.

Leaves predominantly scale-like, imbricate and closely adpressed, 1.5mm long, apex pointed, diverging and with a small dorsal gland; awl-shaped leaves spiny-pointed, opposite or 3 at a node, 5-6(8)mm long and glaucous above; margin entire. Berries ovoid or subglo-bose, about 6mm long, bluish-glaucous. Numerous cultivars.

PATAGONIAN CYPRESS (GENUS FITZROYA)

Fitzroya comprises a single evergreen species (*Fitzroya cupressoides*) from Chile and Argentina where it may live up to an age of 3 000 years. It grows to 50m (164ft) in the wild and the trunk has a diameter of 9m (30ft), with characteristic reddish, furrowed bark.

The leaves are spreading and typically arranged in whorls of three (rarely opposite). They are ternate, dark green, obovate, about 3mm (0.12 in) long narrowing into flat decurrent bases, the free end more or less spreading, but with an incurved tip.

Male and female cones occur separately on the same trees or on different trees, although some cones may be bisexual. The solitary male cones have up to 24 pollen sacs. The female cones comprise three alternating whorls, each whorl of three valvate scales, the lower smallest whorl sterile, the uppermost always fertile and the middle whorl sometimes fertile.

They are finally woody, globose, 6-8mm (0.24-0.32in) in diameter, the fertile scales bearing two to six seeds each with two or three wings.

The mature cone bears a terminal gland which secretes a fragrant resin. The Patagonian Cypress is reasonably hardy when cultivated in temperate zones, but then it is often shrubby.

Propagation is usually from cuttings taken toward the end of summer, since many cultivated trees are only female, thus setting no seed. The wood yields a valuable timber not unlike that of the redwoods and is used for general construction work locally.

AFRICAN CYPRESSES (GENUS WIDDRINGTONIA)

Widdringtonia comprises five species from tropical and southern Africa. They are mostly evergreen trees, rather like *Callitris* but the adult leaves are smaller and decussate (three-ranked in *Callitris*) and the slender, adpressed base of each scale leaf suddenly expands into an obtuse, incurved, broad mucronate apex.

The leaves of juvenile plants are needle-like and spirally arranged. Male and female cones occur on separate trees. Mature cones are woody, more or less globose, mostly comprising four similar cone-scales, each with five or more ovules. The seeds are twowinged.

Cypress pines are not generally hardy in temperate regions although the following two species are marginally hardy in warmer parts of this region. The Berg Cypress (*Widdringtonia cupressoides*) from Table Mountain to Drakensburg in South Africa is a shrub to 3-4m (10-13ft). Its main branches are 10-20cm (4-8in) in thickness, the juvenile leaves 12 × 1 mm (0.48 × 0.04in) and the adult leaves scale-like. The cones comprise virtually smooth scales that are 12-18mm (0.48-0.71in) long; 2030 seeds are produced by each cone.

The Clanwilliam Cedar, Cape Cedar or Cedarboom (*W. juniperoides*) from the Cedarberg mountains, South Africa up to an altitude of 1300m (4300ft), is a tree to nearly tom (66ft) although it is smaller and more bushy in cultivation. The juvenile leaves are 15-18 × 1mm (0.6-0.71 × 0.04in) and the adult leaves are scale-like.

Mature cones are solitary, borne on short laterals, globose, 8-18(25)mm (0.32-0.71(1)in) across, comprising four, exceptionally six, rough and spine-tipped scales.

The timber of this species has some commercial value for furniture and cabinet-making, whilst its good resistance to insect attack makes it suitable for fencing posts.

NEOCALLITROPSIS

The single member of this genus, *Neocallitropsis araucarioides* from New Caledonia, is related to *Callitris*, but has the habit of *Araucaria*. It is a tree to iom (33ft), its branchlets clothed with eight vertical rows of stiff, incurved leaves so that each branchlet has a cylindrical shape.

Each leaf is about 6 × 5mm (0.24 × 0.2in), keeled below with a pointed apex and serrulate margin. The male cones are ovoid, 12 x 6mm (0.48 × 0.24in) comprising about eight rows of bracts bearing sessile pollen sacs.

The female cones are terminal, borne on short laterals, each cone consisting of two alternating whorls of four narrowly-pointed bracts, each bract maturing a single seed. (In *Callitris* there is only one whorl of six or eight alternating long and short scales.)

This species is very rare in cultivation.

TETRACLINIS

Tetraclinis articulata is the only member of this genus and is native to southern Spain, North Africa and Malta. It is related to *Callitris* and *Widdringtonia*, but differs at a glance from these two genera by having the branchlets (phyllomorphs) distinctly flattened and by its scale leaves which are arranged in decussate pairs.

It is an evergreen tree growing up to 15m (soft) and has erect, articulated branches. The lateral scale leaves somewhat exceed the length of the facial ones, but both have long decurrent bases, the upper free parts more or less boat-shaped with pointed tips.

Female cones are solitary, terminal, globose and 8-12mm (0.32-0.48in) in diameter. They are composed of two pairs of nonpeltate woody scales, that are triangular in outline, with a blunt or pointed apex; all the scales are finally grooved or furrowed on the outer surface after separating and bear a very small subapical spine.

Only the upper (inner) pair of scales are fertile, each producing two to nine broadlywinged seeds. Its ability to withstand high temperatures and extended periods of drought has led to the replanting of this species in its native areas. In cultivation it is only hardy in the warmest parts of the north temperate zone.

The wood has been much esteemed, probably from Roman times; it is hard, sweet-smelling, often with attractive markings and has been much used for cabinet-making and high-class furniture. The trunk also yields a resin (Sandarac) which is extensively used for the manufacture of varnish.

DISELMA

Diselma comprises a single species (*Diselma archeri*) which is endemic to western Tasmania and Lake St. Clair, where it grows at altitudes of a little over 1000m (3300ft). It grows to about 8m (26ft) and is characterized by minute, decussate or whorled, closely adpressed scale-like leaves which are blunt, about imm (0.04in) long and pear-shaped.

Male and female cones are borne on separate plants. The female cones are subglobose, about 2mm (0.08in) across comprising four scales, only the upper (inner) pair of which are fertile. Each fertile scale gives rise to two three-winged seeds. *Diselma* is of no known economic value and is very rare in cultivation. It was formerly placed in the genus *Fitzroya.*

FOKIENIA

Fokienia probably contains a single species (*Fokienia hodginsii*) which is native to China, extending westward into Indochina. *Fokienia maclurei is* considered to be a synonym, while *F. kawaii is* doubtfully distinct. *Fokienia hodginsii* is an evergreen tree to ram (43ft), with flattened branchlets arranged in one plane (phyllomorphs).

Leaves are scale-like, 3-8mm (0.12-0.32in) long and dimorphic—the shorter ones on older trees. Their apices are pointed or blunt and they are arranged in four ranks, each set of four leaves of equal length, but with the facial pair narrower than the lateral pair.

The female cones are globose, about 25 mm (tin) in diameter, comprising 12-16 peltate scales, the outside of each scale with a small papilla in a central depression. They ripen during the second year with two seeds per fertile scale. This unusual species is very rare in cultivation.

PODOCARPS AND YELLOW WOODS (GENUS PODOCARPUS)

Podocarpus is a genus of evergreen trees and shrubs commonly called podocarps or yellow woods. Some species were formerly placed in the genus *Taxus* (yews) on account of their similar fleshy edible aril-covered seed. *Podocarpus andinus* of southern Chile, in fact, is known as the Plum-fruited Yew.

Sectioning ofthe genus is not easy and interpretation of the structure of some species is often difficult. In fact, *P. palembanicus* has been regarded as a flowering plant (angiosperm) by some authorities in the past. The genus is unique in having the only known coniferous parasitic species, *P. ustus* which parasitizes *Dacrydium taxoides*, also in the family Podocarpaceae.

About 115 species have been described of which too are generally accepted as 'good.' They are natives of the tropics, subtropics and warm temperate regions of the Old and New Worlds, mainly the Southern Hemisphere, especially of South and East Africa, South America and New Zealand, with a few species extending to Central America, China, India, the West Indies, Japan, Malaysia and the Philippines.

Their leaves are mostly alternate, very variable in form from small and scale-like up to 35 cm (14in) long and 5cm (1in) wide with an equally variable anatomy which is used in sectioning the genus. The sexes are typically on separate plants, rarely on the same.

Male cones are either solitary or clustered. Female 'cones' are often reduced to a short, stout stalk with two to four 'bracts' of which only one is fertile then bearing one, sometimes two, inverted ovules fused to these scale-like bracts.

The latter either remain small or become more or less expanded above into an aril-like structure—the epimatium. In many species the sterile 'bracts' fuse with the upper part of the stout stalk to give an often brightly colored fleshy receptacle on which the seed matures. In some species this fleshy receptacle is edible.

The seed is commonly ovoid or globose and resembles a

drupe or nut with an outer layer which may be skin-like or more or less fleshy, surrounding a hard inner shell or 'kernel.' The homologies of thi-, 'cone' structure are not clear: the 'bract' is thought to be a bract-scale and the epimatium an ovuliferous-scale.

Podocarps are important timber trees in their native areas. Fine timber—known as yellow wood—is obtained from the South African species *Ps falcatus* and *P. latifolius*, the Australian *P. elatus* and *P. amarus* and *in* New Zealand from *P. totara*—locally known as 'Totara,' which is deeply rooted in the traditions of the Maoris.

Most species are not hardy in temperate regions, although there are some clear exceptions to this rule. The Plum-fruited Yew forms a bushy tree which makes an excellent hedge, often being a welcome alternative to the Common Yew (*Taxus baccata*). It grows well on good soils overlying chalk.

Other hardy species include *P. salignus*, *P. totara*, *P. alpinus* and *P. nivalis*—the Alpine Totara which is normally seen as a low-growing shrub forming a mound of prostrate stems. Other species, such as *P. dacryoides* and *P. elatus*, grow well in conservatories.

THE MAIN SPECIES OF PODOCARPUS

Section *Dacrycarpus*

Leaves awl-shaped or flattened or both. Bract fused with outer seed coat and as long as seed; receptacle fleshy.

P. dacrydioides White Pine. New Zealand. Tree to 50m. Leaves of young trees soft, flat, to 8mm in a single row on each side of shoot (on mature trees scale-like, spirally arranged - trees may show both types). Seed a black nut, 4-6mm, on red fleshy stalk. Important timber tree.

Section *Microcarpus*

Leaves scale-like only and overlapping. Bract free from outer seed coat and shorter than seed.

P. ustus New Caledonia. Densely branched shrub to 1 m. Scale leaves to 2mm, copperyred to purple. Seeds globose, 2.5mm in diameter, purplish, without fleshy receptacle. Parasitic on *Dacrydium taxoides*.

Section *Nageia*

Leaves many-nerved, to about 5 × 2.5cm, about half as broad as long; opposite or almost so.

P. nagi China, Japan, Taiwan. Tree to about 25m, but mostly a bush in cultivation. Leaves leathery, ovate, 5 × 2.5cm. Seeds plum-like about 1.25cm across on slightly thickened stalk.

Section *Afrocarpus*

Leaves alternate, more or less spirally arranged; stomata on both leaf surfaces. *P. dawei* Uganda. Tree to 33m. Leaves leathery, 1.25-4.75 × 0.3-0.4cm. Seeds brown to purple, bloomed, subglobose, about 2cm long. Important timber tree.

Section *Polypodiopsis*

Leaves opposite and decussate, but appearing mostly in one plane of 2 ranks; stomata on both leaf surfaces. This section contains species from widely different areas including S America, S Pacific Islands, New Guinea, New Caledonia and Fiji. They are of little economic value and little known in cultivation.

Section *Sundacarpus*

Leaves lacking a hypoderm and at least 5 × 0.6cm, more or less spirally arranged around the branchlets; transfusion tissue present. Receptacle little developed and typically not fleshy. Species from NE Australia (Cape York Peninsula), New Guinea, Philippines and Indonesia (East Indies). Of no economic or ornamental importance.

Section *Stachycarpus*

Leaves lacking a hypoderm and not exceeding 3.6 × 0.5cm, typically appearing to be arranged in 2 ranks; transfusion tissue absent.

Receptacle little developed and typically not fleshy.

P. andinus Plum-fruited Yew. Andes region of S Chile. Tree to about 17m but mostly a much-branched shrub in cultivation. Leaves linear, 2-3 × 0.5-0.7cm, often distinctly 2-ranked with 2 glaucous bands beneath. Female 'cone' arising from upper leaf axils on a scaly stalk; seeds with yellowishgreen, white-speckled outer fleshy coating, subglobose, about 2cm across.

P. spicatus New Zealand. Tree 20-25m with dense, finally erect shoots. Leaves somewhat scale-like, 6-12mm long, glaucous on each side of midrib below. Male cones sessile, each about 4mm long, about 20 grouped together on short (2.5cm) stiff shoot; seeds globose, about 8mm across, black with glaucous bloom and without fleshy base. Wood like ordinary deal and in general use.

P. ferrugineus New Zealand (mainly South Island). Tree 1 7-30m. Leaves like those of the Common Yew (*Taxus baccata*), 18-30 × 2mm (about half this size on old trees), the margins more or less revolute.

Male cones 6-18mm long, borne singly; female 'cones' subsessile, also borne singly, about 18mm long, with short point, bright red with waxy bloom. Wood strong and hard and much used for indoor purposes, but requires treating with preservative for outdoor staking etc.

Section *Podocarpus*

The typical section of the genus. Leaves *either* with hypoderm, hypodermal fibers *or* well-developed transfusion tissue. Receptacle typically well developed, more or less fleshy to leathery.

AA Leaves linear to narrow lanceolate, rarely reaching 25 x 12mm, typically yew-like.

B Typically shrubs. Leaves rounded to slightly mucronate, not tapering; not in spikes.

P. alpinus Mountains of Victoria, New South Wales (Australia) and New Zealand. Dense shrub (rarely low tree 4-5m). Leaves 6-12mm with essentially blunt apex; arranged in 2 ranks. Seed ovoid, 5-6mm long, single or paired, red, on fleshy receptacle.

P. nivalis Alpine Totara. Mountains of New Zealand. Dense shrub to 2m. Leaves irregularly arranged, 6-18mm long, essentially mucronate. Seed a small nutlet on red, fleshy base.

BB Trees with stiff, tapering and acutely pointed leaves.

P. totara Totara. New Zealand. Massive tree to over 30m. Leaves irregularly arranged or 2-ranked, 10-20mm long by up to 4mm wide on adult trees, almost sessile. Seeds mostly solitary, more or less globose, about 12mm across, on a red swollen receptacle. var *hallii* (sometimes regarded as a distinct species) is similar, but smaller and with longer leaves and the seed acute rather than rounded.

AA Leaves lanceolate to oval, exceeding 25mm in length and not yew-like.

P. macrophyllus China, Japan. Small shrub or tree to nearly 20m. Leaves densely and irregularly arranged 10(15) × 0.5cm, with prominent midrib above. Male cones in clusters, female 'cones' solitary; seeds elliptic-ovoid, about 1 cm long on purple, fleshy receptacle. There are a number of varieties.

P. salignus Chile. Tree to about 20m. Leaves 5-10(12) × 0.4-0.6cm, with prominent midrib above, often slightly falcate. Male cones solitary or few but not in spikes; female 'cones' solitary; seeds more or less oblong about 8 x 3mm, red, on slenderstalked fleshy receptacle. Valuable timber tree.

P, nubigenus Chile, S Argentina. Tree to about 25m (in cultivation sometimes a bush) and densely branched. Leaves irregularly arranged but sometimes in

2 ranks, 2.5-3.5 × 0.3-0.4cm, with apical spine, straight to somewhat falcate and glaucous beneath. Male cones in clusters; seeds ovoid-oblong, about 8mm long on a swollen, fleshy receptacle.

RED PINES (GENUS DACRYDIUM)

Dacrydium is a genus of evergreen trees and a few shrubs represented by 20-25 species. These conifers are natives of New Zealand, Tasmania, Australia, New Caledonia, New Guinea, Malaya, the Philippines, Fiji and Chile.

The trees bear two types of foliage—juvenile which is soft and awl-shaped (acicular) and adult which is of small, densely-arranged, overlapping, leathery scale-like leaves. Both types of foliage often occur on the same tree simultaneously.

The two sexes occur on different plants. The male cones are produced in catkins in the axils of upper leaves, and female 'cones' at or near the tips of branchlets. The seeds have an aril. The genus, whilst including many stately trees of ornamental value, for example *Dacrydium cupressinum* and *D. franklinii*, also includes smaller species, for example *D. taxoides*, a shrub or small tree to 15m (50ft) from New Caledonia (parasitized by *Podocarpus ustus*), *D. bidwillii*, the Mountain Pine of New Zealand, an erect or prostrate shrub of 0.6-3m (2-l0ft) and with very widely spreading branches, and *D. laxifolium*, another prostrate shrub of New Zealand, but attaining only a few centimetres in height.

Several species produce timber of economic value, for example the Red Pine (*D. cupressinum*) a native of New Zealand; this tree has a pyramidal shape reaching 1834m (60-100ft) high with *Cupressus*-like branchlets and produces a wood used for building, railway sleepers, furniture and cabinet work.

The Huon Pine of Tasmania (*D. franklinii*), which also attains a height of 34m (i ooft), is an attractive tree with pendulous branchlets. The red timber is fragrant and similarly used for building, furniture and cabinet work. The timber of the Westland Pine (*D. colensoi*) of New Zealand is also of economic value.

PRINCE ALBERT YEW (GENUS SAXEGOTHAEA)

Saxegothaea comprises a single species, the Prince Albert Yew (*Saxegothaea conspicua*) from Chile. It is a remarkable evergreen more or less conical and bushy tree to 13m (45ft) which has yew-like foliage.

The shoots are drooping and either opposite or in whorls of three or four. The leaves are more or less two ranked, spirally inserted, linear, 12-25mm (0.5-1in) long each with a sharp, distinct horny point.

Male and female cones are found on the same tree. The male cones are about imm (0.04in) long and borne near the shoot apex. The female 'cones' are solitary, terminal and comprise overlapping spinetipped fleshy scales.

The mature structure is cone-like but fleshy, subglobose, 1220mm (0.5-0.8in) in diameter, the bluishgray scales more or less connate, the upper ones each with two inverted ovules that ripen into broadly ovoid seeds that are about 4mm (0.16in) long with a small arillate edge.

The Prince Albert Yew is hardy in the warmer parts of the north temperate zone, but shelter is advisable elsewhere. Propagation can be effected by cuttings, but it is a slow grower. The timber is durable and easy to work so that it is used locally for general carpentry.

MICROSTROBOS

This genus comprises two species of evergreen shrubs characteristic of wettish habitats in Tasmania and southeast Australia. Their leaves are scale-like, overlapping and spirally arranged in four or five rows. Female cones are very small, comprising four to eight glume-like bracts.

Both species are rare in cultivation with *M. fitzgeraldi* (New South Wales) the most hardy in temperate zones and hence the most frequently seen. This species is a bushy shrub up to 2m (6.6ft) tall and bears numerous long slender shoots.

The leaves are 2-3mm (0.08-0.12in) long, diverge from the stem and are keeled, with an incurved tip. The female 'cone' is 2-3mm (0.08-0.12in) long and the seed about equal in length to its subtending bract.

The second species *M. niphophilus*, from the mountains of Tasmania, is a shrub to 2m (6.6ft) and is distinguished by its compact, bushy habit and even smaller leaves which are more densely clustered.

ACMOPYLE

Acmopyle comprises three species of evergreen trees with yew-like foliage that are native to New Caledonia and Fiji. They are not hardy in temperate zones, although *Acmopyle pancheri* (New Caledonia) is sometimes grown as a glasshouse subject.

It is a tree up to 16m (soft) tall with erect branches. The leaves are linear lanceolate, 8-20 × 2-3mm (0.32-0.8 × 0.08-0.12in) with obtuse apices and borne in two ranks. The upper leaf surface has broken white stomatic lines and the under surface is more or less silvery.

Male cones are 3-4cm (1.2-1.6in) long borne terminally in clusters of one to three. The female cones are also terminal, each comprising up to nine sterile bracts and a single fertile apical bract which are all fused together to form a fleshy, more or less warty, receptacle. The fertile bract bears a single globose seed that is longer than the receptacle. This genus is related to *Dacrydium* and *Podocarpus*, differing mainly in fruiting cone character, although some authorities place it in the yew family, Taxaceae.

MICROCACRYS

This genus comprises a single species, *Microcachrys tetragona* from the mountains of Tasmania. It is a straggling bush with a prostrate habit and slender fourangled branchlets. The leaves are scalelike with hairy margins, overlapping, 2mm (0.04-0.08in) long and arranged in four ranks. Individual trees may be unisexual or bisexual.

Male cones are ovoid, borne terminally, about 3mm (o.12in) long; female 'cones' are finally 6-8mm (0.24-0.32in) comprising numerous bracts. The mature cones are finally fleshy and a translucent red color—each bract with an inverted seed with a fleshy scarlet aril (or epimatium).

This species is marginally hardy in temperate zones although not common in cultivation, when it is sometimes staked for upright habit. It is particularly unusual in its attractive fruits which yield fertile seeds.

CELERY-TOPPED PINES (GENUS PHYLLOCLADUS)

Phyllocladus comprises some seven species of evergreen trees and shrubs native to the Philippine Islands, Borneo, the Moluccan Islands and Australasia. The striking feature of these plants are the flattened and expanded short shoots which look like and function as leaves (phylloclades as in Butcher's Broom, *Ruscus* spp).

The true leaves are scale-like and borne on the long shoots. Some authorities place the genus in its own family—the Phyllocladaceae. The following species are more or less hardy in the warmest parts of temperate regions.

They are only marginally hardy and, at the limit of cultivation, are often stunted with great reduction in size of the phylloclades.

The Alpine Celery-topped Pine (*P. alpinus*) from the mountains of North and South Islands of New Zealand is a bush or tree to about iom (33ft).

The phylloclades are crenate to somewhat lobed, roughly diamond-shaped, 6-38 × 3-18mm (0.24-1.5 × 0.12-0.7in). The female 'cones,' each with three or four ovules, mature to a globose red fruit 6mm (0.24in) in diameter.

The Celery-topped Pine or Tanekaha (*P. trichomanoides*) is found locally up to altitudes of Boom (2 600ft) throughout New Zealand. It grows to tom (66ft) with a trunk up to 3m (10ft) in diameter.

The branches are arranged in whorls with the phylloclades often reddish-brown when young, up to 25 mm (iin) long, ovate to oblong in outline, more or less lobed. The sexes are borne on the same plant, the female 'cones' in groups of about seven appearing mostly near the apex of terminal phylloclades.

The fruit comprises a nutlike seed with a swollen, basal fleshy cup formed of fused scales. The wood of this species is of good quality and durability and the bark is rich in tannin from which a red dye is obtained.

COW'S TAIL PINES (GENUS CEPHALOTAXUS)

The genus *Cephalotaxus* comprises seven species of evergreen trees and shrubs, native to China, Japan and India (Khasi hills and Assam). The genus resembles *Torreya*, but the leaves are not spiny.

The branches are opposite or whorled with the young branchlets grooved and minutely white-pitted by stomata. The leaves are yew-like, spirally inserted but, at least on lateral shoots, mostly appearing in two ranks, the upper leaf surface with a prominent midrib, the lower with two wide stomatic bands.

The sexes are typically on separate plants, sometimes on the same, with male cones in globose heads in leaf axils and female 'cones' at the base of branchlets, each comprising a few pairs of scales, and each scale bearing two ovules.

Usually only one fertilized ovule in the whole 'cone' matures in the second season to form a stalked, protruding, green to purple, ellipsoid, drupe-like seed up to 2.5cm (1in) long, the outer layer finally fleshy and enclosing an inner woody 'kernel.'

The Chinese Plum Yew (*Cephalotaxus fortunii*) from central China is a small tree to 13111 (43ft) in the wild but in cultivation tends to be a rather untidy shrub. It is grown for its evergreen foliage and the reddish-brown bark which peels away in flakes. The leaves are 5-8cm (2-3in) long, tapering gradually to a point in two horizontal ranks.

The Japanese Plum Yew (*C. drupacea*) is a similar tree to the above and likewise mostly shrubby in cultivation. The leaves are abruptly pointed, 2-5cm (0.8-2in) long, in a V-shaped arrangement on the shoot. The variety *prostrata* provides useful ground cover.

The species is regarded by some authorities as a variety of *C. harringtonia*, a species not found wild but long cultivated in Japan and known by its irregularly pectinate, straight or curved leaves up to 6.5cm (2.5in) long.

The species are hardy in temperate regions and require much the same conditions as yews (*Taxus spp*) although somewhat less tolerant of chalk. Propagation is by seed or cuttings. They stand pruning well and are useful as hedging. The wood has some value, but the yield is low.

YEWS (GENUS TAXUS)

Yew is the popular name for the 10 species (regarded by some as varieties of one species) of *Taxus*, a genus of evergreen trees, shrubs and subshrubs (used for ground cover). Yews are widely distributed throughout the north temperate zone of the Old and New Worlds, with one species, the Chinese Yew (*Taxus celebica*) virtually on the equator on the Indonesian island of Sulawesi (Celebes).

Although placed by many authorities in the order Coniferales, the yews and other genera of the family Taxaceae lack the typical seedbearing cone structure and do not have resin canals in the wood and leaves. For these and other reasons, including fossil evidence, the family is sometimes excluded from the Coniferales and transferred to a separate order—Taxales. The leaves of yews are linear and more or less spirally arranged on erect shoots but appear mostly two-ranked on horizontal shoots. Male and female cones are normally borne on different plants and are small and solitary.

When ripe the seed is nut-like and surrounded by a fleshy cup (aril) which is conspicuous by its usually scarlet color and is commonly referred to as a 'berry' (strictly only angiosperms have berries). In the absence of its seeds, *Taxus* is often confused with *Abies* and *Tsuga*.

It is at once distinguished by the underside of the leaves being uniformly yellow-green without conspicuous white stomatal lines, always evident in the other two genera.

All parts of the plant, except the scarlet aril, are highly poisonous. The enclosed seed or 'stone' of the aril also contains poison, so that children in particular should be discouraged from eating the tempting red fruit in case they swallow the stone.

The poison is a mixture of alkaloids collectively referred to as taxine. Yew poisoning, resulting in gastroenteritis, heart and respiratory failure, is extremely serious, and fatal results in both humans and animals are well documented.

In many temperate countries veterinary surgeons consider the yews to be the most dangerous of all native trees and shrubs. A grim comment on yew poisoning is that the main symptom is sudden death—within five minutes following some sort of convulsion.

Thus, countermeasures are difficult and, in cattle, dangerous: opening the rumen, removing the contents and replacing them with normal foodstuffs. The best approach, as always, is prevention. The poison is also found in dried parts of the plant, so these should be cleared away and burnt.

Yews succeed well on almost any soil from peaty to calcareous, provided it is not liable to waterlogging, which may be fatal. Propagation is by seed, and for the cultivars by cuttings, grafting (on stocks of *Taxus baccata*) or by layering. Apart from Yew Leaf Scorch, caused by *Sphaerulina taxi*, fungus diseases are not especially serious.

Amongst insect pests, the Yew Gall Midge (*Taxomyia taxi*) attacks terminal leaves resulting in up to about 80 leaves becoming closely bunched together like an artichoke head, hence the name 'artichoke' gall.

The attacks do little harm but are unsightly. 'Big bud' is another gall, caused by the mite *Phytopus psilaspis.* Only the buds are infected and these become enlarged and discolored with large numbers of mites at the center. Much more serious are attacks by the Yew Scale Insect (*Parthenolecanium pomeranicum*).

White eggs may be found under females on almost any part of the plant at about midsummer. 'Honeydew' is excreted by the insects and this forms a favorable medium for the growth of 'sooty molds.'

The wood of yews is close-grained, durable and hard but elastic. In Britain it was the traditional material for making bows and is still used today for archery sports, being combined with hickory (*Carya*), the latter for the side facing the 'string,' the former on the side away from it.

In spite of its high quality, the wood is less popular now than formerly; it is used mainly for floor blocks, panels, fence posts, mallet heads etc, and as a veneer in cabinetmaking.

About five species are known in cultivation, the most common being the Common or English Yew (*Taxus baccata*). In Britain this species has been associated with cemeteries and graveyards and many of these trees are of great age, around a thousand years old.

Whatever other reasons may be suggested for this association—religious, bow-making etc—there is the highly practical one that these places are least likely to be frequented by cattle and unaccompanied children who might otherwise be victims of its poisonous properties.

The English Yew is also planted for ornament throughout Western Europe and some of its Cultivars make excellent hedges. It is a favorite subject for topiary work.

THE MAIN SPECIES OF TAXUS

Group I: Leaves gradually tapering, not abruptly pointed (but see *T. celebica*). Winter bud scales not keeled. *T. baccata* Common or English Yew. Europe, N Africa, W Asia. Tree 12—20m with rounded head, sometimes with a few erect stems from the base as well as a main stem. Leaves 1—2.5cm, usually in one plane on either side of stem, suddenly contracted into very short petiole. Seeds with a conspicuous scarlet fleshy edible cup (aril) surrounding an olive-brown poisonous seed 6mm long. Very many garden forms and cultivars.

'Fastigiata' (Irish Yew) is a distinctly compact and columnar cultivar with upwardly directed branches.

Group II: Leaves abruptly pointed (but see *T. celebica*). Winter bud-scales keeled.

T. cuspidata Japanese Yew. Japan. Tree 16-20m. Leaves 1.5—2.5cm × 2—3mm, not obviously in one plane, but ascending on either side of the stem in a V-shape. Seeds much as in *T. baccata.* Several cultivars.

T. canadensis Canada *Yew.* Canada and NE USA. Low, somewhat straggling shrub about 1 m tall. Leaves 1.3—2cm × 1—2mm, arranged horizontally in 2 ranks. Seeds as in *T. baccata.*

T. brevifolia Western or American Yew. W N America, British Columbia, Washington, Oregon, California. Tree 5—15(25)m, rarely shrubby. Leaves 1—2.5cm × 2mm, arranged horizontally in 2 ranks. Seeds as in *T. baccata.*

T. celebica (*T. chinensis*) Chinese Yew. Widely distributed in China but extending to Taiwan (Formosa), the Philippines and Sulawesi (Celebes) although there is doubt whether the extra China distributions represent the same species. Shrub or tree to about 1 2m. Leaves 1.5—4cm × 2—4mm, straight or slightly curved, tapering at the apex or more or less abruptly pointed, the lower surface densely covered with minute papillae. Seeds much as in *T. baccata*. This species is sometimes labeled *T. chinensis.*

NUTMEG TREES (GENUS TORREYA)

The genus *Torreya* comprises six or eight species of evergreen trees from East Africa and the United States of America. They are closely related to the yews (*Taxus* spp), but the branches and branchlets are opposite or almost so, the leaves are pungent with a sharply pointed apex and the lower side, which has a single resin canal, shows two narrow but distinct whitish to off whitish stomatal bands.

The sexes are mostly but not always on separate plants. The seed is drupe-like, being wholly surrounded by a thin fleshy layer, and requires two years to mature. In *Taxus*, the seed has a basal aril and the lower sides of the needles are uniformly pale yellowish-green and there is no resin canal. Nutmeg trees are scarcely hardy except in the warmest parts of temperate regions.

The California Nutmeg (*T. califaornica*) is a tree growing to 20m (66ft) in its native habitat, coastal regions of California, ascending to nearly 2000m (6600ft) in the Sierra Nevada. The second-year shoots are reddish-brown, the crushed leaves strongly aromatic, 3-6cm × 3mm (1.2—2.4 × 0.12in). The seed is ovoid to 3.5cm (1.4in) long and purple streaked.

The other main American species is the Florida Torreya or Stinking Cedar (*T. taxifolia*) which is a tree to 13m (43ft), rarely 18m (60ft), growing in southwestern Florida. The second-year shoots are yellowish-green. The leaves are 2.5-3cm x 3mm (1-1.2 × 0.12in), pungent but not unpleasantly so when crushed and the stomatal bands are not obviously in grooves.

The seeds are obovoid, 2.5-3cm (1-1.2in) long, with the same peculiar smell. It is the least hardy species, not surviving in temperate regions. The Chinese Torreya (*T. grandis* = *T. nucifera* var *grandis*) from eastern and central China, is a tree growing to 25m (82ft) in China, but mostly a shrub in cultivation.

The second-year shoots are yellowish-green. The leaves are virtually without smell when crushed and the stomatal bands are in grooves. The seeds are ellipsoidal.

The hardiest species is the Japanese Nutmeg or Torreya (*T. nucifera*), which is a tree growing to 25m (82ft) but, like the previous species, generally shrubby in cultivation. The second-year shoots are reddish-brown. The leaves are very aromatic when crushed and the stomatal bands are in grooves. The seeds are more or less ovoid, green tinged purplish-red, and are edible.

Index

A

D

E

H

I

J

Q

R

S